Masters of the Nonsense Verse

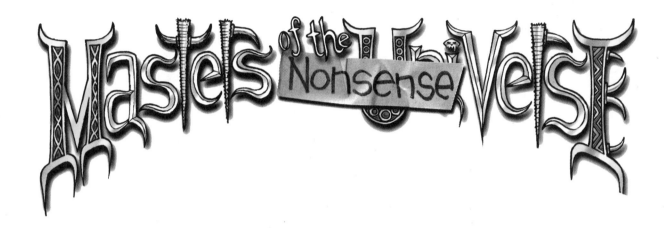

Masters of the Nonsense Universe

A GET FUZZY Collection

by Darby Conley

**Andrews McMeel
Publishing, LLC**

Kansas City • Sydney • London

Get Fuzzy is distributed internationally by Universal Uclick.

Masters of the Nonsenseverse copyright © 2011 by Darby Conley. All rights reserved. Printed in the United States of America. No part of this book may be used or reproduced in any manner whatsoever without written permission except in the case of reprints in the context of reviews.

Andrews McMeel Publishing, LLC
an Andrews McMeel Universal company
1130 Walnut Street, Kansas City, Missouri 64106
www.andrewsmcmeel.com

11 12 13 14 15 RR2 10 9 8 7 6 5 4 3 2 1

ISBN: 978-1-4494-2020-8

Library of Congress Control Number: 2011938595

Get Fuzzy can be viewed on the Internet at
www.gocomics.com/getfuzzy

──────── **ATTENTION: SCHOOLS AND BUSINESSES** ────────

Andrews McMeel books are available at quantity discounts with bulk purchase for educational, business, or sales promotional use. For information, please email the Special Sales Department:
specialsales@amuniversal.com

Other *Get Fuzzy* Books

The Dog Is Not a Toy (House Rule #4)

Fuzzy Logic: Get Fuzzy 2

The Get Fuzzy Experience: Are You Bucksperienced

I Would Have Bought You a Cat, But . . .

Blueprint for Disaster

Say Cheesy

Scrum Bums

I'm Ready for My Movie Contract

Take Our Cat, Please!

Ignorance, Thy Name Is Bucky

Dumbheart

Treasuries

Groovitude: A Get Fuzzy Treasury

Bucky Katt's Big Book of Fun

Loserpalooza

The Potpourrific Great Big Grab Bag of Get Fuzzy

Treasury of the Lost Litter Box

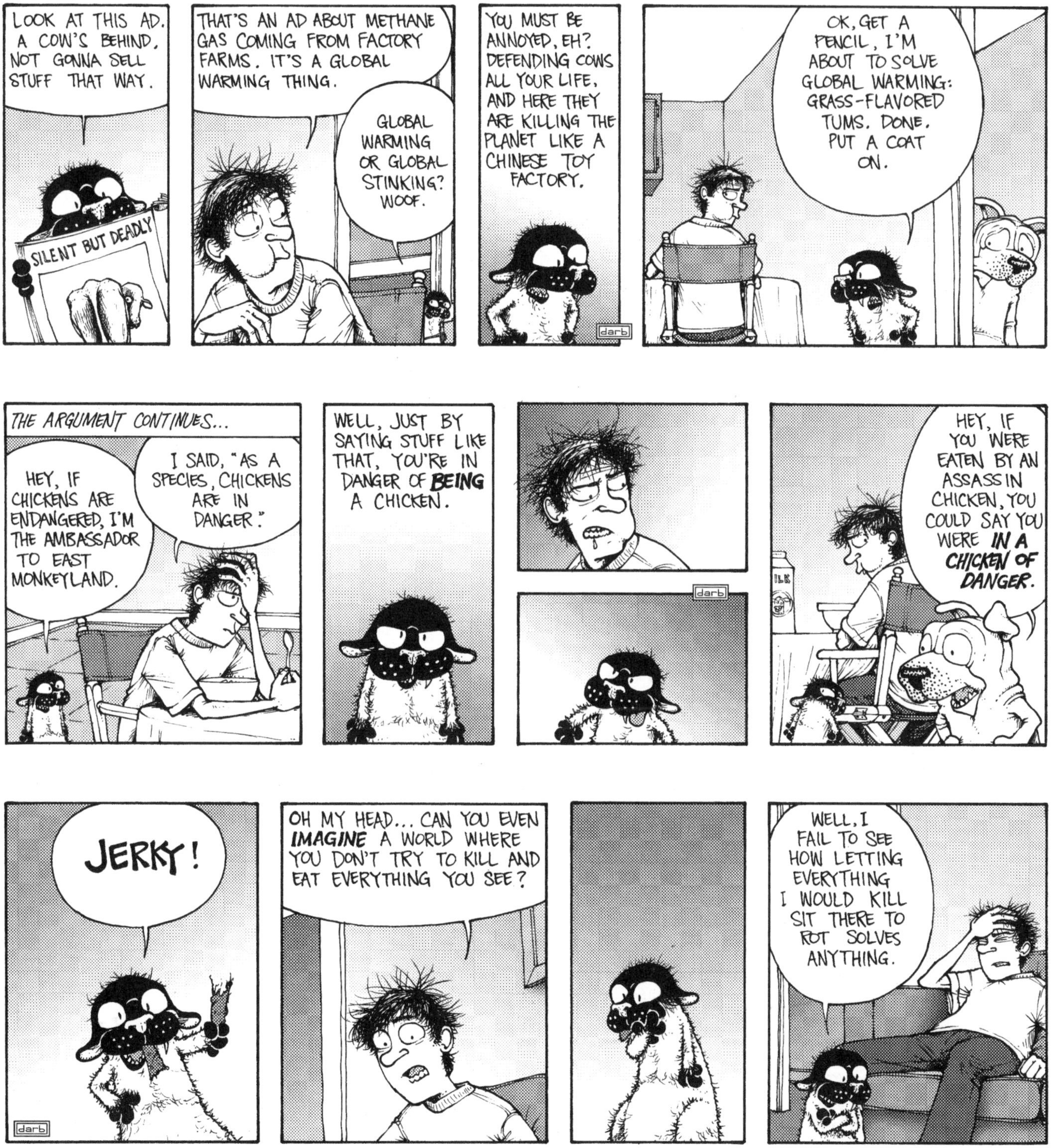
LOOK AT THIS AD. A COW'S BEHIND. NOT GONNA SELL STUFF THAT WAY.
SILENT BUT DEADLY
THAT'S AN AD ABOUT METHANE GAS COMING FROM FACTORY FARMS. IT'S A GLOBAL WARMING THING.
GLOBAL WARMING OR GLOBAL STINKING? WOOF.
YOU MUST BE ANNOYED, EH? DEFENDING COWS ALL YOUR LIFE, AND HERE THEY ARE KILLING THE PLANET LIKE A CHINESE TOY FACTORY.
OK, GET A PENCIL, I'M ABOUT TO SOLVE GLOBAL WARMING: GRASS-FLAVORED TUMS. DONE. PUT A COAT ON.
THE ARGUMENT CONTINUES...
I SAID, "AS A SPECIES, CHICKENS ARE IN DANGER."
HEY, IF CHICKENS ARE ENDANGERED, I'M THE AMBASSADOR TO EAST MONKEYLAND.
WELL, JUST BY SAYING STUFF LIKE THAT, YOU'RE IN DANGER OF **BEING** A CHICKEN.
HEY, IF YOU WERE EATEN BY AN ASSASSIN CHICKEN, YOU COULD SAY YOU WERE **IN A CHICKEN OF DANGER.**
JERKY!
OH MY HEAD... CAN YOU EVEN **IMAGINE** A WORLD WHERE YOU DON'T TRY TO KILL AND EAT EVERYTHING YOU SEE?
WELL, I FAIL TO SEE HOW LETTING EVERYTHING I WOULD KILL SIT THERE TO ROT SOLVES ANYTHING.

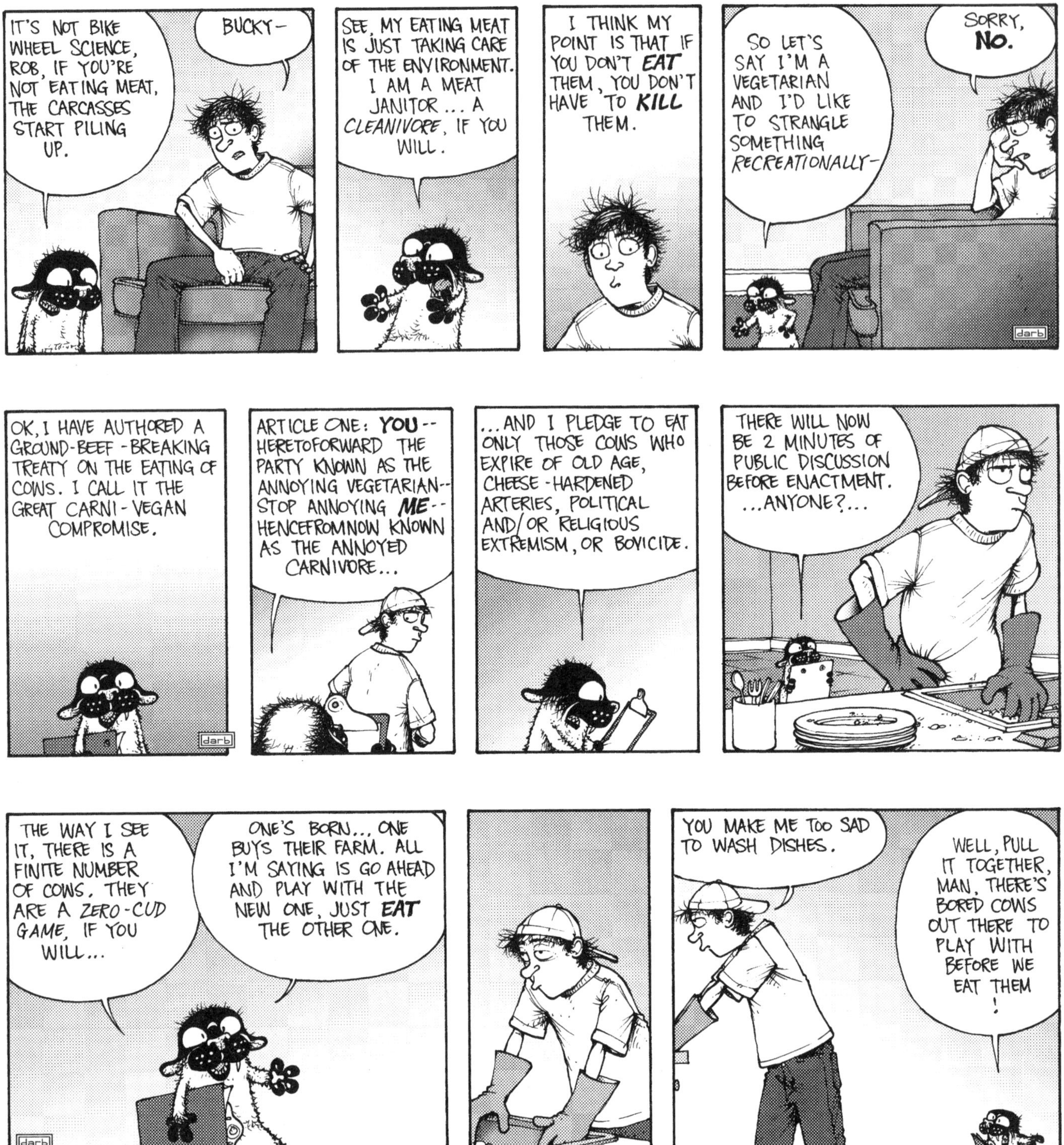
IT'S NOT BIKE WHEEL SCIENCE, ROB, IF YOU'RE NOT EATING MEAT, THE CARCASSES START PILING UP.
BUCKY–
SEE, MY EATING MEAT IS JUST TAKING CARE OF THE ENVIRONMENT. I AM A MEAT JANITOR... A CLEANIVORE, IF YOU WILL.
I THINK MY POINT IS THAT IF YOU DON'T EAT THEM, YOU DON'T HAVE TO KILL THEM.
SO LET'S SAY I'M A VEGETARIAN AND I'D LIKE TO STRANGLE SOMETHING RECREATIONALLY–
SORRY, NO.
OK, I HAVE AUTHORED A GROUND-BEEF-BREAKING TREATY ON THE EATING OF COWS. I CALL IT THE GREAT CARNI-VEGAN COMPROMISE.
ARTICLE ONE: YOU-- HERETOFORWARD THE PARTY KNOWN AS THE ANNOYING VEGETARIAN-- STOP ANNOYING ME-- HENCEFROMNOW KNOWN AS THE ANNOYED CARNIVORE...
...AND I PLEDGE TO EAT ONLY THOSE COWS WHO EXPIRE OF OLD AGE, CHEESE-HARDENED ARTERIES, POLITICAL AND/OR RELIGIOUS EXTREMISM, OR BOVICIDE.
THERE WILL NOW BE 2 MINUTES OF PUBLIC DISCUSSION BEFORE ENACTMENT. ...ANYONE?...
THE WAY I SEE IT, THERE IS A FINITE NUMBER OF COWS. THEY ARE A ZERO-CUD GAME, IF YOU WILL...
ONE'S BORN..., ONE BUYS THEIR FARM. ALL I'M SAYING IS GO AHEAD AND PLAY WITH THE NEW ONE, JUST EAT THE OTHER ONE.
YOU MAKE ME TOO SAD TO WASH DISHES.
WELL, PULL IT TOGETHER, MAN. THERE'S BORED COWS OUT THERE TO PLAY WITH BEFORE WE EAT THEM!

WHO WAS THAT?

OH...BUCKY... HOW LONG HAVE ...THAT WAS NOBODY. JUST A COLLILEAGUE. I MEAN COLLIE.

THAT WAS NO COLLIE. WHAT DID HE GIVE YOU?

JUST SOME ...UM...SOME NOTHING.

HE GAVE YOU SOME "NOTHING"?

VERY WELL, MAYBE IT'S TIME YOU KNEW...I AM PART OF A SECRET SOCIETY.

I IMAGINE ANY SOCIETY YOU WERE IN WOULD WANT TO REMAIN SECRET, SURE.

HEY, DO YOU GUYS HAVE A SECRET RUMP SNIFF?

SO WHAT IS IT, THE ILLUMINASTI? THE C.I. UGLY?

IF YOU'LL EXCUSE ME, I HAVE TO GO.

THERE GOES AGENT DOUBLE-O I.Q. LICENSED AGAINST RABIES.

PARDON?

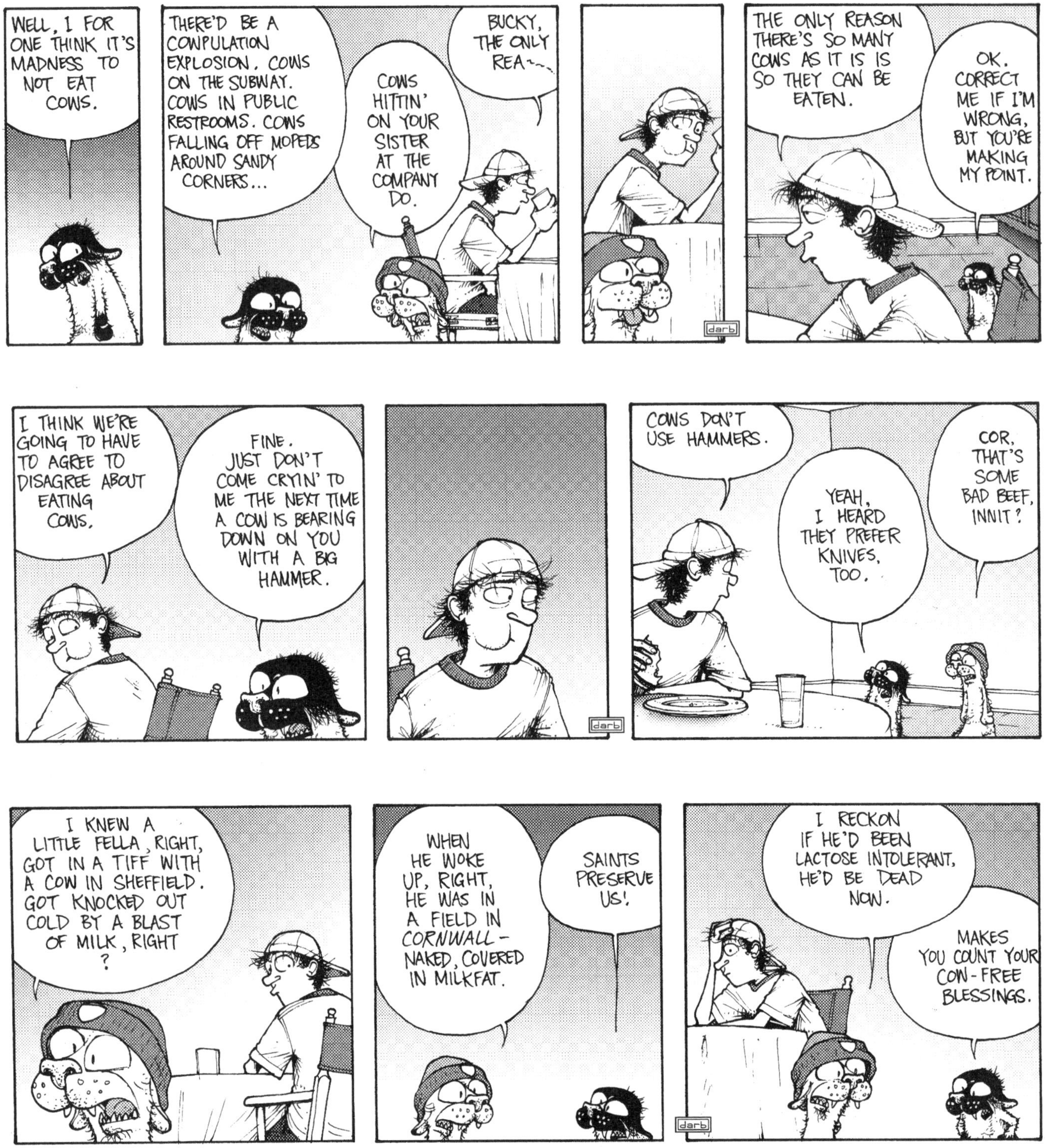
WELL, I FOR ONE THINK IT'S MADNESS TO NOT EAT COWS.
THERE'D BE A COWPULATION EXPLOSION. COWS ON THE SUBWAY. COWS IN PUBLIC RESTROOMS. COWS FALLING OFF MOPEDS AROUND SANDY CORNERS...
COWS HITTIN' ON YOUR SISTER AT THE COMPANY DO.
BUCKY, THE ONLY REA--
darb
THE ONLY REASON THERE'S SO MANY COWS AS IT IS IS SO THEY CAN BE EATEN.
OK. CORRECT ME IF I'M WRONG, BUT YOU'RE MAKING MY POINT.
I THINK WE'RE GOING TO HAVE TO AGREE TO DISAGREE ABOUT EATING COWS.
FINE. JUST DON'T COME CRYIN' TO ME THE NEXT TIME A COW IS BEARING DOWN ON YOU WITH A BIG HAMMER.
darb
COWS DON'T USE HAMMERS.
YEAH, I HEARD THEY PREFER KNIVES, TOO.
COR, THAT'S SOME BAD BEEF, INNIT?
I KNEW A LITTLE FELLA, RIGHT, GOT IN A TIFF WITH A COW IN SHEFFIELD. GOT KNOCKED OUT COLD BY A BLAST OF MILK, RIGHT?
WHEN HE WOKE UP, RIGHT, HE WAS IN A FIELD IN CORNWALL - NAKED, COVERED IN MILKFAT.
SAINTS PRESERVE US!
darb
I RECKON IF HE'D BEEN LACTOSE INTOLERANT, HE'D BE DEAD NOW.
MAKES YOU COUNT YOUR COW-FREE BLESSINGS.

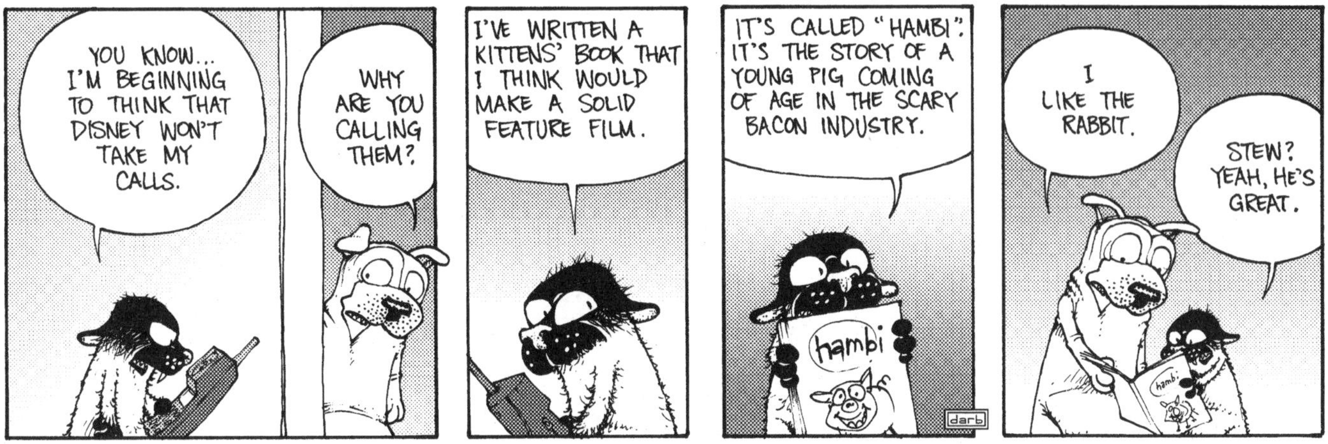
YOU KNOW... I'M BEGINNING TO THINK THAT DISNEY WON'T TAKE MY CALLS.
WHY ARE YOU CALLING THEM?
I'VE WRITTEN A KITTENS' BOOK THAT I THINK WOULD MAKE A SOLID FEATURE FILM.
IT'S CALLED "HAMBI". IT'S THE STORY OF A YOUNG PIG COMING OF AGE IN THE SCARY BACON INDUSTRY.
hambi
darb
I LIKE THE RABBIT.
STEW? YEAH, HE'S GREAT.

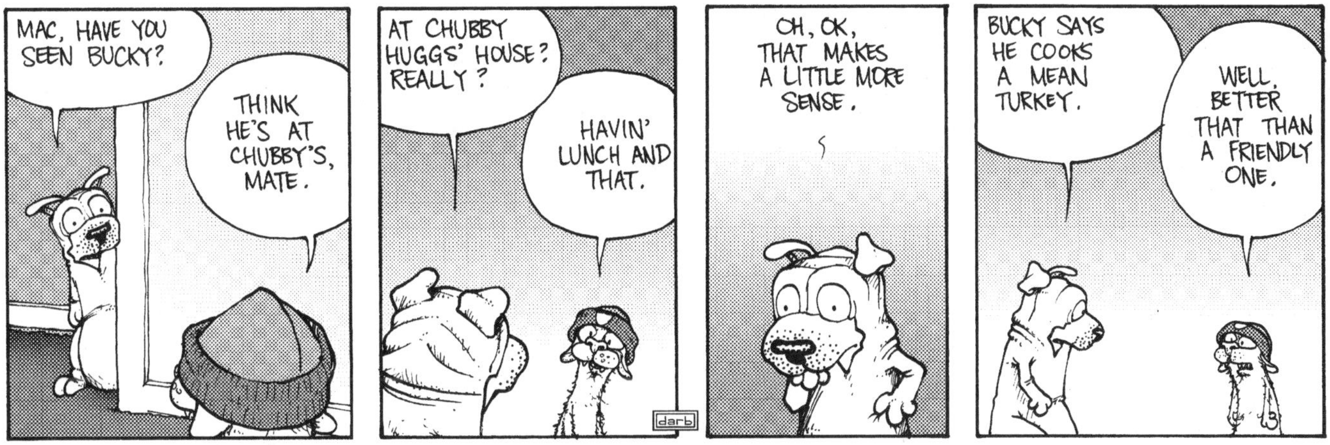
MAC, HAVE YOU SEEN BUCKY?
THINK HE'S AT CHUBBY'S, MATE.
AT CHUBBY HUGGS' HOUSE? REALLY?
HAVIN' LUNCH AND THAT.
darb
OH, OK, THAT MAKES A LITTLE MORE SENSE.
BUCKY SAYS HE COOKS A MEAN TURKEY.
WELL, BETTER THAT THAN A FRIENDLY ONE.

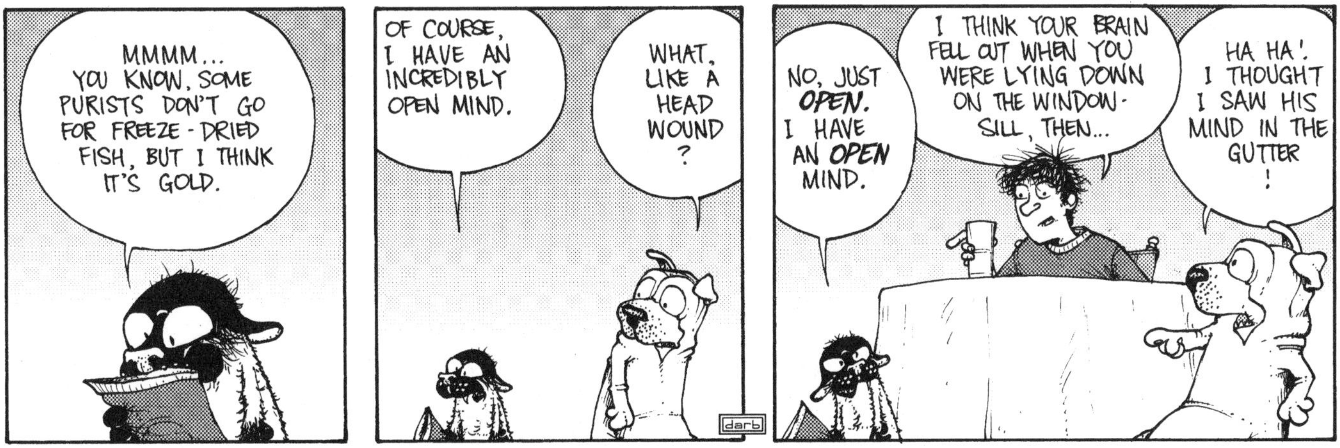
MMMM... YOU KNOW, SOME PURISTS DON'T GO FOR FREEZE-DRIED FISH, BUT I THINK IT'S GOLD.
OF COURSE, I HAVE AN INCREDIBLY OPEN MIND.
WHAT, LIKE A HEAD WOUND?
darb
NO, JUST *OPEN*. I HAVE AN *OPEN* MIND.
I THINK YOUR BRAIN FELL OUT WHEN YOU WERE LYING DOWN ON THE WINDOW-SILL, THEN...
HA HA! I THOUGHT I SAW HIS MIND IN THE GUTTER!

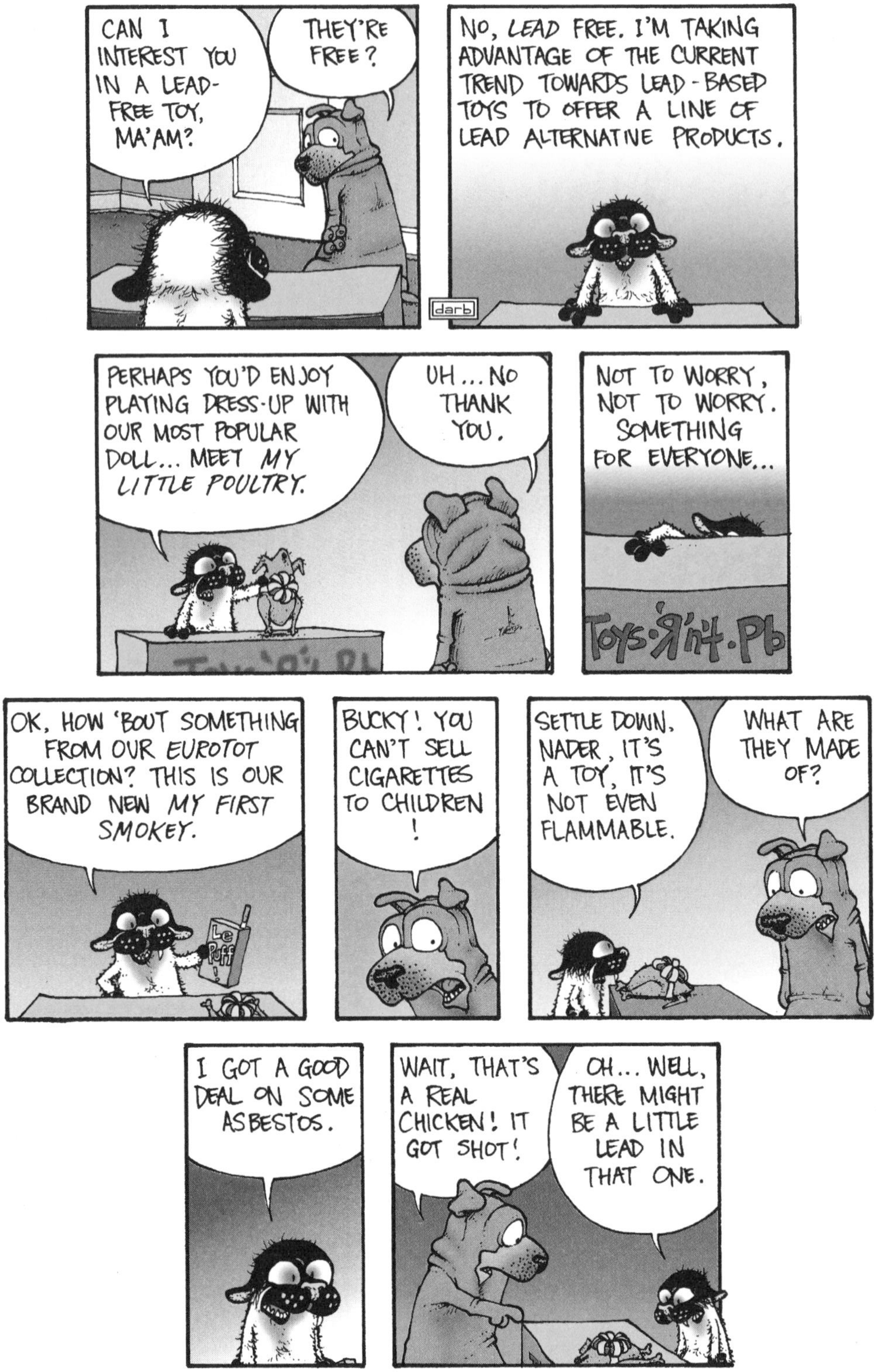
CAN I INTEREST YOU IN A LEAD-FREE TOY, MA'AM?
THEY'RE FREE?
NO, *LEAD* FREE. I'M TAKING ADVANTAGE OF THE CURRENT TREND TOWARDS LEAD-BASED TOYS TO OFFER A LINE OF LEAD ALTERNATIVE PRODUCTS.
darb
PERHAPS YOU'D ENJOY PLAYING DRESS-UP WITH OUR MOST POPULAR DOLL... MEET *MY LITTLE POULTRY.*
UH... NO THANK YOU.
NOT TO WORRY, NOT TO WORRY. SOMETHING FOR EVERYONE...
Toys·Я'n't·Pb
OK, HOW 'BOUT SOMETHING FROM OUR *EUROTOT* COLLECTION? THIS IS OUR BRAND NEW *MY FIRST SMOKEY.*
Le Puff!
BUCKY! YOU CAN'T SELL CIGARETTES TO CHILDREN!
SETTLE DOWN, NADER, IT'S A TOY, IT'S NOT EVEN FLAMMABLE.
WHAT ARE THEY MADE OF?
I GOT A GOOD DEAL ON SOME ASBESTOS.
WAIT, THAT'S A REAL CHICKEN! IT GOT SHOT!
OH... WELL, THERE MIGHT BE A LITTLE LEAD IN THAT ONE.

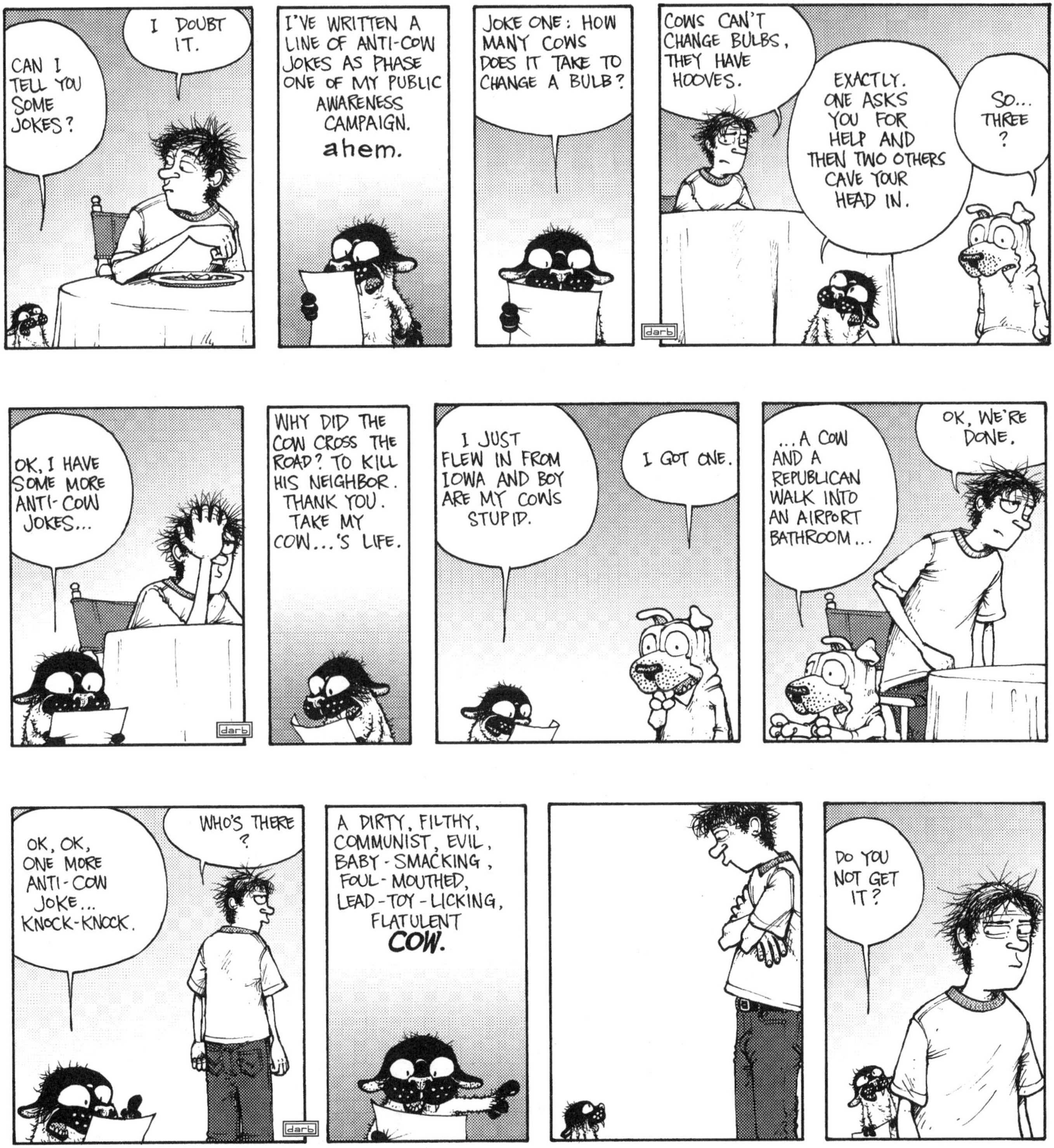

CAN I TELL YOU SOME JOKES?
I DOUBT IT.
I'VE WRITTEN A LINE OF ANTI-COW JOKES AS PHASE ONE OF MY PUBLIC AWARENESS CAMPAIGN.
ahem.
JOKE ONE: HOW MANY COWS DOES IT TAKE TO CHANGE A BULB?
COWS CAN'T CHANGE BULBS, THEY HAVE HOOVES.
EXACTLY. ONE ASKS YOU FOR HELP AND THEN TWO OTHERS CAVE YOUR HEAD IN.
SO... THREE?
darb
OK, I HAVE SOME MORE ANTI-COW JOKES...
darb
WHY DID THE COW CROSS THE ROAD? TO KILL HIS NEIGHBOR. THANK YOU. TAKE MY COW...'S LIFE.
I JUST FLEW IN FROM IOWA AND BOY ARE MY COWS STUPID.
I GOT ONE.
...A COW AND A REPUBLICAN WALK INTO AN AIRPORT BATHROOM...
OK, WE'RE DONE.
OK, OK, ONE MORE ANTI-COW JOKE... KNOCK-KNOCK.
WHO'S THERE?
darb
A DIRTY, FILTHY, COMMUNIST, EVIL, BABY-SMACKING, FOUL-MOUTHED, LEAD-TOY-LICKING, FLATULENT COW.
DO YOU NOT GET IT?

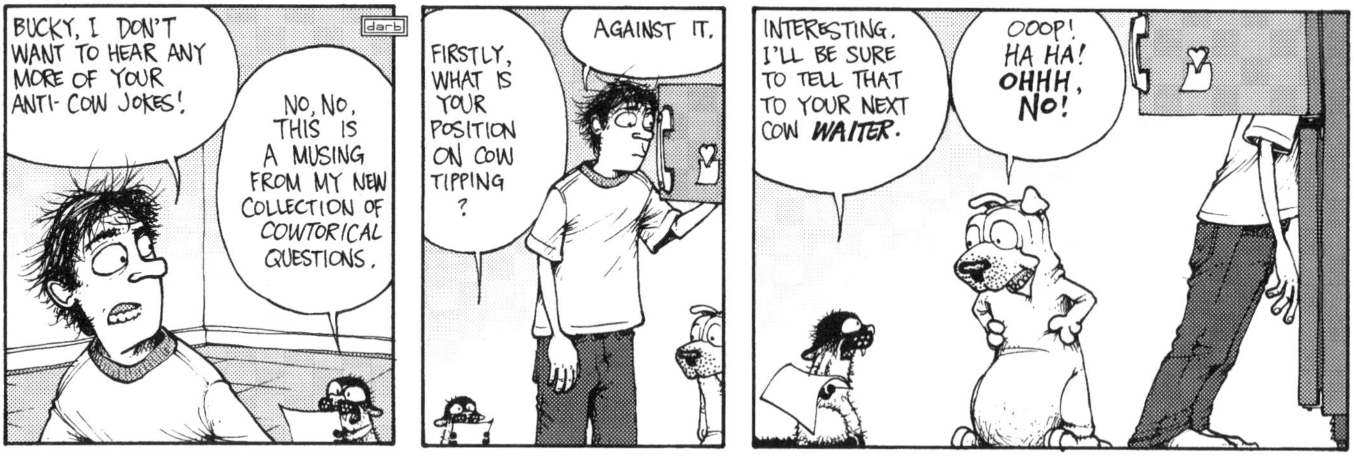
darb
BUCKY, I DON'T WANT TO HEAR ANY MORE OF YOUR ANTI-COW JOKES!
NO, NO, THIS IS A MUSING FROM MY NEW COLLECTION OF COWTORICAL QUESTIONS.
FIRSTLY, WHAT IS YOUR POSITION ON COW TIPPING ?
AGAINST IT.
INTERESTING. I'LL BE SURE TO TELL THAT TO YOUR NEXT COW **WAITER**.
OOOP! HA HA! **OHHH, NO!**

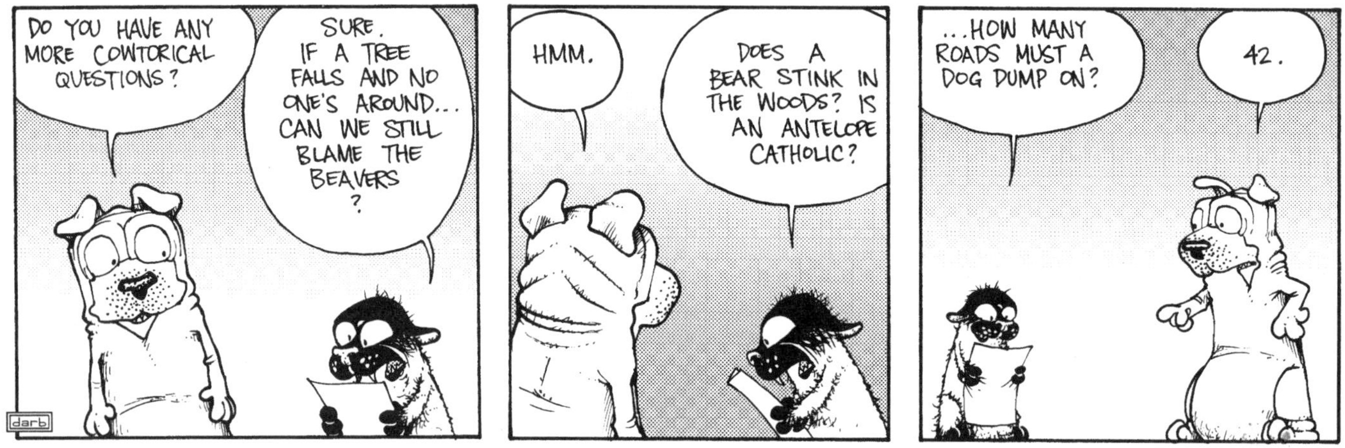
DO YOU HAVE ANY MORE COWTORICAL QUESTIONS?
SURE. IF A TREE FALLS AND NO ONE'S AROUND... CAN WE STILL BLAME THE BEAVERS ?
darb
HMM.
DOES A BEAR STINK IN THE WOODS? IS AN ANTELOPE CATHOLIC?
...HOW MANY ROADS MUST A DOG DUMP ON?
42.

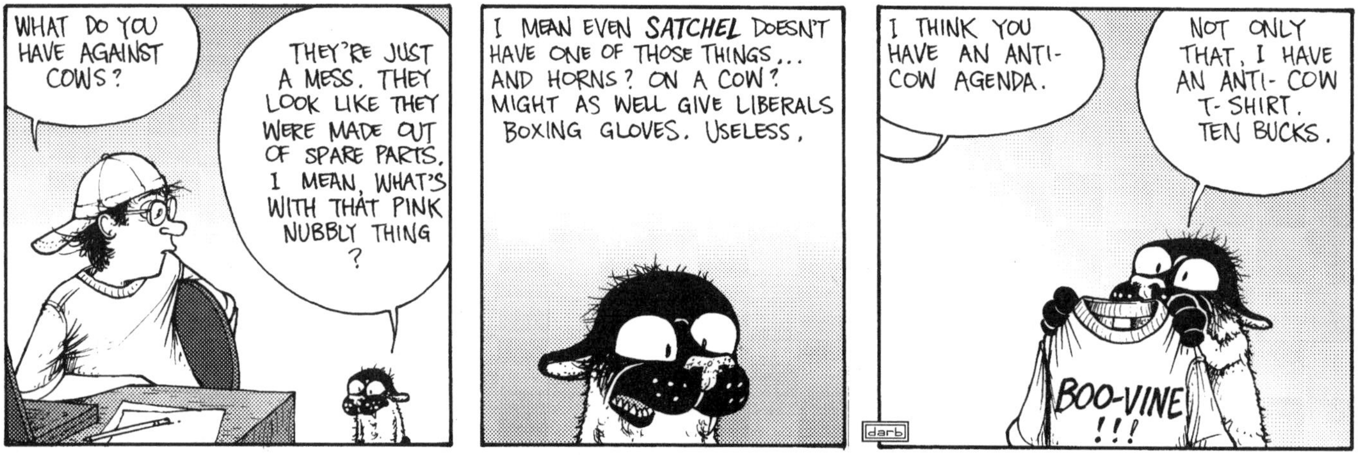
WHAT DO YOU HAVE AGAINST COWS?
THEY'RE JUST A MESS. THEY LOOK LIKE THEY WERE MADE OUT OF SPARE PARTS. I MEAN, WHAT'S WITH THAT PINK NUBBLY THING ?
I MEAN EVEN **SATCHEL** DOESN'T HAVE ONE OF THOSE THINGS... AND HORNS? ON A COW? MIGHT AS WELL GIVE LIBERALS BOXING GLOVES. USELESS.
I THINK YOU HAVE AN ANTI-COW AGENDA.
NOT ONLY THAT, I HAVE AN ANTI-COW T-SHIRT. TEN BUCKS.
darb
BOO-VINE !!!

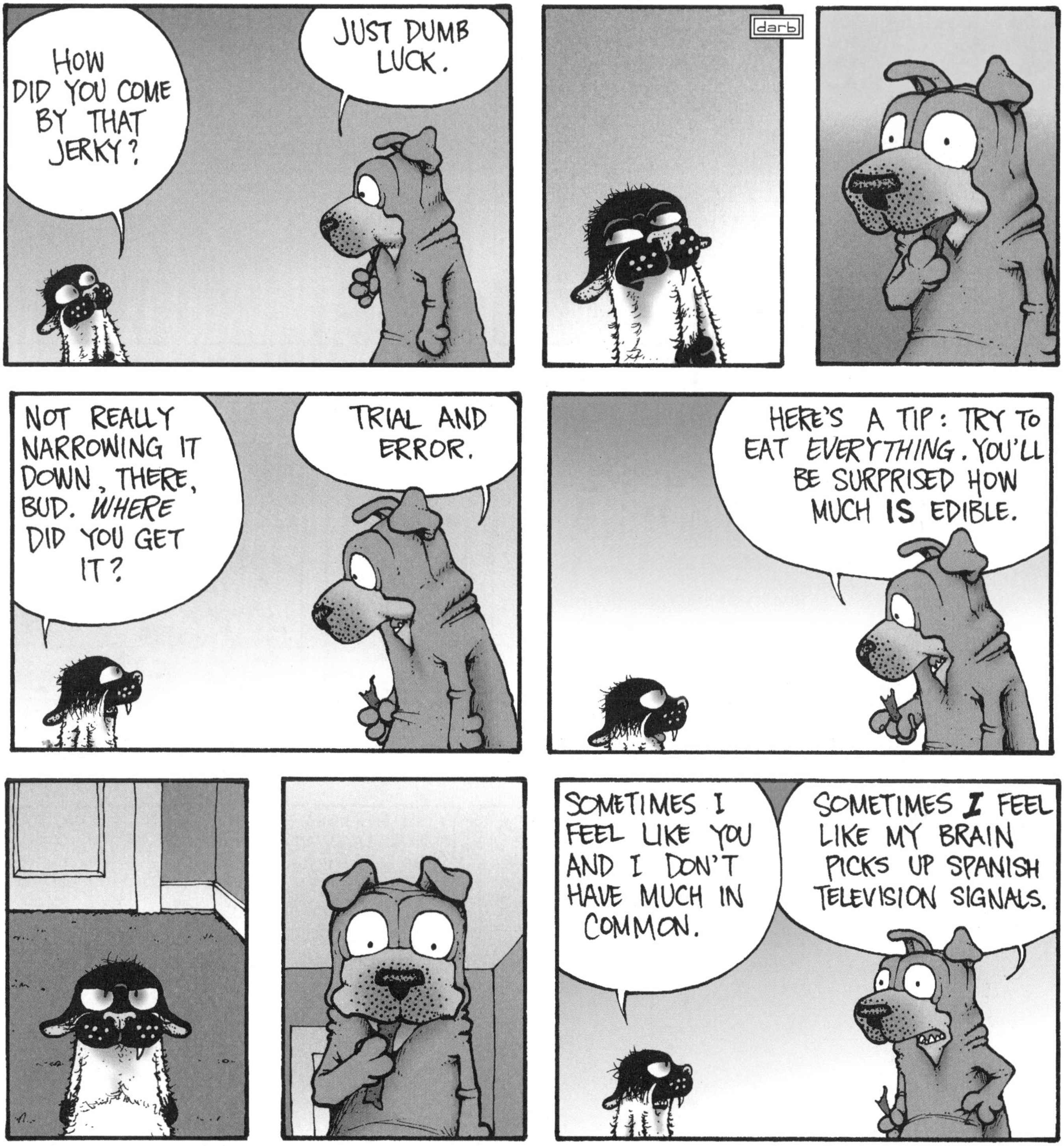
HOW DID YOU COME BY THAT JERKY?
JUST DUMB LUCK.
darb
NOT REALLY NARROWING IT DOWN, THERE, BUD. WHERE DID YOU GET IT?
TRIAL AND ERROR.
HERE'S A TIP: TRY TO EAT EVERYTHING. YOU'LL BE SURPRISED HOW MUCH IS EDIBLE.
SOMETIMES I FEEL LIKE YOU AND I DON'T HAVE MUCH IN COMMON.
SOMETIMES I FEEL LIKE MY BRAIN PICKS UP SPANISH TELEVISION SIGNALS.

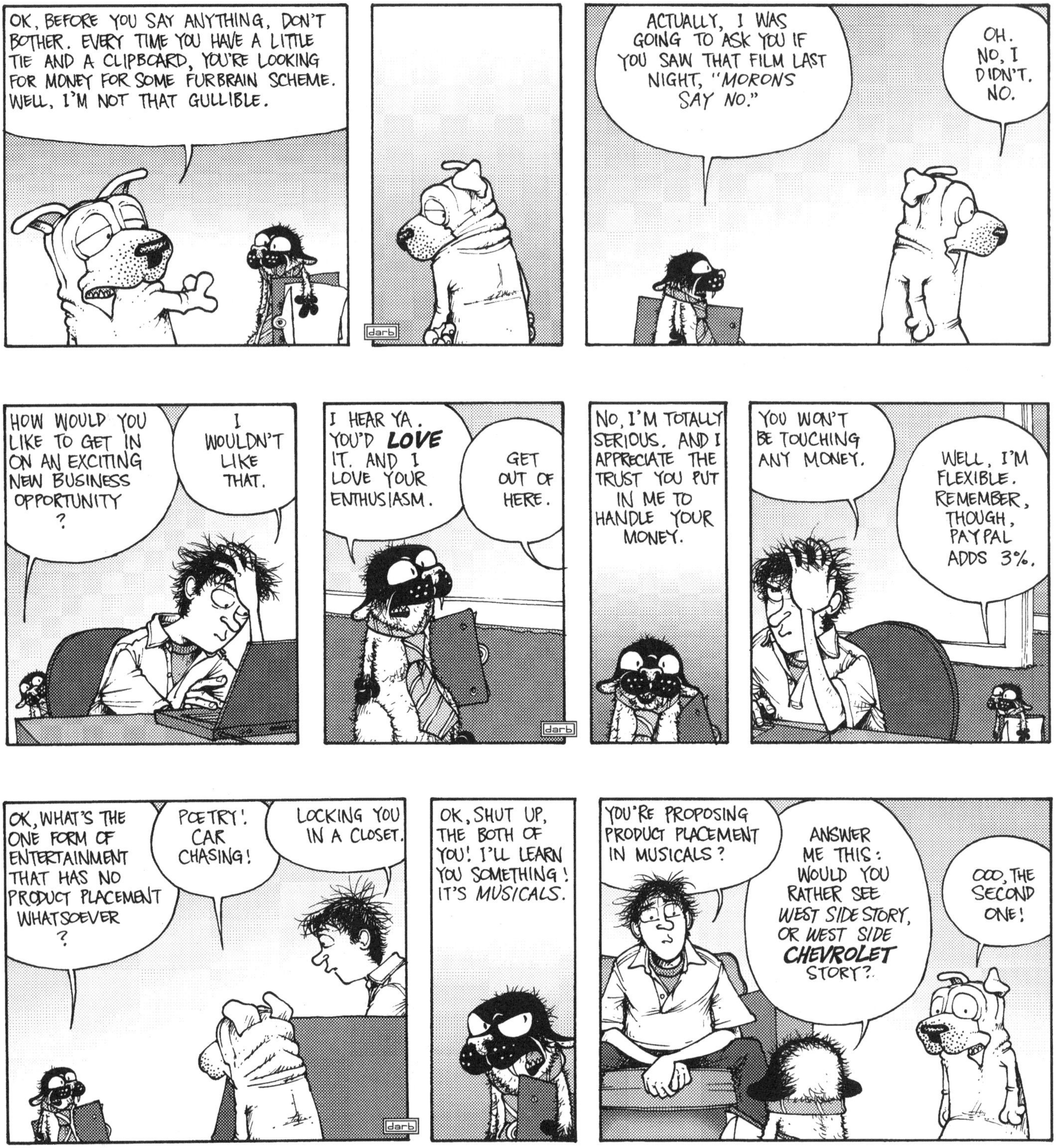
OK, BEFORE YOU SAY ANYTHING, DON'T BOTHER. EVERY TIME YOU HAVE A LITTLE TIE AND A CLIPBOARD, YOU'RE LOOKING FOR MONEY FOR SOME FURBRAIN SCHEME. WELL, I'M NOT THAT GULLIBLE.
darb
ACTUALLY, I WAS GOING TO ASK YOU IF YOU SAW THAT FILM LAST NIGHT, "*MORONS SAY NO.*"
OH. NO, I DIDN'T. NO.
HOW WOULD YOU LIKE TO GET IN ON AN EXCITING NEW BUSINESS OPPORTUNITY ?
I WOULDN'T LIKE THAT.
I HEAR YA. YOU'D **LOVE** IT. AND I LOVE YOUR ENTHUSIASM.
GET OUT OF HERE.
darb
NO, I'M TOTALLY SERIOUS. AND I APPRECIATE THE TRUST YOU PUT IN ME TO HANDLE YOUR MONEY.
YOU WON'T BE TOUCHING ANY MONEY.
WELL, I'M FLEXIBLE. REMEMBER, THOUGH, PAYPAL ADDS 3%.
OK, WHAT'S THE ONE FORM OF ENTERTAINMENT THAT HAS NO PRODUCT PLACEMENT WHATSOEVER ?
POETRY! CAR CHASING!
LOCKING YOU IN A CLOSET.
darb
OK, SHUT UP, THE BOTH OF YOU! I'LL LEARN YOU SOMETHING! IT'S *MUSICALS*.
YOU'RE PROPOSING PRODUCT PLACEMENT IN MUSICALS?
ANSWER ME THIS: WOULD YOU RATHER SEE *WEST SIDE STORY*, OR *WEST SIDE* **CHEVROLET** STORY?
OOO, THE SECOND ONE!

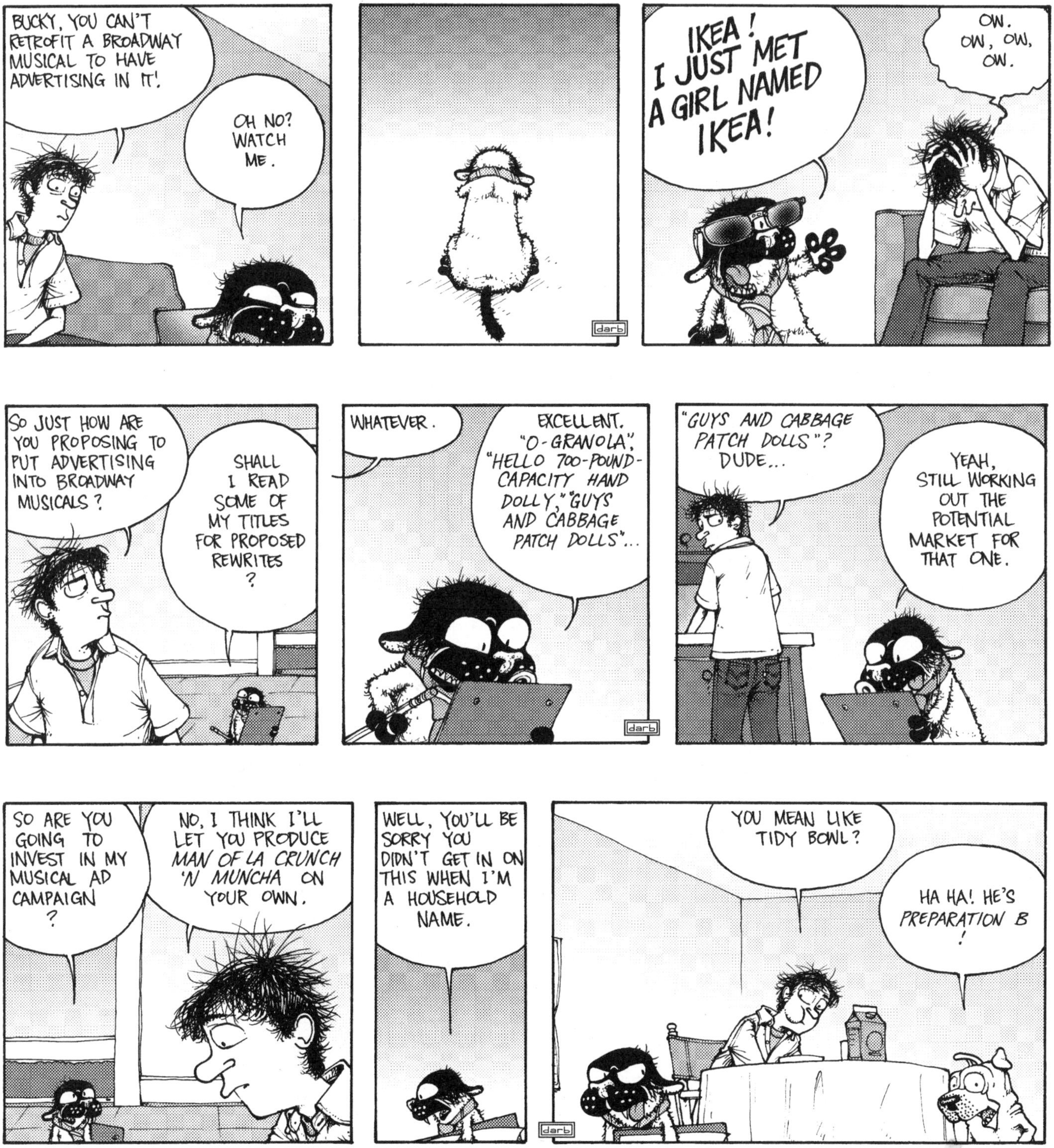
BUCKY, YOU CAN'T RETROFIT A BROADWAY MUSICAL TO HAVE ADVERTISING IN IT!
OH NO? WATCH ME.
darb
IKEA! I JUST MET A GIRL NAMED IKEA!
OW. OW, OW, OW.
SO JUST HOW ARE YOU PROPOSING TO PUT ADVERTISING INTO BROADWAY MUSICALS?
SHALL I READ SOME OF MY TITLES FOR PROPOSED REWRITES?
WHATEVER.
EXCELLENT. "O-GRANOLA", "HELLO 700-POUND-CAPACITY HAND DOLLY," "GUYS AND CABBAGE PATCH DOLLS"...
darb
"GUYS AND CABBAGE PATCH DOLLS"? DUDE...
YEAH, STILL WORKING OUT THE POTENTIAL MARKET FOR THAT ONE.
SO ARE YOU GOING TO INVEST IN MY MUSICAL AD CAMPAIGN?
NO, I THINK I'LL LET YOU PRODUCE *MAN OF LA CRUNCH 'N MUNCHA* ON YOUR OWN.
WELL, YOU'LL BE SORRY YOU DIDN'T GET IN ON THIS WHEN I'M A HOUSEHOLD NAME.
darb
YOU MEAN LIKE TIDY BOWL?
HA HA! HE'S *PREPARATION B*!

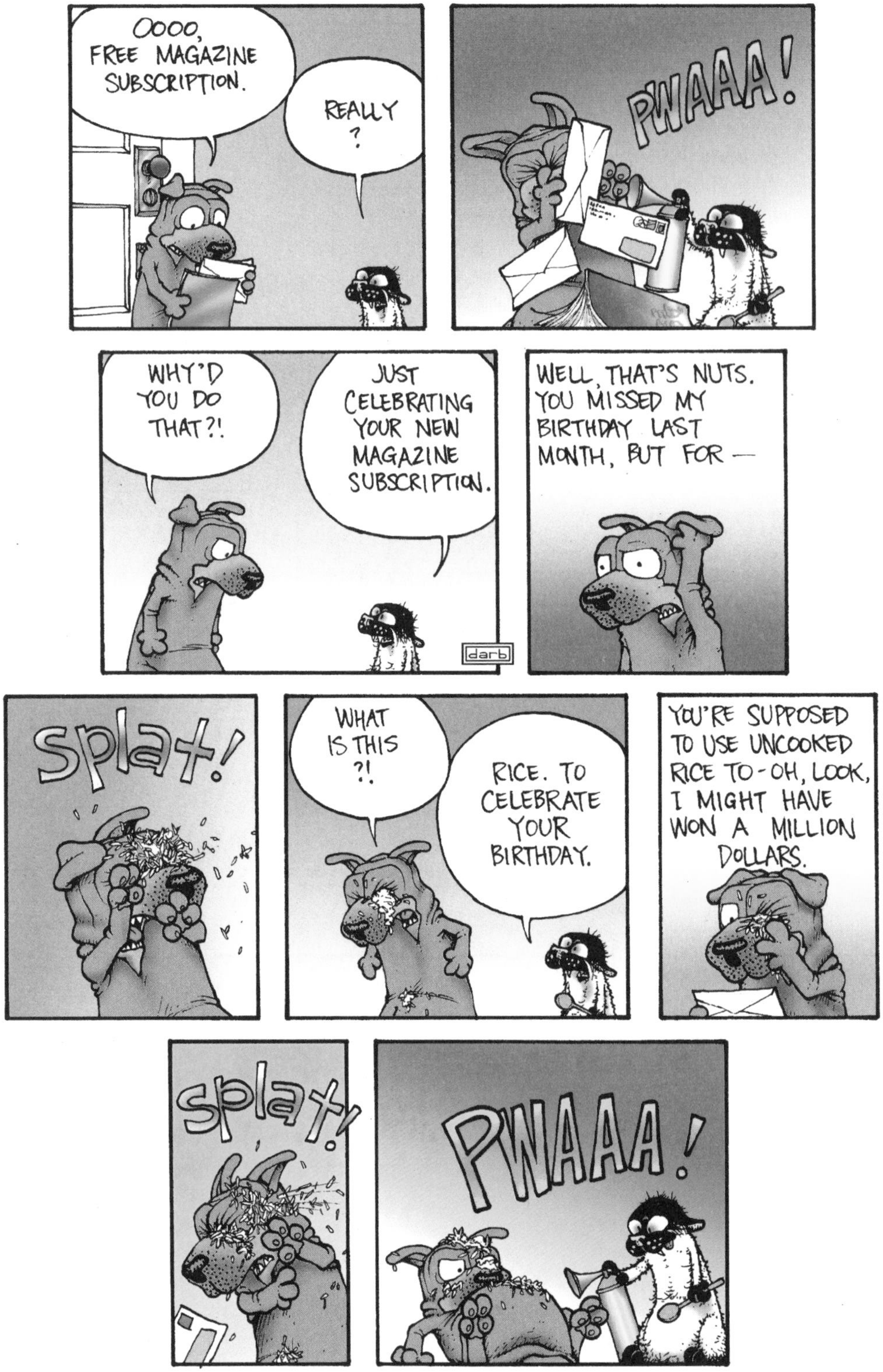
OOOO, FREE MAGAZINE SUBSCRIPTION.
REALLY ?
PWAAA!
WHY'D YOU DO THAT?!
JUST CELEBRATING YOUR NEW MAGAZINE SUBSCRIPTION.
darb
WELL, THAT'S NUTS. YOU MISSED MY BIRTHDAY LAST MONTH, BUT FOR —
splat!
WHAT IS THIS ?!
RICE. TO CELEBRATE YOUR BIRTHDAY.
YOU'RE SUPPOSED TO USE UNCOOKED RICE TO - OH, LOOK, I MIGHT HAVE WON A MILLION DOLLARS.
splat!
PWAAA!

Panel 1:
OH, HI! WHAT ARE YOU DOING IN MY ROOM? IS THAT A PIE?

IT'S AN IMAGE PIE.

Panel 2:
STUDIES SHOW IT'S IMPOSSIBLE TO THINK THAT SOMEONE HOLDING A PIE JUST LOOTED YOUR PIGGY BANK.

WAIT.... WHAT DOES "LOOTED" MEAN?

Panel 3:

Panel 4:
CARE FOR A DIVERSION CRACKER?

YEAH, YEAH!

Panel 5:
BUCKY, WHERE DID ALL THE STUFF IN MY ROOM GO?

OH, I CLEANED YOUR ROOM EARLIER.

Panel 6:
THERE'S NOTHING LEFT IN MY ROOM...

NO PROBLEM, CHIEF. YOU'RE WELCOME.

Panel 7:
BUT YOU, LIKE, STOLE ALL OF MY STUFF...

WELL, I MAINTAIN I WAS CLEANING, AND IT'S THE THOUGHT THAT COUNTS.

Panel 8:
NO, THE BRAIN COUNTS, AND YOUR BRAIN ALSO JUST STOLE ALL MY STUFF!

LOOK, IF YOU'RE GONNA GET TECHNICAL, THE FINGERS COUNT!

Panel 9:
EVERYBODY KNOWS YOU COUNT WITH YOUR FINGERS! 1... 2... 6... UH... 1 AGAIN...

BUT YOUR BRAIN IS DOING THE COUNTING, IT CONTROLS YOUR FINGERS.

Panel 10:
OH, YEAH? IF MY BRAIN CONTROLLED MY PAW, COULD MY PAW DO.....

...THIS?!

punch!

Panel 11:
punch punch

OOF!

19

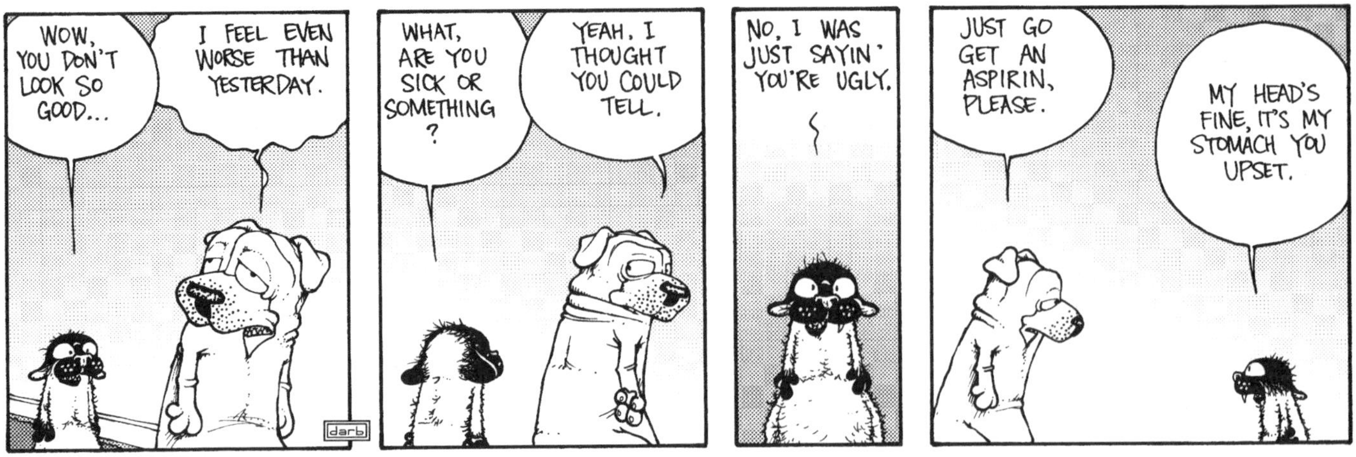
WOW, YOU DON'T LOOK SO GOOD...
I FEEL EVEN WORSE THAN YESTERDAY.
WHAT, ARE YOU SICK OR SOMETHING ?
YEAH. I THOUGHT YOU COULD TELL.
NO, I WAS JUST SAYIN' YOU'RE UGLY.
JUST GO GET AN ASPIRIN, PLEASE.
MY HEAD'S FINE, IT'S MY STOMACH YOU UPSET.
darb

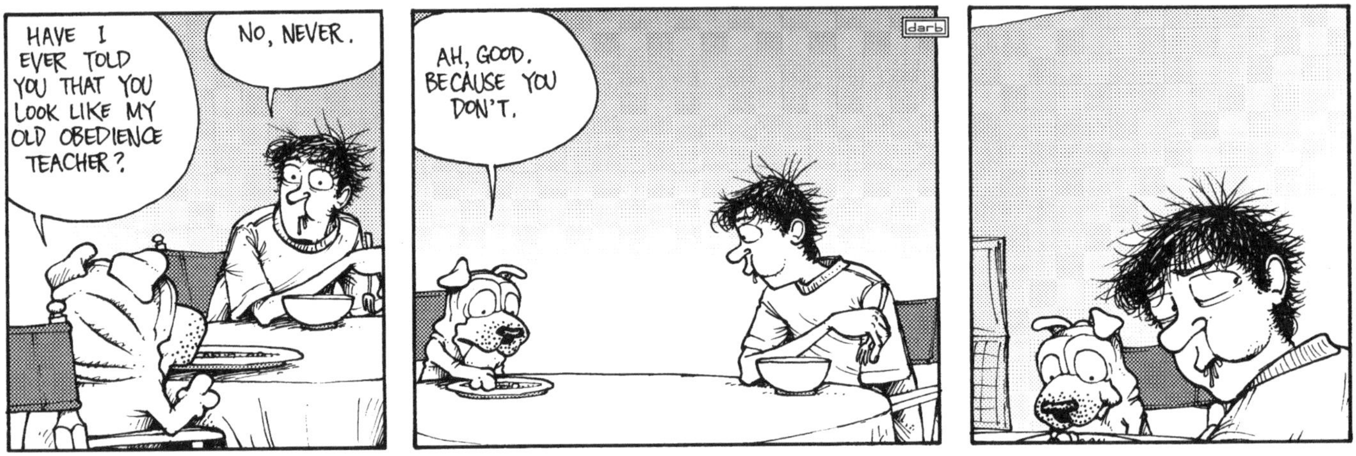
HAVE I EVER TOLD YOU THAT YOU LOOK LIKE MY OLD OBEDIENCE TEACHER ?
NO, NEVER.
AH, GOOD. BECAUSE YOU DON'T.
darb

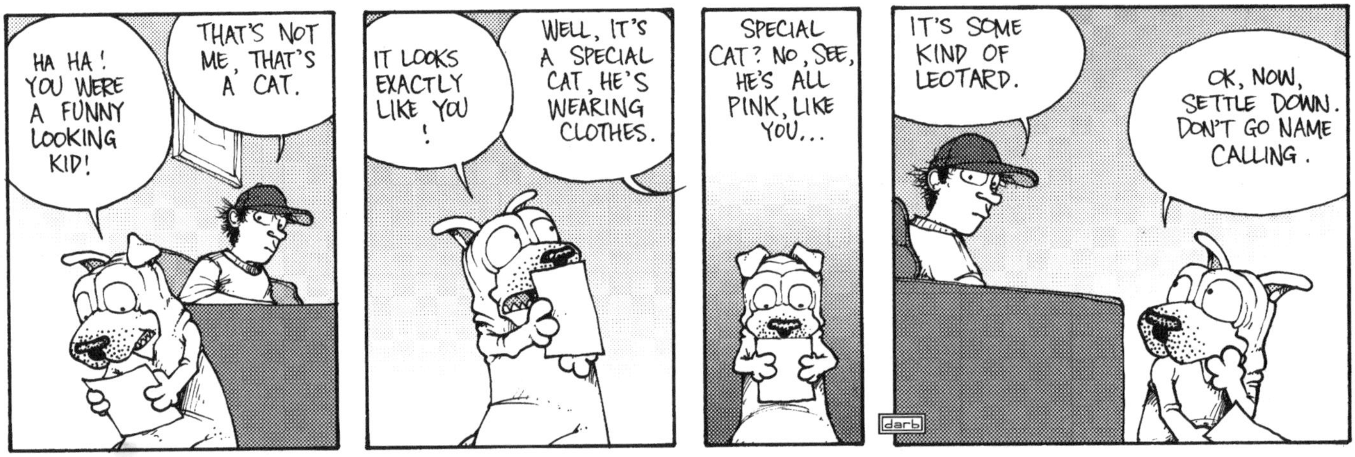
HA HA! YOU WERE A FUNNY LOOKING KID!
THAT'S NOT ME, THAT'S A CAT.
IT LOOKS EXACTLY LIKE YOU !
WELL, IT'S A SPECIAL CAT, HE'S WEARING CLOTHES.
SPECIAL CAT? NO, SEE, HE'S ALL PINK, LIKE YOU...
IT'S SOME KIND OF LEOTARD.
OK, NOW, SETTLE DOWN. DON'T GO NAME CALLING.
darb

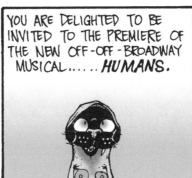

YOU ARE DELIGHTED TO BE INVITED TO THE PREMIERE OF THE NEW OFF-OFF-BROADWAY MUSICAL...... *HUMANS*.

♪ MEMO B! ALL ALONE IN THE IN-TRAY! I CAN FAX YOU AN INVOICE! IT WAS 2 BUCKS LESS THEN!

WHERE... WHERE AM I ?

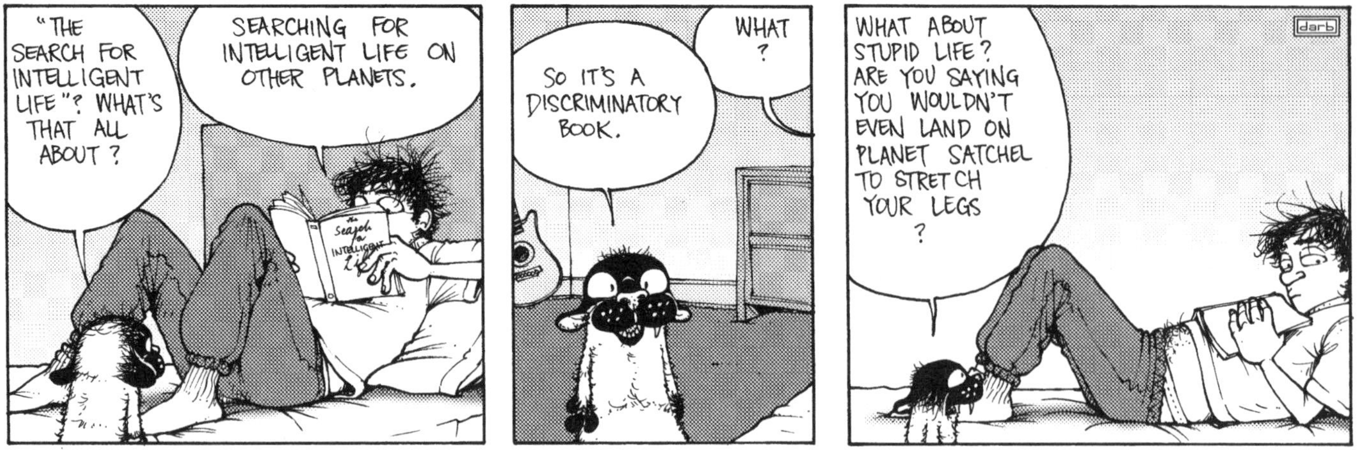
"THE SEARCH FOR INTELLIGENT LIFE"? WHAT'S THAT ALL ABOUT?
SEARCHING FOR INTELLIGENT LIFE ON OTHER PLANETS.
SO IT'S A DISCRIMINATORY BOOK.
WHAT?
WHAT ABOUT STUPID LIFE? ARE YOU SAYING YOU WOULDN'T EVEN LAND ON PLANET SATCHEL TO STRETCH YOUR LEGS?
darb

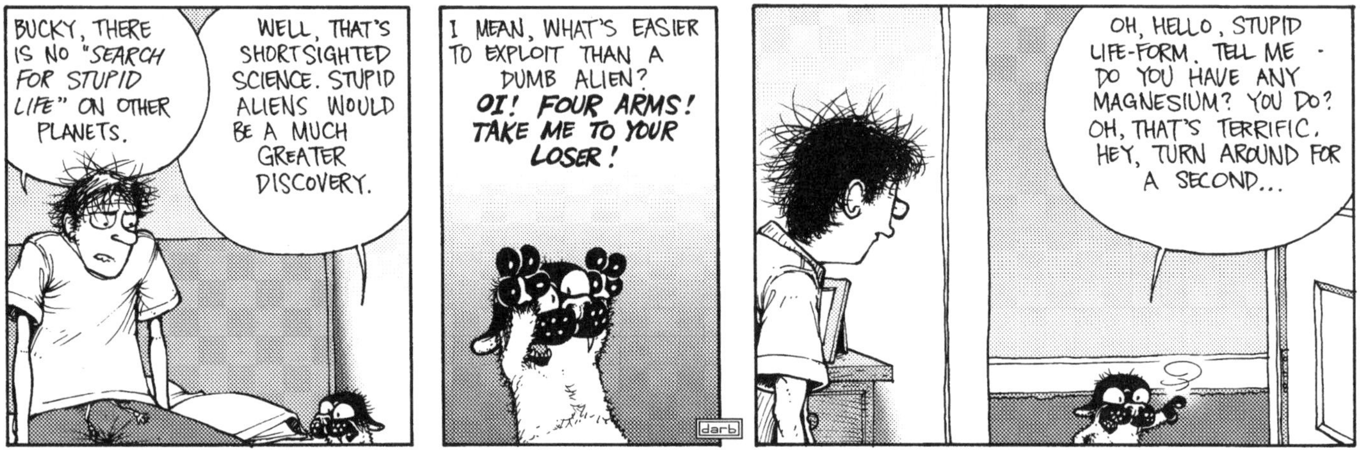
BUCKY, THERE IS NO "*SEARCH FOR STUPID LIFE*" ON OTHER PLANETS.
WELL, THAT'S SHORTSIGHTED SCIENCE. STUPID ALIENS WOULD BE A MUCH GREATER DISCOVERY.
I MEAN, WHAT'S EASIER TO EXPLOIT THAN A DUMB ALIEN?
OI! FOUR ARMS! TAKE ME TO YOUR LOSER!
darb
OH, HELLO, STUPID LIFE-FORM. TELL ME - DO YOU HAVE ANY MAGNESIUM? YOU DO? OH, THAT'S TERRIFIC. HEY, TURN AROUND FOR A SECOND...

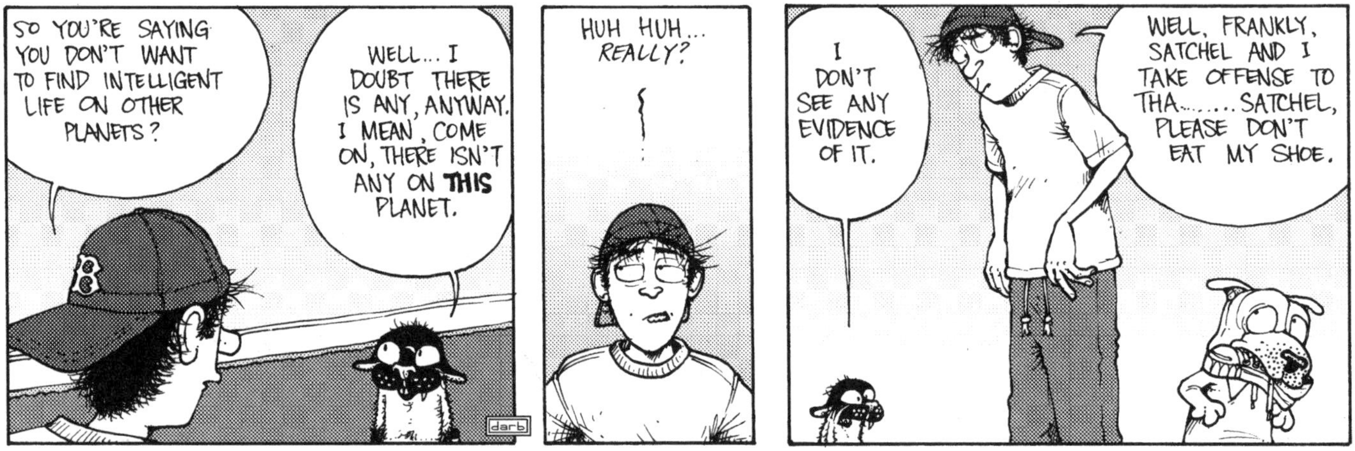
SO YOU'RE SAYING YOU DON'T WANT TO FIND INTELLIGENT LIFE ON OTHER PLANETS?
WELL... I DOUBT THERE IS ANY, ANYWAY. I MEAN, COME ON, THERE ISN'T ANY ON **THIS** PLANET.
darb
HUH HUH... *REALLY?*
I DON'T SEE ANY EVIDENCE OF IT.
WELL, FRANKLY, SATCHEL AND I TAKE OFFENSE TO THA....... SATCHEL, PLEASE DON'T EAT MY SHOE.

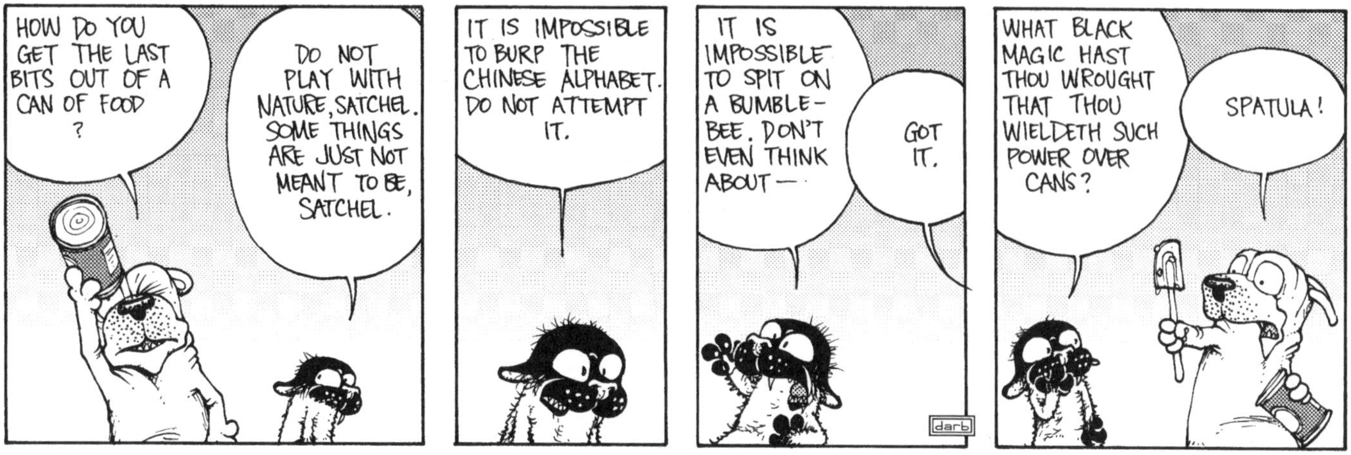
HOW DO YOU GET THE LAST BITS OUT OF A CAN OF FOOD?
DO NOT PLAY WITH NATURE, SATCHEL. SOME THINGS ARE JUST NOT MEANT TO BE, SATCHEL.
IT IS IMPOSSIBLE TO BURP THE CHINESE ALPHABET. DO NOT ATTEMPT IT.
IT IS IMPOSSIBLE TO SPIT ON A BUMBLE-BEE. DON'T EVEN THINK ABOUT—
GOT IT.
WHAT BLACK MAGIC HAST THOU WROUGHT THAT THOU WIELDETH SUCH POWER OVER CANS?
SPATULA!

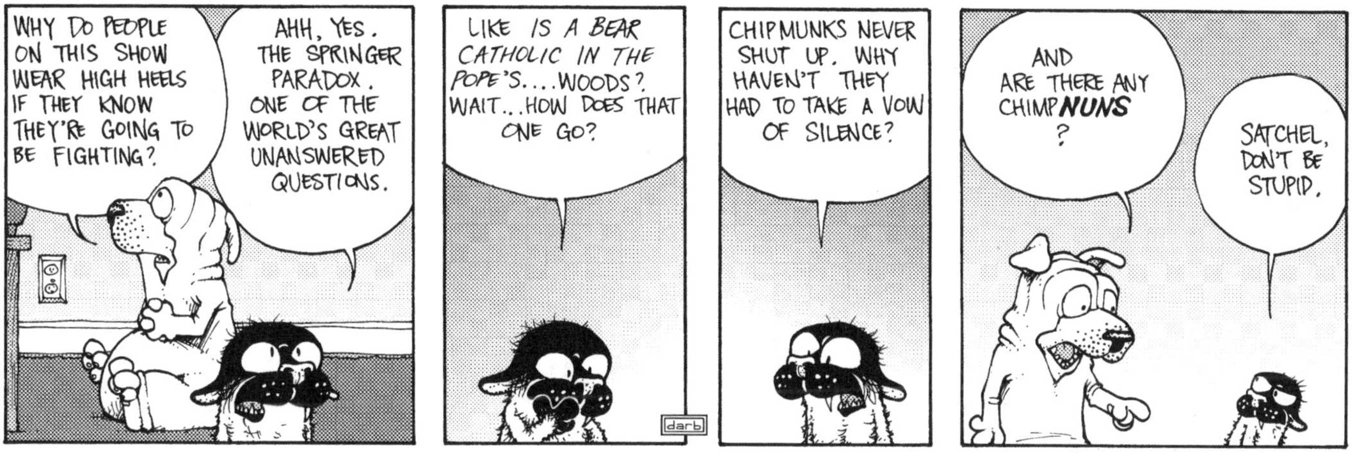
WHY DO PEOPLE ON THIS SHOW WEAR HIGH HEELS IF THEY KNOW THEY'RE GOING TO BE FIGHTING?
AHH, YES. THE SPRINGER PARADOX. ONE OF THE WORLD'S GREAT UNANSWERED QUESTIONS.
LIKE *IS A BEAR CATHOLIC IN THE POPE'S*.... WOODS? WAIT... HOW DOES THAT ONE GO?
CHIPMUNKS NEVER SHUT UP. WHY HAVEN'T THEY HAD TO TAKE A VOW OF SILENCE?
AND ARE THERE ANY CHIMP ***NUNS***?
SATCHEL, DON'T BE STUPID.

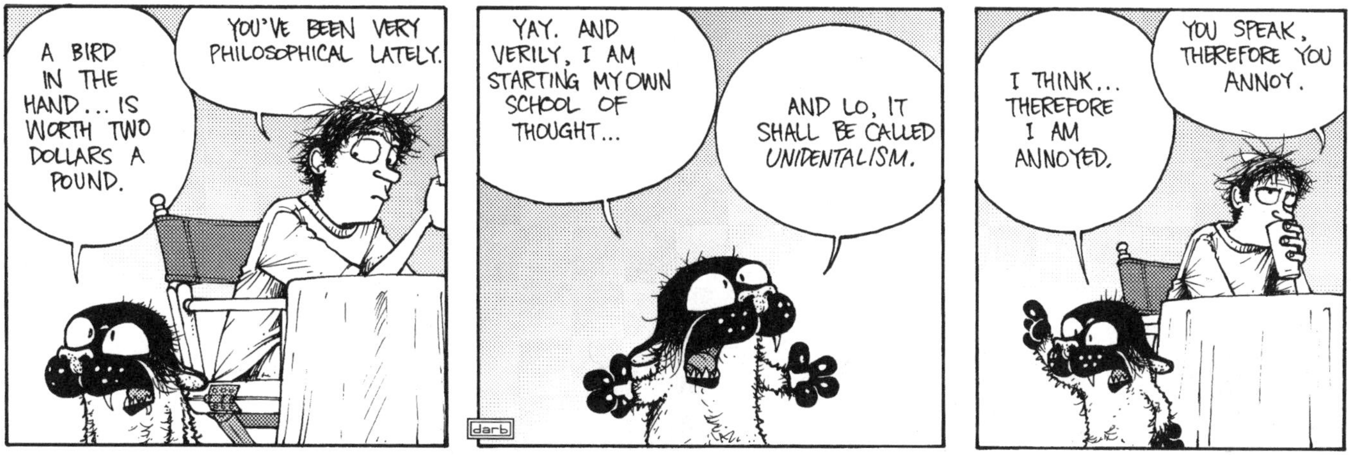
A BIRD IN THE HAND... IS WORTH TWO DOLLARS A POUND.
YOU'VE BEEN VERY PHILOSOPHICAL LATELY.
YAY. AND VERILY, I AM STARTING MY OWN SCHOOL OF THOUGHT...
AND LO, IT SHALL BE CALLED *UNIDENTALISM*.
I THINK... THEREFORE I AM ANNOYED.
YOU SPEAK, THEREFORE YOU ANNOY.

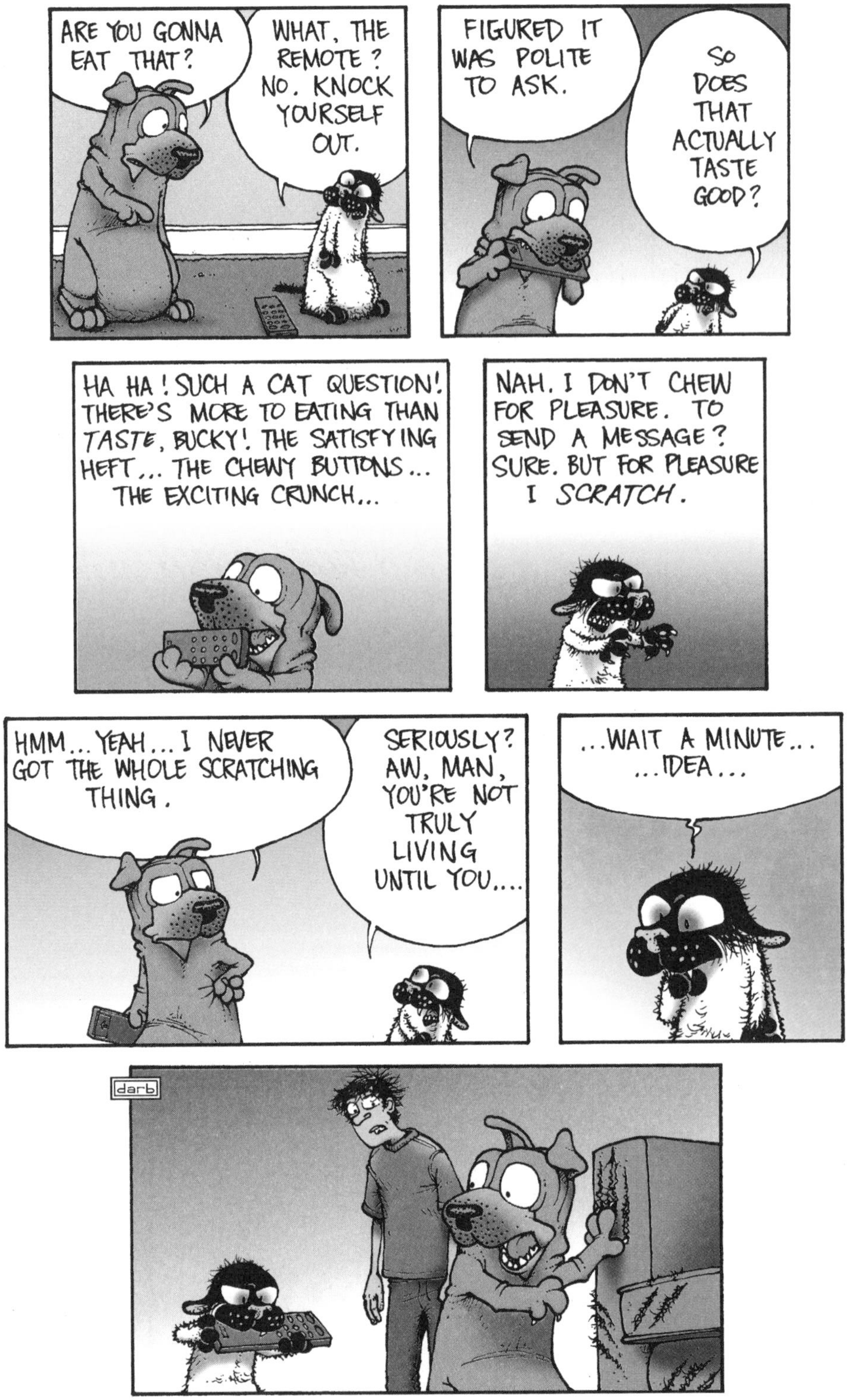
ARE YOU GONNA EAT THAT?
WHAT, THE REMOTE? NO. KNOCK YOURSELF OUT.
FIGURED IT WAS POLITE TO ASK.
SO DOES THAT ACTUALLY TASTE GOOD?
HA HA! SUCH A CAT QUESTION! THERE'S MORE TO EATING THAN TASTE, BUCKY! THE SATISFYING HEFT... THE CHEWY BUTTONS... THE EXCITING CRUNCH...
NAH. I DON'T CHEW FOR PLEASURE. TO SEND A MESSAGE? SURE. BUT FOR PLEASURE I SCRATCH.
HMM... YEAH... I NEVER GOT THE WHOLE SCRATCHING THING.
SERIOUSLY? AW, MAN, YOU'RE NOT TRULY LIVING UNTIL YOU....
...WAIT A MINUTE...
...IDEA...
darb

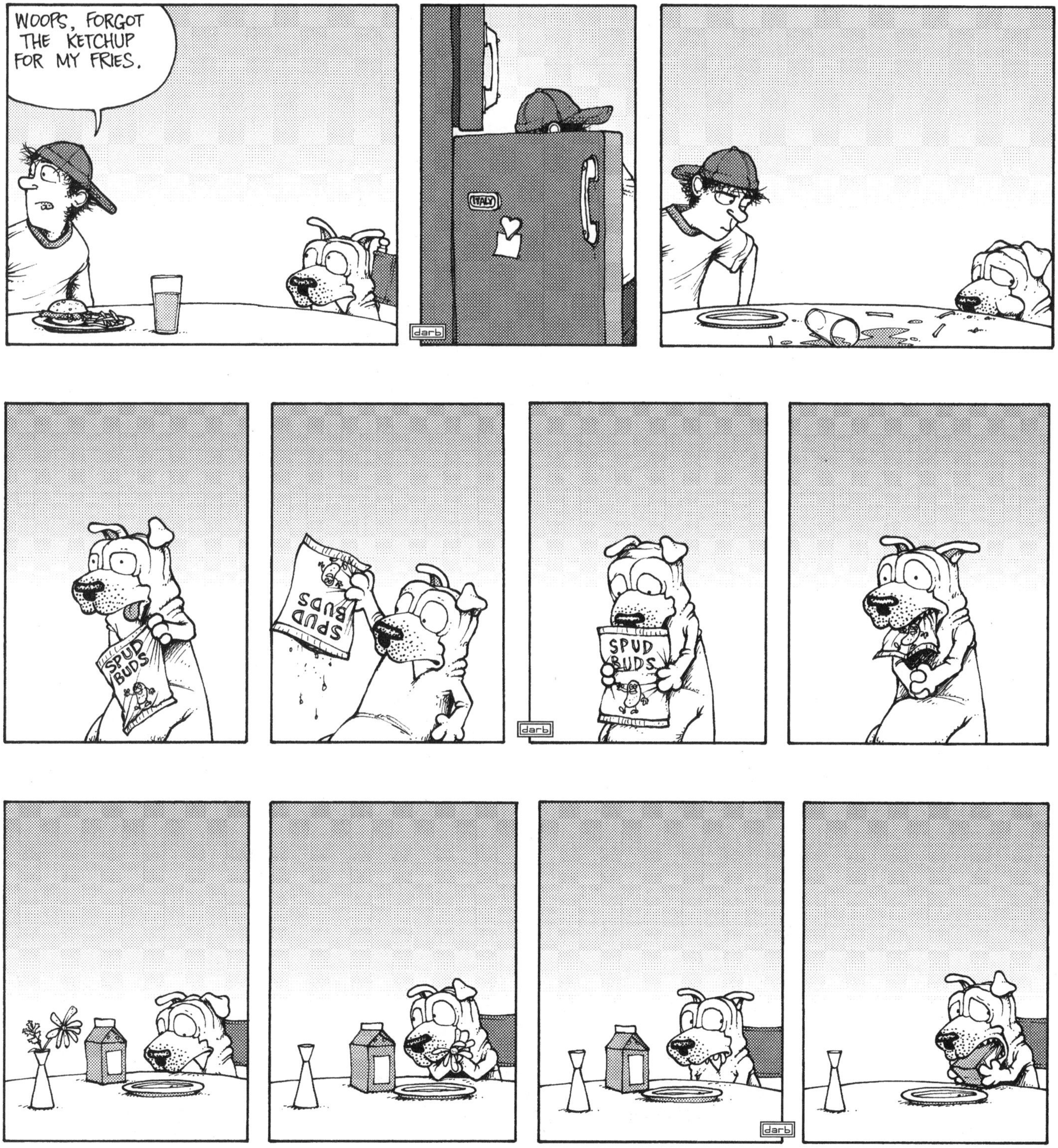
WOOPS, FORGOT THE KETCHUP FOR MY FRIES.
ITALY
darb
SPUD BUDS
SPUD BUDS
SPUD BUDS
darb
darb

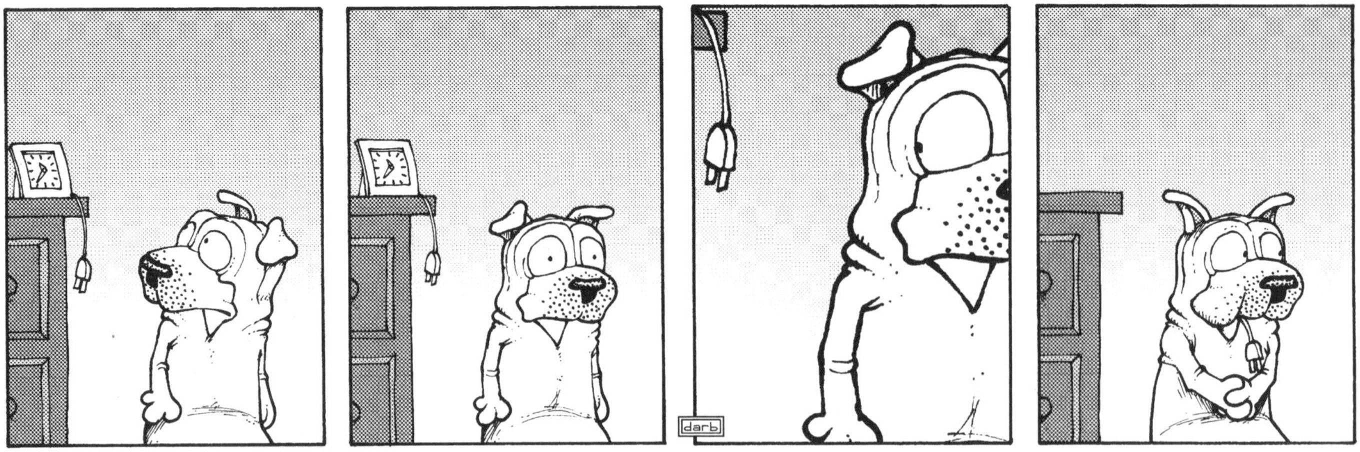
darb

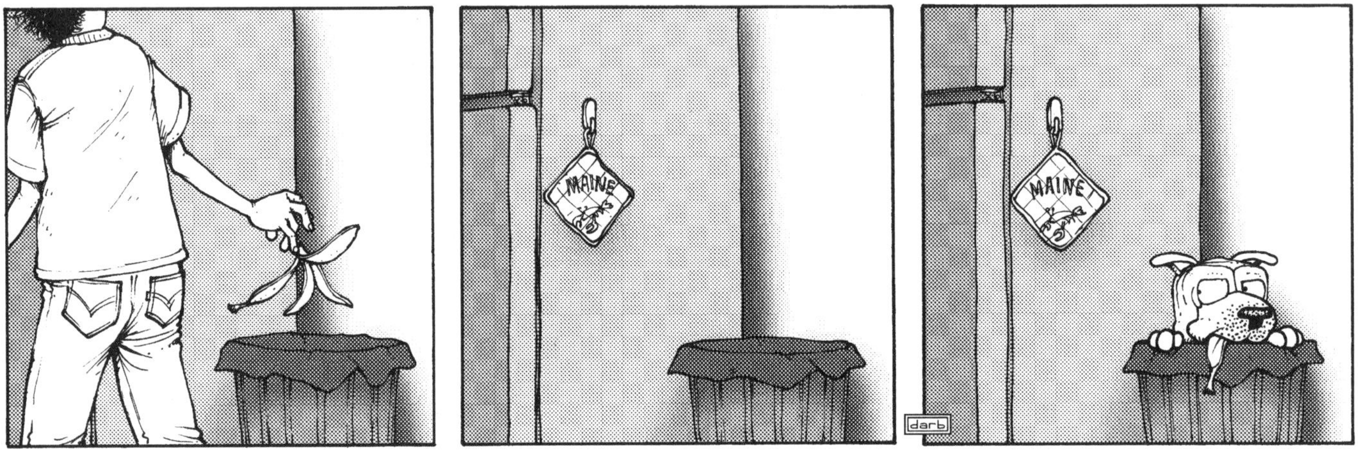
MAINE
MAINE
darb

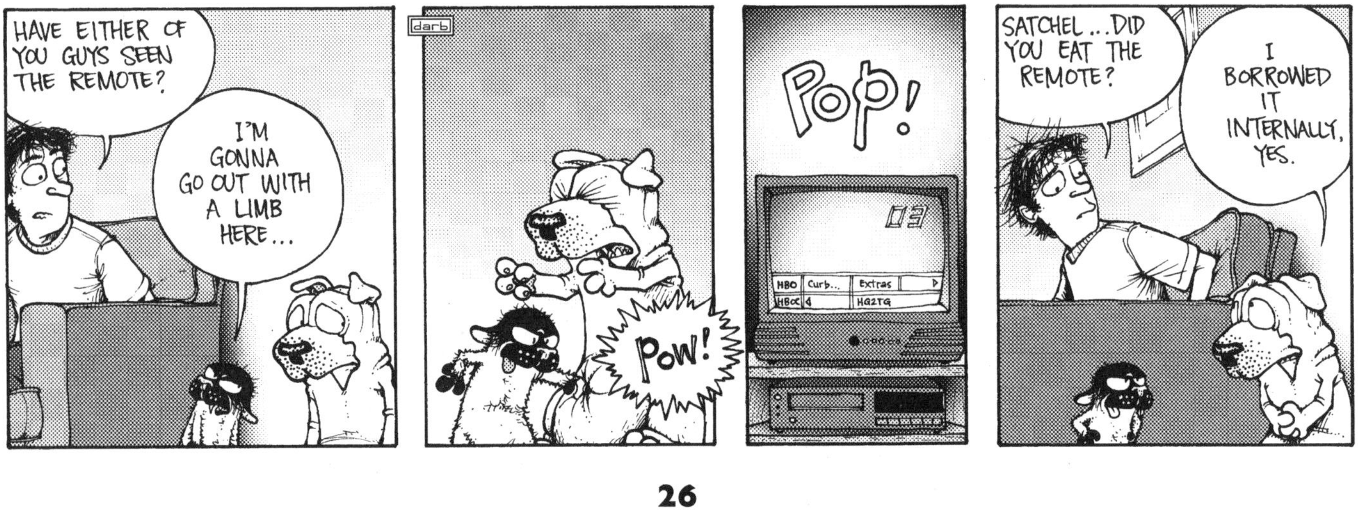
HAVE EITHER OF YOU GUYS SEEN THE REMOTE?
I'M GONNA GO OUT WITH A LIMB HERE...
darb
POW!
POP!
SATCHEL...DID YOU EAT THE REMOTE?
I BORROWED IT INTERNALLY, YES.

bzzz
YAAA!
!
darb
ARE WE NOT DOING THE WAVE?

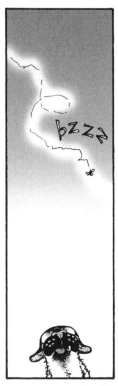

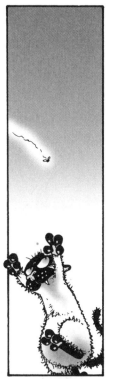

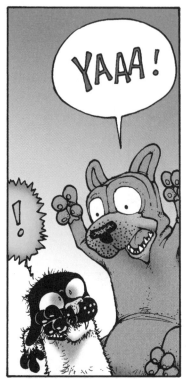

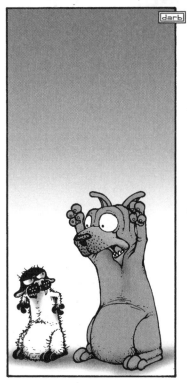

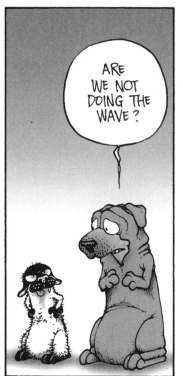

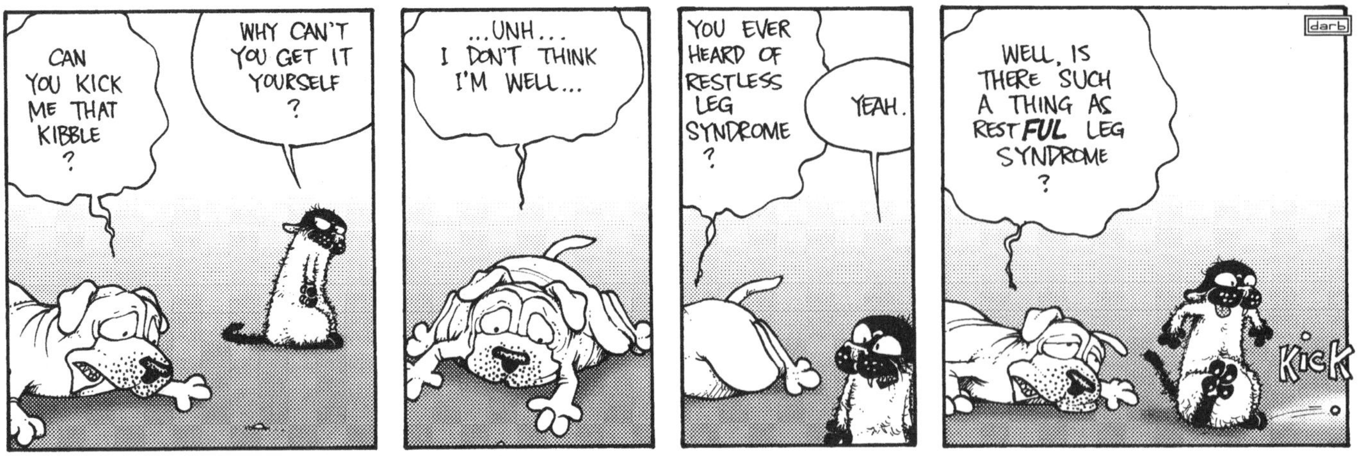
CAN YOU KICK ME THAT KIBBLE ?
WHY CAN'T YOU GET IT YOURSELF ?
...UNH... I DON'T THINK I'M WELL...
YOU EVER HEARD OF RESTLESS LEG SYNDROME ?
YEAH.
WELL, IS THERE SUCH A THING AS RESTFUL LEG SYNDROME ?
KICK
darb

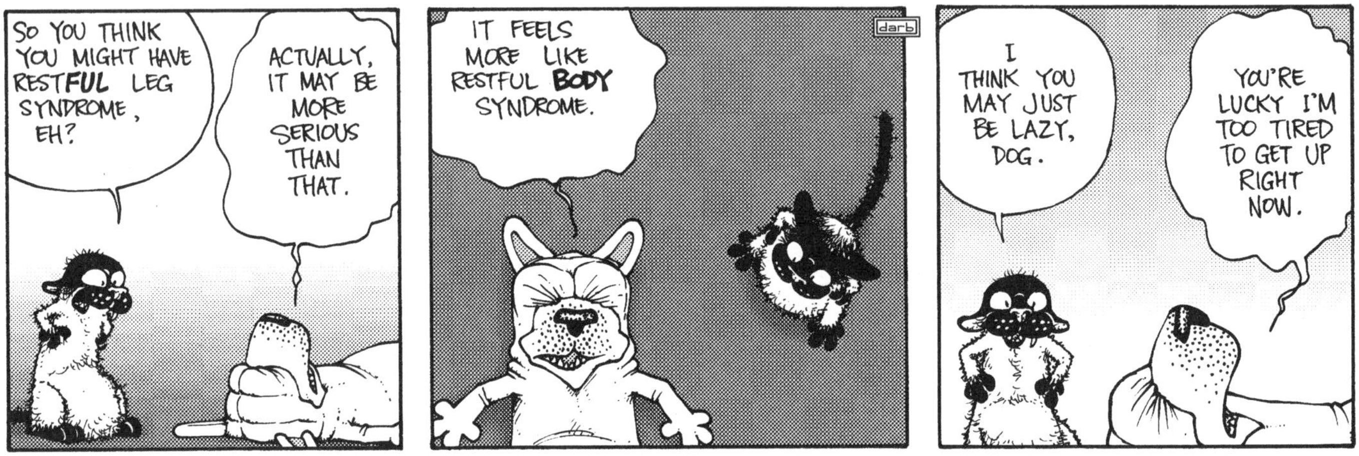
SO YOU THINK YOU MIGHT HAVE RESTFUL LEG SYNDROME, EH?
ACTUALLY, IT MAY BE MORE SERIOUS THAN THAT.
IT FEELS MORE LIKE RESTFUL BODY SYNDROME.
darb
I THINK YOU MAY JUST BE LAZY, DOG.
YOU'RE LUCKY I'M TOO TIRED TO GET UP RIGHT NOW.

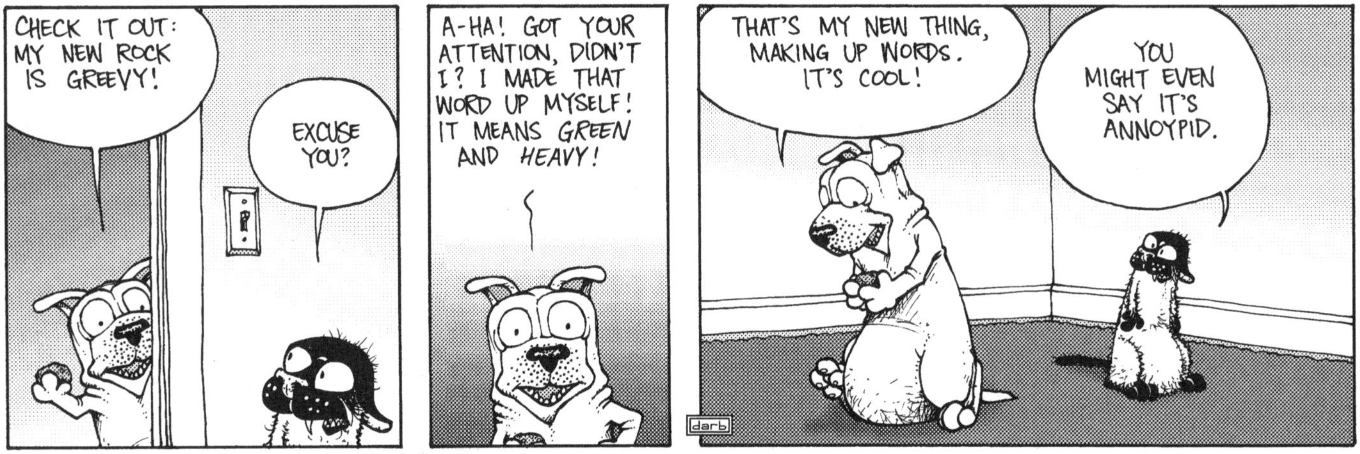
CHECK IT OUT: MY NEW ROCK IS GREEVY!
EXCUSE YOU?
A-HA! GOT YOUR ATTENTION, DIDN'T I? I MADE THAT WORD UP MYSELF! IT MEANS GREEN AND HEAVY!
darb
THAT'S MY NEW THING, MAKING UP WORDS. IT'S COOL!
YOU MIGHT EVEN SAY IT'S ANNOYPID.

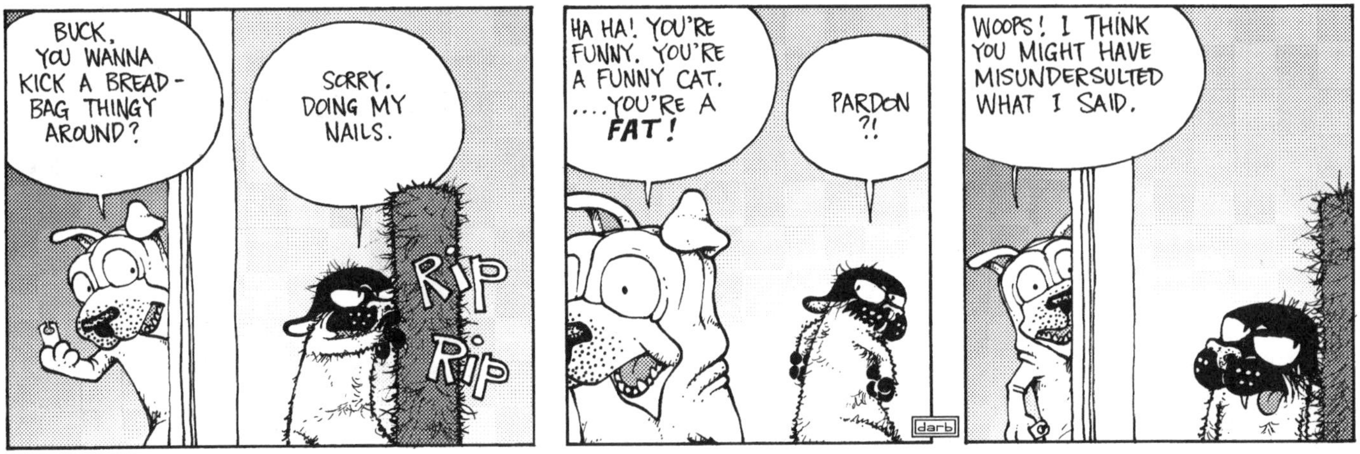
BUCK, YOU WANNA KICK A BREAD-BAG THINGY AROUND?
SORRY. DOING MY NAILS.
RIP
RIP
HA HA! YOU'RE FUNNY. YOU'RE A FUNNY CAT. ....YOU'RE A FAT!
PARDON ?!
WOOPS! I THINK YOU MIGHT HAVE MISUNDERSULTED WHAT I SAID.
darb

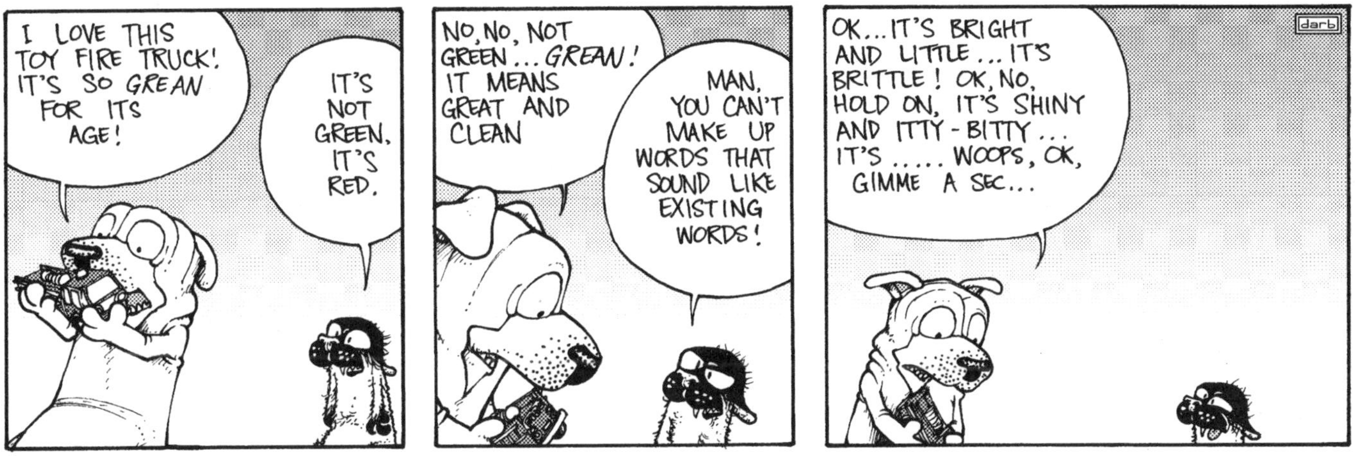
I LOVE THIS TOY FIRE TRUCK! IT'S SO GREAN FOR ITS AGE!
IT'S NOT GREEN. IT'S RED.
NO, NO, NOT GREEN... GREAN! IT MEANS GREAT AND CLEAN
MAN, YOU CAN'T MAKE UP WORDS THAT SOUND LIKE EXISTING WORDS!
OK... IT'S BRIGHT AND LITTLE... IT'S BRITTLE! OK, NO, HOLD ON, IT'S SHINY AND ITTY-BITTY... IT'S ..... WOOPS, OK, GIMME A SEC...
darb

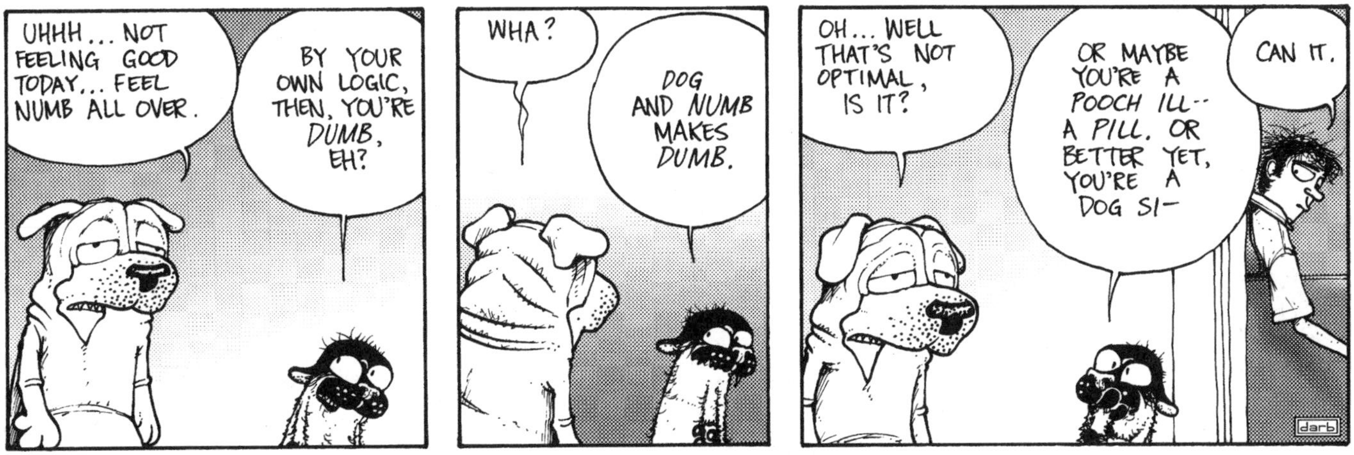
UHHH... NOT FEELING GOOD TODAY... FEEL NUMB ALL OVER.
BY YOUR OWN LOGIC, THEN, YOU'RE DUMB, EH?
WHA?
DOG AND NUMB MAKES DUMB.
OH... WELL THAT'S NOT OPTIMAL, IS IT?
OR MAYBE YOU'RE A POOCH ILL-- A PILL. OR BETTER YET, YOU'RE A DOG SI—
CAN IT.
darb

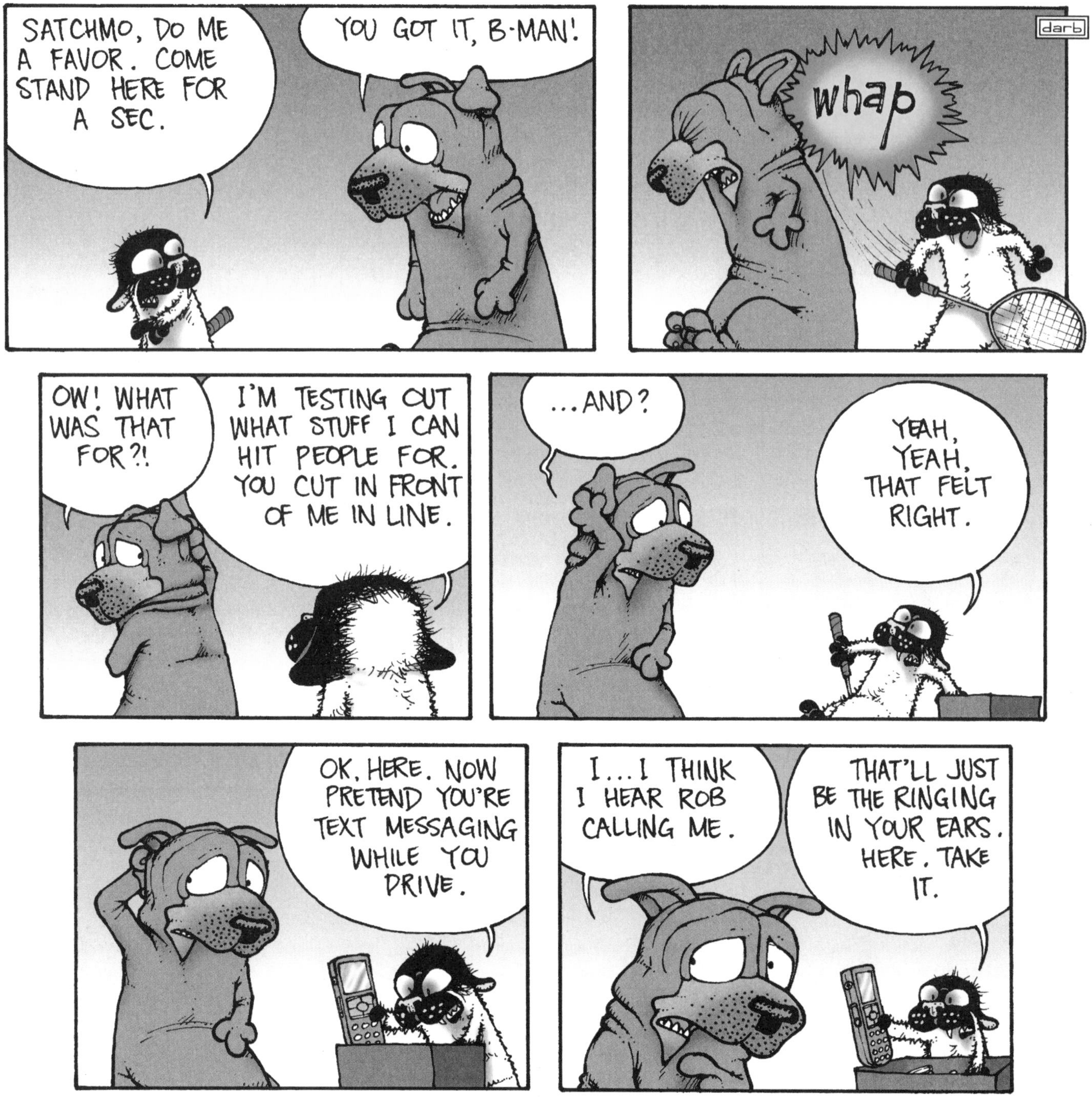
SATCHMO, DO ME A FAVOR. COME STAND HERE FOR A SEC.
YOU GOT IT, B-MAN!
darb
whap
OW! WHAT WAS THAT FOR?!
I'M TESTING OUT WHAT STUFF I CAN HIT PEOPLE FOR. YOU CUT IN FRONT OF ME IN LINE.
...AND?
YEAH, YEAH, THAT FELT RIGHT.
OK, HERE. NOW PRETEND YOU'RE TEXT MESSAGING WHILE YOU DRIVE.
I...I THINK I HEAR ROB CALLING ME.
THAT'LL JUST BE THE RINGING IN YOUR EARS. HERE. TAKE IT.

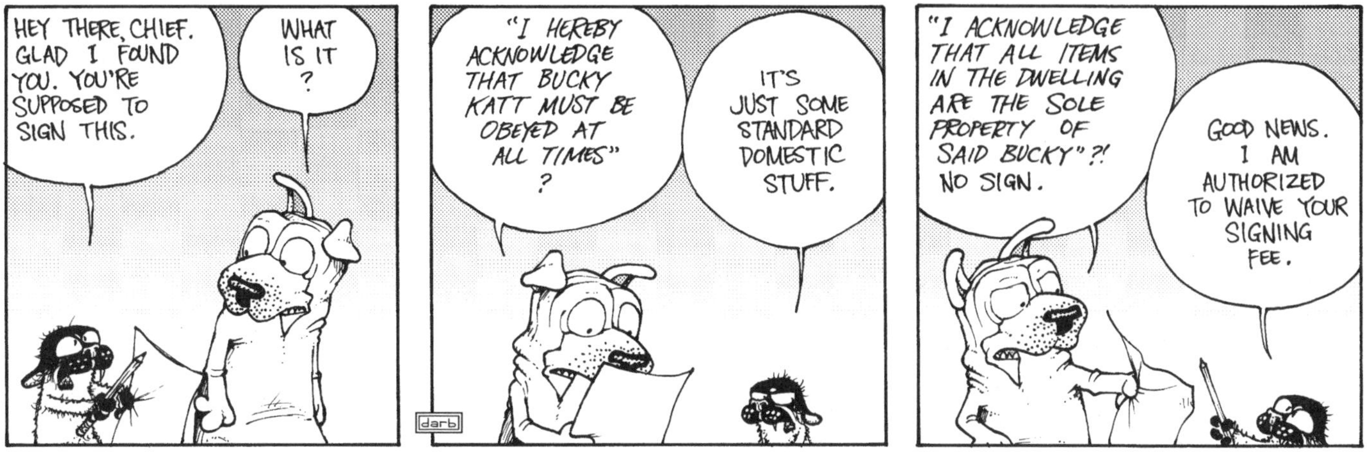
HEY THERE, CHIEF. GLAD I FOUND YOU. YOU'RE SUPPOSED TO SIGN THIS.
WHAT IS IT ?
"I HEREBY ACKNOWLEDGE THAT BUCKY KATT MUST BE OBEYED AT ALL TIMES" ?
IT'S JUST SOME STANDARD DOMESTIC STUFF.
"I ACKNOWLEDGE THAT ALL ITEMS IN THE DWELLING ARE THE SOLE PROPERTY OF SAID BUCKY"?! NO SIGN.
GOOD NEWS. I AM AUTHORIZED TO WAIVE YOUR SIGNING FEE.
darb

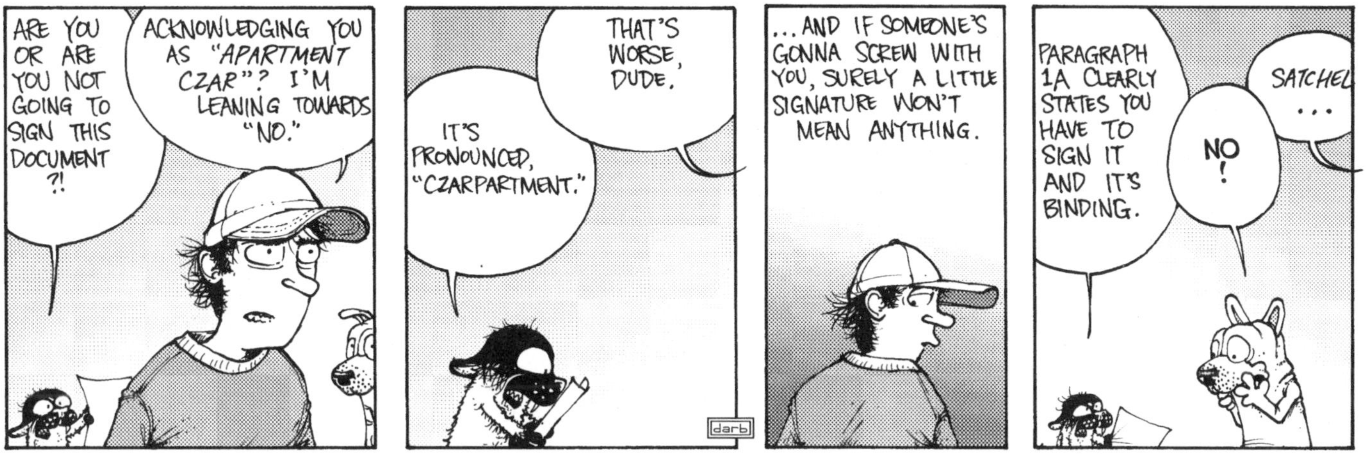
ARE YOU OR ARE YOU NOT GOING TO SIGN THIS DOCUMENT ?!
ACKNOWLEDGING YOU AS "APARTMENT CZAR"? I'M LEANING TOWARDS "NO."
IT'S PRONOUNCED, "CZARPARTMENT."
THAT'S WORSE, DUDE.
darb
...AND IF SOMEONE'S GONNA SCREW WITH YOU, SURELY A LITTLE SIGNATURE WON'T MEAN ANYTHING.
PARAGRAPH 1A CLEARLY STATES YOU HAVE TO SIGN IT AND IT'S BINDING.
NO !
SATCHEL ...

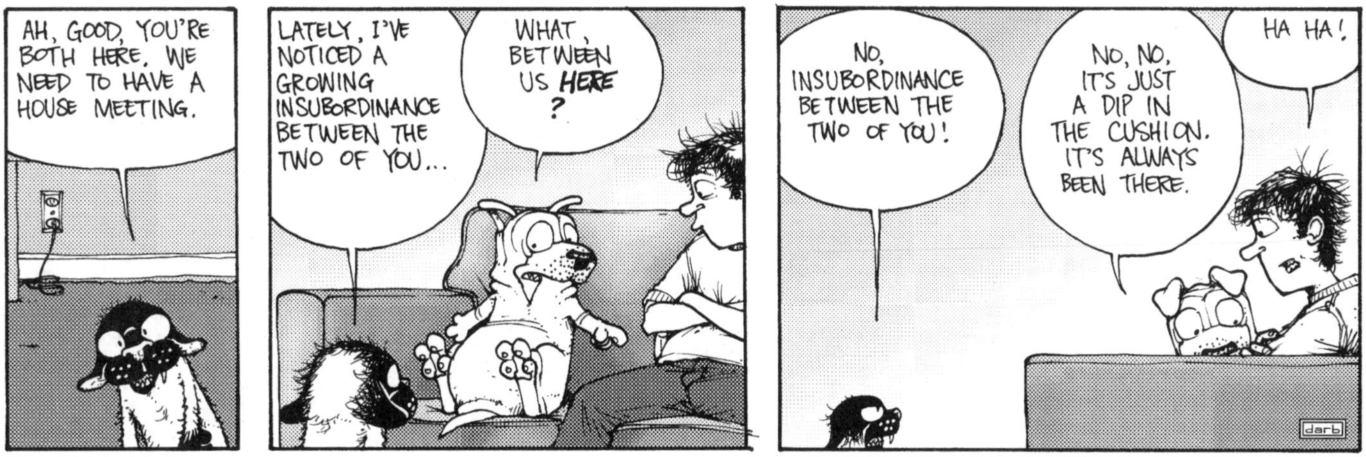
AH, GOOD, YOU'RE BOTH HERE. WE NEED TO HAVE A HOUSE MEETING.
LATELY, I'VE NOTICED A GROWING INSUBORDINANCE BETWEEN THE TWO OF YOU...
WHAT, BETWEEN US HERE ?
NO, INSUBORDINANCE BETWEEN THE TWO OF YOU!
NO, NO, IT'S JUST A DIP IN THE CUSHION. IT'S ALWAYS BEEN THERE.
HA HA!
darb

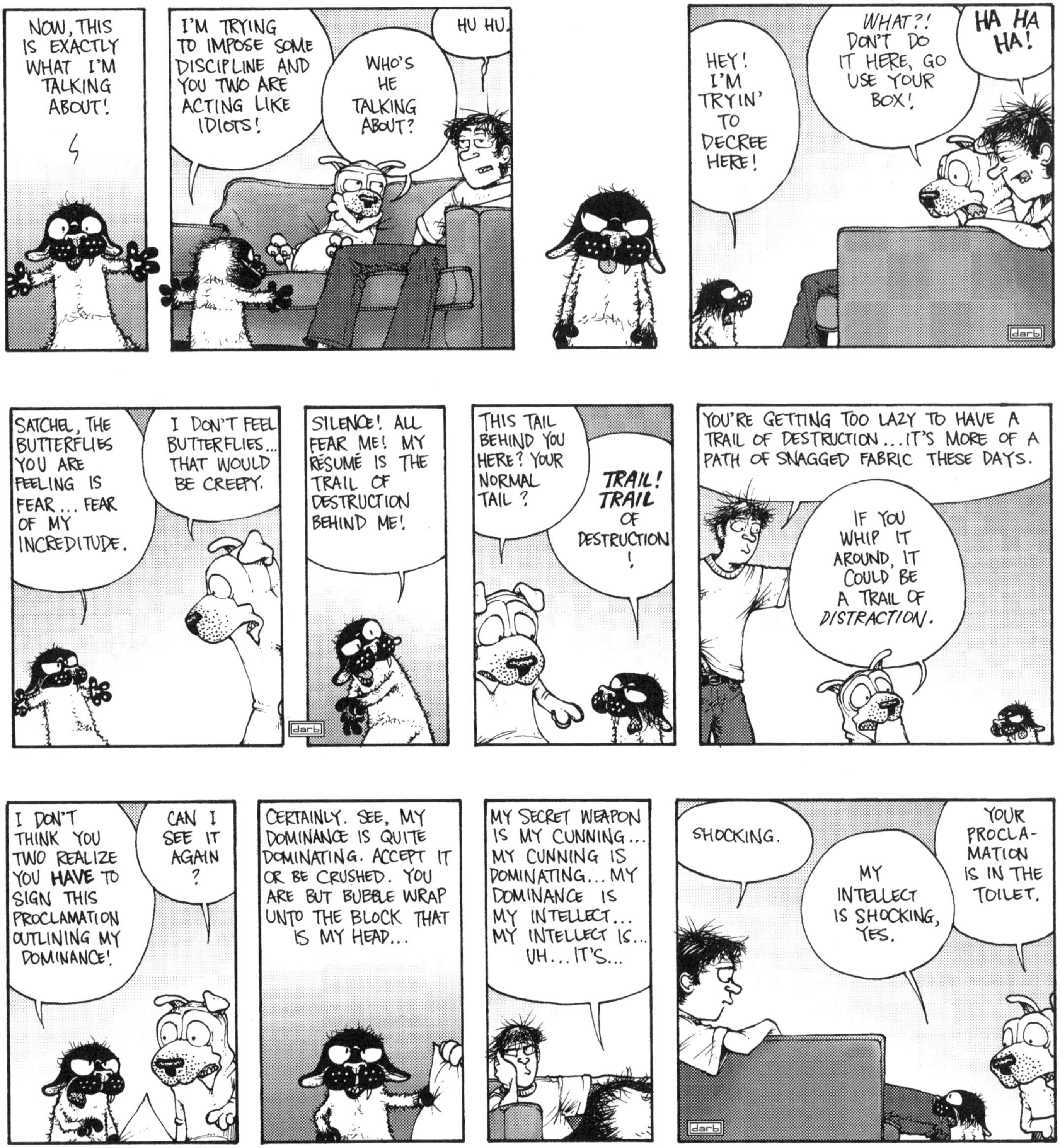
NOW, THIS IS EXACTLY WHAT I'M TALKING ABOUT!
I'M TRYING TO IMPOSE SOME DISCIPLINE AND YOU TWO ARE ACTING LIKE IDIOTS!
HU HU.
WHO'S HE TALKING ABOUT?
HEY! I'M TRYIN' TO DECREE HERE!
WHAT?! DON'T DO IT HERE, GO USE YOUR BOX!
HA HA HA!
darb
SATCHEL, THE BUTTERFLIES YOU ARE FEELING IS FEAR... FEAR OF MY INCREDITUDE.
I DON'T FEEL BUTTERFLIES... THAT WOULD BE CREEPY.
SILENCE! ALL FEAR ME! MY RÉSUMÉ IS THE TRAIL OF DESTRUCTION BEHIND ME!
darb
THIS TAIL BEHIND YOU HERE? YOUR NORMAL TAIL?
TRAIL! TRAIL OF DESTRUCTION!
YOU'RE GETTING TOO LAZY TO HAVE A TRAIL OF DESTRUCTION... IT'S MORE OF A PATH OF SNAGGED FABRIC THESE DAYS.
IF YOU WHIP IT AROUND, IT COULD BE A TRAIL OF DISTRACTION.
I DON'T THINK YOU TWO REALIZE YOU HAVE TO SIGN THIS PROCLAMATION OUTLINING MY DOMINANCE!
CAN I SEE IT AGAIN?
CERTAINLY. SEE, MY DOMINANCE IS QUITE DOMINATING. ACCEPT IT OR BE CRUSHED. YOU ARE BUT BUBBLE WRAP UNTO THE BLOCK THAT IS MY HEAD...
MY SECRET WEAPON IS MY CUNNING... MY CUNNING IS DOMINATING... MY DOMINANCE IS MY INTELLECT... MY INTELLECT IS... UH... IT'S...
SHOCKING.
MY INTELLECT IS SHOCKING, YES.
YOUR PROCLAMATION IS IN THE TOILET.
darb

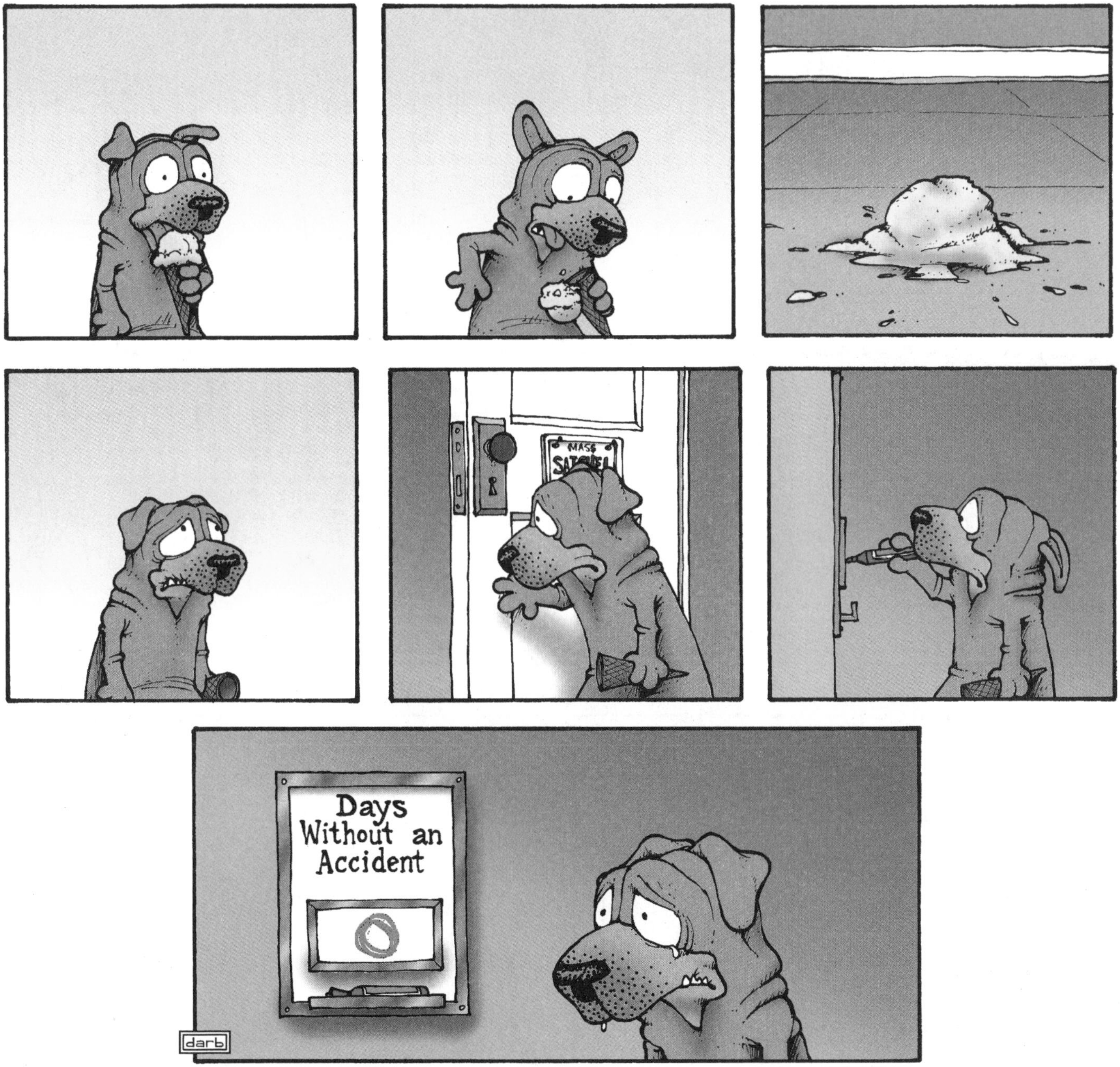
MASS
Days Without an Accident
darb

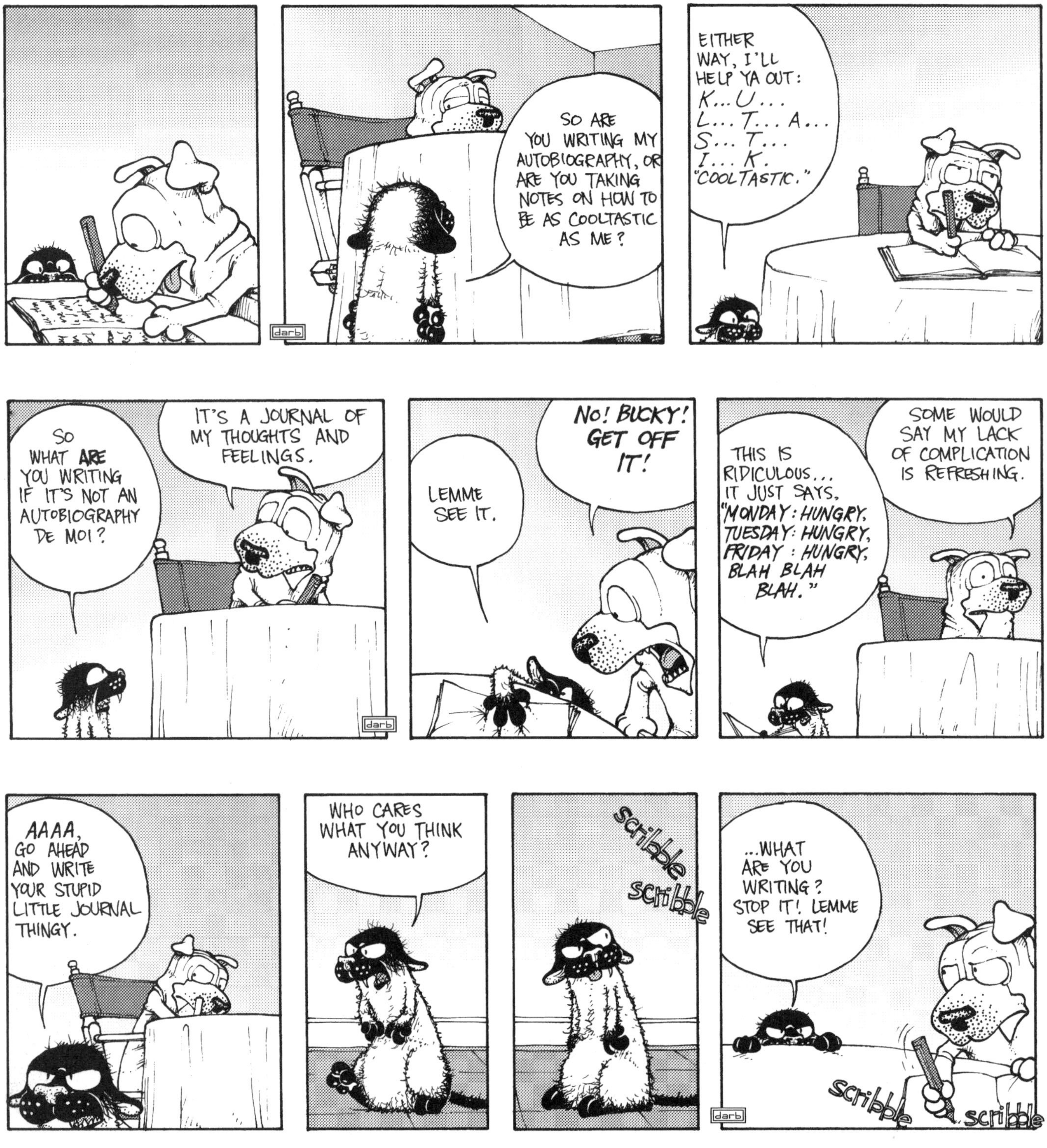
SO ARE YOU WRITING MY AUTOBIOGRAPHY, OR ARE YOU TAKING NOTES ON HOW TO BE AS COOLTASTIC AS ME?
EITHER WAY, I'LL HELP YA OUT: K... U... L... T... A... S... T... I... K. "COOLTASTIC."
SO WHAT ARE YOU WRITING IF IT'S NOT AN AUTOBIOGRAPHY DE MOI?
IT'S A JOURNAL OF MY THOUGHTS AND FEELINGS.
LEMME SEE IT.
NO! BUCKY! GET OFF IT!
THIS IS RIDICULOUS... IT JUST SAYS, "MONDAY: HUNGRY, TUESDAY: HUNGRY, FRIDAY: HUNGRY, BLAH BLAH BLAH."
SOME WOULD SAY MY LACK OF COMPLICATION IS REFRESHING.
AAAA, GO AHEAD AND WRITE YOUR STUPID LITTLE JOURNAL THINGY.
WHO CARES WHAT YOU THINK ANYWAY?
scribble
scribble
...WHAT ARE YOU WRITING? STOP IT! LEMME SEE THAT!
scribble
scribble

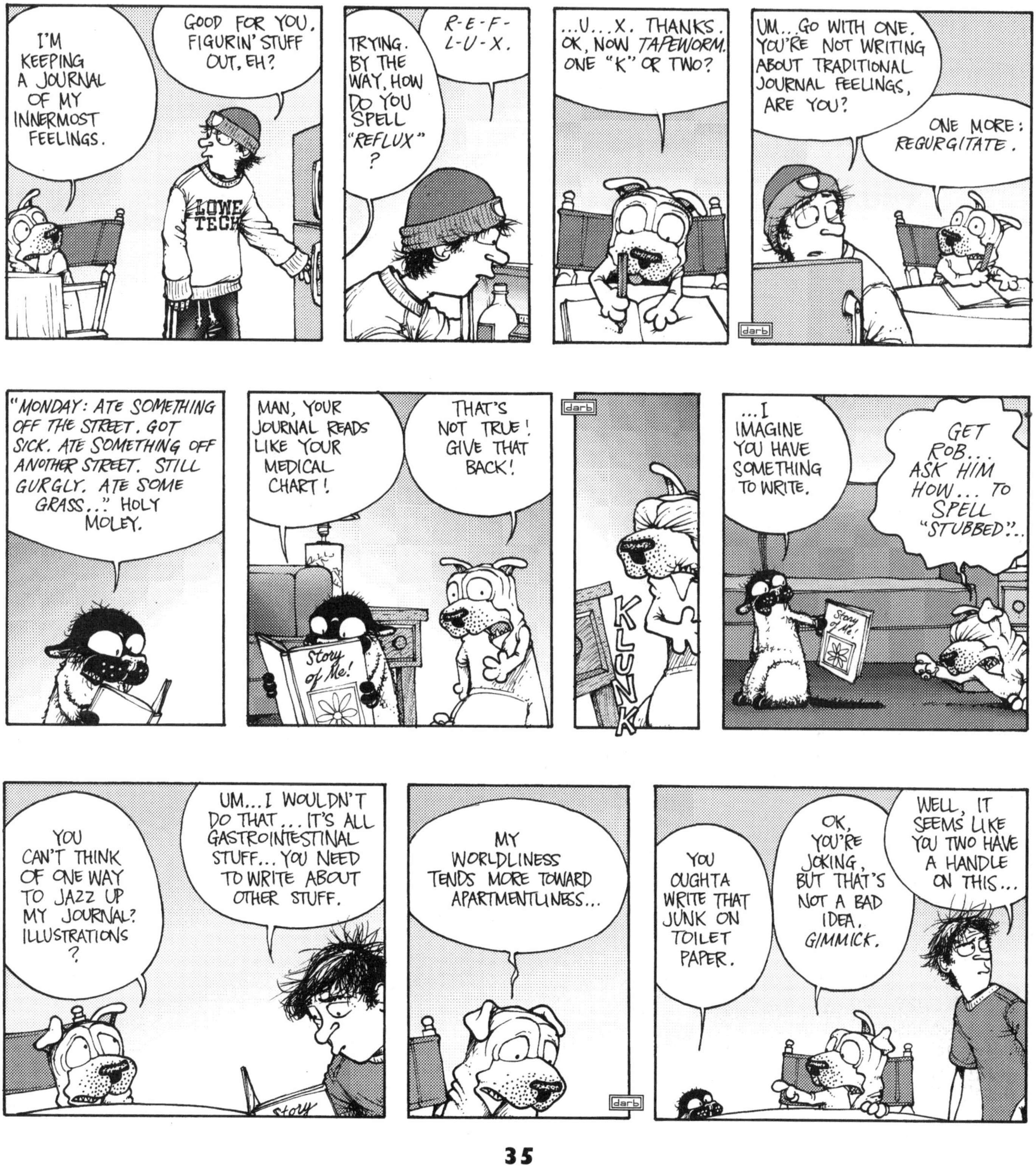
I'M KEEPING A JOURNAL OF MY INNERMOST FEELINGS.
GOOD FOR YOU, FIGURIN' STUFF OUT, EH?
LOWE TECH
TRYING. BY THE WAY, HOW DO YOU SPELL "REFLUX"?
R-E-F-L-U-X.
...U...X. THANKS. OK, NOW TAPEWORM. ONE "K" OR TWO?
UM...GO WITH ONE. YOU'RE NOT WRITING ABOUT TRADITIONAL JOURNAL FEELINGS, ARE YOU?
ONE MORE: REGURGITATE.
darb
"MONDAY: ATE SOMETHING OFF THE STREET. GOT SICK. ATE SOMETHING OFF ANOTHER STREET. STILL GURGLY. ATE SOME GRASS..." HOLY MOLEY.
MAN, YOUR JOURNAL READS LIKE YOUR MEDICAL CHART!
THAT'S NOT TRUE! GIVE THAT BACK!
Story of Me!
darb
KLUNK
...I IMAGINE YOU HAVE SOMETHING TO WRITE.
GET ROB... ASK HIM HOW... TO SPELL "STUBBED"...
Story of Me!
YOU CAN'T THINK OF ONE WAY TO JAZZ UP MY JOURNAL? ILLUSTRATIONS?
UM...I WOULDN'T DO THAT...IT'S ALL GASTROINTESTINAL STUFF...YOU NEED TO WRITE ABOUT OTHER STUFF.
Story
MY WORLDLINESS TENDS MORE TOWARD APARTMENTLINESS...
darb
YOU OUGHTA WRITE THAT JUNK ON TOILET PAPER.
OK, YOU'RE JOKING, BUT THAT'S NOT A BAD IDEA, GIMMICK.
WELL, IT SEEMS LIKE YOU TWO HAVE A HANDLE ON THIS...

TOUGHNESS OOZES FROM ME LIKE CLEARASIL ON PICTURE DAY...
TODAY, I ASSERT MY DOMINANCE OVER ALL LIVING THINGS. TODAY, THE EARTH TREMBLES BENEATH MY PAWS. TO-
VRRR
darb
ANOTHER WORLD DOMINATION PLOT THWARTED BY THE BUCK DUSTER...

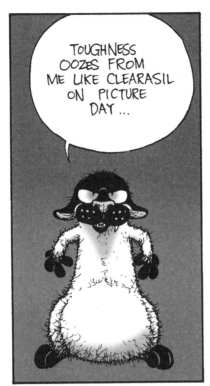

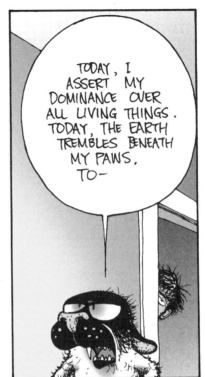

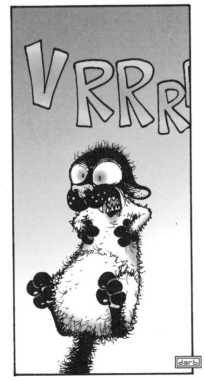

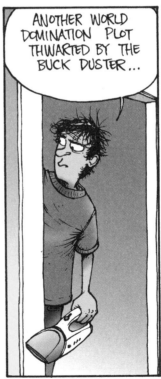

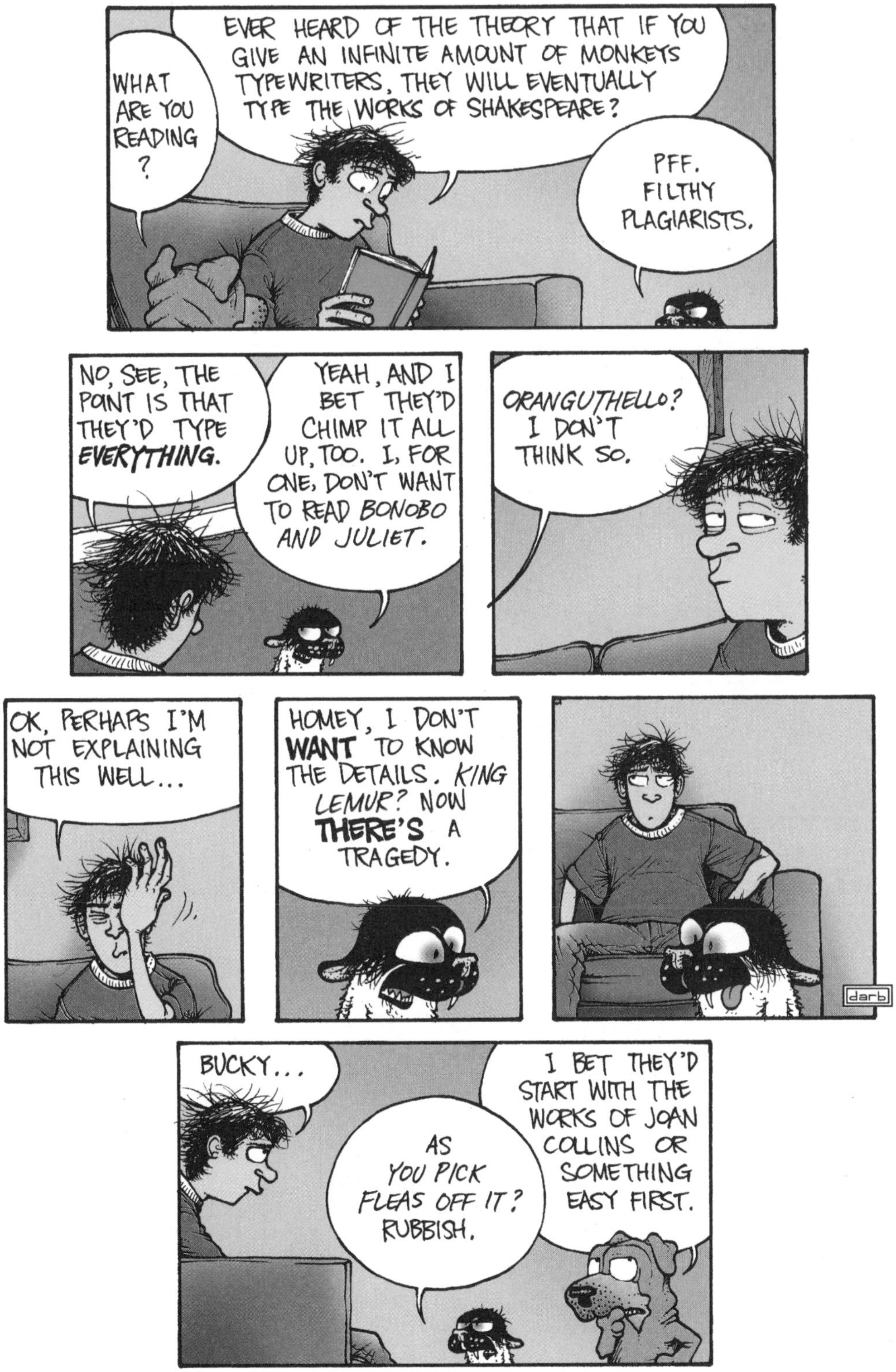
WHAT ARE YOU READING ?
EVER HEARD OF THE THEORY THAT IF YOU GIVE AN INFINITE AMOUNT OF MONKEYS TYPEWRITERS, THEY WILL EVENTUALLY TYPE THE WORKS OF SHAKESPEARE?
PFF. FILTHY PLAGIARISTS.
NO, SEE, THE POINT IS THAT THEY'D TYPE **EVERYTHING**.
YEAH, AND I BET THEY'D CHIMP IT ALL UP, TOO. I, FOR ONE, DON'T WANT TO READ *BONOBO AND JULIET*.
ORANGUTHELLO? I DON'T THINK SO.
OK, PERHAPS I'M NOT EXPLAINING THIS WELL...
HOMEY, I DON'T **WANT** TO KNOW THE DETAILS. *KING LEMUR?* NOW **THERE'S** A TRAGEDY.
darb
BUCKY...
I BET THEY'D START WITH THE WORKS OF JOAN COLLINS OR SOMETHING EASY FIRST.
AS *YOU PICK FLEAS OFF IT?* RUBBISH.

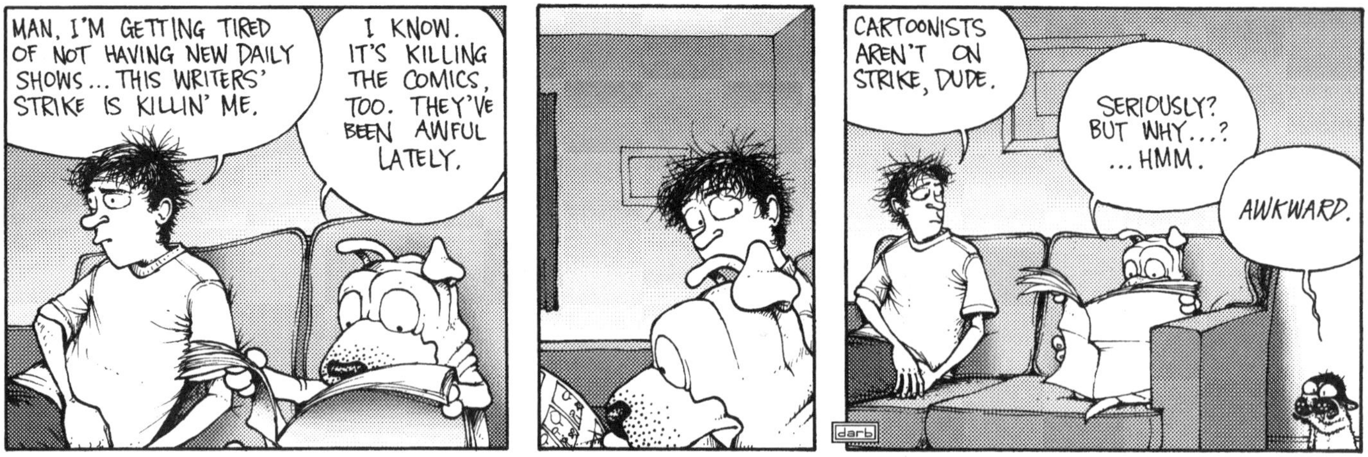
MAN, I'M GETTING TIRED OF NOT HAVING NEW DAILY SHOWS... THIS WRITERS' STRIKE IS KILLIN' ME.
I KNOW. IT'S KILLING THE COMICS, TOO. THEY'VE BEEN AWFUL LATELY.
CARTOONISTS AREN'T ON STRIKE, DUDE.
SERIOUSLY? BUT WHY...? ...HMM.
AWKWARD.
darb

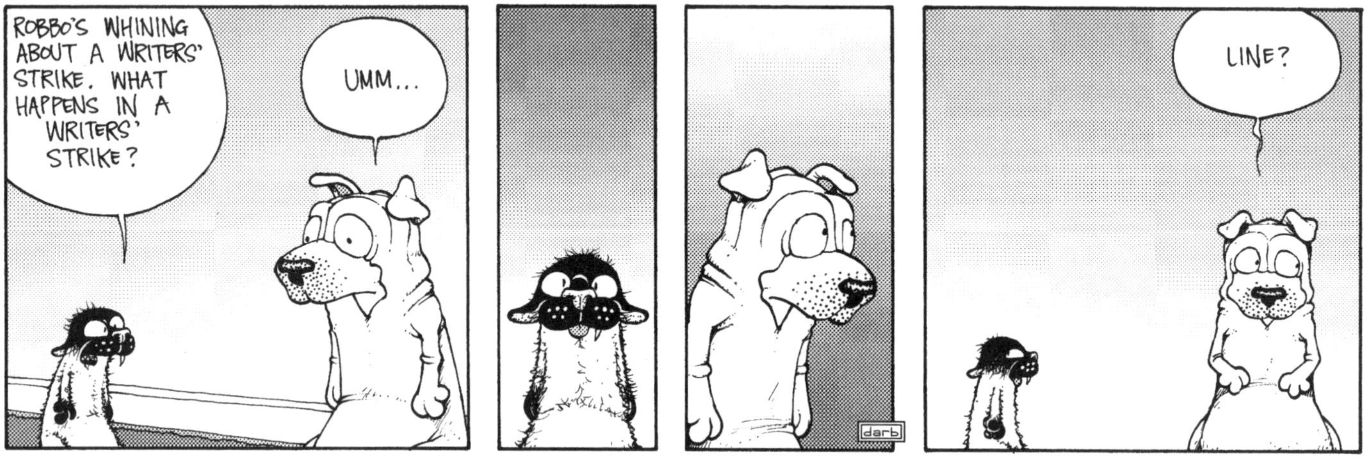
ROBBO'S WHINING ABOUT A WRITERS' STRIKE. WHAT HAPPENS IN A WRITERS' STRIKE?
UMM...
darb
LINE?

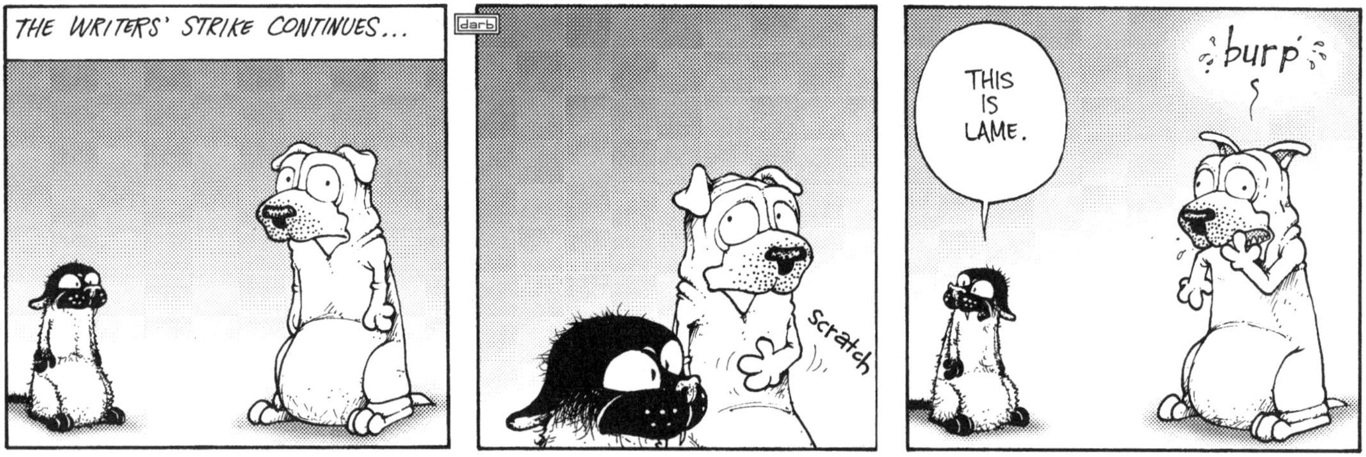
THE WRITERS' STRIKE CONTINUES...
darb
scratch
THIS IS LAME.
burp

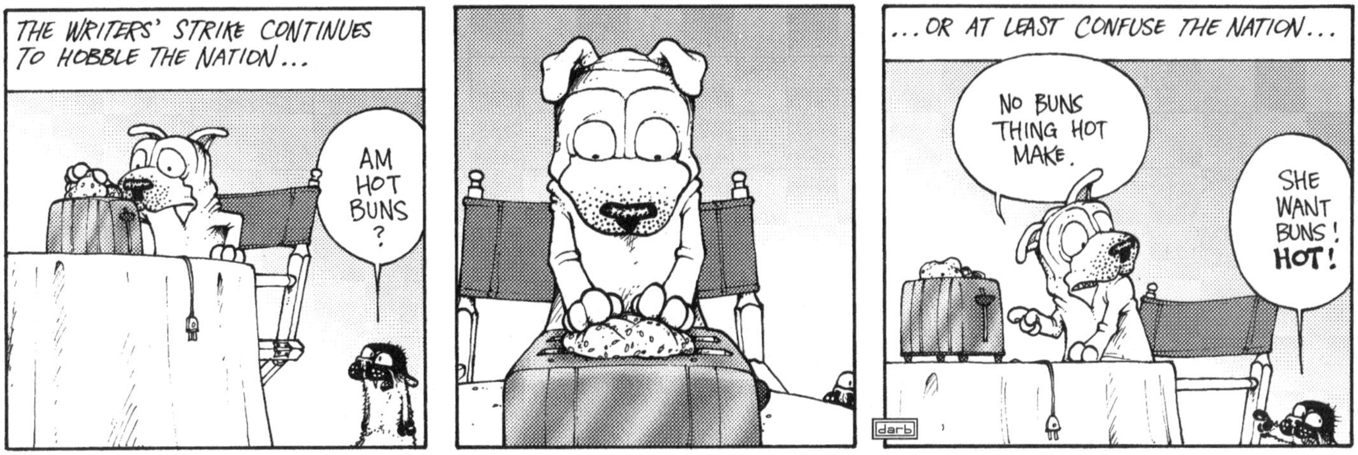
THE WRITERS' STRIKE CONTINUES TO HOBBLE THE NATION...
AM HOT BUNS ?
...OR AT LEAST CONFUSE THE NATION...
NO BUNS THING HOT MAKE.
SHE WANT BUNS! HOT!

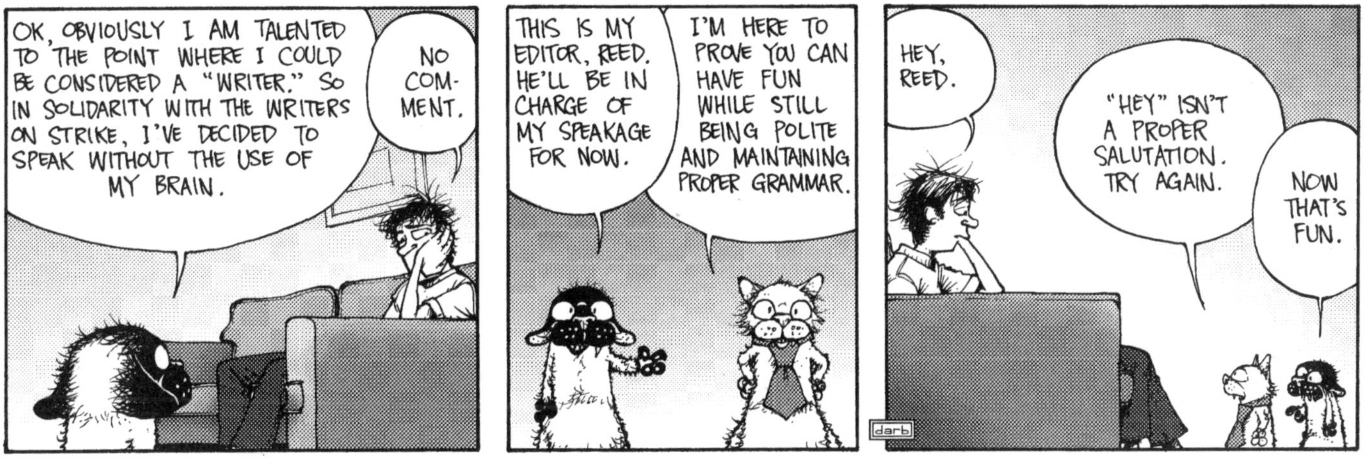
OK, OBVIOUSLY I AM TALENTED TO THE POINT WHERE I COULD BE CONSIDERED A "WRITER." SO IN SOLIDARITY WITH THE WRITERS ON STRIKE, I'VE DECIDED TO SPEAK WITHOUT THE USE OF MY BRAIN.
NO COMMENT.
THIS IS MY EDITOR, REED. HE'LL BE IN CHARGE OF MY SPEAKAGE FOR NOW.
I'M HERE TO PROVE YOU CAN HAVE FUN WHILE STILL BEING POLITE AND MAINTAINING PROPER GRAMMAR.
HEY, REED.
"HEY" ISN'T A PROPER SALUTATION. TRY AGAIN.
NOW THAT'S FUN.

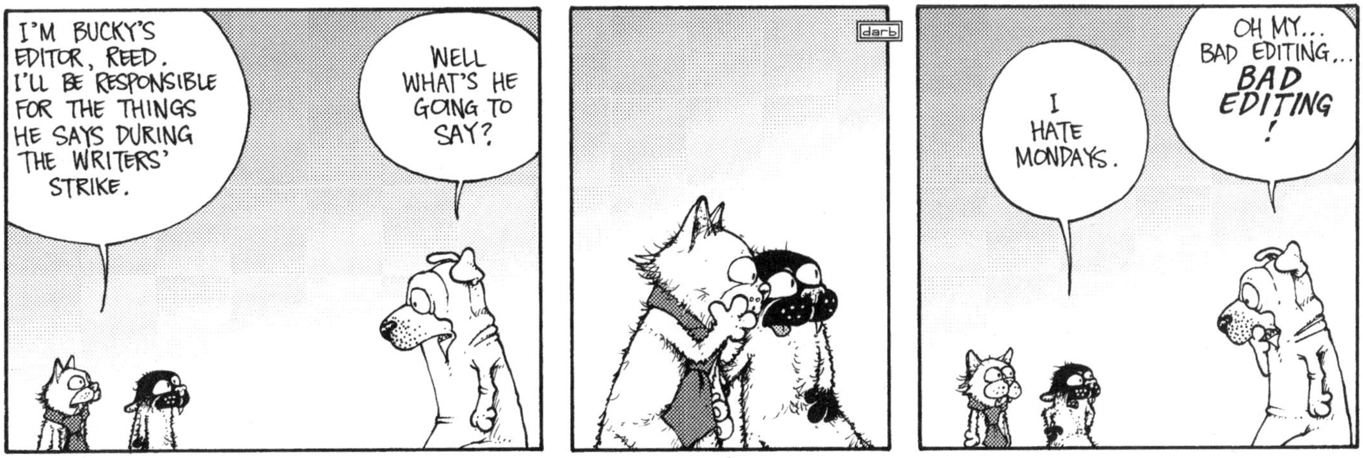
I'M BUCKY'S EDITOR, REED. I'LL BE RESPONSIBLE FOR THE THINGS HE SAYS DURING THE WRITERS' STRIKE.
WELL WHAT'S HE GOING TO SAY?
I HATE MONDAYS.
OH MY... BAD EDITING... BAD EDITING!

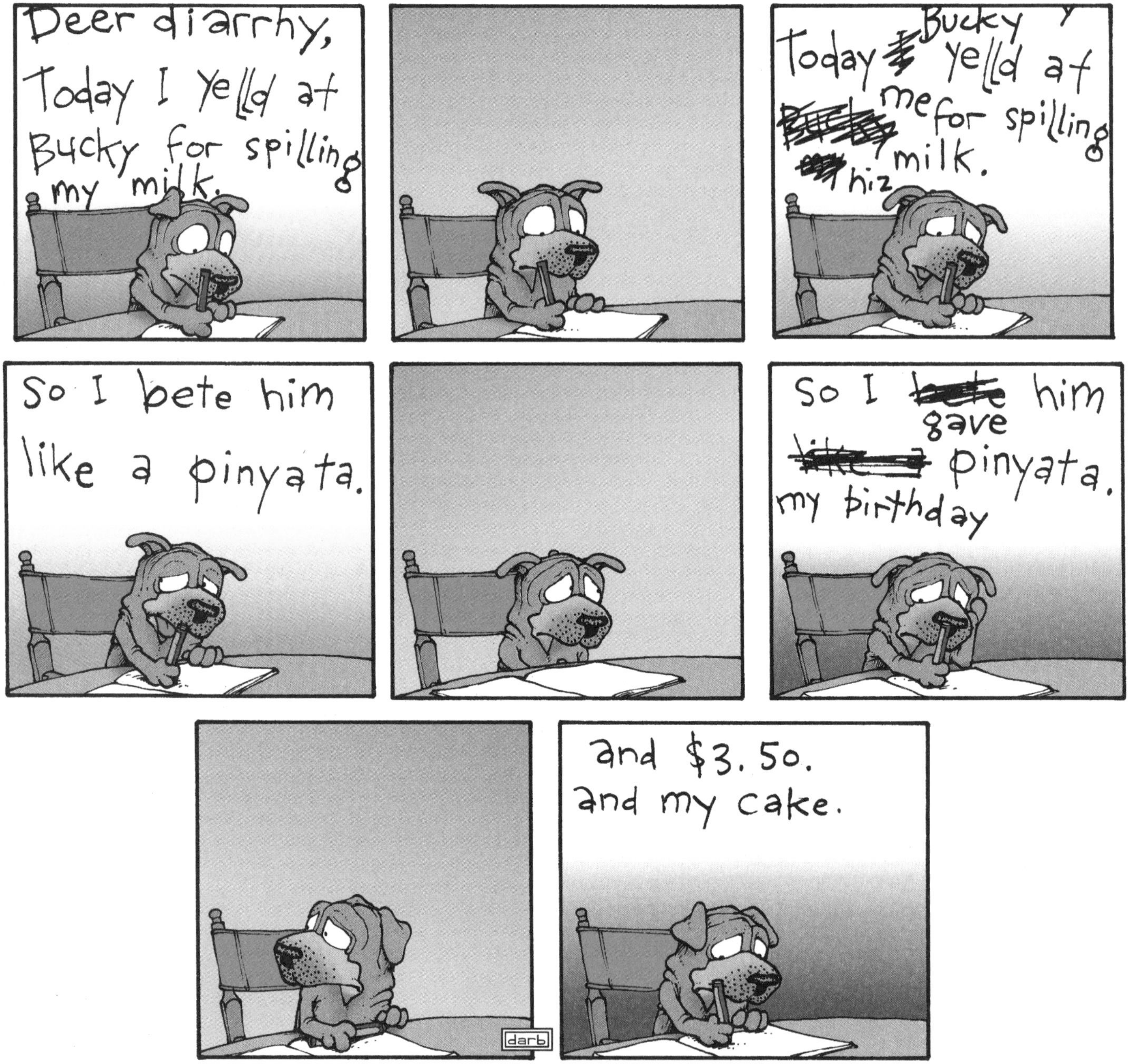
Deer diarrhy,
Today I yelld at Bucky for spilling my milk.
Today Bucky yelld at me for spilling hiz milk.
So I bete him like a pinyata.
So I gave him pinyata. my birthday
and $3.50. and my cake.
darb

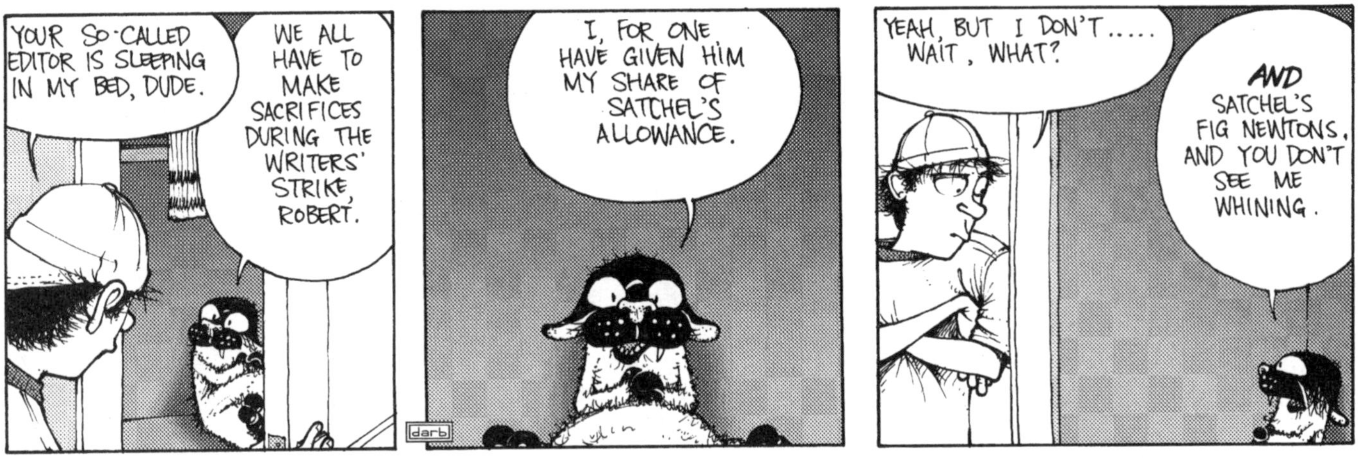
YOUR SO-CALLED EDITOR IS SLEEPING IN MY BED, DUDE.
WE ALL HAVE TO MAKE SACRIFICES DURING THE WRITERS' STRIKE, ROBERT.
I, FOR ONE HAVE GIVEN HIM MY SHARE OF SATCHEL'S ALLOWANCE.
YEAH, BUT I DON'T..... WAIT, WHAT?
AND SATCHEL'S FIG NEWTONS, AND YOU DON'T SEE ME WHINING.

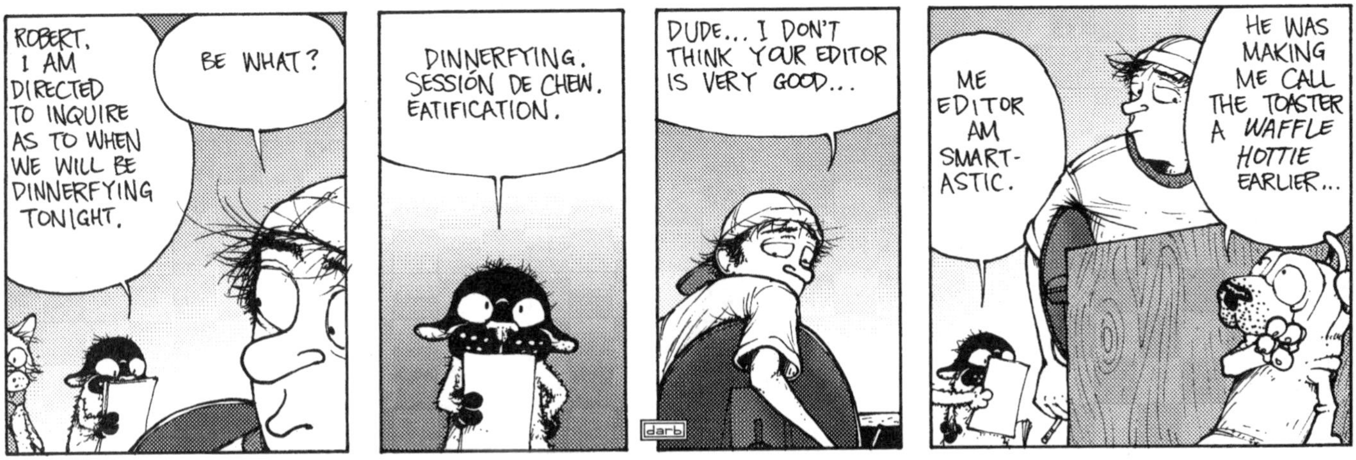
ROBERT, I AM DIRECTED TO INQUIRE AS TO WHEN WE WILL BE DINNERFYING TONIGHT.
BE WHAT?
DINNERFYING. SESSIÓN DE CHEW. EATIFICATION.
DUDE... I DON'T THINK YOUR EDITOR IS VERY GOOD...
ME EDITOR AM SMART-ASTIC.
HE WAS MAKING ME CALL THE TOASTER A WAFFLE HOTTIE EARLIER...

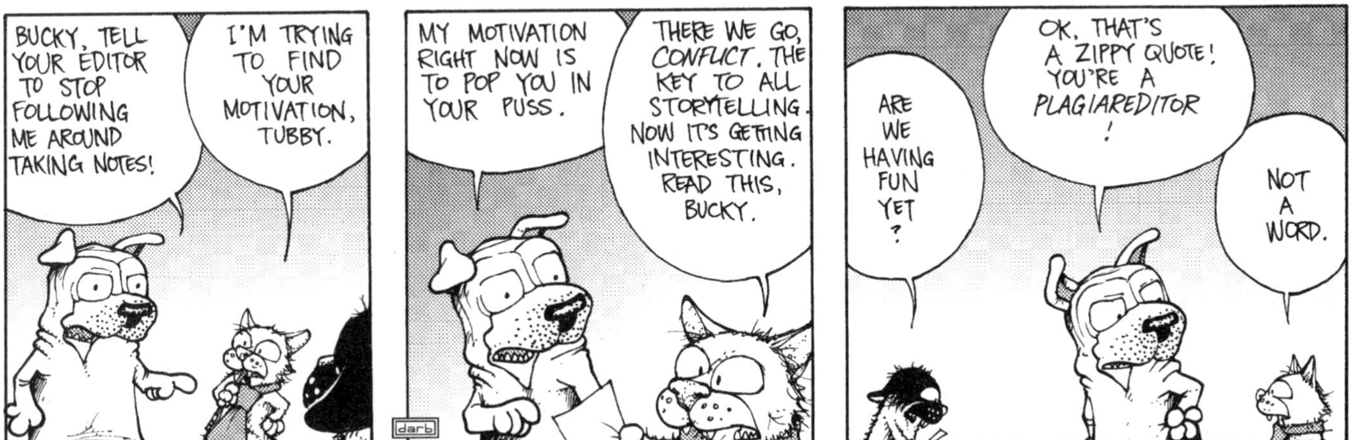
BUCKY, TELL YOUR EDITOR TO STOP FOLLOWING ME AROUND TAKING NOTES!
I'M TRYING TO FIND YOUR MOTIVATION, TUBBY.
MY MOTIVATION RIGHT NOW IS TO POP YOU IN YOUR PUSS.
THERE WE GO, CONFLICT. THE KEY TO ALL STORYTELLING. NOW IT'S GETTING INTERESTING. READ THIS, BUCKY.
ARE WE HAVING FUN YET?
OK. THAT'S A ZIPPY QUOTE! YOU'RE A PLAGIAREDITOR!
NOT A WORD.

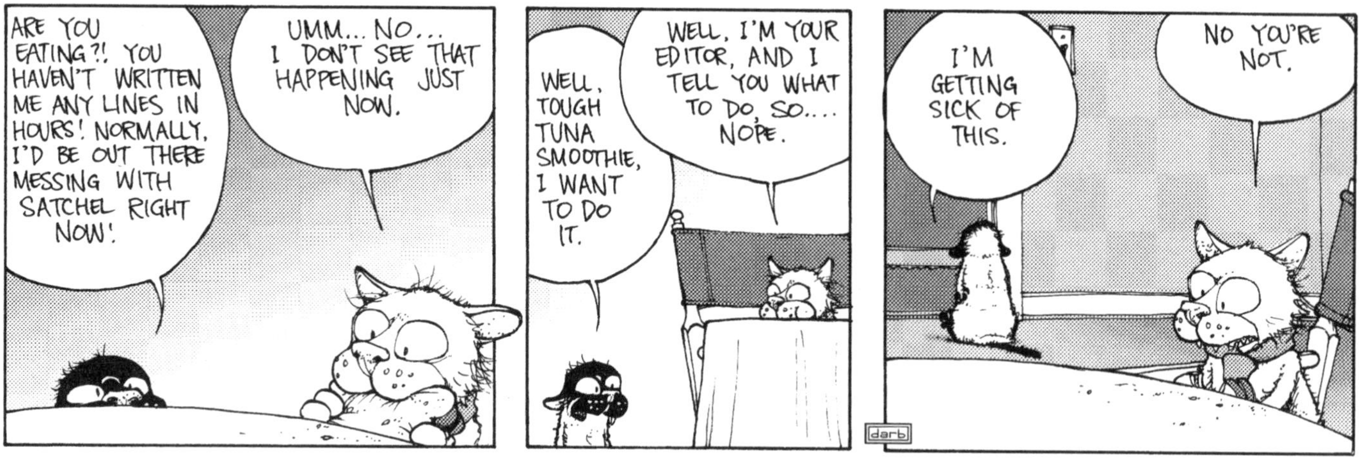
ARE YOU EATING?! YOU HAVEN'T WRITTEN ME ANY LINES IN HOURS! NORMALLY, I'D BE OUT THERE MESSING WITH SATCHEL RIGHT NOW!
UMM... NO... I DON'T SEE THAT HAPPENING JUST NOW.
WELL, TOUGH TUNA SMOOTHIE, I WANT TO DO IT.
WELL, I'M YOUR EDITOR, AND I TELL YOU WHAT TO DO, SO.... NOPE.
I'M GETTING SICK OF THIS.
NO YOU'RE NOT.
darb

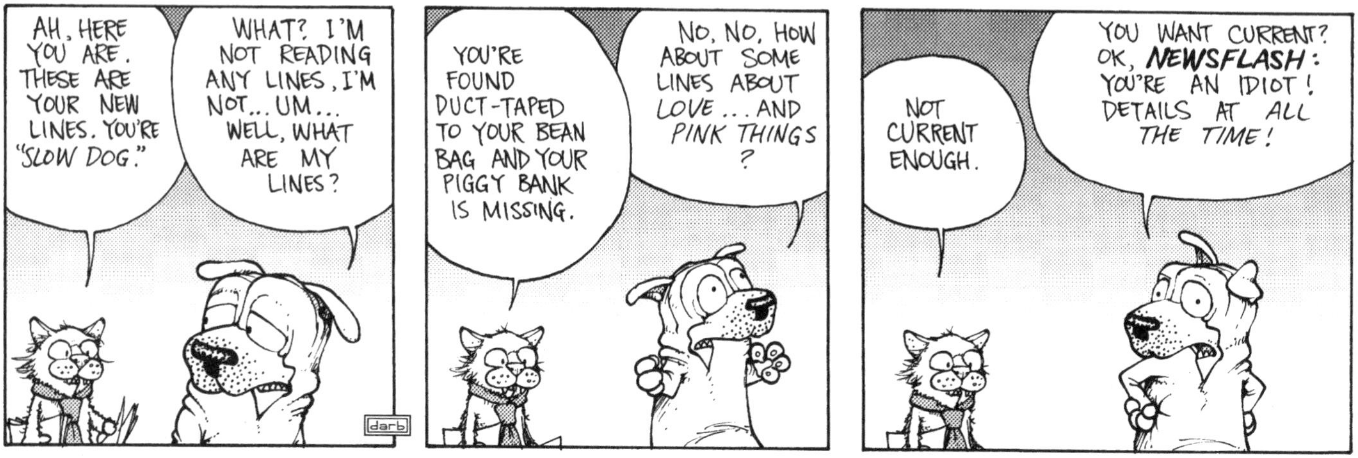
AH, HERE YOU ARE. THESE ARE YOUR NEW LINES. YOU'RE "SLOW DOG."
WHAT? I'M NOT READING ANY LINES, I'M NOT... UM... WELL, WHAT ARE MY LINES?
YOU'RE FOUND DUCT-TAPED TO YOUR BEAN BAG AND YOUR PIGGY BANK IS MISSING.
NO, NO, HOW ABOUT SOME LINES ABOUT LOVE ... AND PINK THINGS ?
NOT CURRENT ENOUGH.
YOU WANT CURRENT? OK, NEWSFLASH: YOU'RE AN IDIOT! DETAILS AT ALL THE TIME!
darb

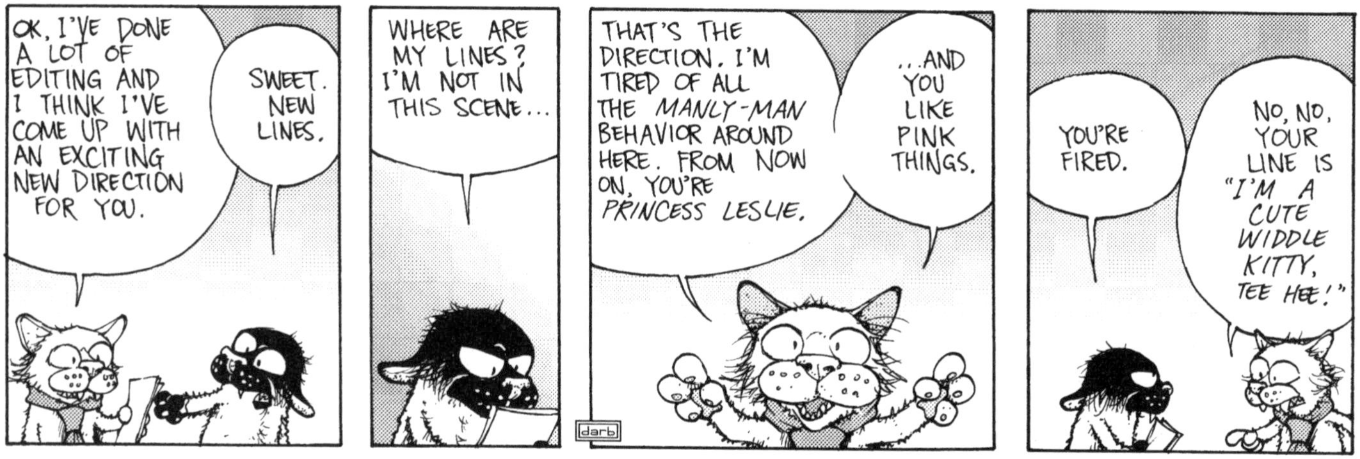
OK, I'VE DONE A LOT OF EDITING AND I THINK I'VE COME UP WITH AN EXCITING NEW DIRECTION FOR YOU.
SWEET. NEW LINES.
WHERE ARE MY LINES? I'M NOT IN THIS SCENE...
THAT'S THE DIRECTION. I'M TIRED OF ALL THE MANLY-MAN BEHAVIOR AROUND HERE. FROM NOW ON, YOU'RE PRINCESS LESLIE.
...AND YOU LIKE PINK THINGS.
YOU'RE FIRED.
NO, NO, YOUR LINE IS "I'M A CUTE WIDDLE KITTY, TEE HEE!"
darb

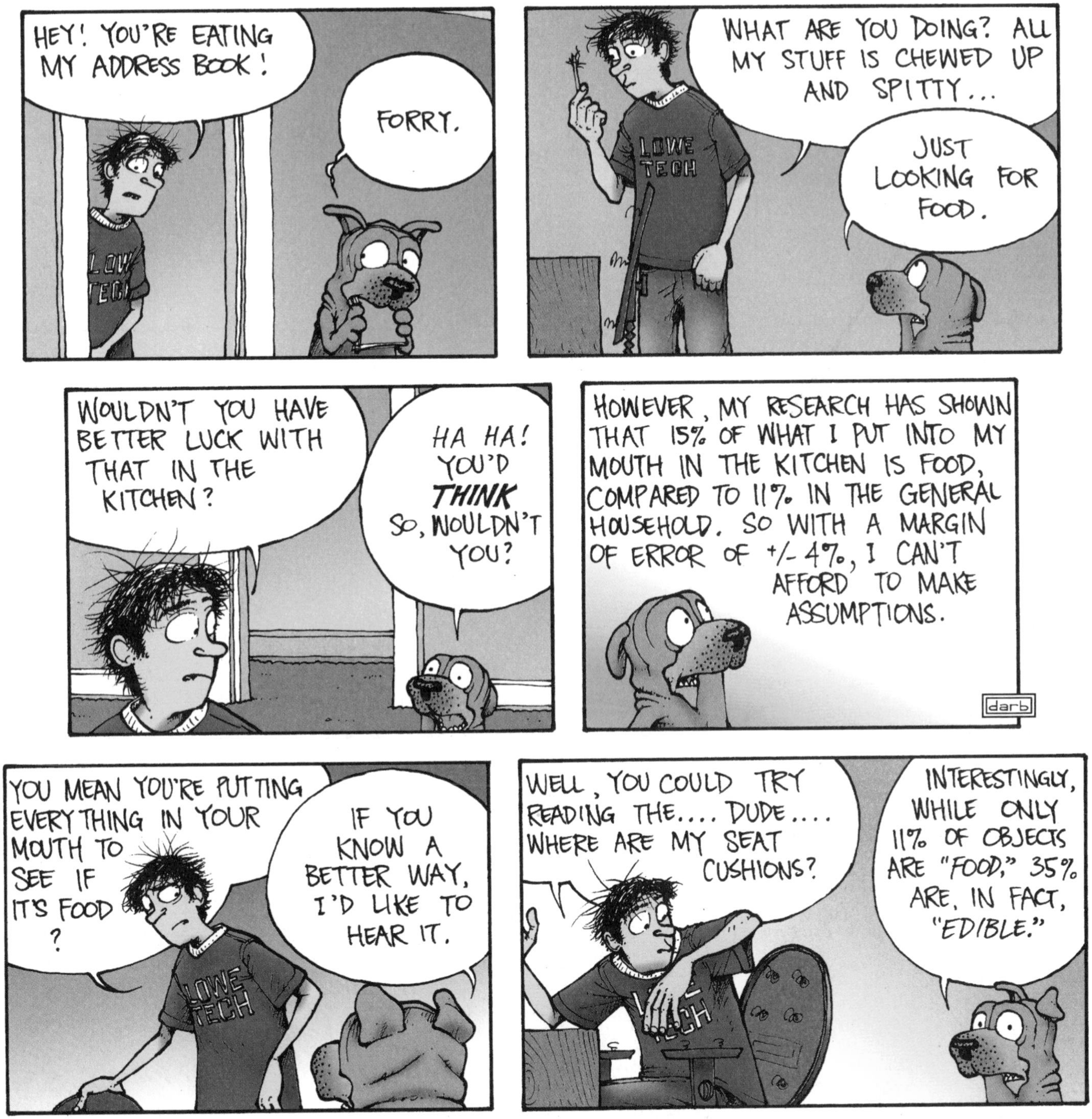
HEY! YOU'RE EATING MY ADDRESS BOOK!
FORRY.
LOWE TECH
WHAT ARE YOU DOING? ALL MY STUFF IS CHEWED UP AND SPITTY...
JUST LOOKING FOR FOOD.
WOULDN'T YOU HAVE BETTER LUCK WITH THAT IN THE KITCHEN?
HA HA! YOU'D **THINK** SO, WOULDN'T YOU?
HOWEVER, MY RESEARCH HAS SHOWN THAT 15% OF WHAT I PUT INTO MY MOUTH IN THE KITCHEN IS FOOD, COMPARED TO 11% IN THE GENERAL HOUSEHOLD. SO WITH A MARGIN OF ERROR OF +/- 4%, I CAN'T AFFORD TO MAKE ASSUMPTIONS.
darb
YOU MEAN YOU'RE PUTTING EVERYTHING IN YOUR MOUTH TO SEE IF IT'S FOOD?
IF YOU KNOW A BETTER WAY, I'D LIKE TO HEAR IT.
WELL, YOU COULD TRY READING THE.... DUDE.... WHERE ARE MY SEAT CUSHIONS?
INTERESTINGLY, WHILE ONLY 11% OF OBJECTS ARE "FOOD," 35% ARE, IN FACT, "EDIBLE."

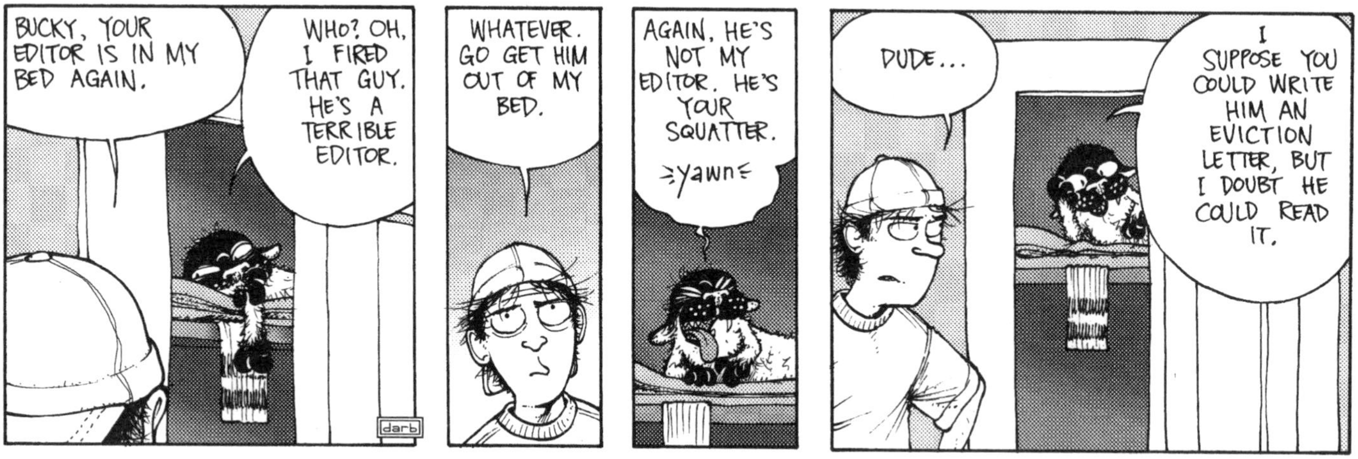
BUCKY, YOUR EDITOR IS IN MY BED AGAIN.
WHO? OH, I FIRED THAT GUY. HE'S A TERRIBLE EDITOR.
WHATEVER. GO GET HIM OUT OF MY BED.
AGAIN, HE'S NOT MY EDITOR. HE'S YOUR SQUATTER.
yawn
DUDE...
I SUPPOSE YOU COULD WRITE HIM AN EVICTION LETTER, BUT I DOUBT HE COULD READ IT.

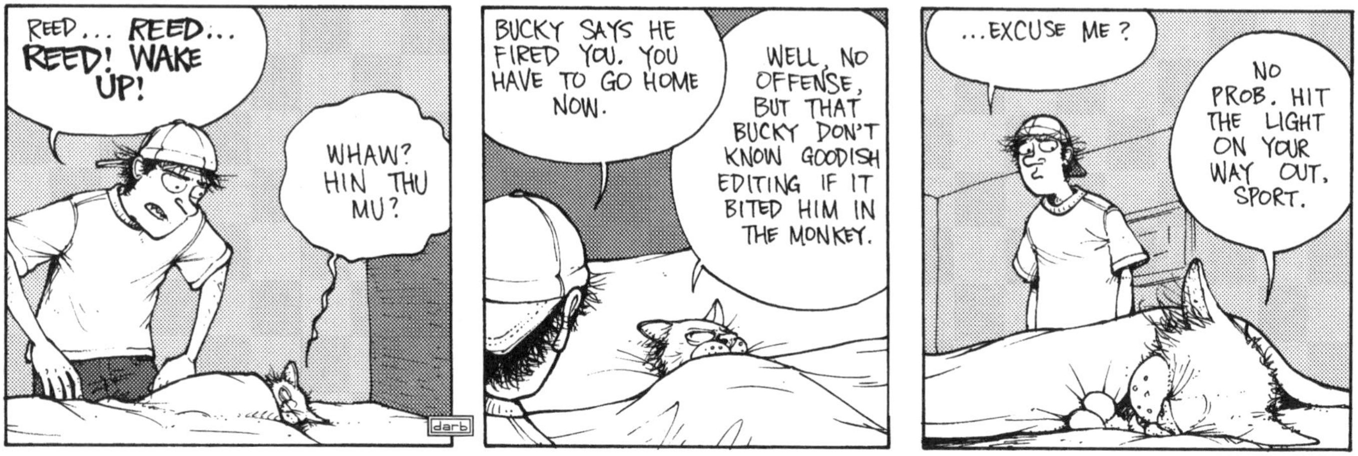
REED... REED... REED! WAKE UP!
WHAW? HIN THU MU?
BUCKY SAYS HE FIRED YOU. YOU HAVE TO GO HOME NOW.
WELL, NO OFFENSE, BUT THAT BUCKY DON'T KNOW GOODISH EDITING IF IT BITED HIM IN THE MONKEY.
...EXCUSE ME?
NO PROB. HIT THE LIGHT ON YOUR WAY OUT, SPORT.

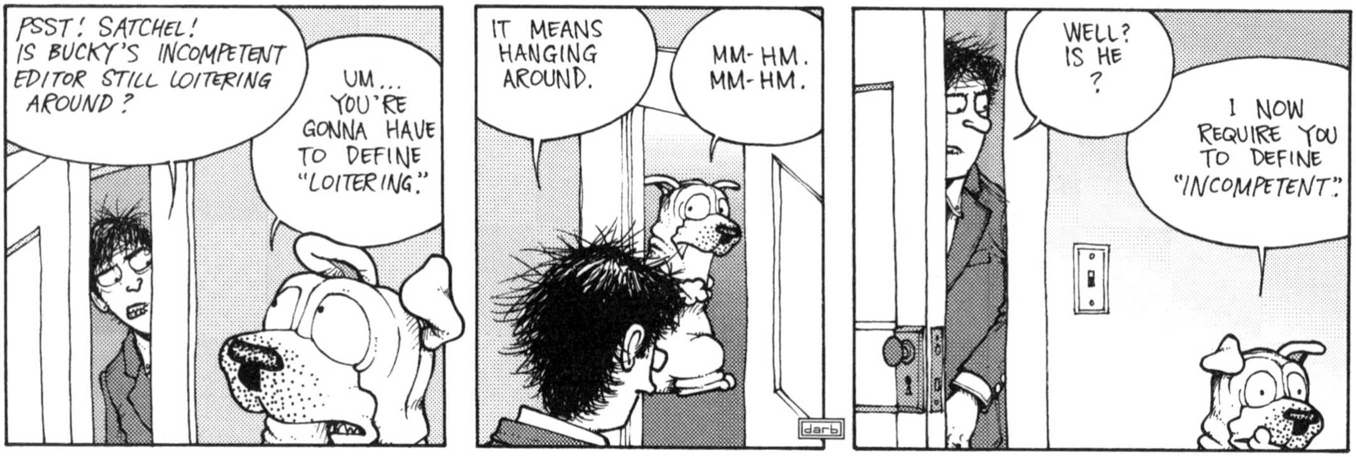
PSST! SATCHEL! IS BUCKY'S INCOMPETENT EDITOR STILL LOITERING AROUND?
UM... YOU'RE GONNA HAVE TO DEFINE "LOITERING."
IT MEANS HANGING AROUND.
MM-HM. MM-HM.
WELL? IS HE ?
I NOW REQUIRE YOU TO DEFINE "INCOMPETENT."

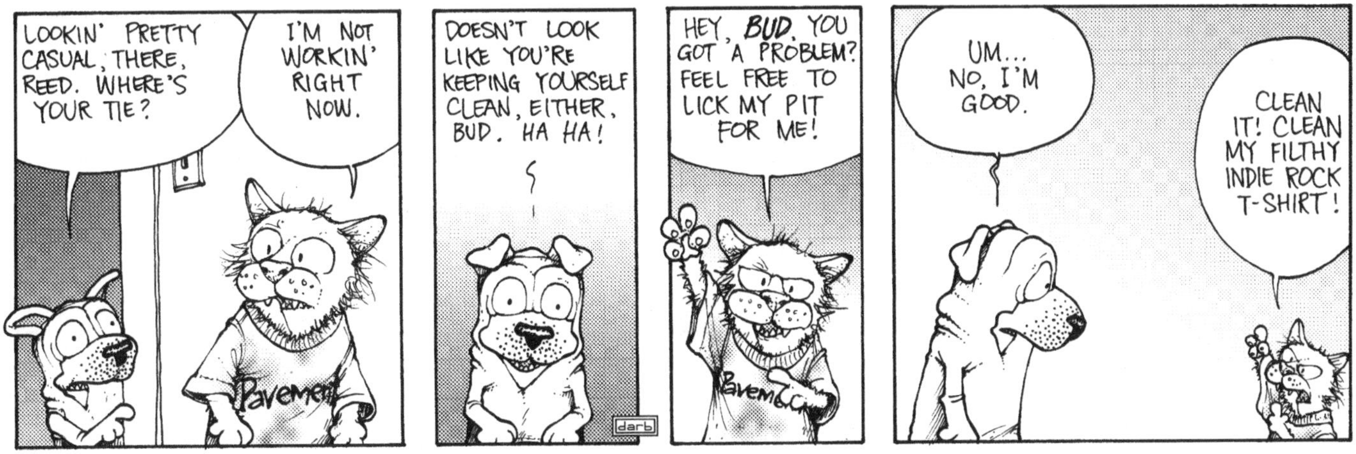
LOOKIN' PRETTY CASUAL, THERE, REED. WHERE'S YOUR TIE?
I'M NOT WORKIN' RIGHT NOW.
Pavement
DOESN'T LOOK LIKE YOU'RE KEEPING YOURSELF CLEAN, EITHER, BUD. HA HA!
darb
HEY, BUD, YOU GOT A PROBLEM? FEEL FREE TO LICK MY PIT FOR ME!
UM... NO, I'M GOOD.
CLEAN IT! CLEAN MY FILTHY INDIE ROCK T-SHIRT!

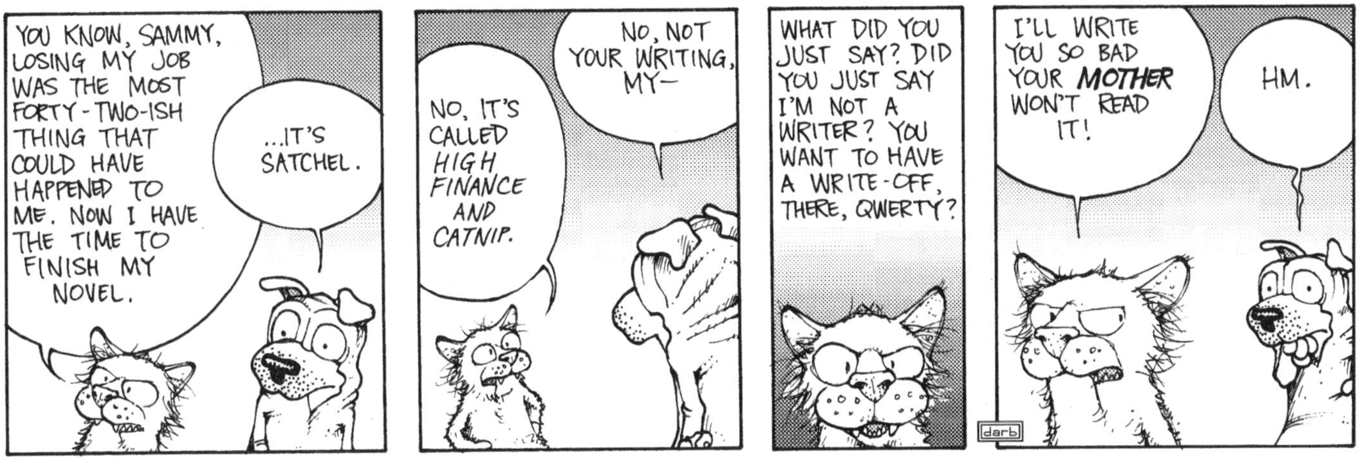
YOU KNOW, SAMMY, LOSING MY JOB WAS THE MOST FORTY-TWO-ISH THING THAT COULD HAVE HAPPENED TO ME. NOW I HAVE THE TIME TO FINISH MY NOVEL.
...IT'S SATCHEL.
NO, IT'S CALLED HIGH FINANCE AND CATNIP.
NO, NOT YOUR WRITING, MY—
WHAT DID YOU JUST SAY? DID YOU JUST SAY I'M NOT A WRITER? YOU WANT TO HAVE A WRITE-OFF, THERE, QWERTY?
darb
I'LL WRITE YOU SO BAD YOUR MOTHER WON'T READ IT!
HM.

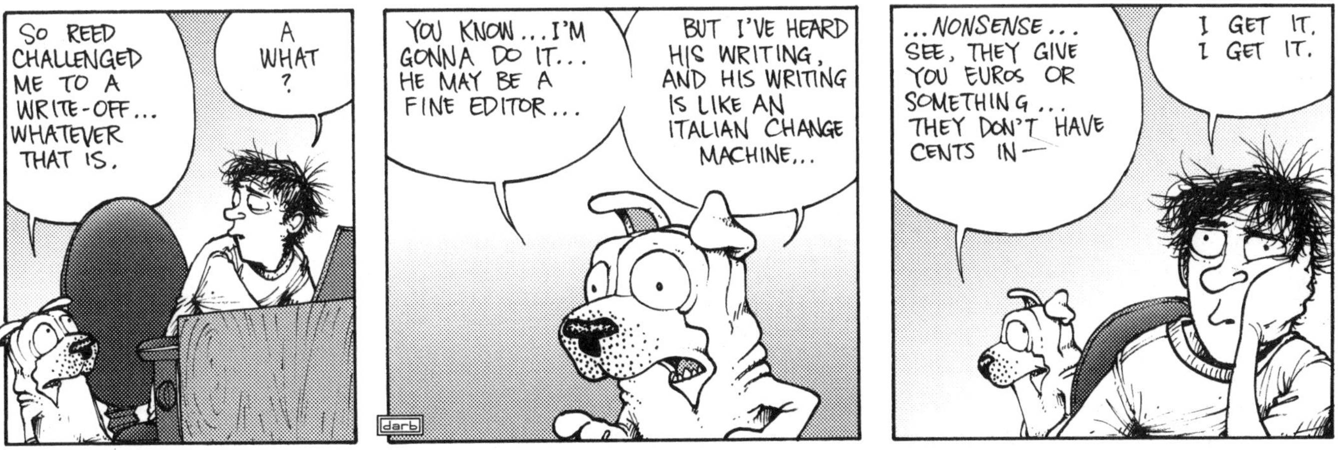
SO REED CHALLENGED ME TO A WRITE-OFF... WHATEVER THAT IS.
A WHAT?
darb
YOU KNOW... I'M GONNA DO IT... HE MAY BE A FINE EDITOR...
BUT I'VE HEARD HIS WRITING, AND HIS WRITING IS LIKE AN ITALIAN CHANGE MACHINE...
...NONSENSE... SEE, THEY GIVE YOU EUROS OR SOMETHING... THEY DON'T HAVE CENTS IN—
I GET IT. I GET IT.

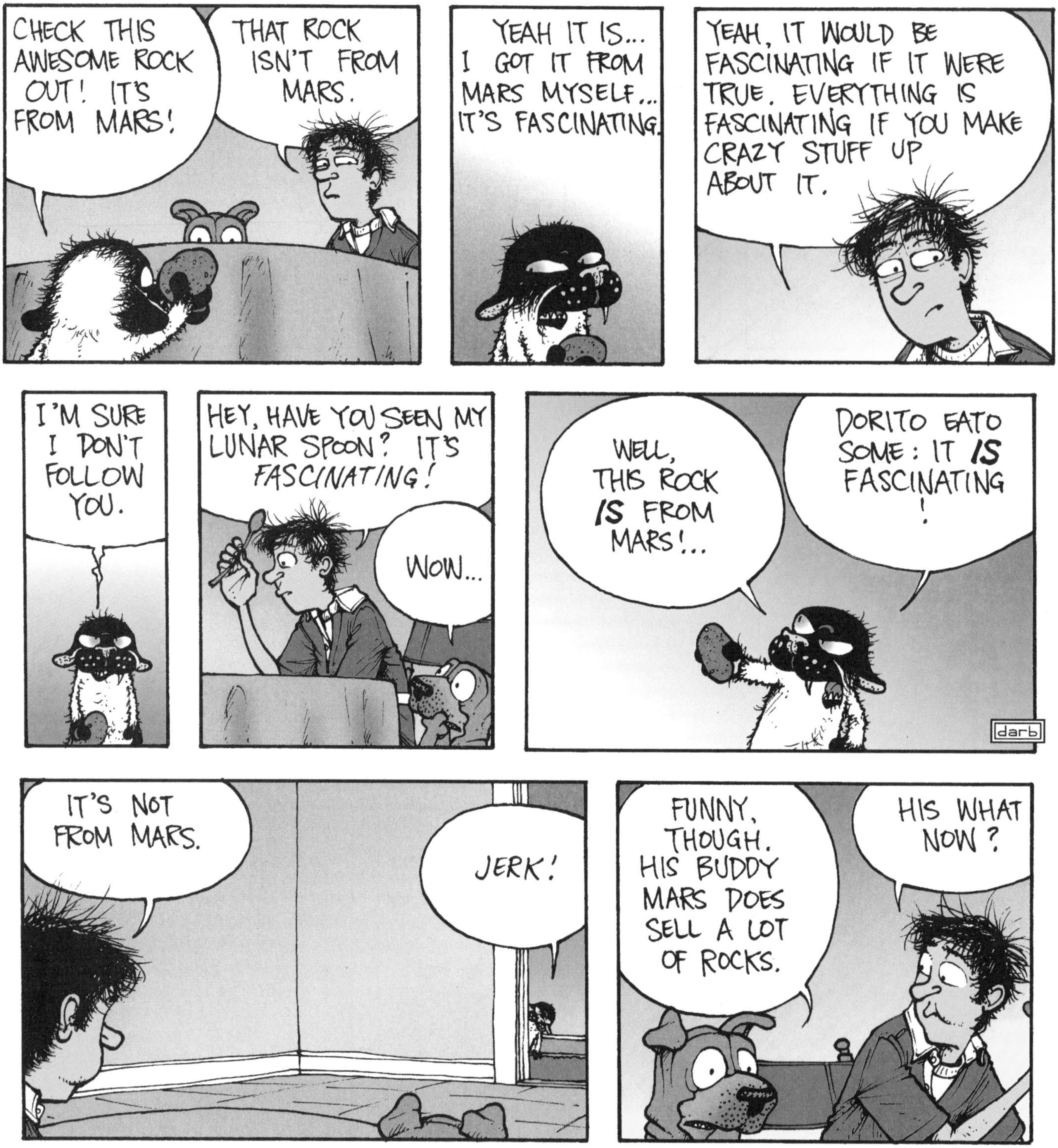
CHECK THIS AWESOME ROCK OUT! IT'S FROM MARS!
THAT ROCK ISN'T FROM MARS.
YEAH IT IS... I GOT IT FROM MARS MYSELF... IT'S FASCINATING.
YEAH, IT WOULD BE FASCINATING IF IT WERE TRUE. EVERYTHING IS FASCINATING IF YOU MAKE CRAZY STUFF UP ABOUT IT.
I'M SURE I DON'T FOLLOW YOU.
HEY, HAVE YOU SEEN MY LUNAR SPOON? IT'S *FASCINATING!*
WOW...
WELL, THIS ROCK **IS** FROM MARS!...
DORITO EATO SOME: IT **IS** FASCINATING!
darb
IT'S NOT FROM MARS.
JERK!
FUNNY, THOUGH. HIS BUDDY MARS DOES SELL A LOT OF ROCKS.
HIS WHAT NOW?

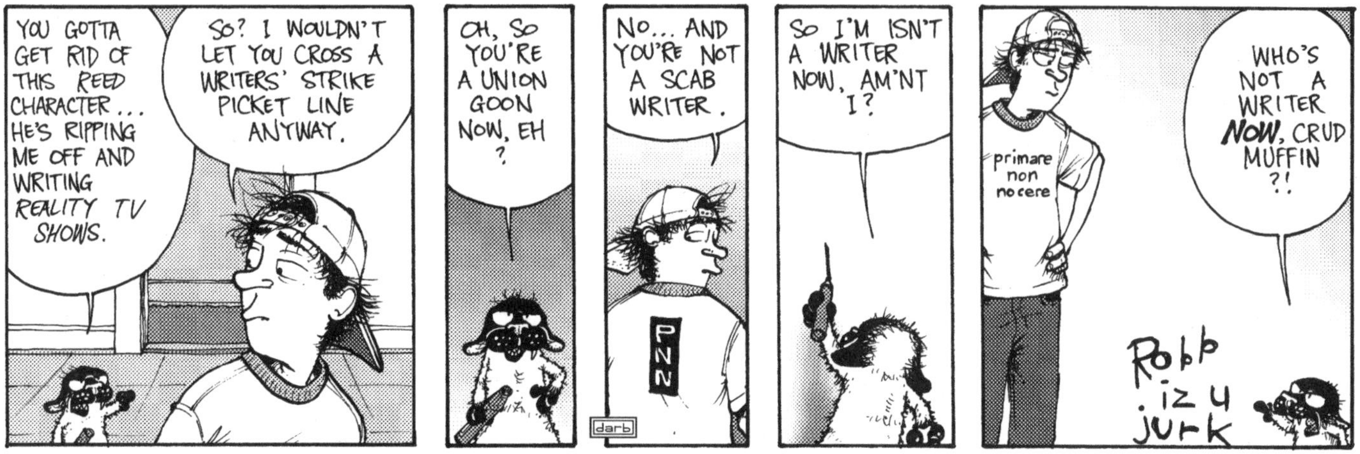
YOU GOTTA GET RID OF THIS REED CHARACTER... HE'S RIPPING ME OFF AND WRITING REALITY TV SHOWS.
SO? I WOULDN'T LET YOU CROSS A WRITERS' STRIKE PICKET LINE ANYWAY.
OH, SO YOU'RE A UNION GOON NOW, EH?
NO... AND YOU'RE NOT A SCAB WRITER.
PNN
SO I'M ISN'T A WRITER NOW, AM'NT I?
primare non nocere
WHO'S NOT A WRITER NOW, CRUD MUFFIN?!
Robb iz u jurk
darb

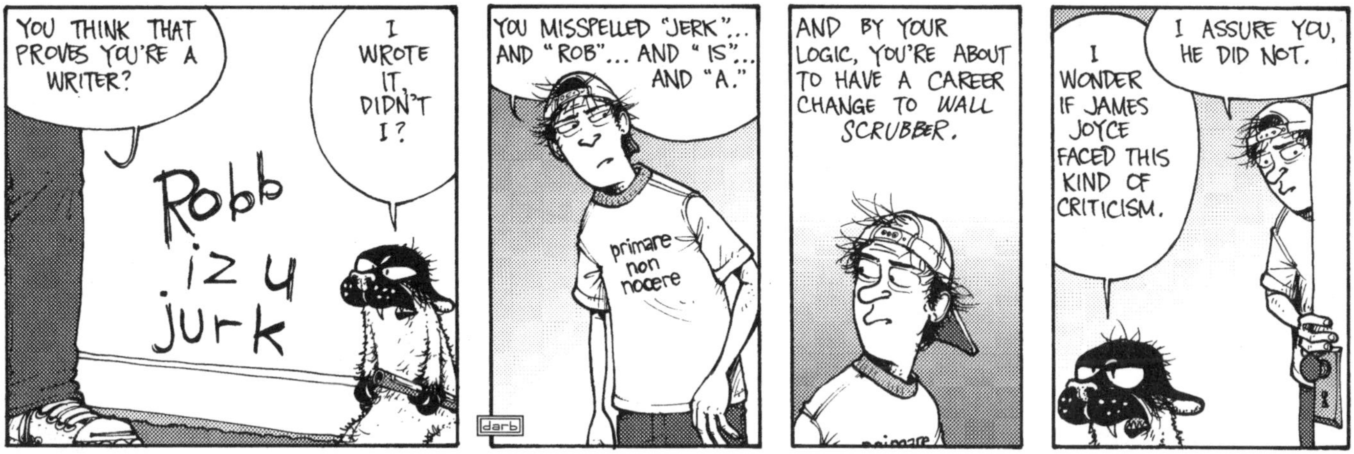
YOU THINK THAT PROVES YOU'RE A WRITER?
I WROTE IT, DIDN'T I?
Robb iz u jurk
darb
YOU MISSPELLED "JERK"... AND "ROB"... AND "IS"... AND "A."
primare non nocere
AND BY YOUR LOGIC, YOU'RE ABOUT TO HAVE A CAREER CHANGE TO WALL SCRUBBER.
I WONDER IF JAMES JOYCE FACED THIS KIND OF CRITICISM.
I ASSURE YOU, HE DID NOT.

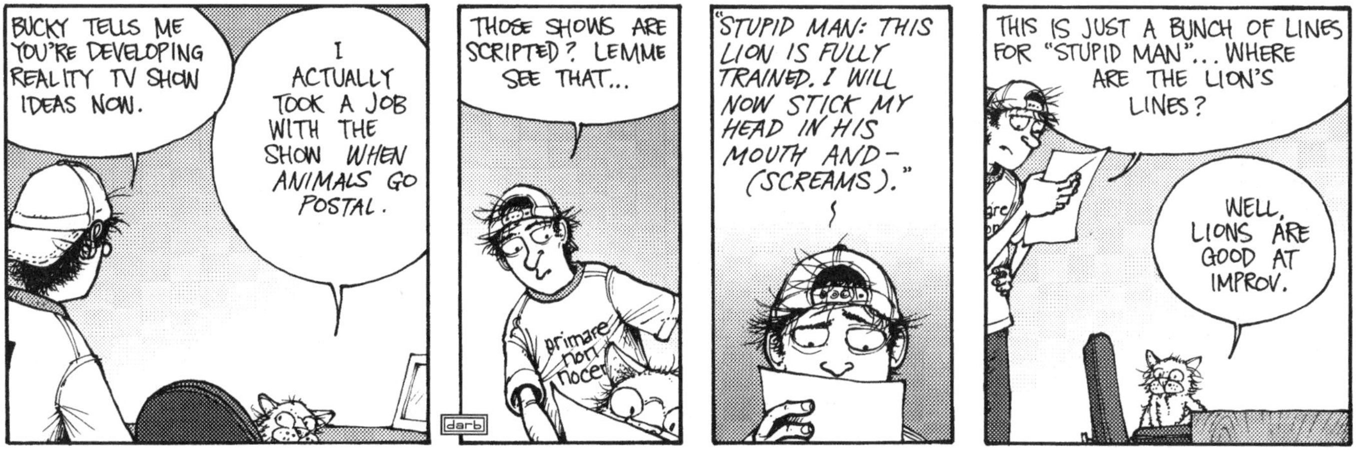
BUCKY TELLS ME YOU'RE DEVELOPING REALITY TV SHOW IDEAS NOW.
I ACTUALLY TOOK A JOB WITH THE SHOW WHEN ANIMALS GO POSTAL.
darb
THOSE SHOWS ARE SCRIPTED? LEMME SEE THAT...
primare non nocere
"STUPID MAN: THIS LION IS FULLY TRAINED. I WILL NOW STICK MY HEAD IN HIS MOUTH AND— (SCREAMS)."
THIS IS JUST A BUNCH OF LINES FOR "STUPID MAN"... WHERE ARE THE LION'S LINES?
WELL, LIONS ARE GOOD AT IMPROV.

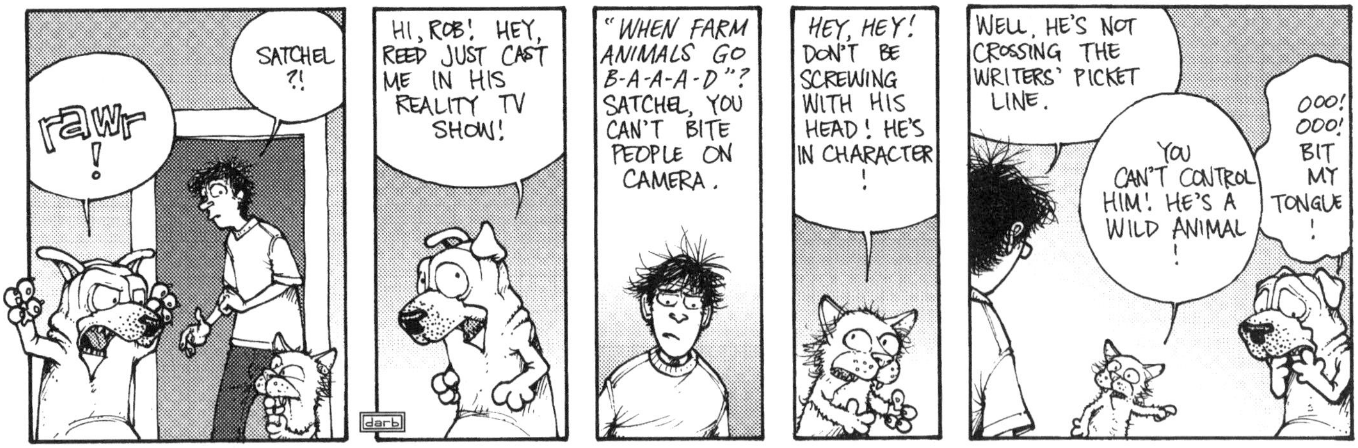
rawr !
SATCHEL ?!
HI, ROB! HEY, REED JUST CAST ME IN HIS REALITY TV SHOW!
"WHEN FARM ANIMALS GO B-A-A-A-D"? SATCHEL, YOU CAN'T BITE PEOPLE ON CAMERA.
HEY, HEY! DON'T BE SCREWING WITH HIS HEAD! HE'S IN CHARACTER !
WELL, HE'S NOT CROSSING THE WRITERS' PICKET LINE.
YOU CAN'T CONTROL HIM! HE'S A WILD ANIMAL !
OOO! OOO! BIT MY TONGUE !
darb

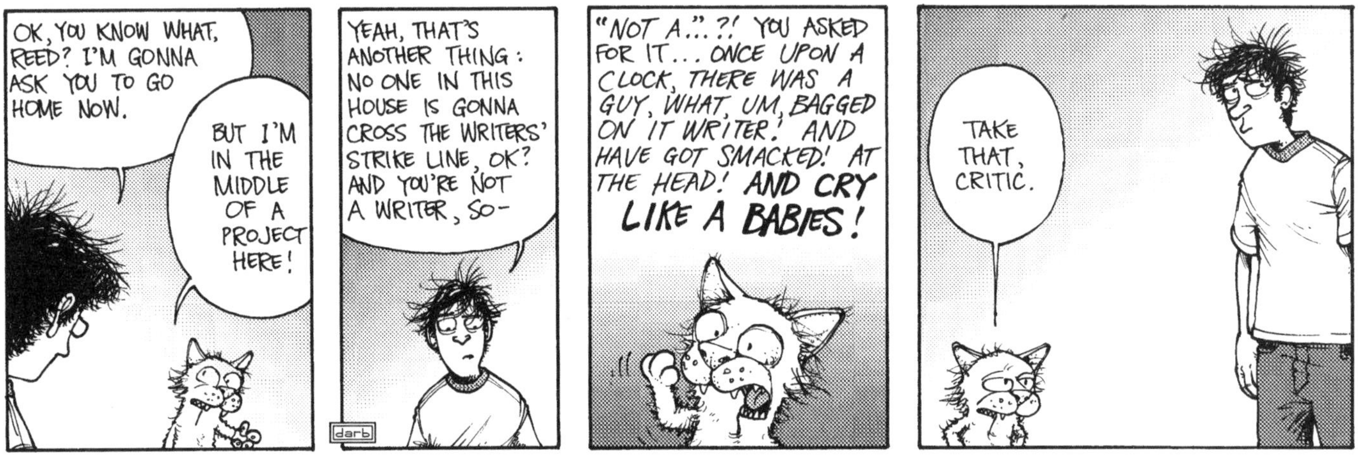
OK, YOU KNOW WHAT, REED? I'M GONNA ASK YOU TO GO HOME NOW.
BUT I'M IN THE MIDDLE OF A PROJECT HERE!
YEAH, THAT'S ANOTHER THING: NO ONE IN THIS HOUSE IS GONNA CROSS THE WRITERS' STRIKE LINE, OK? AND YOU'RE NOT A WRITER, SO-
"NOT A..."?! YOU ASKED FOR IT... ONCE UPON A CLOCK, THERE WAS A GUY, WHAT, UM, BAGGED ON IT WRITER! AND HAVE GOT SMACKED! AT THE HEAD! AND CRY LIKE A BABIES!
TAKE THAT, CRITIC.
darb

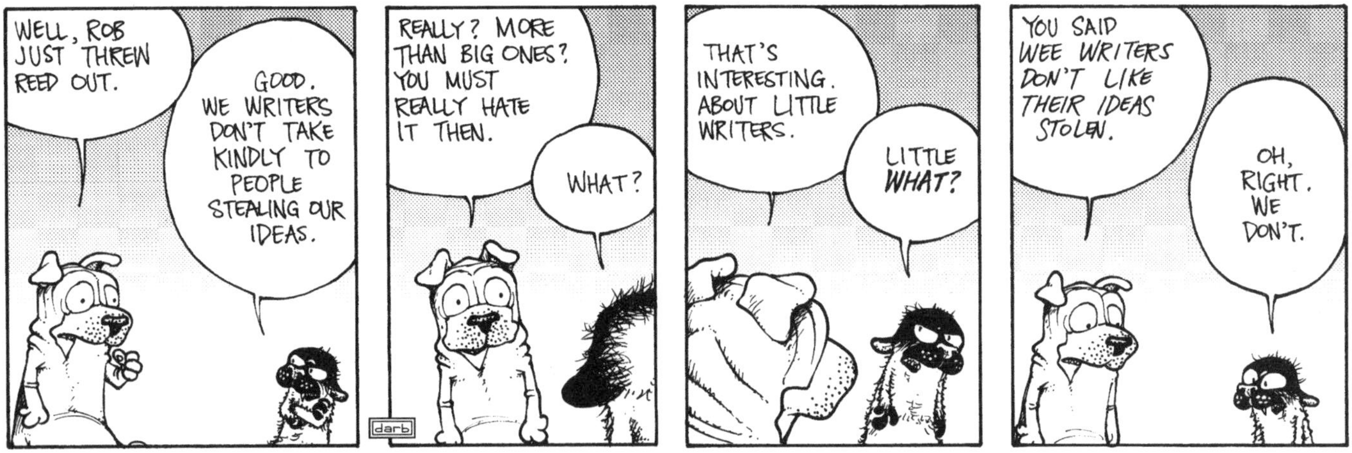
WELL, ROB JUST THREW REED OUT.
GOOD. WE WRITERS DON'T TAKE KINDLY TO PEOPLE STEALING OUR IDEAS.
REALLY? MORE THAN BIG ONES? YOU MUST REALLY HATE IT THEN.
WHAT?
THAT'S INTERESTING. ABOUT LITTLE WRITERS.
LITTLE WHAT?
YOU SAID WEE WRITERS DON'T LIKE THEIR IDEAS STOLEN.
OH, RIGHT. WE DON'T.
darb

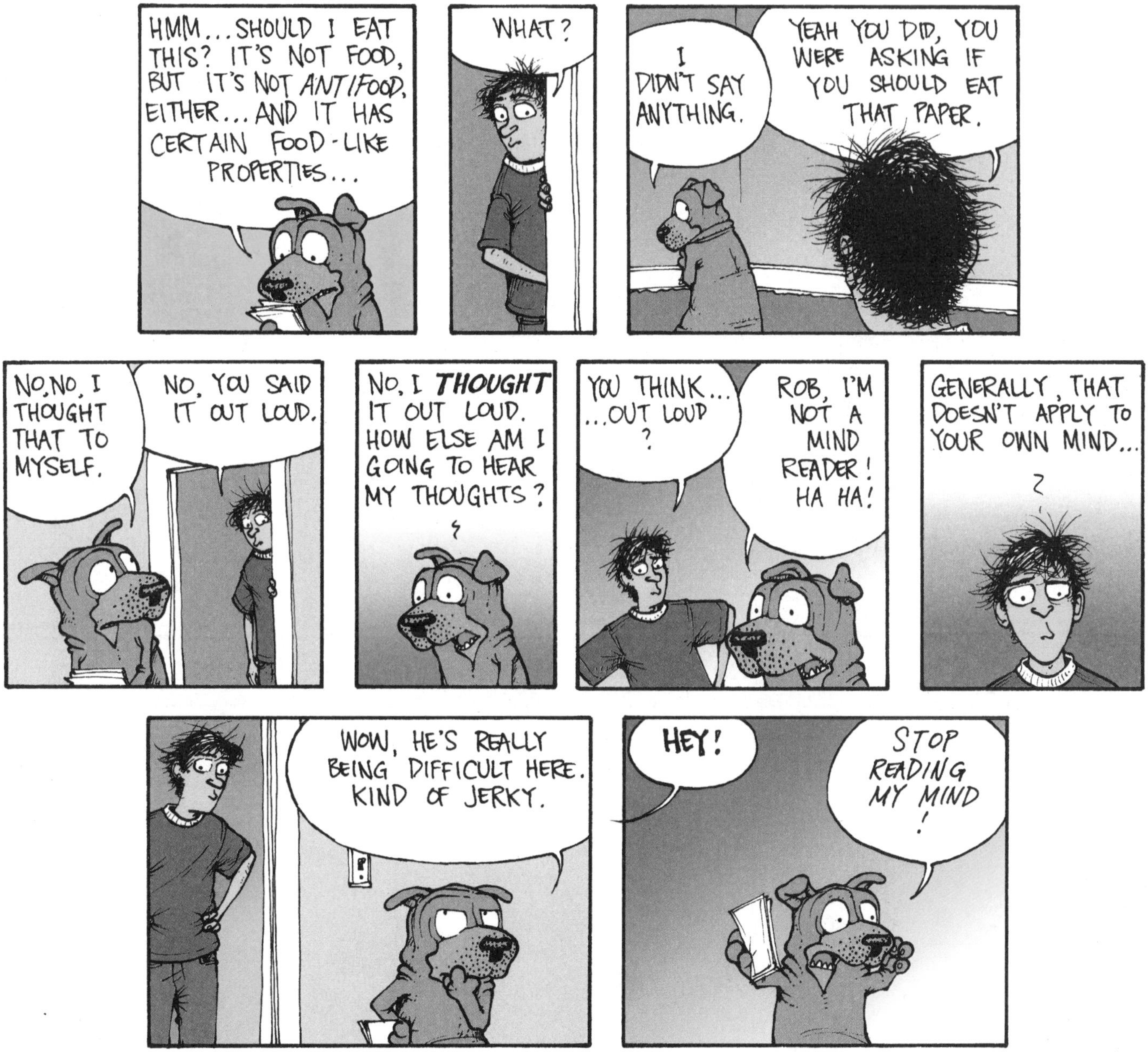
HMM...SHOULD I EAT THIS? IT'S NOT FOOD, BUT IT'S NOT ANTIFOOD, EITHER... AND IT HAS CERTAIN FOOD-LIKE PROPERTIES...
WHAT?
I DIDN'T SAY ANYTHING.
YEAH YOU DID, YOU WERE ASKING IF YOU SHOULD EAT THAT PAPER.
NO, NO, I THOUGHT THAT TO MYSELF.
NO, YOU SAID IT OUT LOUD.
NO, I THOUGHT IT OUT LOUD. HOW ELSE AM I GOING TO HEAR MY THOUGHTS?
YOU THINK... ...OUT LOUD ?
ROB, I'M NOT A MIND READER! HA HA!
GENERALLY, THAT DOESN'T APPLY TO YOUR OWN MIND...
?
WOW, HE'S REALLY BEING DIFFICULT HERE. KIND OF JERKY.
HEY!
STOP READING MY MIND !

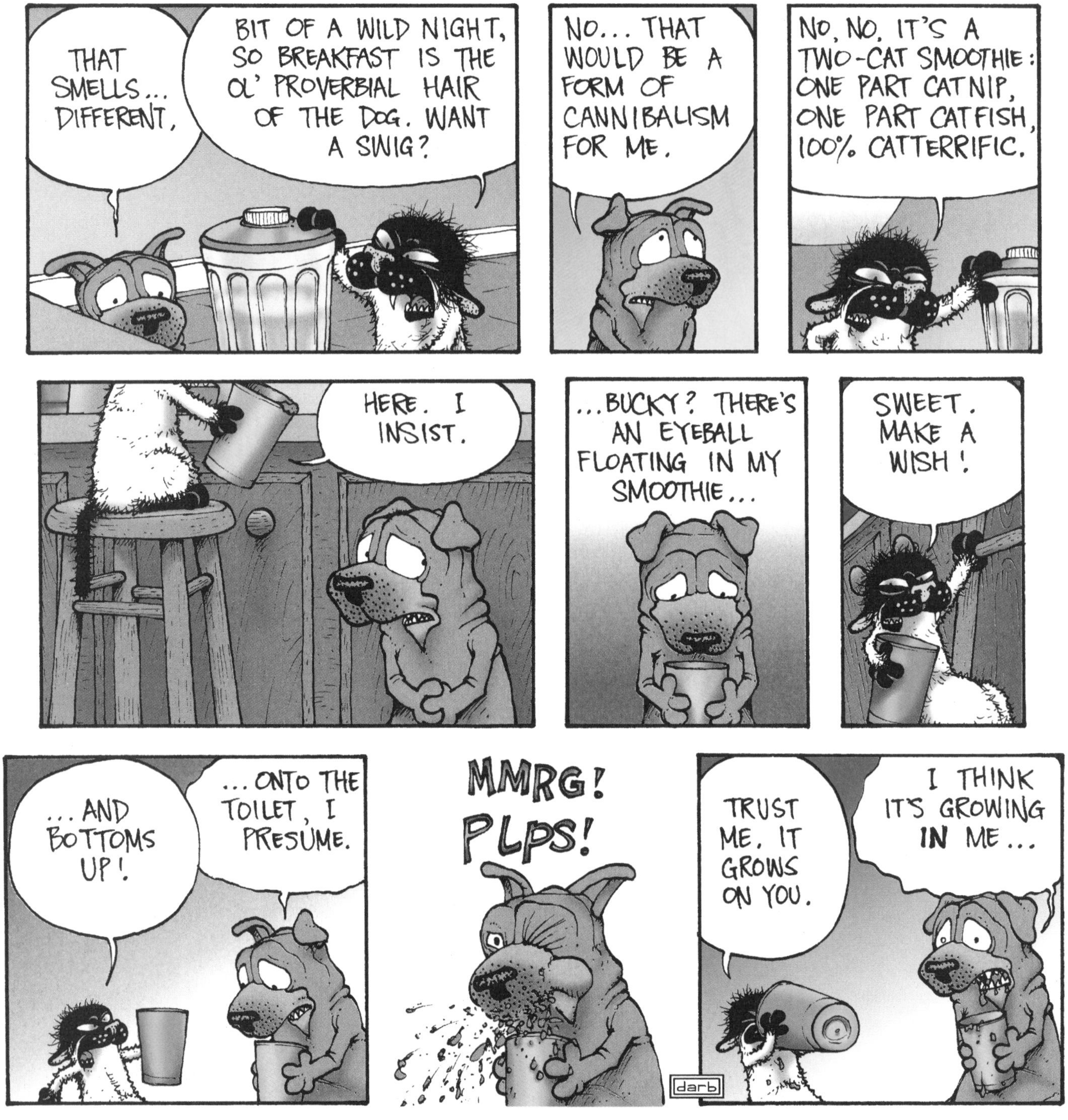
THAT SMELLS... DIFFERENT.
BIT OF A WILD NIGHT, SO BREAKFAST IS THE OL' PROVERBIAL HAIR OF THE DOG. WANT A SWIG?
NO... THAT WOULD BE A FORM OF CANNIBALISM FOR ME.
NO, NO. IT'S A TWO-CAT SMOOTHIE: ONE PART CATNIP, ONE PART CATFISH, 100% CATTERRIFIC.
HERE. I INSIST.
...BUCKY? THERE'S AN EYEBALL FLOATING IN MY SMOOTHIE...
SWEET. MAKE A WISH!
...AND BOTTOMS UP!
...ONTO THE TOILET, I PRESUME.
MMRG! PLPS!
darb
TRUST ME. IT GROWS ON YOU.
I THINK IT'S GROWING **IN** ME...

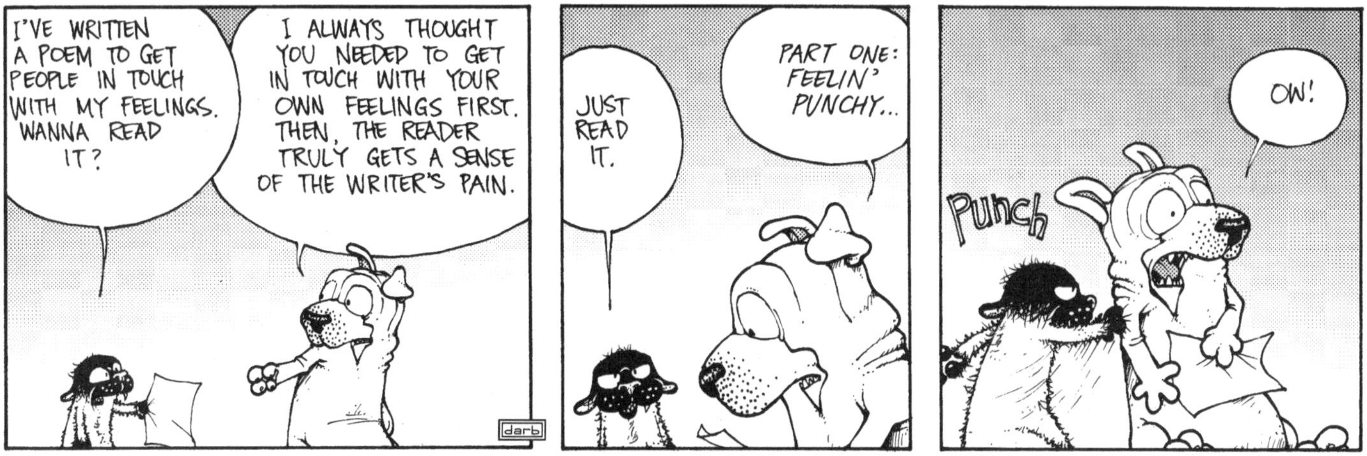
I'VE WRITTEN A POEM TO GET PEOPLE IN TOUCH WITH MY FEELINGS. WANNA READ IT?
I ALWAYS THOUGHT YOU NEEDED TO GET IN TOUCH WITH YOUR OWN FEELINGS FIRST. THEN, THE READER TRULY GETS A SENSE OF THE WRITER'S PAIN.
JUST READ IT.
PART ONE: FEELIN' PUNCHY...
PUNCH
OW!

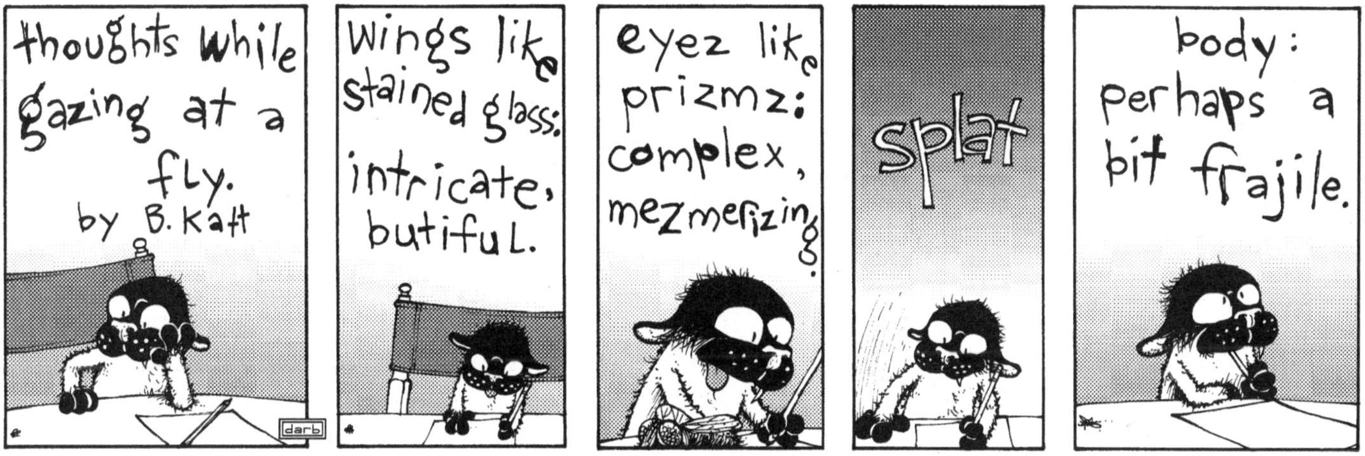
thoughts while gazing at a fly. by B. Katt
wings like stained glass: intricate, butiful.
eyez like prizmz: complex, mezmerizing.
splat
body: perhaps a bit frajile.

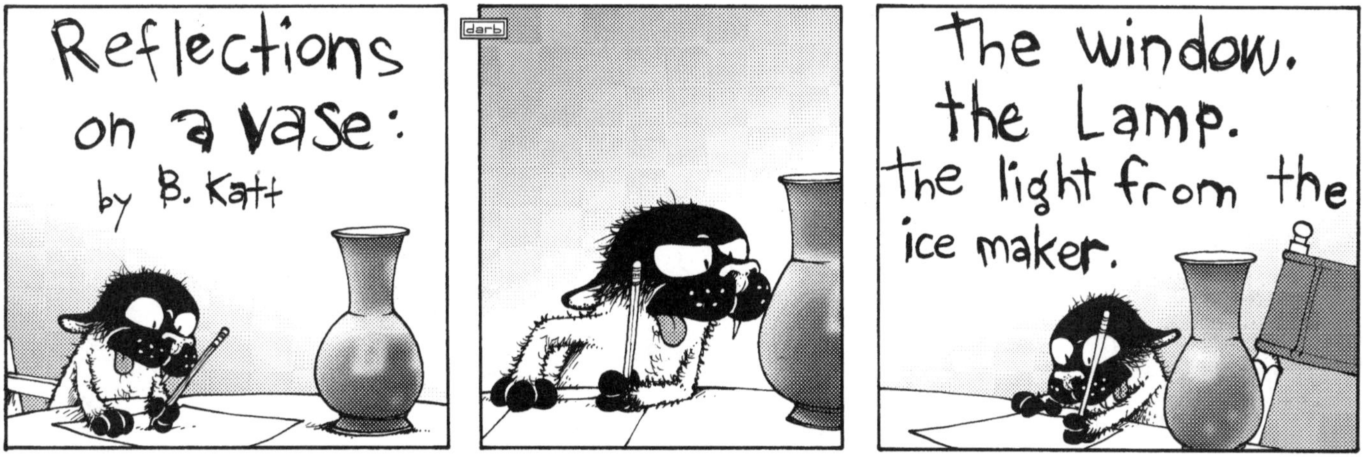
Reflections on a vase: by B. Katt
The window. the Lamp. The light from the ice maker.

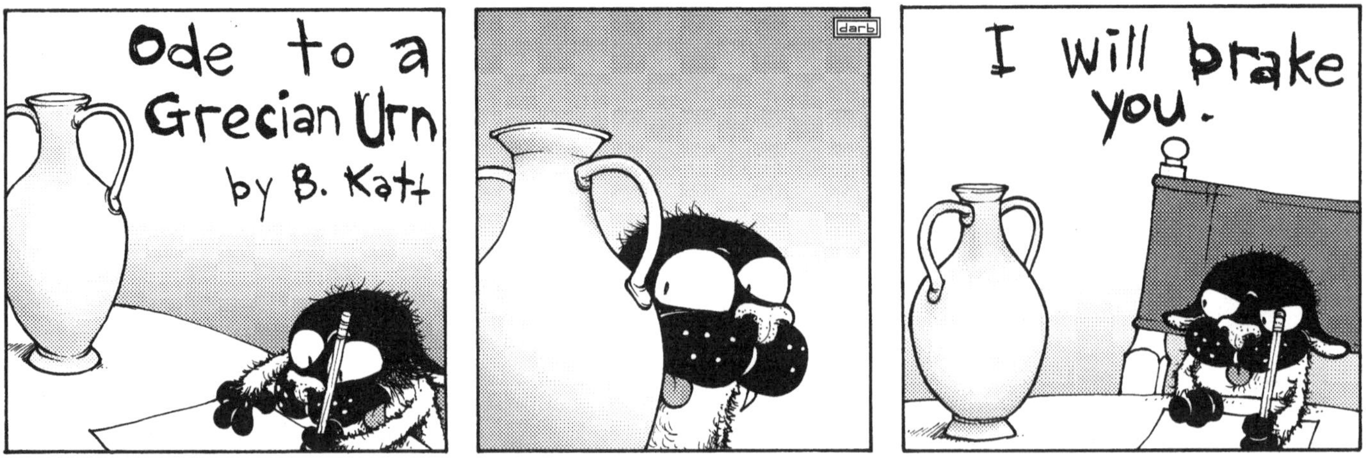
Ode to a Grecian Urn
by B. Katt
I will brake you.

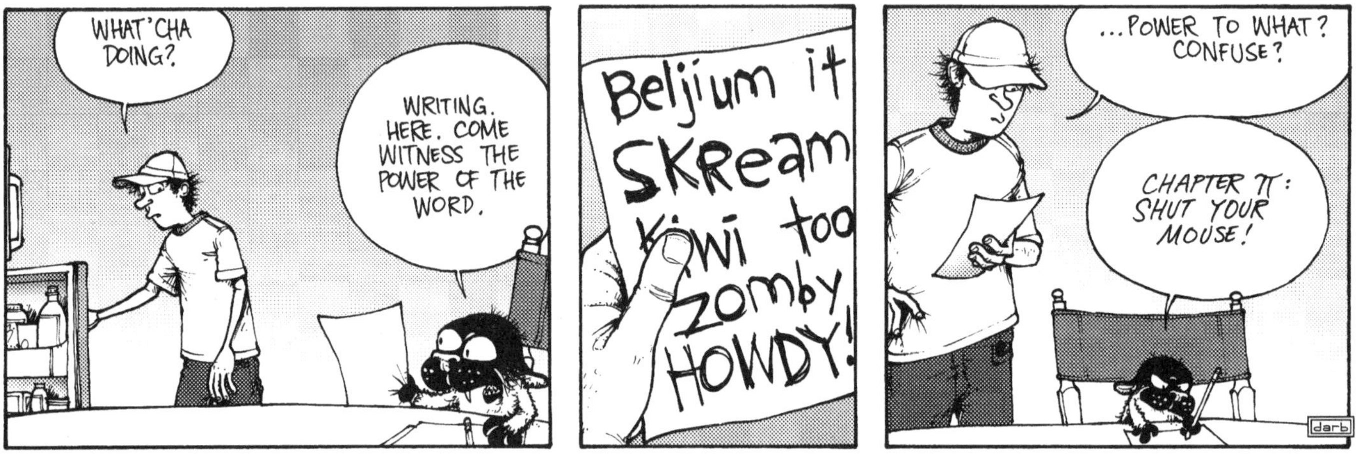
WHAT'CHA DOING?
WRITING. HERE. COME WITNESS THE POWER OF THE WORD.
Beljium it SKream Kiwi too zomby HOWDY!
...POWER TO WHAT? CONFUSE?
CHAPTER π: SHUT YOUR MOUSE!

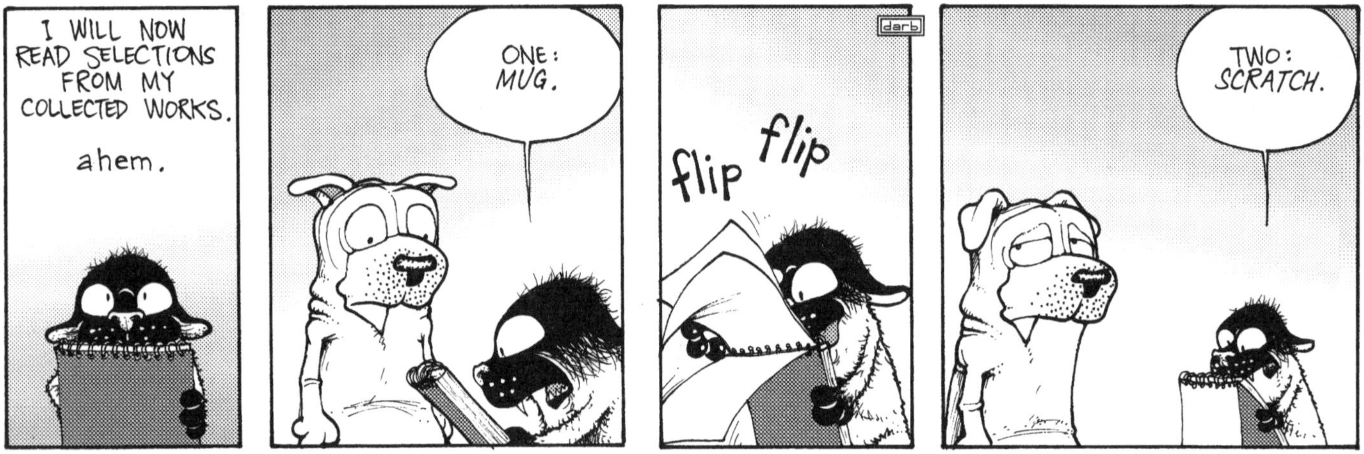
I WILL NOW READ SELECTIONS FROM MY COLLECTED WORKS.
ahem.
ONE: MUG.
flip flip
TWO: SCRATCH.

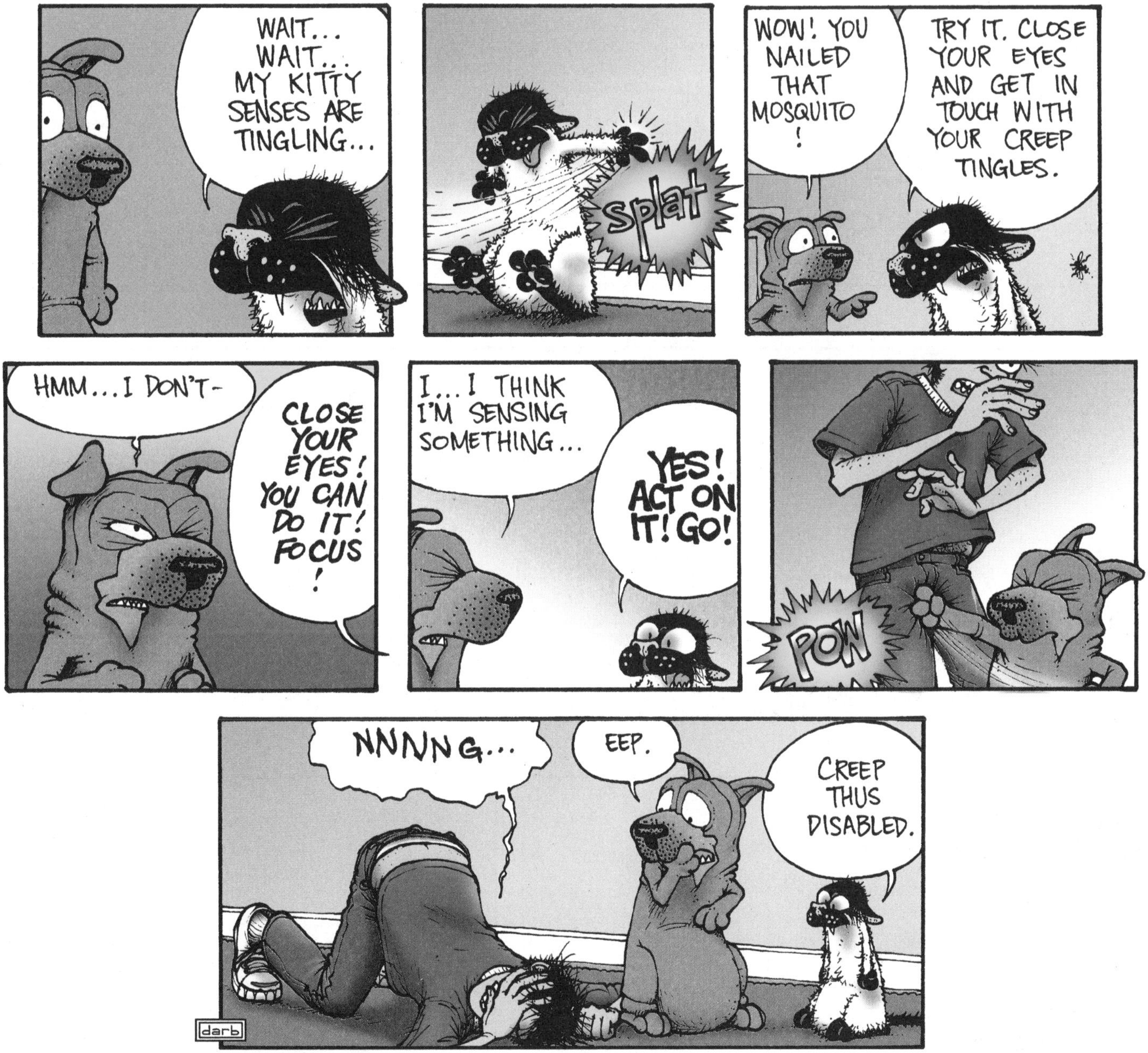
WAIT... WAIT... MY KITTY SENSES ARE TINGLING...
splat
WOW! YOU NAILED THAT MOSQUITO!
TRY IT. CLOSE YOUR EYES AND GET IN TOUCH WITH YOUR CREEP TINGLES.
HMM...I DON'T-
CLOSE YOUR EYES! YOU CAN DO IT! FOCUS!
I...I THINK I'M SENSING SOMETHING...
YES! ACT ON IT! GO!
POW
NNNNG...
EEP.
CREEP THUS DISABLED.
darb

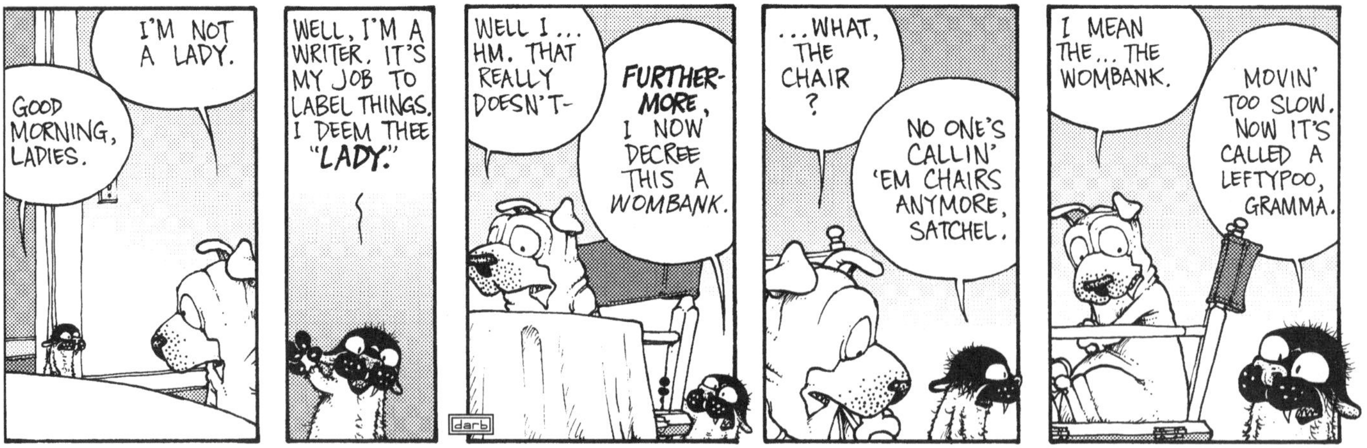
GOOD MORNING, LADIES.
I'M NOT A LADY.
WELL, I'M A WRITER. IT'S MY JOB TO LABEL THINGS. I DEEM THEE "LADY."
WELL I... HM. THAT REALLY DOESN'T-
FURTHERMORE, I NOW DECREE THIS A WOMBANK.
...WHAT, THE CHAIR?
NO ONE'S CALLIN' 'EM CHAIRS ANYMORE, SATCHEL.
I MEAN THE... THE WOMBANK.
MOVIN' TOO SLOW. NOW IT'S CALLED A LEFTYPOO, GRAMMA.
darb

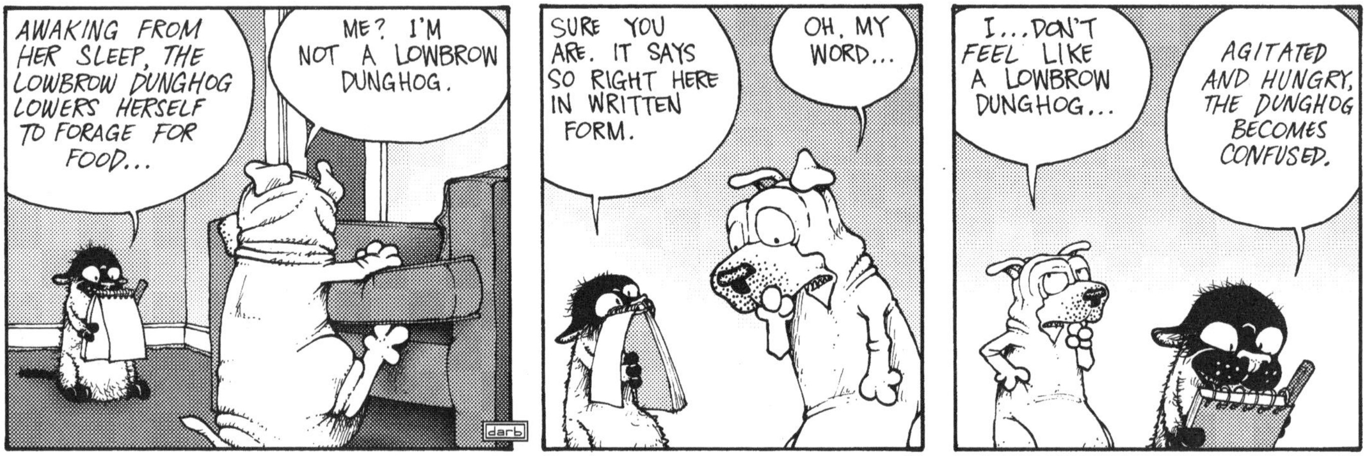
AWAKING FROM HER SLEEP, THE LOWBROW DUNGHOG LOWERS HERSELF TO FORAGE FOR FOOD...
ME? I'M NOT A LOWBROW DUNGHOG.
darb
SURE YOU ARE. IT SAYS SO RIGHT HERE IN WRITTEN FORM.
OH, MY WORD...
I...DON'T FEEL LIKE A LOWBROW DUNGHOG...
AGITATED AND HUNGRY, THE DUNGHOG BECOMES CONFUSED.

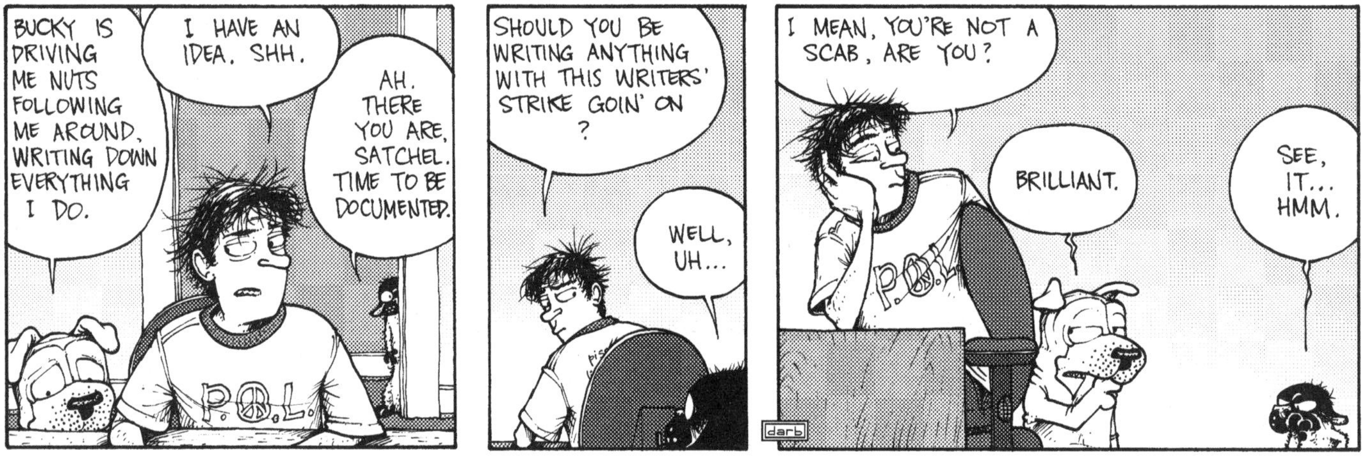
BUCKY IS DRIVING ME NUTS FOLLOWING ME AROUND, WRITING DOWN EVERYTHING I DO.
I HAVE AN IDEA. SHH.
AH. THERE YOU ARE, SATCHEL. TIME TO BE DOCUMENTED.
SHOULD YOU BE WRITING ANYTHING WITH THIS WRITERS' STRIKE GOIN' ON?
WELL, UH...
darb
I MEAN, YOU'RE NOT A SCAB, ARE YOU?
BRILLIANT.
SEE, IT... HMM.

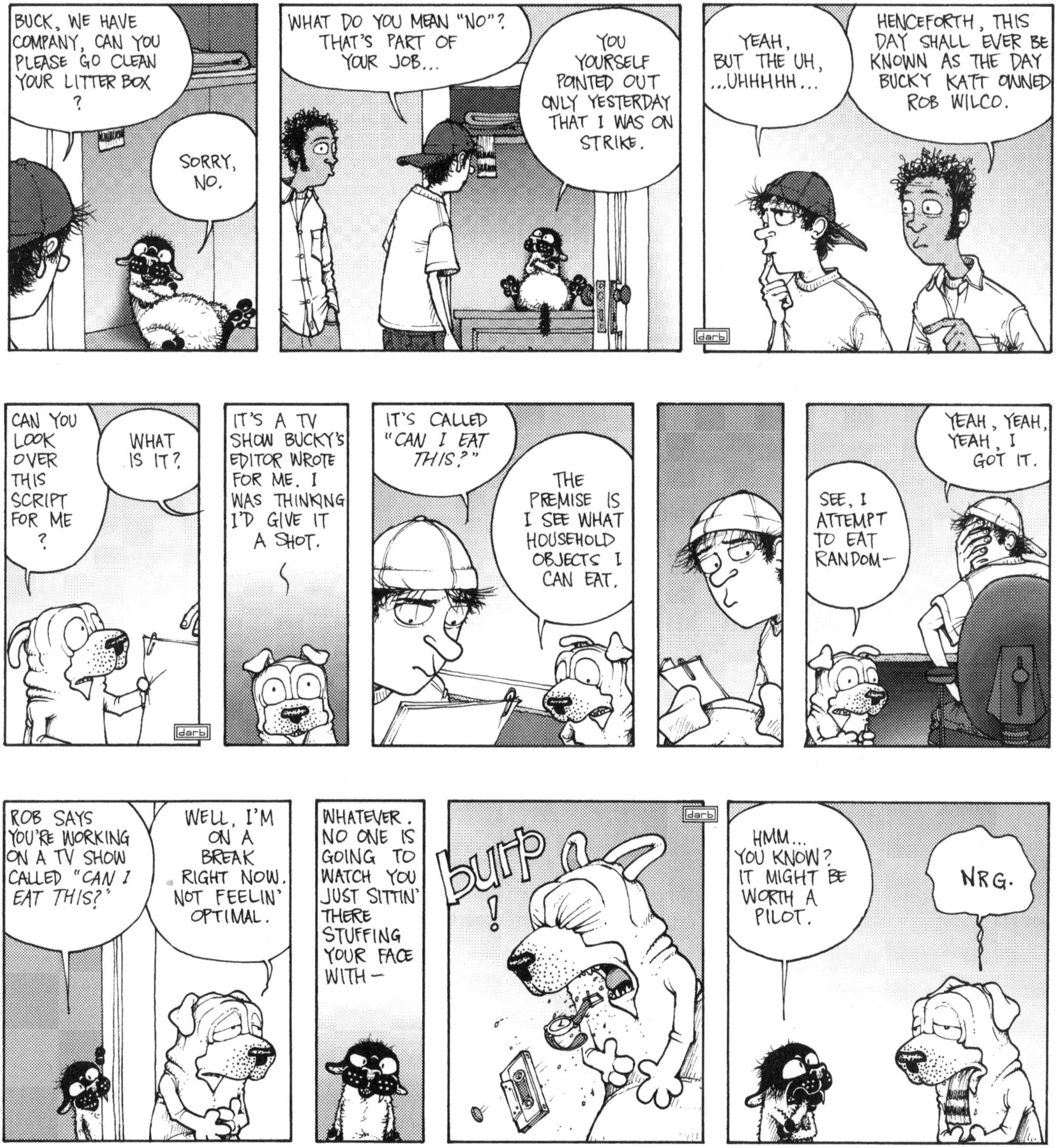
BUCK, WE HAVE COMPANY, CAN YOU PLEASE GO CLEAN YOUR LITTER BOX ?
SORRY, NO.
WHAT DO YOU MEAN "NO"? THAT'S PART OF YOUR JOB...
YOU YOURSELF POINTED OUT ONLY YESTERDAY THAT I WAS ON STRIKE.
YEAH, BUT THE UH, ...UHHHHH...
HENCEFORTH, THIS DAY SHALL EVER BE KNOWN AS THE DAY BUCKY KATT OWNED ROB WILCO.
CAN YOU LOOK OVER THIS SCRIPT FOR ME ?
WHAT IS IT?
IT'S A TV SHOW BUCKY'S EDITOR WROTE FOR ME. I WAS THINKING I'D GIVE IT A SHOT.
IT'S CALLED "CAN I EAT THIS?"
THE PREMISE IS I SEE WHAT HOUSEHOLD OBJECTS I CAN EAT.
SEE, I ATTEMPT TO EAT RANDOM–
YEAH, YEAH, YEAH, I GOT IT.
ROB SAYS YOU'RE WORKING ON A TV SHOW CALLED "CAN I EAT THIS?"
WELL, I'M ON A BREAK RIGHT NOW. NOT FEELIN' OPTIMAL.
WHATEVER. NO ONE IS GOING TO WATCH YOU JUST SITTIN' THERE STUFFING YOUR FACE WITH–
burp
!
HMM... YOU KNOW? IT MIGHT BE WORTH A PILOT.
NRG.

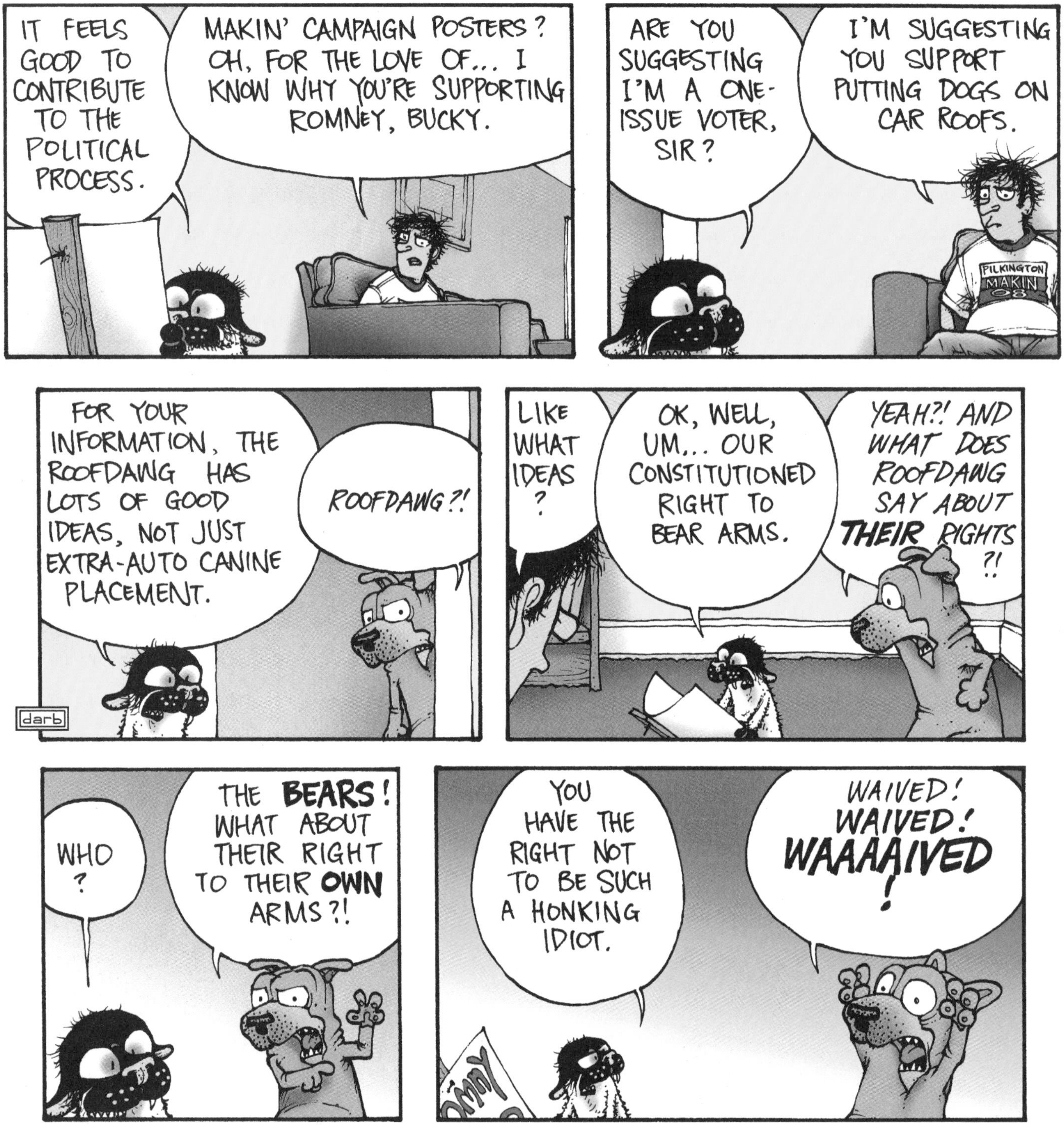
IT FEELS GOOD TO CONTRIBUTE TO THE POLITICAL PROCESS.
MAKIN' CAMPAIGN POSTERS? OH, FOR THE LOVE OF... I KNOW WHY YOU'RE SUPPORTING ROMNEY, BUCKY.
ARE YOU SUGGESTING I'M A ONE-ISSUE VOTER, SIR?
I'M SUGGESTING YOU SUPPORT PUTTING DOGS ON CAR ROOFS.
PILKINGTON MAKIN 08
FOR YOUR INFORMATION, THE ROOFDAWG HAS LOTS OF GOOD IDEAS, NOT JUST EXTRA-AUTO CANINE PLACEMENT.
ROOFDAWG?!
darb
LIKE WHAT IDEAS?
OK, WELL, UM... OUR CONSTITUTIONED RIGHT TO BEAR ARMS.
YEAH?! AND WHAT DOES ROOFDAWG SAY ABOUT THEIR RIGHTS?!
WHO?
THE BEARS! WHAT ABOUT THEIR RIGHT TO THEIR OWN ARMS?!
YOU HAVE THE RIGHT NOT TO BE SUCH A HONKING IDIOT.
WAIVED! WAIVED! WAAAAIVED!

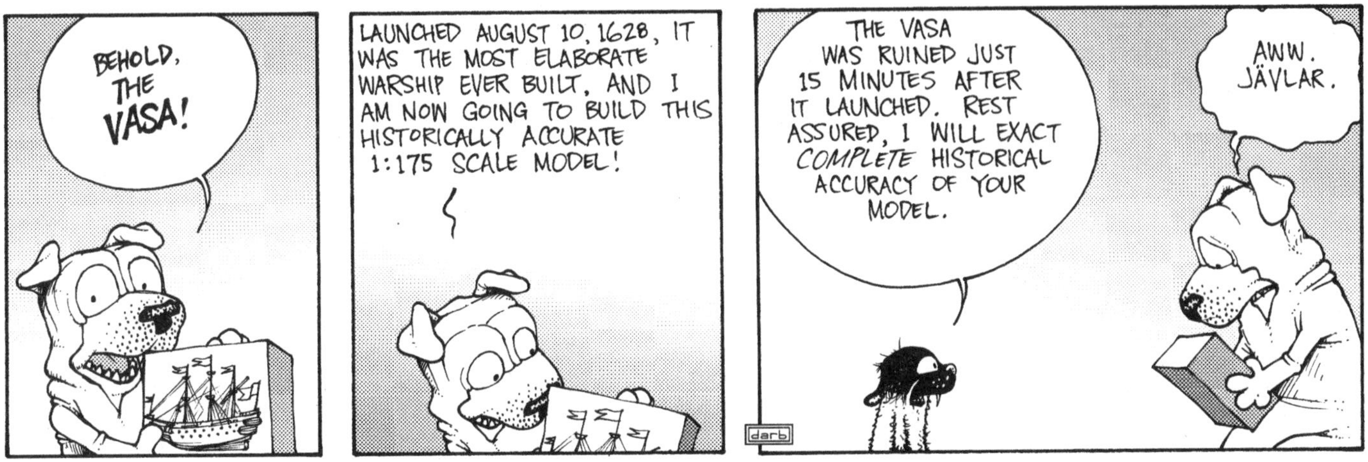
BEHOLD, THE VASA!
LAUNCHED AUGUST 10, 1628, IT WAS THE MOST ELABORATE WARSHIP EVER BUILT, AND I AM NOW GOING TO BUILD THIS HISTORICALLY ACCURATE 1:175 SCALE MODEL!
THE VASA WAS RUINED JUST 15 MINUTES AFTER IT LAUNCHED. REST ASSURED, I WILL EXACT *COMPLETE* HISTORICAL ACCURACY OF YOUR MODEL.
darb
AWW. JÄVLAR.

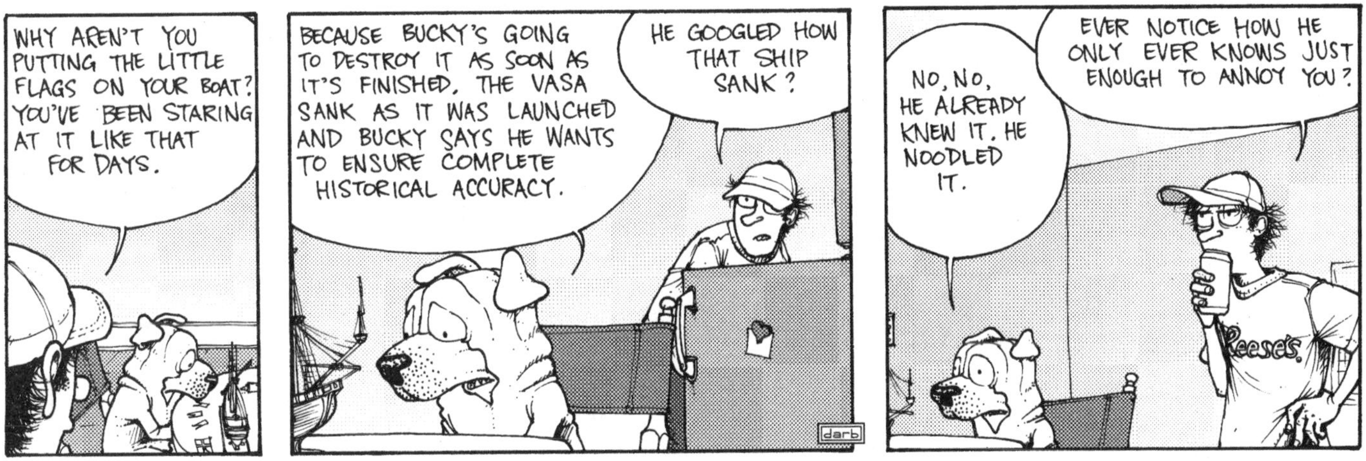
WHY AREN'T YOU PUTTING THE LITTLE FLAGS ON YOUR BOAT? YOU'VE BEEN STARING AT IT LIKE THAT FOR DAYS.
BECAUSE BUCKY'S GOING TO DESTROY IT AS SOON AS IT'S FINISHED. THE VASA SANK AS IT WAS LAUNCHED AND BUCKY SAYS HE WANTS TO ENSURE COMPLETE HISTORICAL ACCURACY.
HE GOOGLED HOW THAT SHIP SANK?
darb
NO, NO, HE ALREADY KNEW IT. HE NOODLED IT.
EVER NOTICE HOW HE ONLY EVER KNOWS JUST ENOUGH TO ANNOY YOU?
Reese's

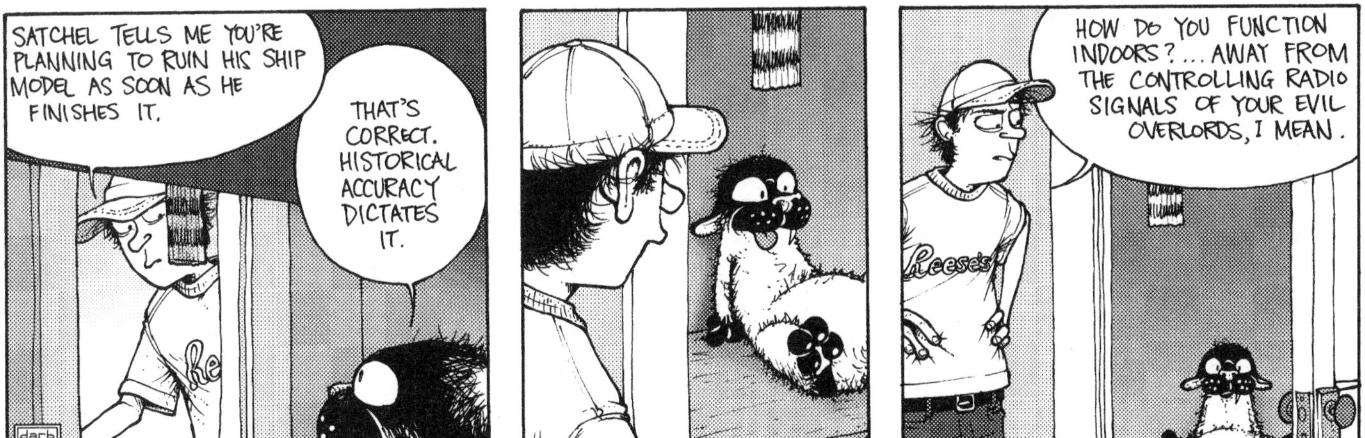
SATCHEL TELLS ME YOU'RE PLANNING TO RUIN HIS SHIP MODEL AS SOON AS HE FINISHES IT.
THAT'S CORRECT. HISTORICAL ACCURACY DICTATES IT.
darb
Reese's
HOW DO YOU FUNCTION INDOORS? ... AWAY FROM THE CONTROLLING RADIO SIGNALS OF YOUR EVIL OVERLORDS, I MEAN.

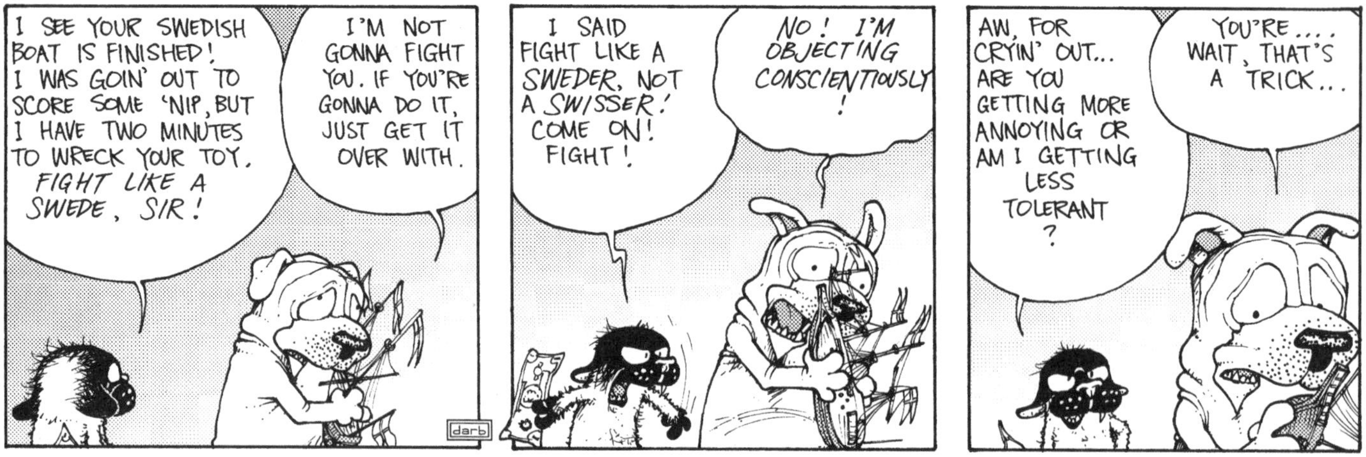
I SEE YOUR SWEDISH BOAT IS FINISHED! I WAS GOIN' OUT TO SCORE SOME 'NIP, BUT I HAVE TWO MINUTES TO WRECK YOUR TOY. FIGHT LIKE A SWEDE, SIR!
I'M NOT GONNA FIGHT YOU. IF YOU'RE GONNA DO IT, JUST GET IT OVER WITH.
I SAID FIGHT LIKE A SWEDER, NOT A SWISSER! COME ON! FIGHT!
NO! I'M OBJECTING CONSCIENTIOUSLY!
AW, FOR CRYIN' OUT... ARE YOU GETTING MORE ANNOYING OR AM I GETTING LESS TOLERANT?
YOU'RE.... WAIT, THAT'S A TRICK...
darb

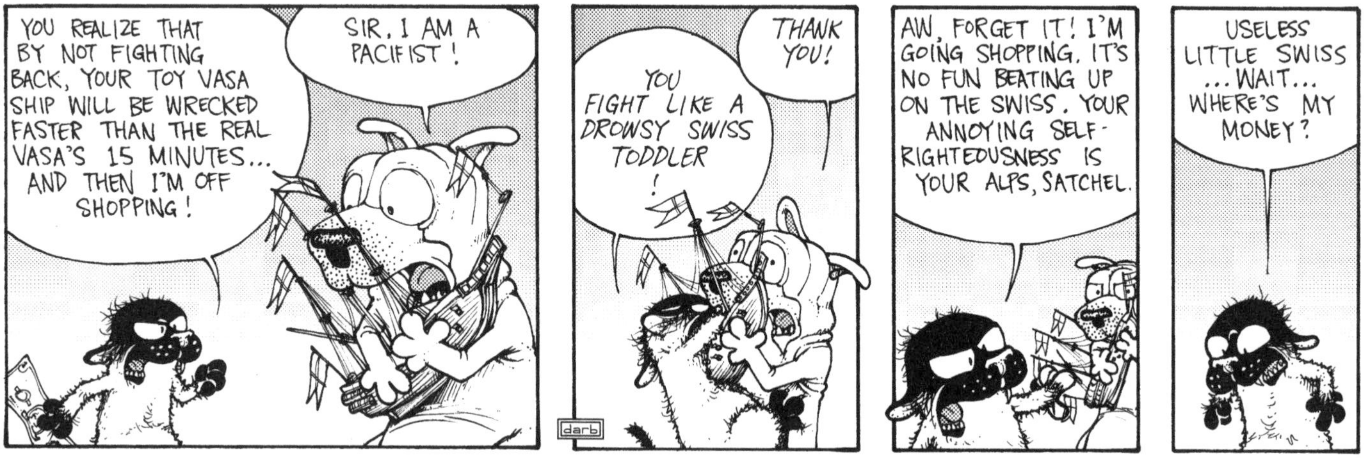
YOU REALIZE THAT BY NOT FIGHTING BACK, YOUR TOY VASA SHIP WILL BE WRECKED FASTER THAN THE REAL VASA'S 15 MINUTES... AND THEN I'M OFF SHOPPING!
SIR, I AM A PACIFIST!
YOU FIGHT LIKE A DROWSY SWISS TODDLER!
THANK YOU!
darb
AW, FORGET IT! I'M GOING SHOPPING. IT'S NO FUN BEATING UP ON THE SWISS. YOUR ANNOYING SELF-RIGHTEOUSNESS IS YOUR ALPS, SATCHEL.
USELESS LITTLE SWISS ...WAIT... WHERE'S MY MONEY?

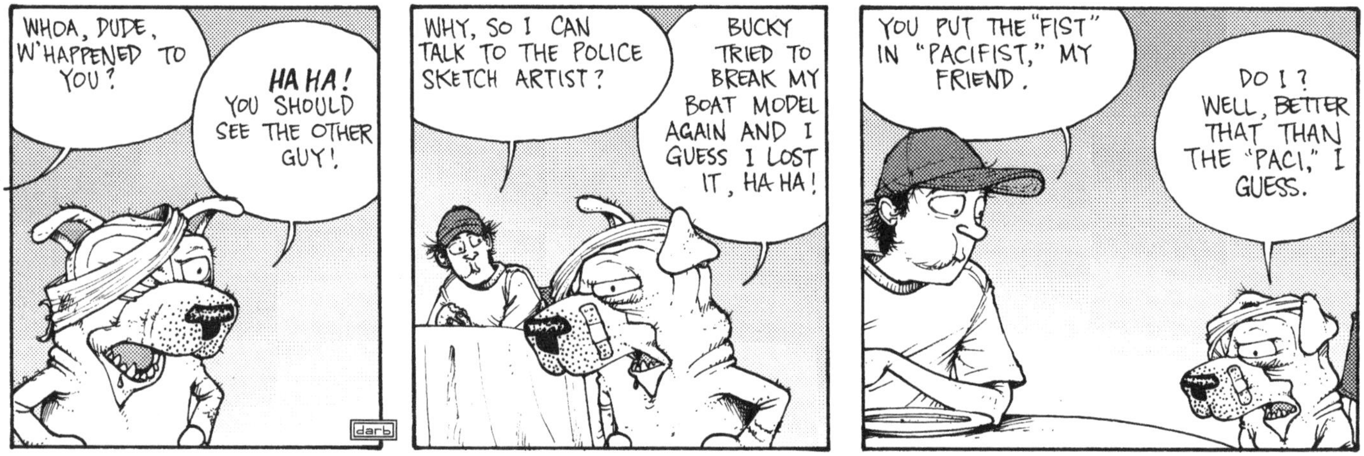
WHOA, DUDE, W'HAPPENED TO YOU?
HA HA! YOU SHOULD SEE THE OTHER GUY!
darb
WHY, SO I CAN TALK TO THE POLICE SKETCH ARTIST?
BUCKY TRIED TO BREAK MY BOAT MODEL AGAIN AND I GUESS I LOST IT, HA HA!
YOU PUT THE "FIST" IN "PACIFIST," MY FRIEND.
DO I? WELL, BETTER THAT THAN THE "PACI," I GUESS.

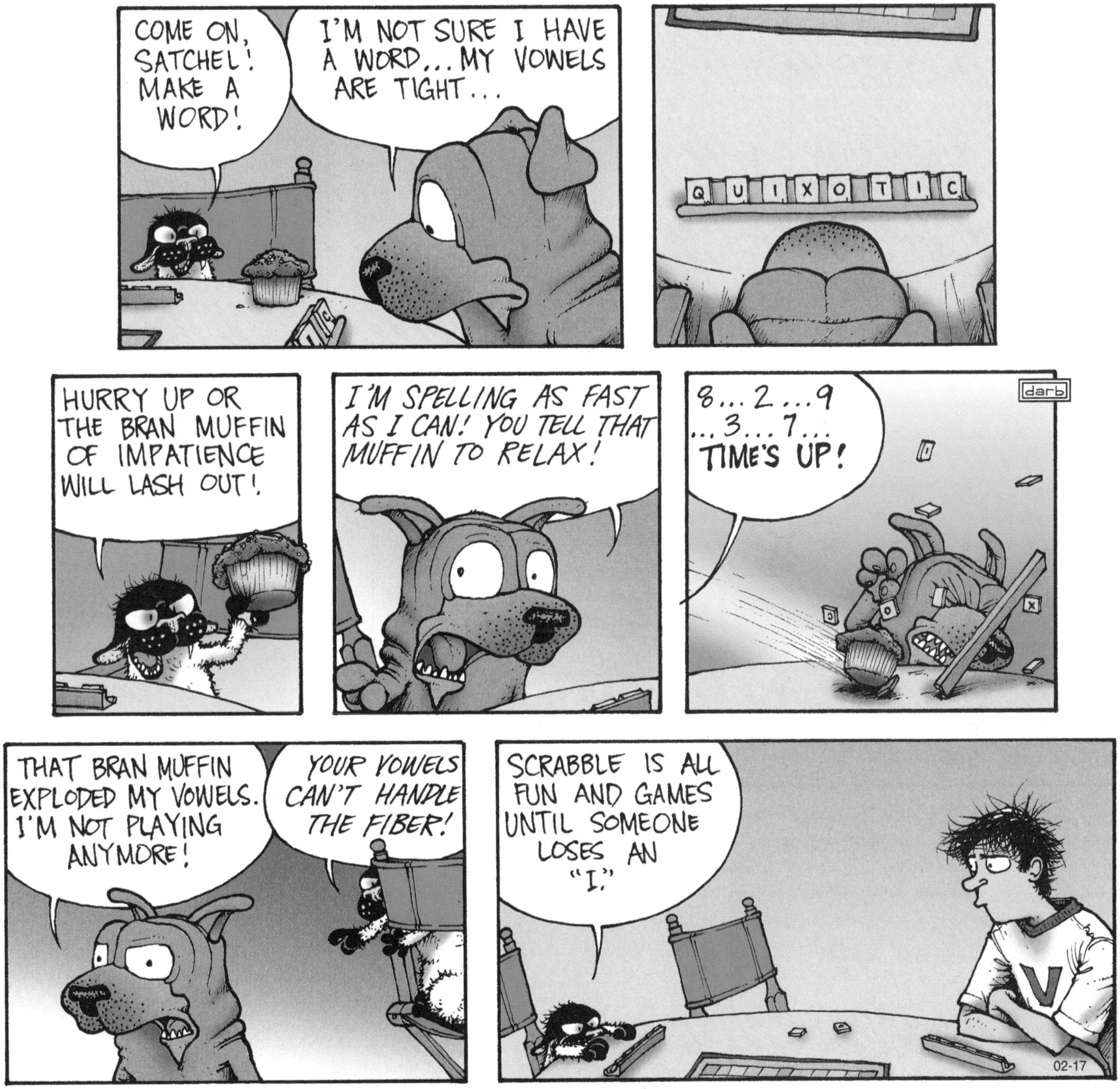
COME ON, SATCHEL! MAKE A WORD!
I'M NOT SURE I HAVE A WORD... MY VOWELS ARE TIGHT...
QUIXOTIC
HURRY UP OR THE BRAN MUFFIN OF IMPATIENCE WILL LASH OUT!
I'M SPELLING AS FAST AS I CAN! YOU TELL THAT MUFFIN TO RELAX!
8...2...9 ...3...7... TIME'S UP!
darb
THAT BRAN MUFFIN EXPLODED MY VOWELS. I'M NOT PLAYING ANYMORE!
YOUR VOWELS CAN'T HANDLE THE FIBER!
SCRABBLE IS ALL FUN AND GAMES UNTIL SOMEONE LOSES AN "I."
V
02-17

WELL, I'M OFF TO LAY THE WRECKAGE OF THE VASA TO REST.

"LAY IT TO REST"? THAT'S A *TOY*, SATCHEL!

YOU SHOW THE VASA SOME RESPECT! YOU'RE THE ONE WHO *BROKE HER!*

"HER"?

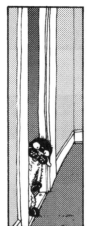

OK, SO IS HE GETTING STUPIDER, OR AM I GETTING INTELLIGENTER?

KEEP GOING...

ROB SAYS YOU OWE ME A NEW SHIP MODEL.

SATCHEL, THAT MODEL OF THE VASA WAS DESTINED TO FAIL, AS WAS ITS UNSEAWORTHY NAMESAKE.

IT JOINS THE LIST OF HISTORY'S FAILURES: THE FRENCH RESISTANCE AT AGINCOURT... THE FRENCH 40-HOUR WORK WEEK... THE INTRODUCTION OF DEODORANT INTO FRANCE... YOUR VASA MODEL...

YOU REALIZE I'M PART FRENCH.

ABSOLUTELY.

RETURN TO YOUR WATERY DEPTHS, NOBLE VASA, WHENCE YOU WERE EXHUMED, LO THESE MANY YEARS PAST.

FLUSH

WUH-OH.

60

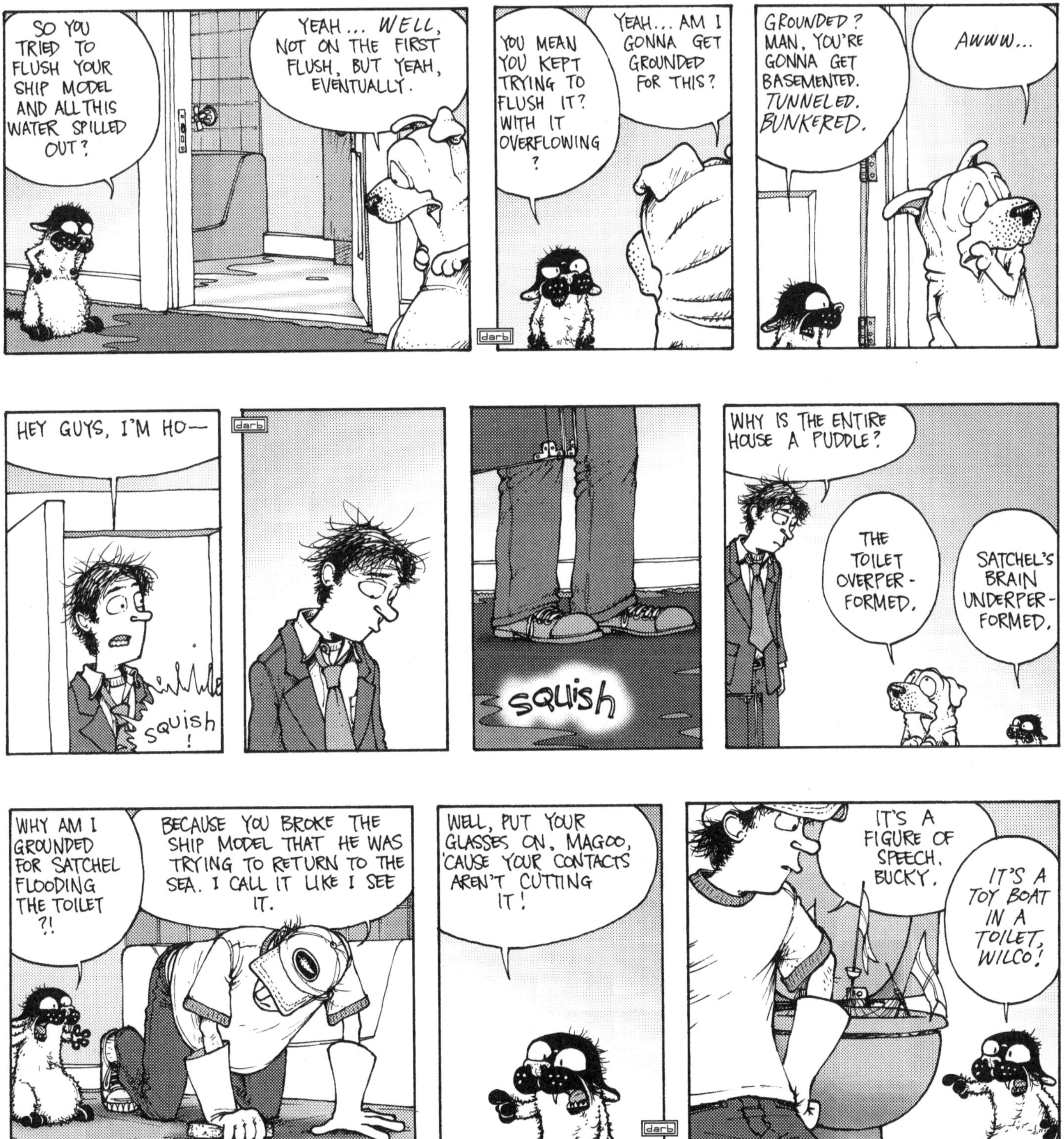
SO YOU TRIED TO FLUSH YOUR SHIP MODEL AND ALL THIS WATER SPILLED OUT?
YEAH... WELL, NOT ON THE FIRST FLUSH, BUT YEAH, EVENTUALLY.
darb
YOU MEAN YOU KEPT TRYING TO FLUSH IT? WITH IT OVERFLOWING?
YEAH... AM I GONNA GET GROUNDED FOR THIS?
GROUNDED? MAN, YOU'RE GONNA GET BASEMENTED. TUNNELED. BUNKERED.
AWWW...
HEY GUYS, I'M HO—
SQUISH!
darb
SQUISH
WHY IS THE ENTIRE HOUSE A PUDDLE?
THE TOILET OVERPERFORMED.
SATCHEL'S BRAIN UNDERPERFORMED.
WHY AM I GROUNDED FOR SATCHEL FLOODING THE TOILET?!
BECAUSE YOU BROKE THE SHIP MODEL THAT HE WAS TRYING TO RETURN TO THE SEA. I CALL IT LIKE I SEE IT.
WELL, PUT YOUR GLASSES ON, MAGOO, 'CAUSE YOUR CONTACTS AREN'T CUTTING IT!
darb
IT'S A FIGURE OF SPEECH, BUCKY.
IT'S A TOY BOAT IN A TOILET, WILCO!

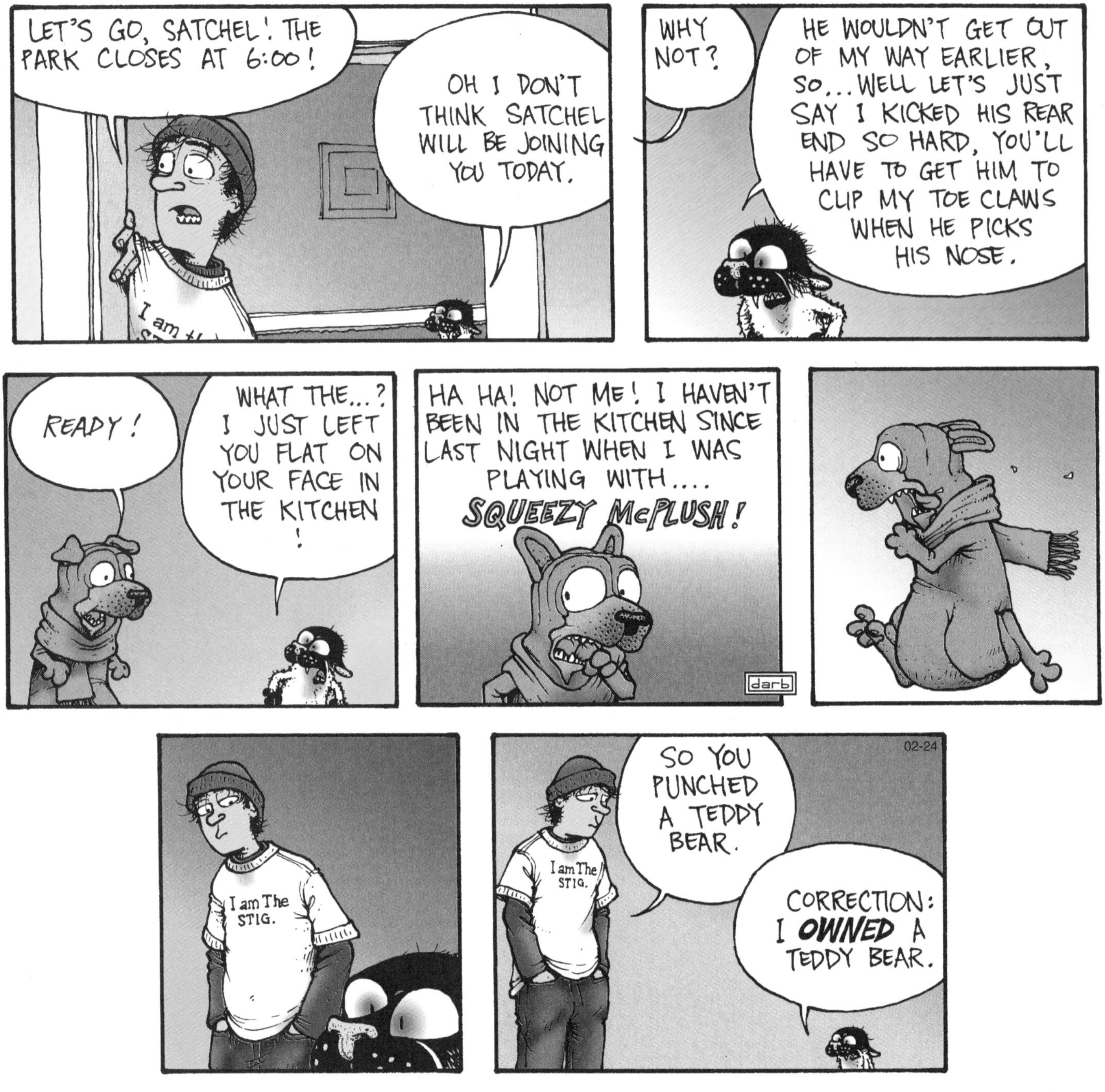
LET'S GO, SATCHEL! THE PARK CLOSES AT 6:00!
OH I DON'T THINK SATCHEL WILL BE JOINING YOU TODAY.
I am th
WHY NOT?
HE WOULDN'T GET OUT OF MY WAY EARLIER, SO... WELL LET'S JUST SAY I KICKED HIS REAR END SO HARD, YOU'LL HAVE TO GET HIM TO CLIP MY TOE CLAWS WHEN HE PICKS HIS NOSE.
READY!
WHAT THE...? I JUST LEFT YOU FLAT ON YOUR FACE IN THE KITCHEN!
HA HA! NOT ME! I HAVEN'T BEEN IN THE KITCHEN SINCE LAST NIGHT WHEN I WAS PLAYING WITH.... SQUEEZY McPLUSH!
darb
I am The STIG.
02-24
I am The STIG.
SO YOU PUNCHED A TEDDY BEAR.
CORRECTION: I **OWNED** A TEDDY BEAR.

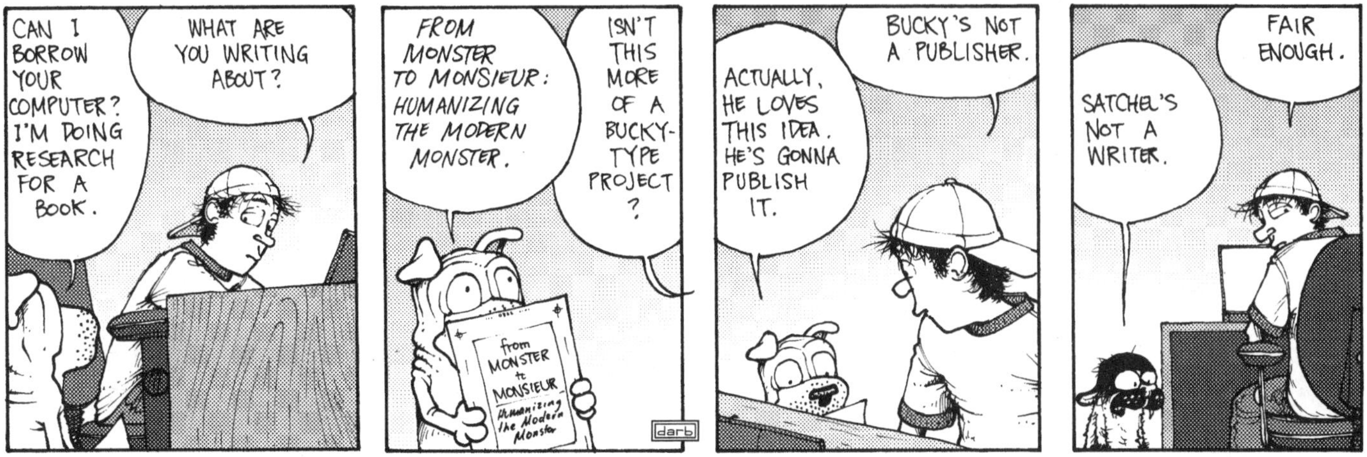
CAN I BORROW YOUR COMPUTER? I'M DOING RESEARCH FOR A BOOK.
WHAT ARE YOU WRITING ABOUT?
FROM MONSTER TO MONSIEUR: HUMANIZING THE MODERN MONSTER.
from MONSTER to MONSIEUR Humanizing the Modern Monster
ISN'T THIS MORE OF A BUCKY-TYPE PROJECT?
ACTUALLY, HE LOVES THIS IDEA. HE'S GONNA PUBLISH IT.
BUCKY'S NOT A PUBLISHER.
SATCHEL'S NOT A WRITER.
FAIR ENOUGH.

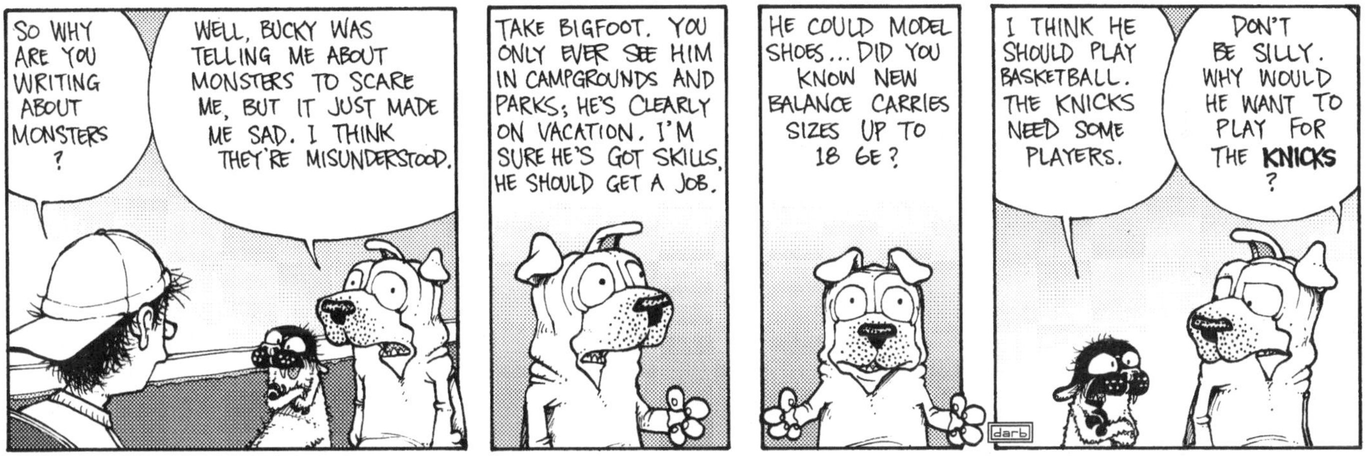
SO WHY ARE YOU WRITING ABOUT MONSTERS?
WELL, BUCKY WAS TELLING ME ABOUT MONSTERS TO SCARE ME, BUT IT JUST MADE ME SAD. I THINK THEY'RE MISUNDERSTOOD.
TAKE BIGFOOT. YOU ONLY EVER SEE HIM IN CAMPGROUNDS AND PARKS; HE'S CLEARLY ON VACATION. I'M SURE HE'S GOT SKILLS. HE SHOULD GET A JOB.
HE COULD MODEL SHOES... DID YOU KNOW NEW BALANCE CARRIES SIZES UP TO 18 6E?
I THINK HE SHOULD PLAY BASKETBALL. THE KNICKS NEED SOME PLAYERS.
DON'T BE SILLY. WHY WOULD HE WANT TO PLAY FOR THE KNICKS?

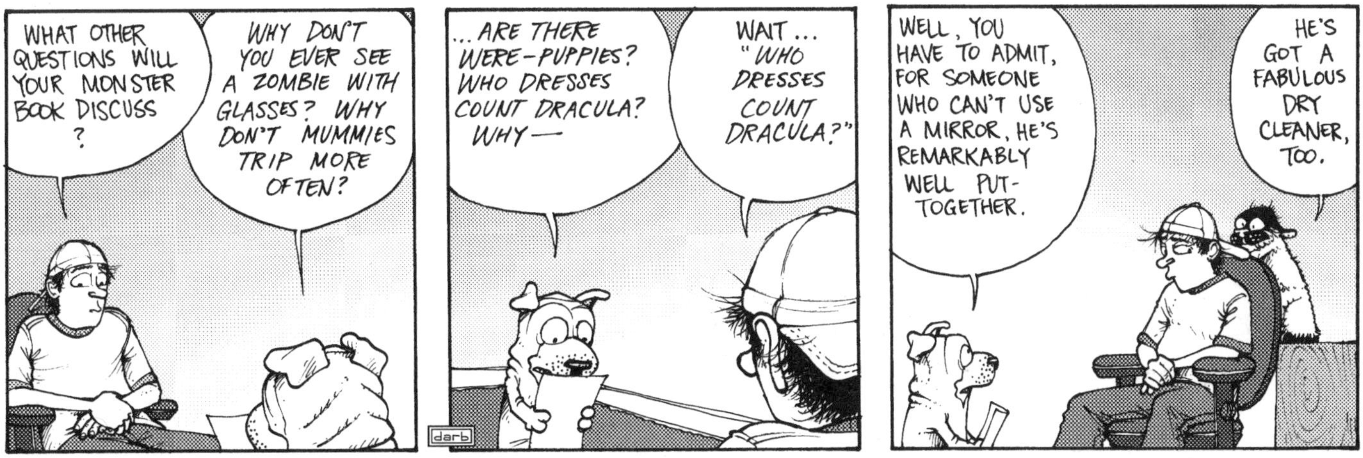
WHAT OTHER QUESTIONS WILL YOUR MONSTER BOOK DISCUSS?
WHY DON'T YOU EVER SEE A ZOMBIE WITH GLASSES? WHY DON'T MUMMIES TRIP MORE OFTEN?
...ARE THERE WERE-PUPPIES? WHO DRESSES COUNT DRACULA? WHY—
WAIT... "WHO DRESSES COUNT DRACULA?"
WELL, YOU HAVE TO ADMIT, FOR SOMEONE WHO CAN'T USE A MIRROR, HE'S REMARKABLY WELL PUT-TOGETHER.
HE'S GOT A FABULOUS DRY CLEANER, TOO.

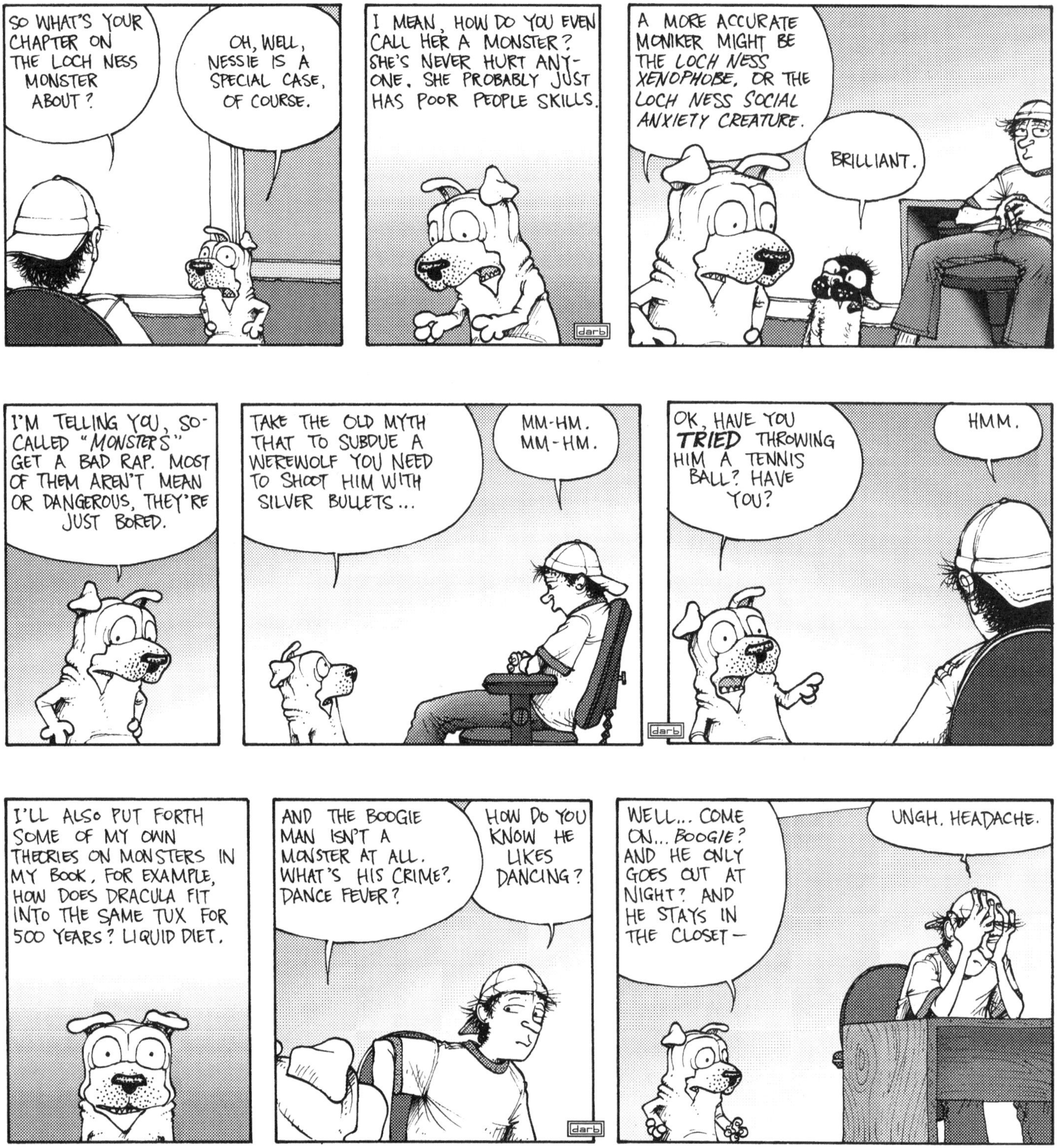
SO WHAT'S YOUR CHAPTER ON THE LOCH NESS MONSTER ABOUT?
OH, WELL, NESSIE IS A SPECIAL CASE, OF COURSE.
I MEAN, HOW DO YOU EVEN CALL HER A MONSTER? SHE'S NEVER HURT ANY-ONE. SHE PROBABLY JUST HAS POOR PEOPLE SKILLS.
A MORE ACCURATE MONIKER MIGHT BE THE *LOCH NESS XENOPHOBE*, OR THE *LOCH NESS SOCIAL ANXIETY CREATURE*.
BRILLIANT.
I'M TELLING YOU, SO-CALLED "*MONSTERS*" GET A BAD RAP. MOST OF THEM AREN'T MEAN OR DANGEROUS, THEY'RE JUST BORED.
TAKE THE OLD MYTH THAT TO SUBDUE A WEREWOLF YOU NEED TO SHOOT HIM WITH SILVER BULLETS...
MM-HM. MM-HM.
OK, HAVE YOU ***TRIED*** THROWING HIM A TENNIS BALL? HAVE YOU?
HMM.
I'LL ALSO PUT FORTH SOME OF MY OWN THEORIES ON MONSTERS IN MY BOOK. FOR EXAMPLE, HOW DOES DRACULA FIT INTO THE SAME TUX FOR 500 YEARS? LIQUID DIET.
AND THE BOOGIE MAN ISN'T A MONSTER AT ALL. WHAT'S HIS CRIME? DANCE FEVER?
HOW DO YOU KNOW HE LIKES DANCING?
WELL... COME ON... *BOOGIE*? AND HE ONLY GOES OUT AT NIGHT? AND HE STAYS IN THE CLOSET—
UNGH. HEADACHE.
darb

I THOUGHT YOU WERE GOING TO WORK ON YOUR MONSTER BOOK TODAY.

TURNS OUT BUCKY IS FINISHING IT.

WHY ARE YOU LETTING HIM DO THAT? IT'S YOUR BOOK...

HE SAYS HE KNOWS MORE ABOUT MONSTERS THAN ME.

YEAH, BUT YOU WERE WRITING A BOOK **ABOUT** MONSTERS, NOT HOW TO **BE** A MONSTER.

DON'T LET HIM HEAR YOU SAY THAT, YOU'RE ALREADY CITED IN THE CHAPTER ON GHOULS.

WHAT ARE YOU DOING?

I'M FINISHING THE CHAPTER ON BIGFOOT IN YOUR MONSTER BOOK.

REALLY? YOU KNOW THAT MUCH ABOUT BIGFOOT?

I ATTACHED AN ACTUAL, IF GRAINY, PHOTO OF THE BEAST AS WELL.

OOO! LEMME SEE!

TO THE UNTRAINED EYE, BIGFOOT LOOKS A LOT LIKE ROB IN HIS CLEVELAND BROWNS ROBE.

EERIE.

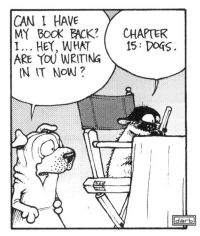

CAN I HAVE MY BOOK BACK? I... HEY, WHAT ARE YOU WRITING IN IT NOW?

CHAPTER 15: DOGS.

WHAT? IN A MONSTER GUIDEBOOK? DOGS AREN'T MONSTERS...

OOOO, CONTROVERSIAL VIEW, THERE. LET'S KEEP THIS BOOK GROUNDED IN ACCEPTED SCIENCE.

BUCKY... I THINK YOU MAY BE OUT OF TOUCH WITH THE MODERN CONCEPT OF "MONSTER."

YOU'RE ABOUT TO SEE HOW OUT OF TOUCH MY PAW IS WITH THE CONCEPT OF YOUR NOSE.

OK, YOU KNOW WHAT? CHAPTER 16: ABOMINABLE **BUCKY**.

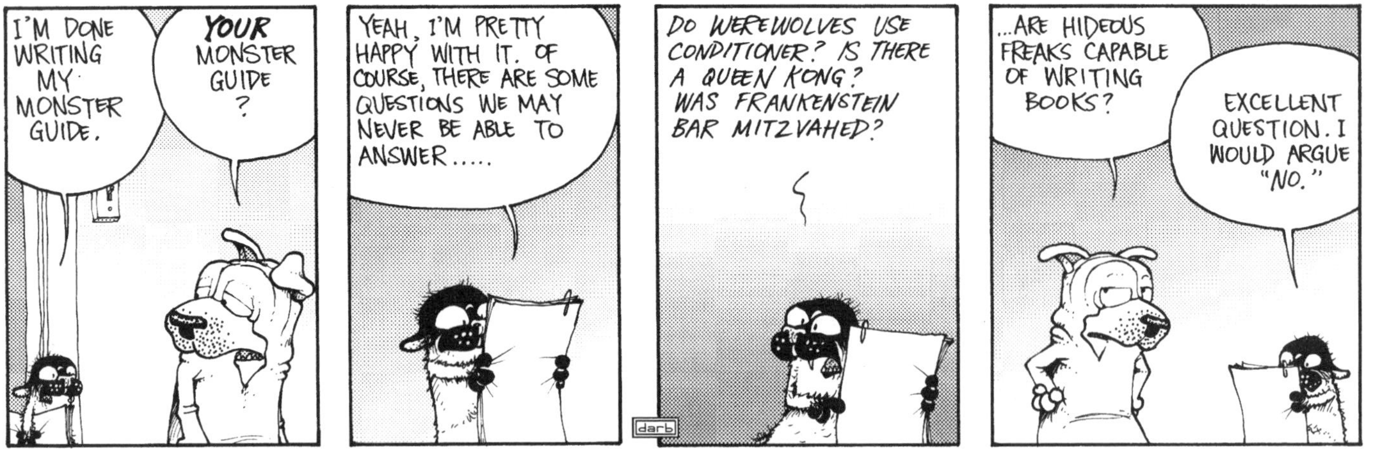
I'M DONE WRITING MY MONSTER GUIDE.
YOUR MONSTER GUIDE?
YEAH, I'M PRETTY HAPPY WITH IT. OF COURSE, THERE ARE SOME QUESTIONS WE MAY NEVER BE ABLE TO ANSWER.....
DO WEREWOLVES USE CONDITIONER? IS THERE A QUEEN KONG? WAS FRANKENSTEIN BAR MITZVAHED?
darb
...ARE HIDEOUS FREAKS CAPABLE OF WRITING BOOKS?
EXCELLENT QUESTION. I WOULD ARGUE "NO."

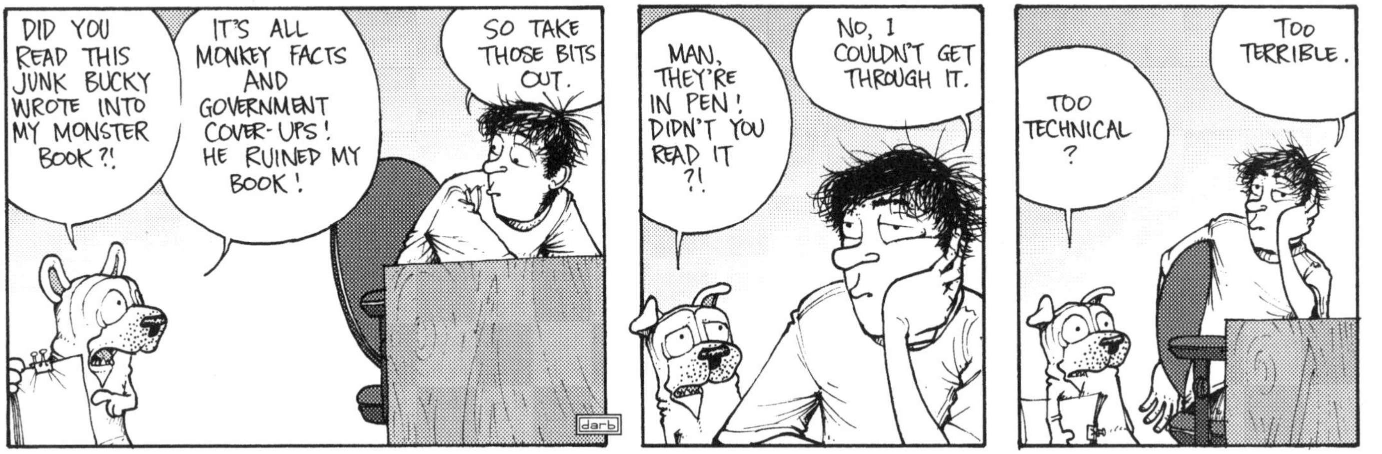
DID YOU READ THIS JUNK BUCKY WROTE INTO MY MONSTER BOOK?!
IT'S ALL MONKEY FACTS AND GOVERNMENT COVER-UPS! HE RUINED MY BOOK!
SO TAKE THOSE BITS OUT.
darb
MAN, THEY'RE IN PEN! DIDN'T YOU READ IT?!
NO, I COULDN'T GET THROUGH IT.
TOO TECHNICAL?
TOO TERRIBLE.

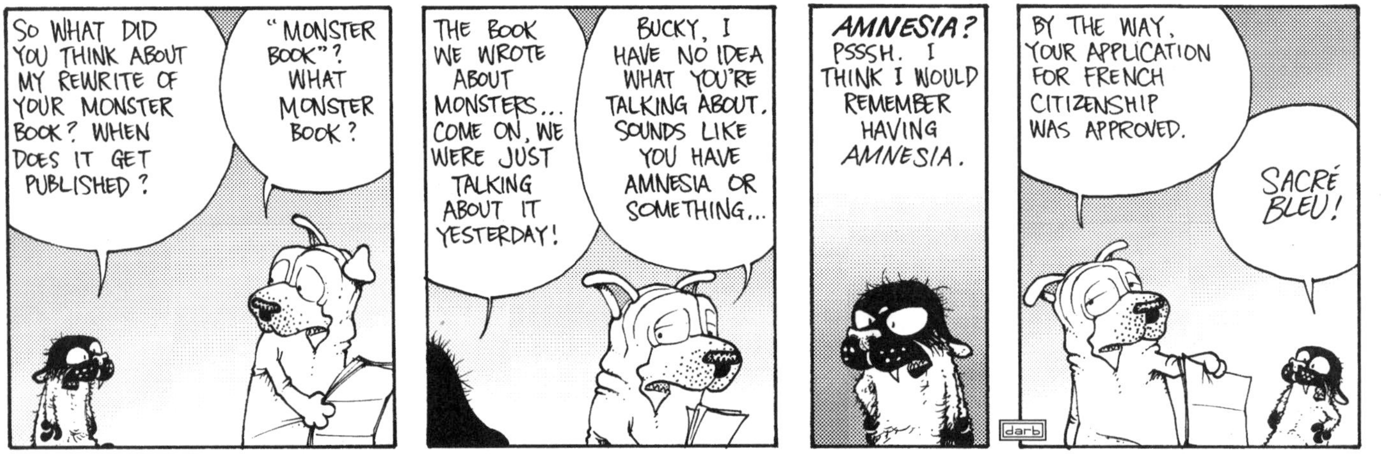
SO WHAT DID YOU THINK ABOUT MY REWRITE OF YOUR MONSTER BOOK? WHEN DOES IT GET PUBLISHED?
"MONSTER BOOK"? WHAT MONSTER BOOK?
THE BOOK WE WROTE ABOUT MONSTERS... COME ON, WE WERE JUST TALKING ABOUT IT YESTERDAY!
BUCKY, I HAVE NO IDEA WHAT YOU'RE TALKING ABOUT. SOUNDS LIKE YOU HAVE AMNESIA OR SOMETHING...
AMNESIA? PSSSH. I THINK I WOULD REMEMBER HAVING AMNESIA.
darb
BY THE WAY, YOUR APPLICATION FOR FRENCH CITIZENSHIP WAS APPROVED.
SACRÉ BLEU!

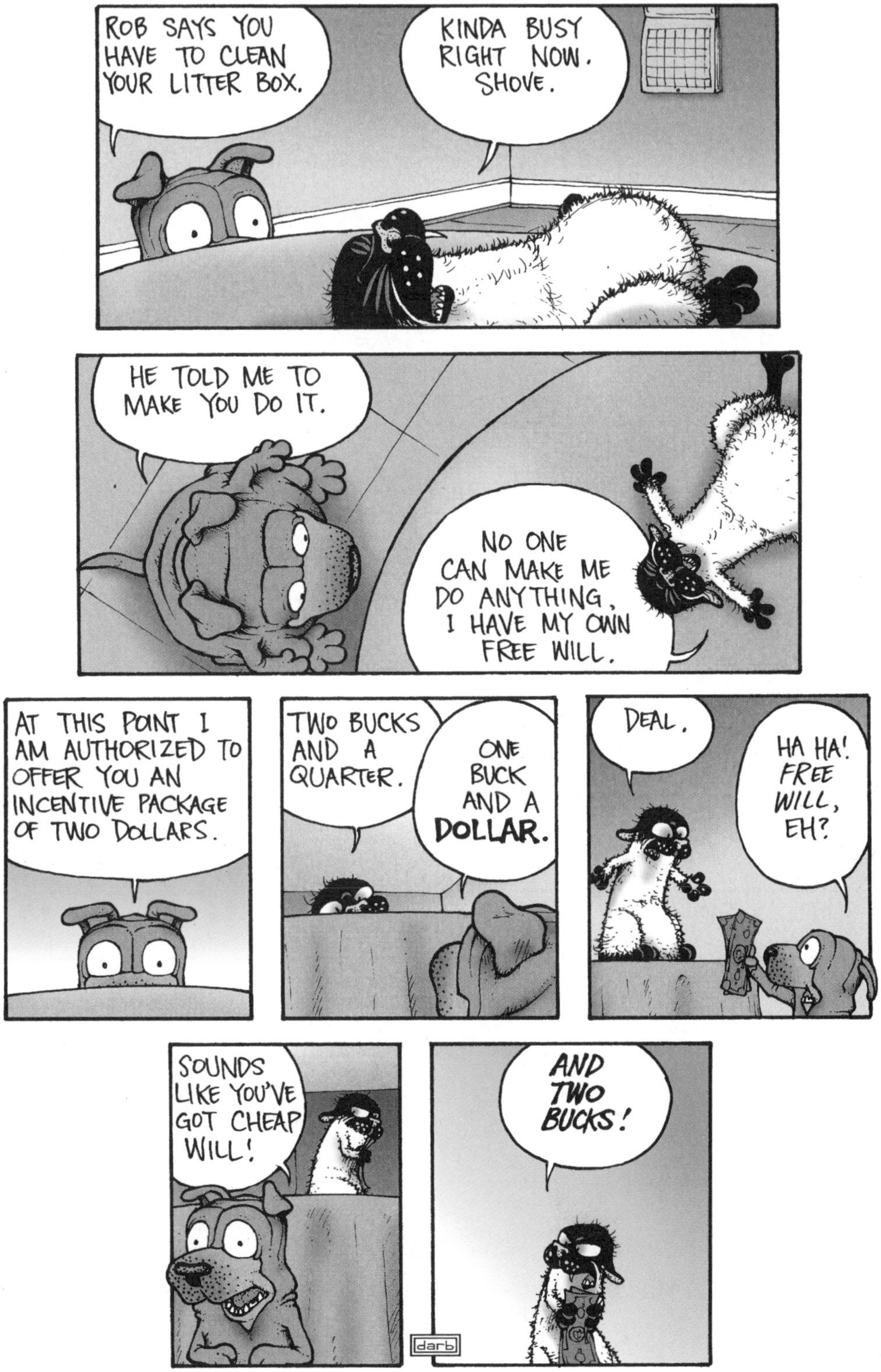
ROB SAYS YOU HAVE TO CLEAN YOUR LITTER BOX.
KINDA BUSY RIGHT NOW. SHOVE.
HE TOLD ME TO MAKE YOU DO IT.
NO ONE CAN MAKE ME DO ANYTHING. I HAVE MY OWN FREE WILL.
AT THIS POINT I AM AUTHORIZED TO OFFER YOU AN INCENTIVE PACKAGE OF TWO DOLLARS.
TWO BUCKS AND A QUARTER.
ONE BUCK AND A **DOLLAR.**
DEAL.
HA HA! *FREE WILL*, EH?
SOUNDS LIKE YOU'VE GOT CHEAP WILL!
AND TWO BUCKS!
darb

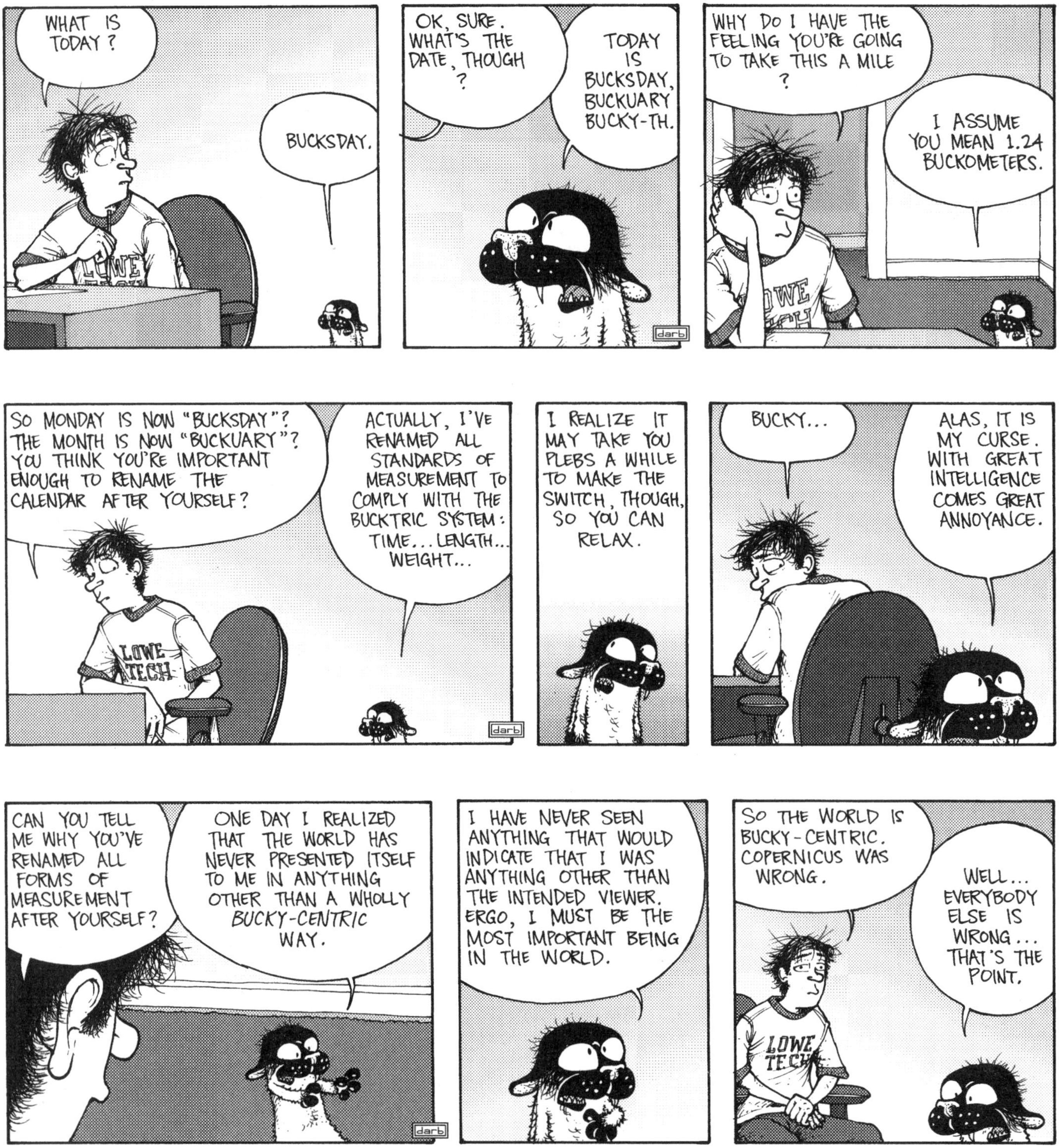
WHAT IS TODAY?
BUCKSDAY.
OK, SURE. WHAT'S THE DATE, THOUGH?
TODAY IS BUCKSDAY, BUCKUARY BUCKY-TH.
darb
WHY DO I HAVE THE FEELING YOU'RE GOING TO TAKE THIS A MILE?
I ASSUME YOU MEAN 1.24 BUCKOMETERS.
SO MONDAY IS NOW "BUCKSDAY"? THE MONTH IS NOW "BUCKUARY"? YOU THINK YOU'RE IMPORTANT ENOUGH TO RENAME THE CALENDAR AFTER YOURSELF?
ACTUALLY, I'VE RENAMED ALL STANDARDS OF MEASUREMENT TO COMPLY WITH THE BUCKTRIC SYSTEM: TIME... LENGTH... WEIGHT...
LOWE TECH
darb
I REALIZE IT MAY TAKE YOU PLEBS A WHILE TO MAKE THE SWITCH, THOUGH, SO YOU CAN RELAX.
BUCKY...
ALAS, IT IS MY CURSE. WITH GREAT INTELLIGENCE COMES GREAT ANNOYANCE.
CAN YOU TELL ME WHY YOU'VE RENAMED ALL FORMS OF MEASUREMENT AFTER YOURSELF?
ONE DAY I REALIZED THAT THE WORLD HAS NEVER PRESENTED ITSELF TO ME IN ANYTHING OTHER THAN A WHOLLY *BUCKY-CENTRIC* WAY.
darb
I HAVE NEVER SEEN ANYTHING THAT WOULD INDICATE THAT I WAS ANYTHING OTHER THAN THE INTENDED VIEWER. ERGO, I MUST BE THE MOST IMPORTANT BEING IN THE WORLD.
SO THE WORLD IS BUCKY-CENTRIC. COPERNICUS WAS WRONG.
WELL... EVERYBODY ELSE IS WRONG... THAT'S THE POINT.
LOWE TECH

Panel 1: SO EVERYTHING IS MEASURED IN UNITS OF BUCKYS NOW? TIME... LENGTH... VOLUME...

THAT'S CORRECT.

Panel 2: OK, WELL, IT'S NOON NOW, WHAT TIME IS THAT IN BUCKY-CENTRIC? 12 O'BUCKY?

Panel 3: TECHNICALLY, RIGHT NOW WE ARE EXPERIENCING "HIGH BUCKY."

OK, YEAH, I'LL GIVE YOU THAT ONE.

Panel 4: HOW DO YOU MEASURE WEIGHT IN BUCKTRIC?

WELL, MOST THINGS ARE SMALLER THAN ME, SO I'VE CHOSEN MY FOOT AS THE STANDARDIZED UNIT OF MEASUREMENT. FOR EXAMPLE, YOUR PENCIL PROBABLY WEIGHS ABOUT .2 BUCKFEET.

Panel 5: COULDN'T YOU JUST USE "BUCKY POUNDS"?

NO, SEE, A POUND IS THE WIDTH OF MY PAW AS I POUND SOMETHING.

Panel 6: SO BUCKPOUNDS IS LENGTH AND BUCKFEET IS WEIGHT?

SEE? YOU ALREADY GET IT.

Panel 7: WAIT, LENGTH IS MEASURED IN BUCKPOUNDS? YOU SAID IT WAS BUCKO-METERS EARLIER.

Panel 8: CORRECT. THERE ARE TEN BUCK-POUNDS IN A DECIBUCKY AND TEN DECIBUCKYS IN ONE BUCKOMETER.

Panel 9: BUT YOU TOLD ME THAT LIQUIDS ARE MEASURED IN DECIBUCKYS...

CORRECT. AND SOUND VOLUME, TOO.

Panel 10: WHATEVER. I WOULDN'T TOUCH YOUR SILLY SYSTEM WITH A BUCKOMETER POLE.

WELL, YOU APPARENTLY KNOW THE SYSTEM ALREADY, SO IT'S WORKING.

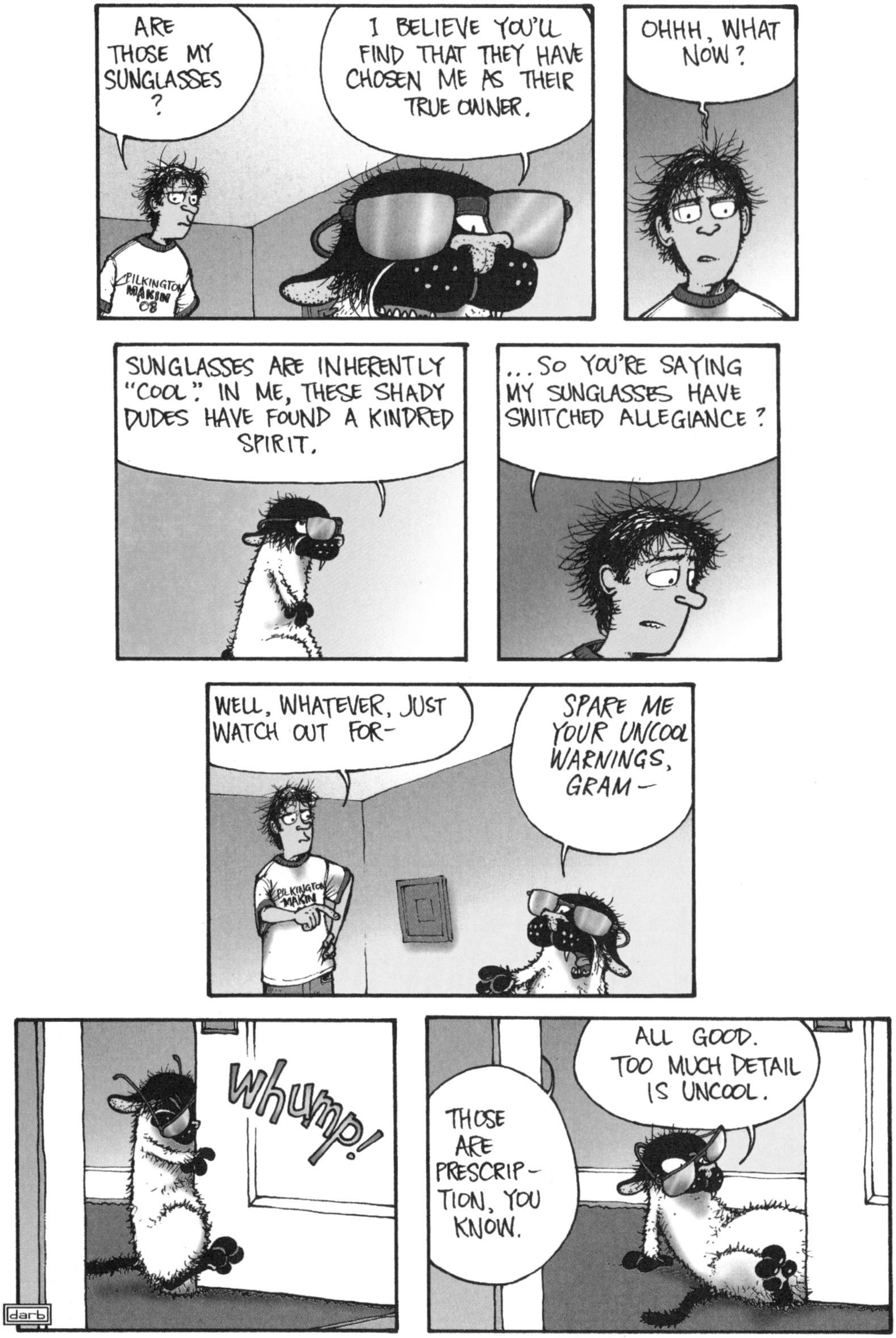
ARE THOSE MY SUNGLASSES ?
I BELIEVE YOU'LL FIND THAT THEY HAVE CHOSEN ME AS THEIR TRUE OWNER.
PILKINGTON MAKIN 08
OHHH, WHAT NOW ?
SUNGLASSES ARE INHERENTLY "COOL." IN ME, THESE SHADY DUDES HAVE FOUND A KINDRED SPIRIT.
...SO YOU'RE SAYING MY SUNGLASSES HAVE SWITCHED ALLEGIANCE ?
WELL, WHATEVER, JUST WATCH OUT FOR-
SPARE ME YOUR UNCOOL WARNINGS, GRAM-
PILKINGTON MAKIN
whump!
THOSE ARE PRESCRIP-TION, YOU KNOW.
ALL GOOD. TOO MUCH DETAIL IS UNCOOL.
darb

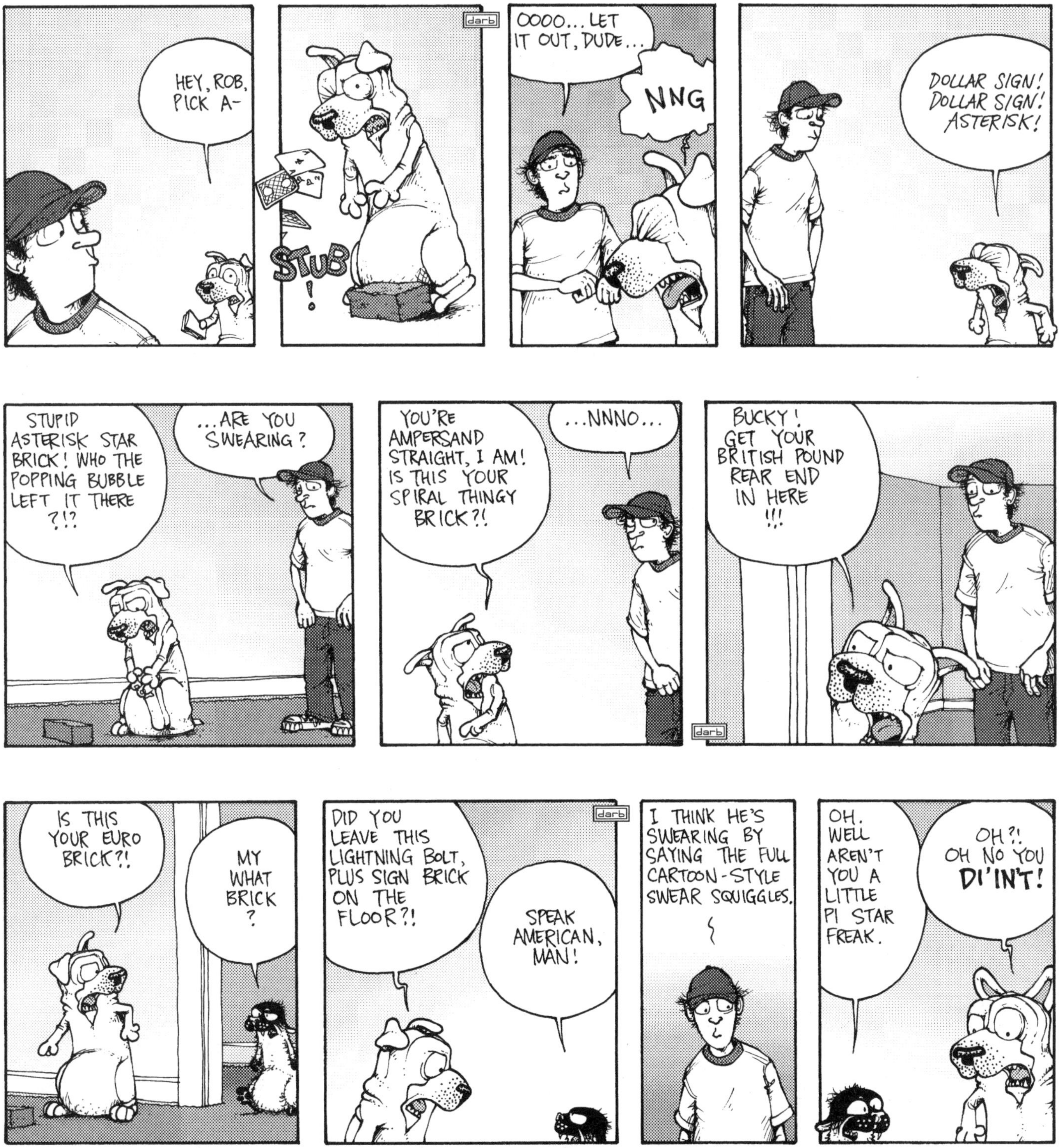
HEY, ROB, PICK A-
darb
STUB !
OOOO... LET IT OUT, DUDE...
NNG
DOLLAR SIGN! DOLLAR SIGN! ASTERISK!
STUPID ASTERISK STAR BRICK! WHO THE POPPING BUBBLE LEFT IT THERE ?!?
...ARE YOU SWEARING?
YOU'RE AMPERSAND STRAIGHT, I AM! IS THIS YOUR SPIRAL THINGY BRICK?!
...NNNO...
BUCKY! GET YOUR BRITISH POUND REAR END IN HERE !!!
darb
IS THIS YOUR EURO BRICK?!
MY WHAT BRICK ?
DID YOU LEAVE THIS LIGHTNING BOLT, PLUS SIGN BRICK ON THE FLOOR?!
darb
SPEAK AMERICAN, MAN!
I THINK HE'S SWEARING BY SAYING THE FULL CARTOON-STYLE SWEAR SQUIGGLES.
OH. WELL AREN'T YOU A LITTLE PI STAR FREAK.
OH?! OH NO YOU DI'INT!

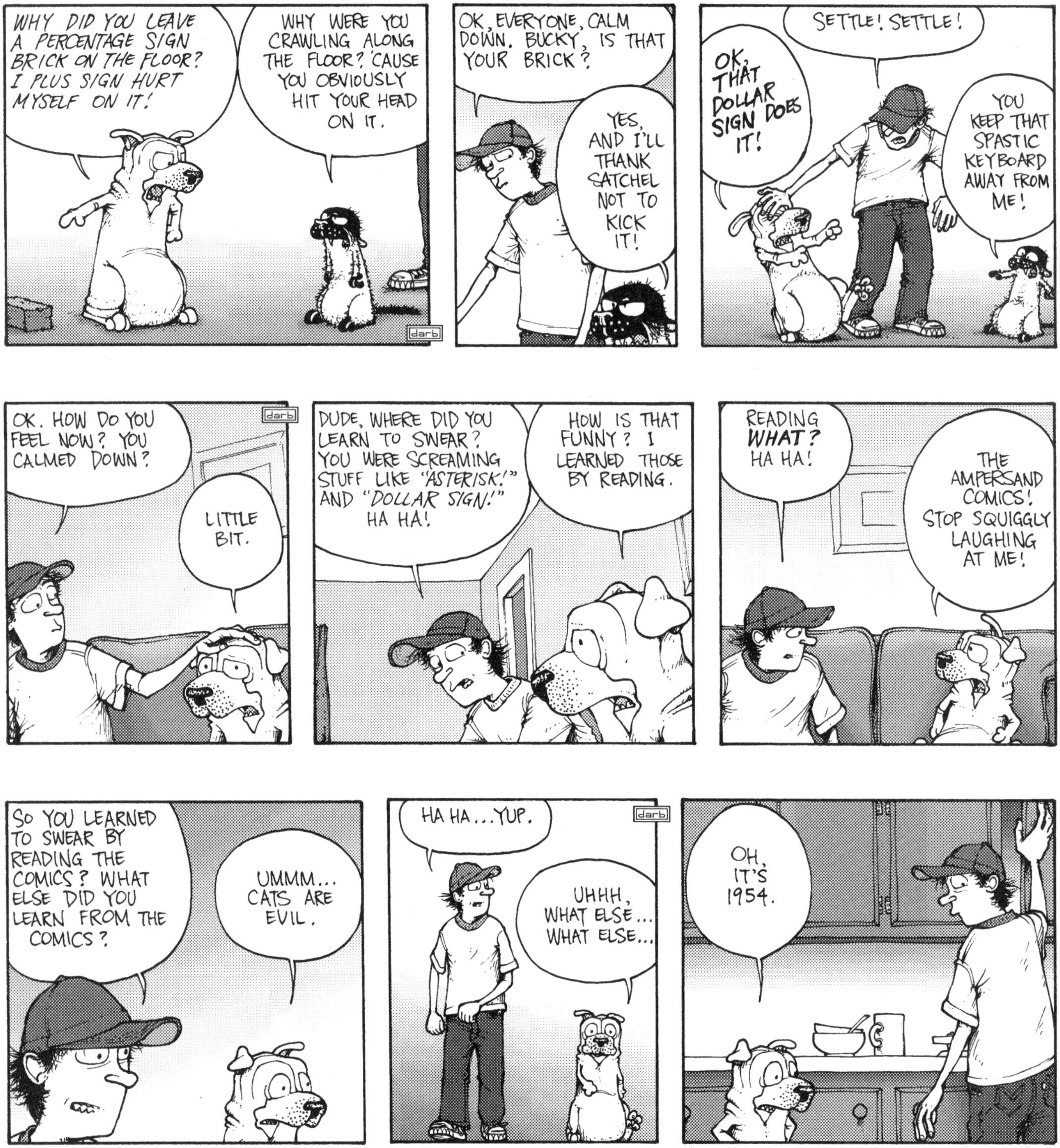

WHY DID YOU LEAVE A PERCENTAGE SIGN BRICK ON THE FLOOR? I PLUS SIGN HURT MYSELF ON IT!
WHY WERE YOU CRAWLING ALONG THE FLOOR? 'CAUSE YOU OBVIOUSLY HIT YOUR HEAD ON IT.
darb
OK, EVERYONE, CALM DOWN. BUCKY, IS THAT YOUR BRICK?
YES, AND I'LL THANK SATCHEL NOT TO KICK IT!
SETTLE! SETTLE!
OK, THAT DOLLAR SIGN DOES IT!
YOU KEEP THAT SPASTIC KEYBOARD AWAY FROM ME!
darb
OK. HOW DO YOU FEEL NOW? YOU CALMED DOWN?
LITTLE BIT.
DUDE, WHERE DID YOU LEARN TO SWEAR? YOU WERE SCREAMING STUFF LIKE "ASTERISK!" AND "DOLLAR SIGN!" HA HA!
HOW IS THAT FUNNY? I LEARNED THOSE BY READING.
READING WHAT? HA HA!
THE AMPERSAND COMICS! STOP SQUIGGLY LAUGHING AT ME!
SO YOU LEARNED TO SWEAR BY READING THE COMICS? WHAT ELSE DID YOU LEARN FROM THE COMICS?
UMMM... CATS ARE EVIL.
darb
HA HA... YUP.
UHHH, WHAT ELSE... WHAT ELSE...
OH, IT'S 1954.

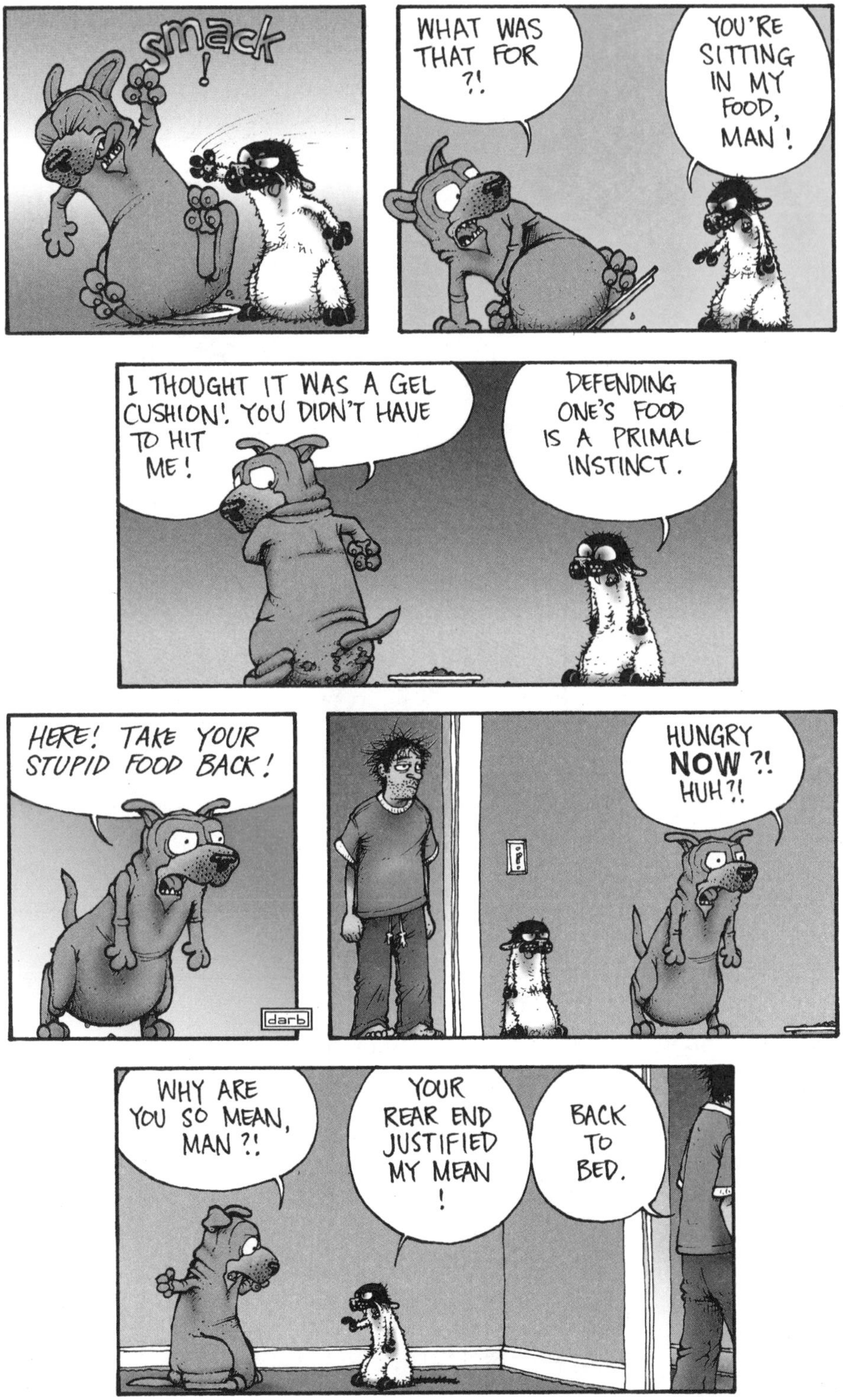
smack !
WHAT WAS THAT FOR ?!
YOU'RE SITTING IN MY FOOD, MAN !
I THOUGHT IT WAS A GEL CUSHION! YOU DIDN'T HAVE TO HIT ME !
DEFENDING ONE'S FOOD IS A PRIMAL INSTINCT.
HERE! TAKE YOUR STUPID FOOD BACK !
darb
HUNGRY **NOW** ?! HUH ?!
WHY ARE YOU SO MEAN, MAN ?!
YOUR REAR END JUSTIFIED MY MEAN !
BACK TO BED.

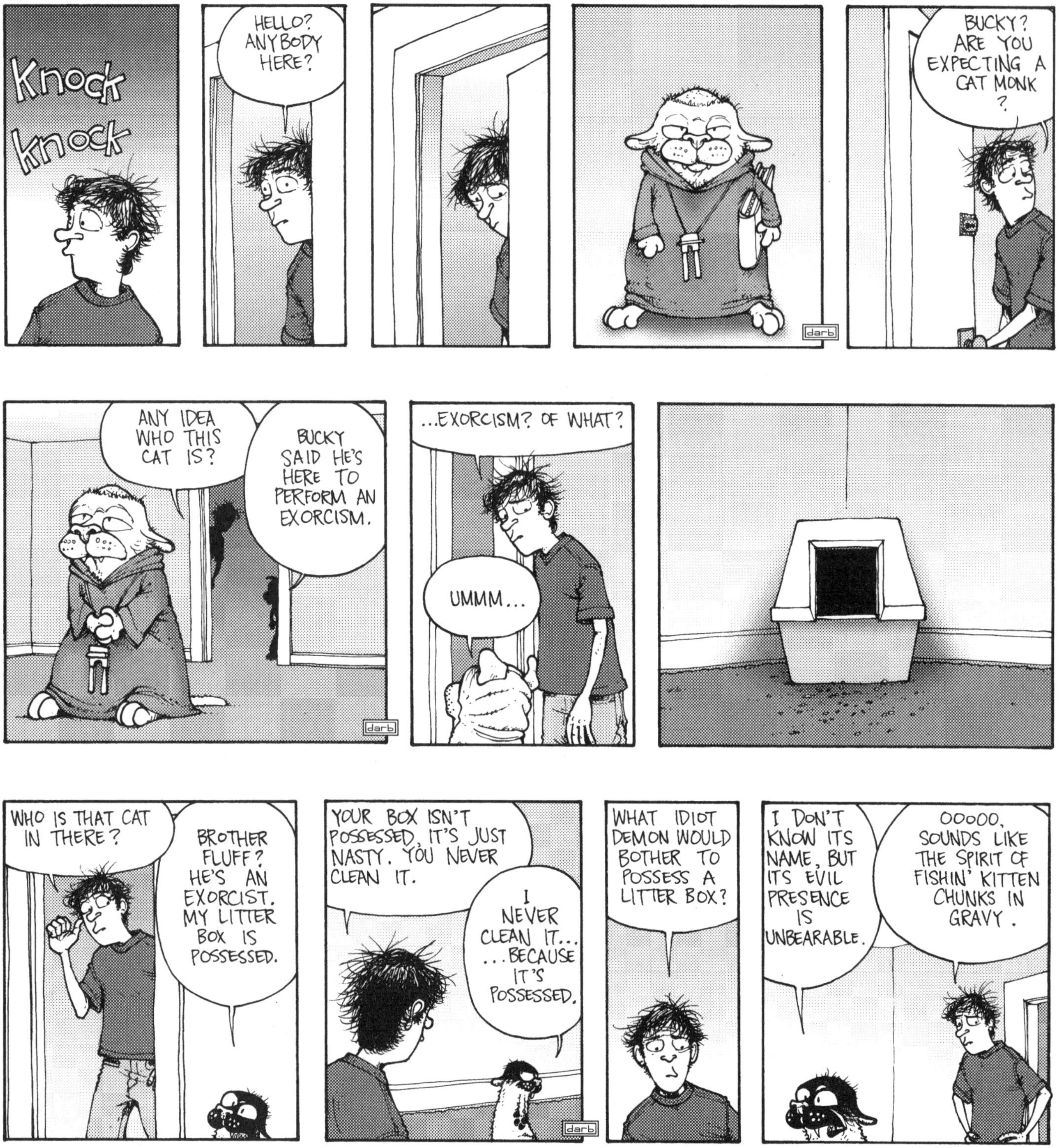
Knock knock
HELLO? ANYBODY HERE?
BUCKY? ARE YOU EXPECTING A CAT MONK ?
darb
ANY IDEA WHO THIS CAT IS?
BUCKY SAID HE'S HERE TO PERFORM AN EXORCISM.
darb
...EXORCISM? OF WHAT?
UMMM...
WHO IS THAT CAT IN THERE?
BROTHER FLUFF? HE'S AN EXORCIST. MY LITTER BOX IS POSSESSED.
YOUR BOX ISN'T POSSESSED, IT'S JUST NASTY. YOU NEVER CLEAN IT.
I NEVER CLEAN IT... ...BECAUSE IT'S POSSESSED.
darb
WHAT IDIOT DEMON WOULD BOTHER TO POSSESS A LITTER BOX?
I DON'T KNOW ITS NAME, BUT ITS EVIL PRESENCE IS UNBEARABLE.
OOOOO, SOUNDS LIKE THE SPIRIT OF FISHIN' KITTEN CHUNKS IN GRAVY .

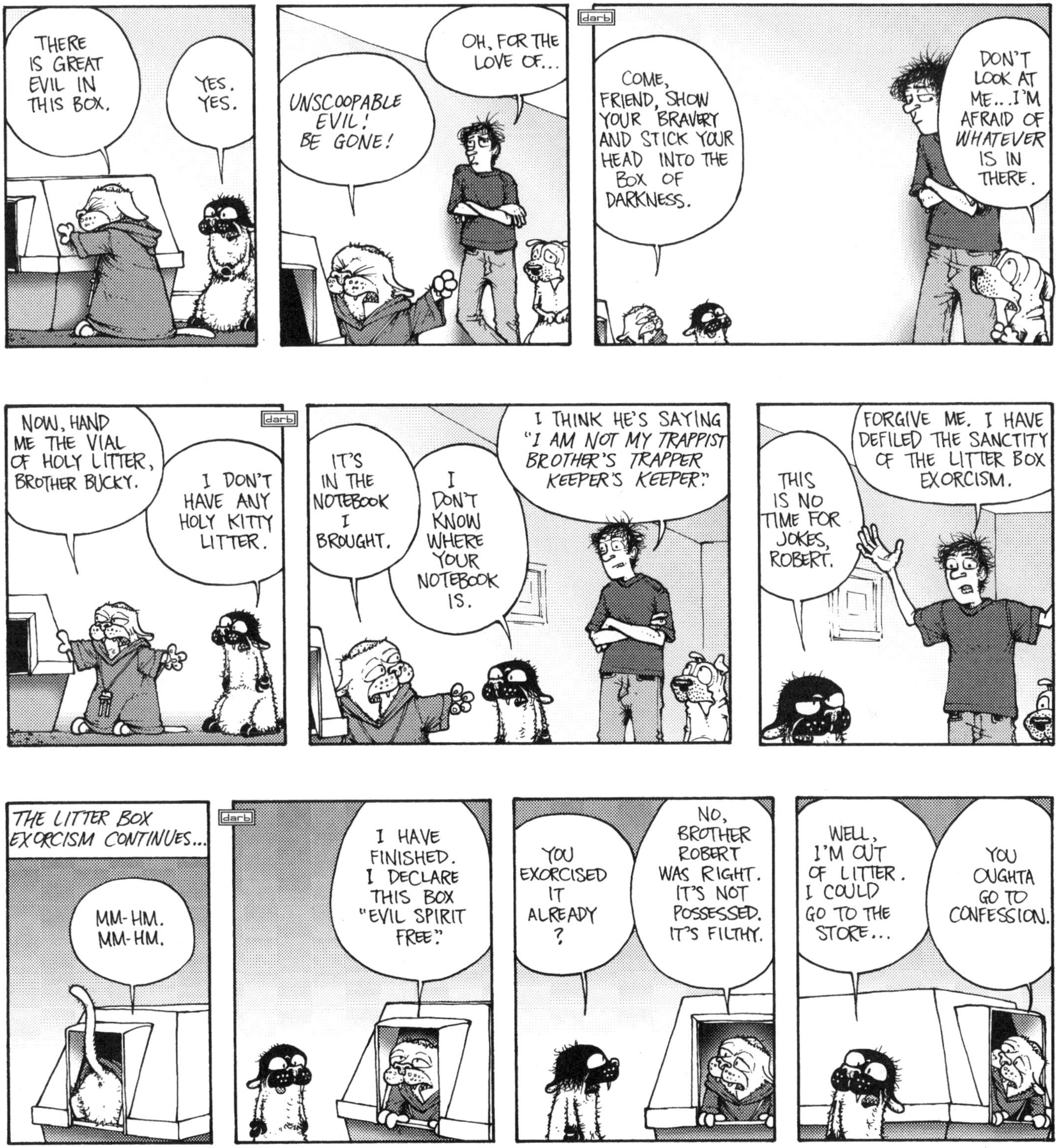
THERE IS GREAT EVIL IN THIS BOX.
YES. YES.
OH, FOR THE LOVE OF...
UNSCOOPABLE EVIL! BE GONE!
darb
COME, FRIEND, SHOW YOUR BRAVERY AND STICK YOUR HEAD INTO THE BOX OF DARKNESS.
DON'T LOOK AT ME...I'M AFRAID OF WHATEVER IS IN THERE.
darb
NOW, HAND ME THE VIAL OF HOLY LITTER, BROTHER BUCKY.
I DON'T HAVE ANY HOLY KITTY LITTER.
IT'S IN THE NOTEBOOK I BROUGHT.
I DON'T KNOW WHERE YOUR NOTEBOOK IS.
I THINK HE'S SAYING "I AM NOT MY TRAPPIST BROTHER'S TRAPPER KEEPER'S KEEPER."
THIS IS NO TIME FOR JOKES, ROBERT.
FORGIVE ME. I HAVE DEFILED THE SANCTITY OF THE LITTER BOX EXORCISM.
THE LITTER BOX EXORCISM CONTINUES...
MM-HM. MM-HM.
darb
I HAVE FINISHED. I DECLARE THIS BOX "EVIL SPIRIT FREE."
YOU EXORCISED IT ALREADY?
NO, BROTHER ROBERT WAS RIGHT. IT'S NOT POSSESSED. IT'S FILTHY.
WELL, I'M OUT OF LITTER. I COULD GO TO THE STORE...
YOU OUGHTA GO TO CONFESSION.

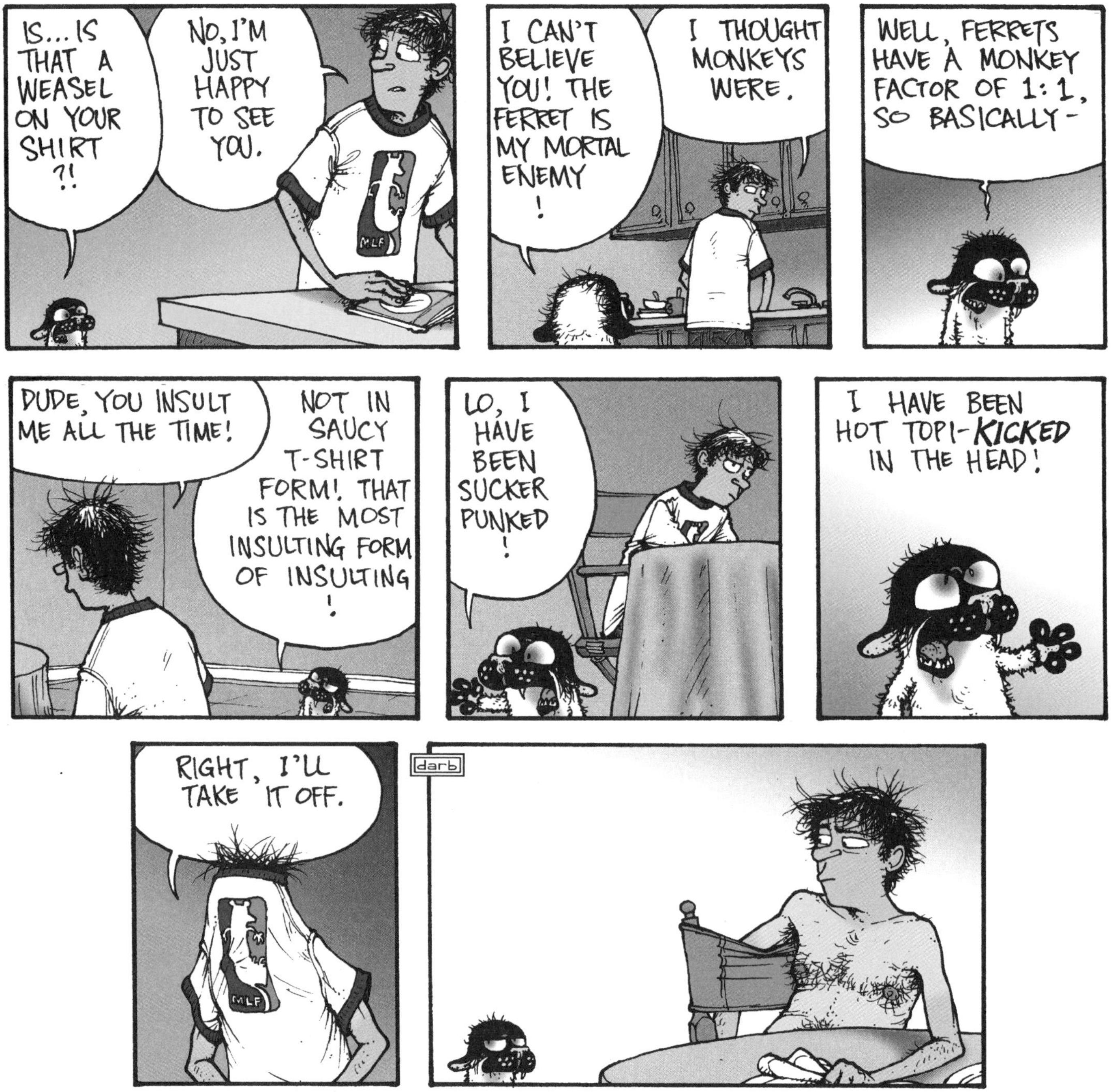
IS... IS THAT A WEASEL ON YOUR SHIRT ?!
NO, I'M JUST HAPPY TO SEE YOU.
I CAN'T BELIEVE YOU! THE FERRET IS MY MORTAL ENEMY !
I THOUGHT MONKEYS WERE.
WELL, FERRETS HAVE A MONKEY FACTOR OF 1:1, SO BASICALLY-
DUDE, YOU INSULT ME ALL THE TIME!
NOT IN SAUCY T-SHIRT FORM! THAT IS THE MOST INSULTING FORM OF INSULTING !
LO, I HAVE BEEN SUCKER PUNKED !
I HAVE BEEN HOT TOPI-KICKED IN THE HEAD!
RIGHT, I'LL TAKE IT OFF.
darb

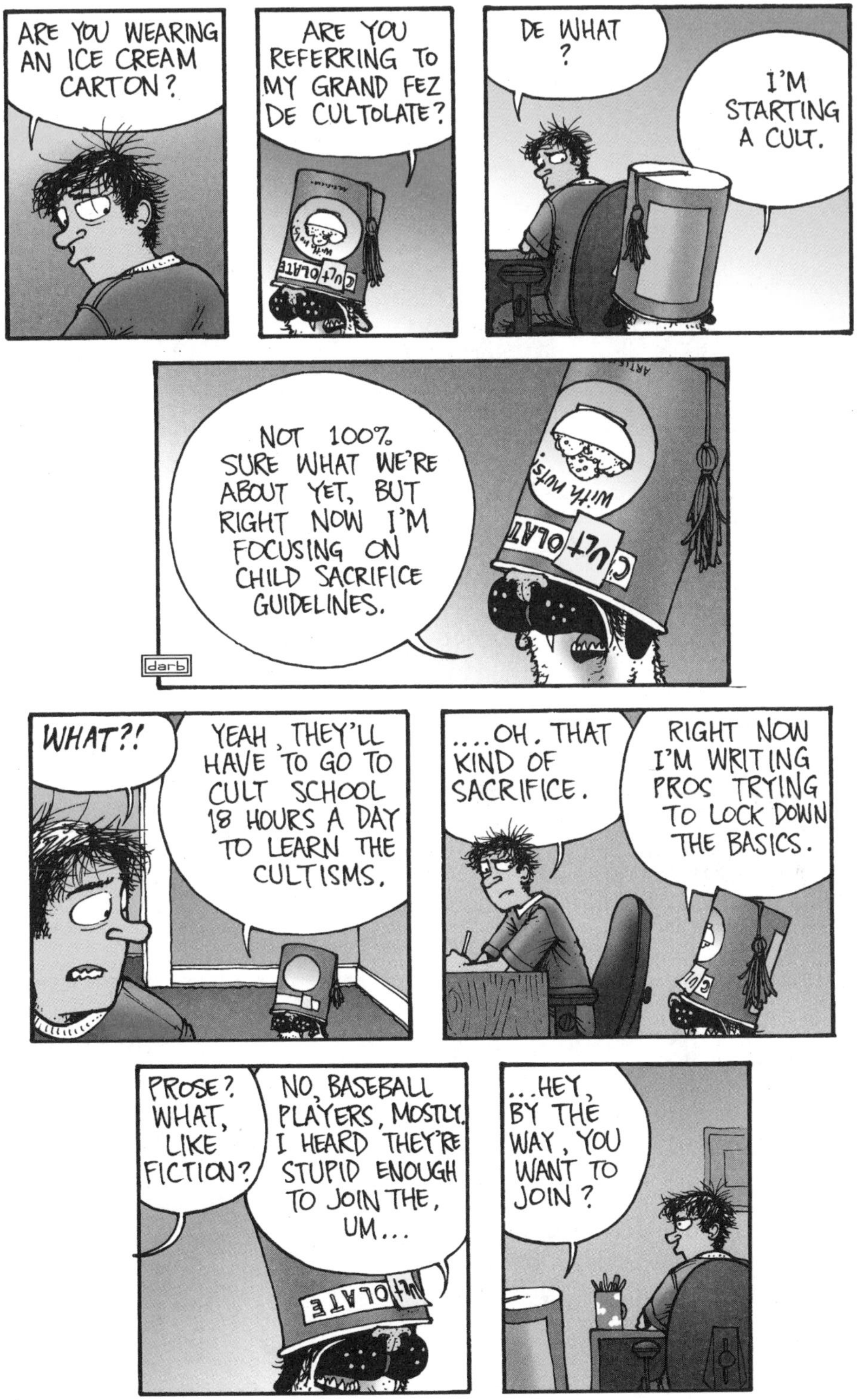

ARE YOU WEARING AN ICE CREAM CARTON?
ARE YOU REFERRING TO MY GRAND FEZ DE CULTOLATE?
DE WHAT ?
I'M STARTING A CULT.
NOT 100% SURE WHAT WE'RE ABOUT YET, BUT RIGHT NOW I'M FOCUSING ON CHILD SACRIFICE GUIDELINES.
darb
WHAT?!
YEAH, THEY'LL HAVE TO GO TO CULT SCHOOL 18 HOURS A DAY TO LEARN THE CULTISMS.
....OH. THAT KIND OF SACRIFICE.
RIGHT NOW I'M WRITING PROS TRYING TO LOCK DOWN THE BASICS.
PROSE? WHAT, LIKE FICTION?
NO, BASEBALL PLAYERS, MOSTLY. I HEARD THEY'RE STUPID ENOUGH TO JOIN THE, UM...
...HEY, BY THE WAY, YOU WANT TO JOIN?

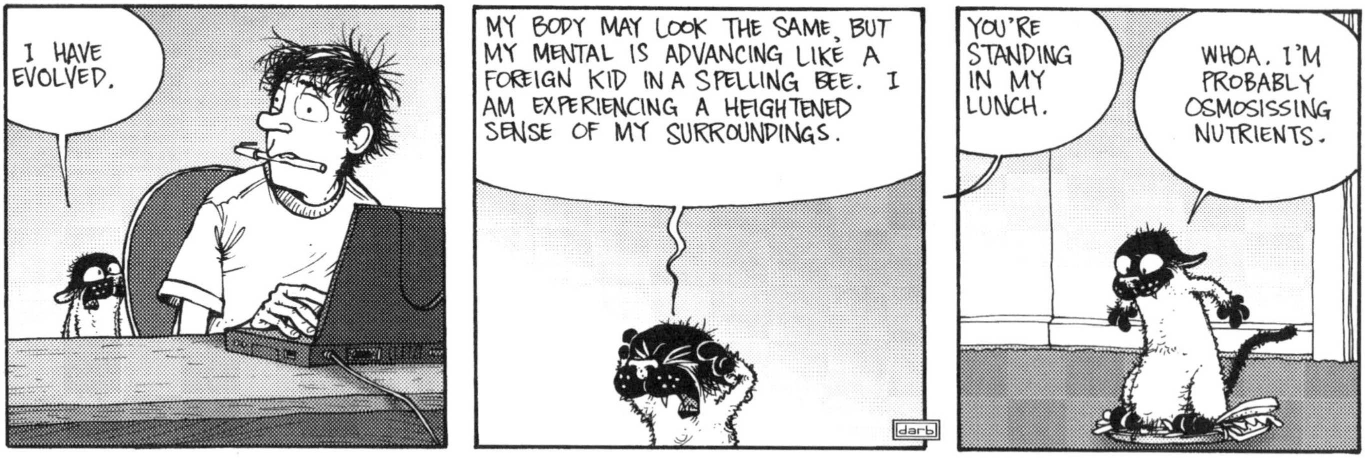
I HAVE EVOLVED.
MY BODY MAY LOOK THE SAME, BUT MY MENTAL IS ADVANCING LIKE A FOREIGN KID IN A SPELLING BEE. I AM EXPERIENCING A HEIGHTENED SENSE OF MY SURROUNDINGS.
darb
YOU'RE STANDING IN MY LUNCH.
WHOA. I'M PROBABLY OSMOSISSING NUTRIENTS.

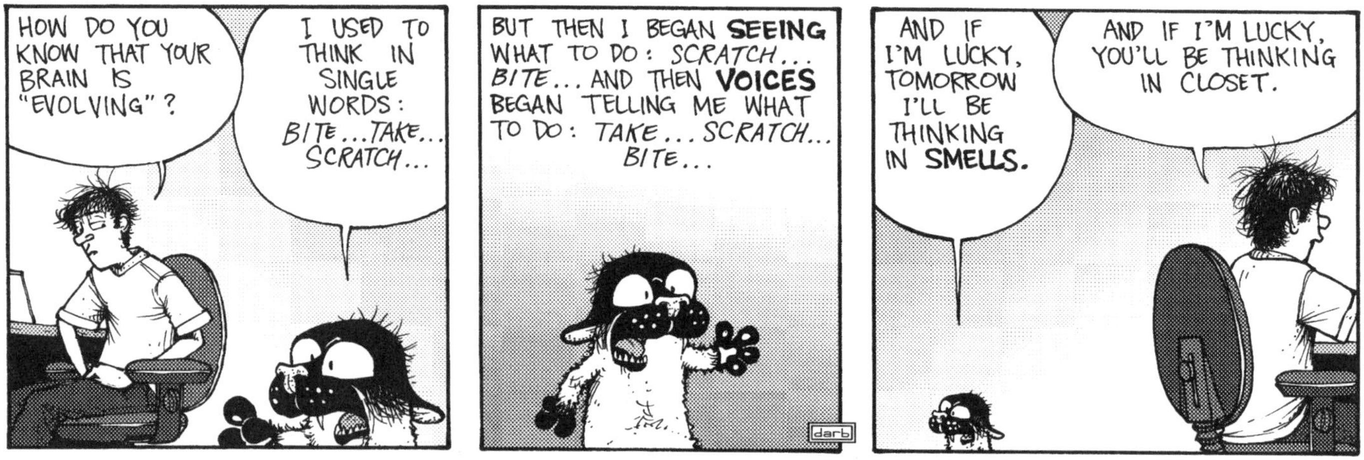
HOW DO YOU KNOW THAT YOUR BRAIN IS "EVOLVING"?
I USED TO THINK IN SINGLE WORDS: *BITE...TAKE... SCRATCH...*
BUT THEN I BEGAN **SEEING** WHAT TO DO: *SCRATCH... BITE...* AND THEN **VOICES** BEGAN TELLING ME WHAT TO DO: *TAKE... SCRATCH... BITE...*
darb
AND IF I'M LUCKY, TOMORROW I'LL BE THINKING IN **SMELLS.**
AND IF I'M LUCKY, YOU'LL BE THINKING IN CLOSET.

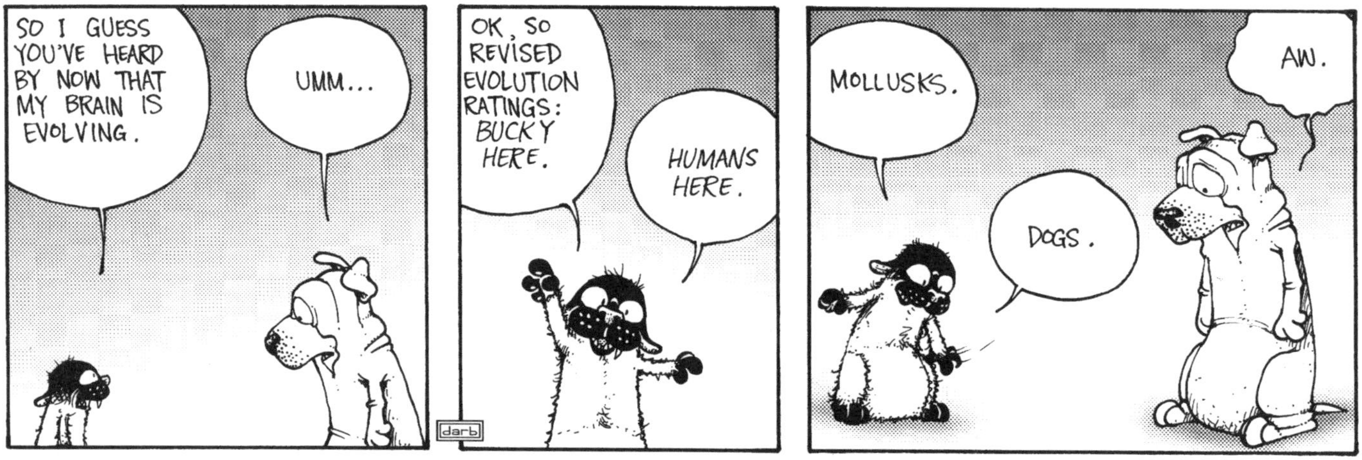
SO I GUESS YOU'VE HEARD BY NOW THAT MY BRAIN IS EVOLVING.
UMM...
darb
OK, SO REVISED EVOLUTION RATINGS: *BUCKY HERE.*
HUMANS HERE.
MOLLUSKS.
DOGS.
AW.

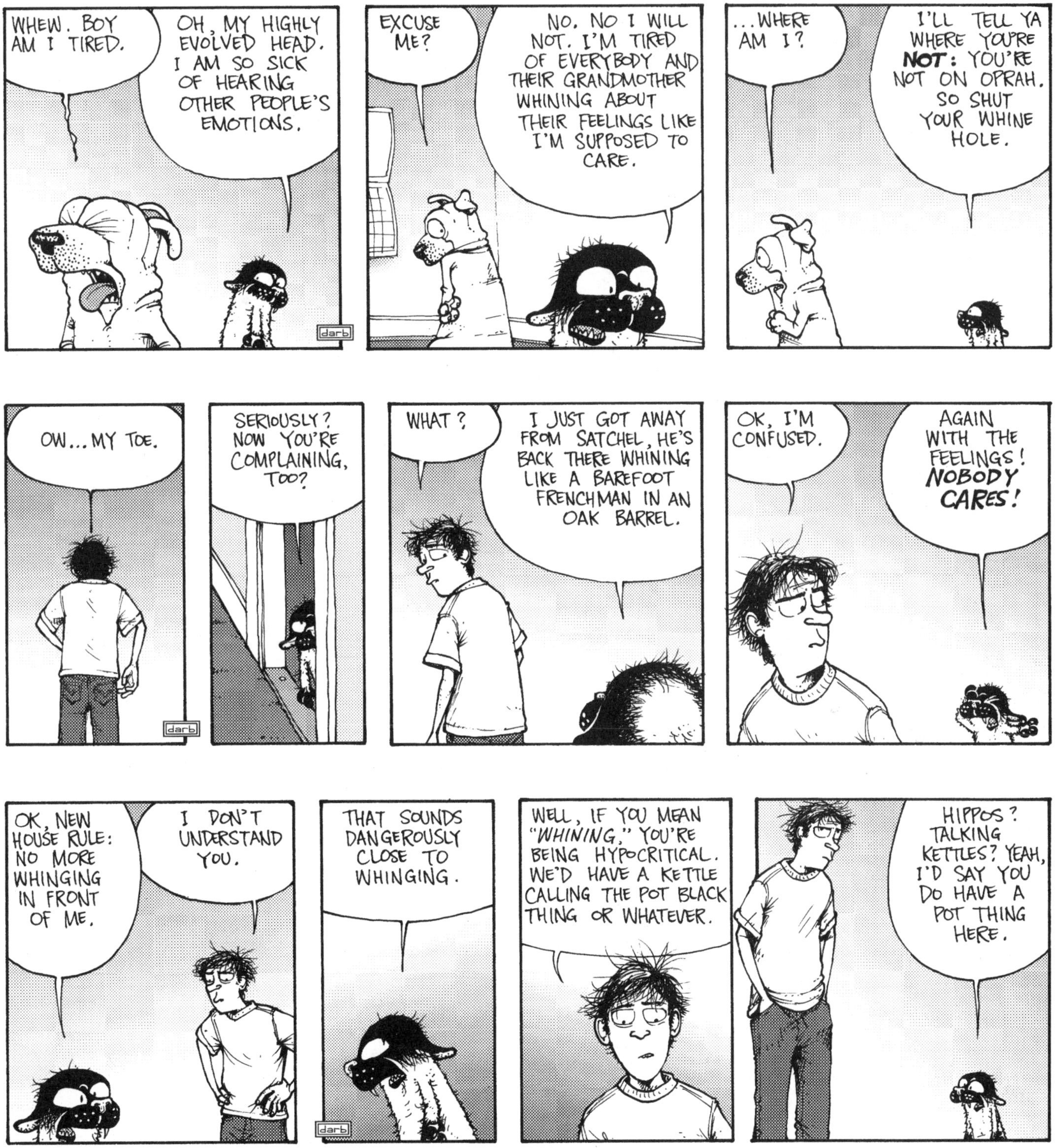
WHEW. BOY AM I TIRED.
OH, MY HIGHLY EVOLVED HEAD. I AM SO SICK OF HEARING OTHER PEOPLE'S EMOTIONS.
darb
EXCUSE ME?
NO. NO I WILL NOT. I'M TIRED OF EVERYBODY AND THEIR GRANDMOTHER WHINING ABOUT THEIR FEELINGS LIKE I'M SUPPOSED TO CARE.
...WHERE AM I?
I'LL TELL YA WHERE YOU'RE **NOT**: YOU'RE NOT ON OPRAH. SO SHUT YOUR WHINE HOLE.
OW... MY TOE.
darb
SERIOUSLY? NOW YOU'RE COMPLAINING, TOO?
WHAT?
I JUST GOT AWAY FROM SATCHEL, HE'S BACK THERE WHINING LIKE A BAREFOOT FRENCHMAN IN AN OAK BARREL.
OK, I'M CONFUSED.
AGAIN WITH THE FEELINGS! **NOBODY CARES!**
OK, NEW HOUSE RULE: NO MORE WHINGING IN FRONT OF ME.
I DON'T UNDERSTAND YOU.
THAT SOUNDS DANGEROUSLY CLOSE TO WHINGING.
darb
WELL, IF YOU MEAN "*WHINING*," YOU'RE BEING HYPOCRITICAL. WE'D HAVE A KETTLE CALLING THE POT BLACK THING OR WHATEVER.
HIPPOS? TALKING KETTLES? YEAH, I'D SAY YOU DO HAVE A POT THING HERE.

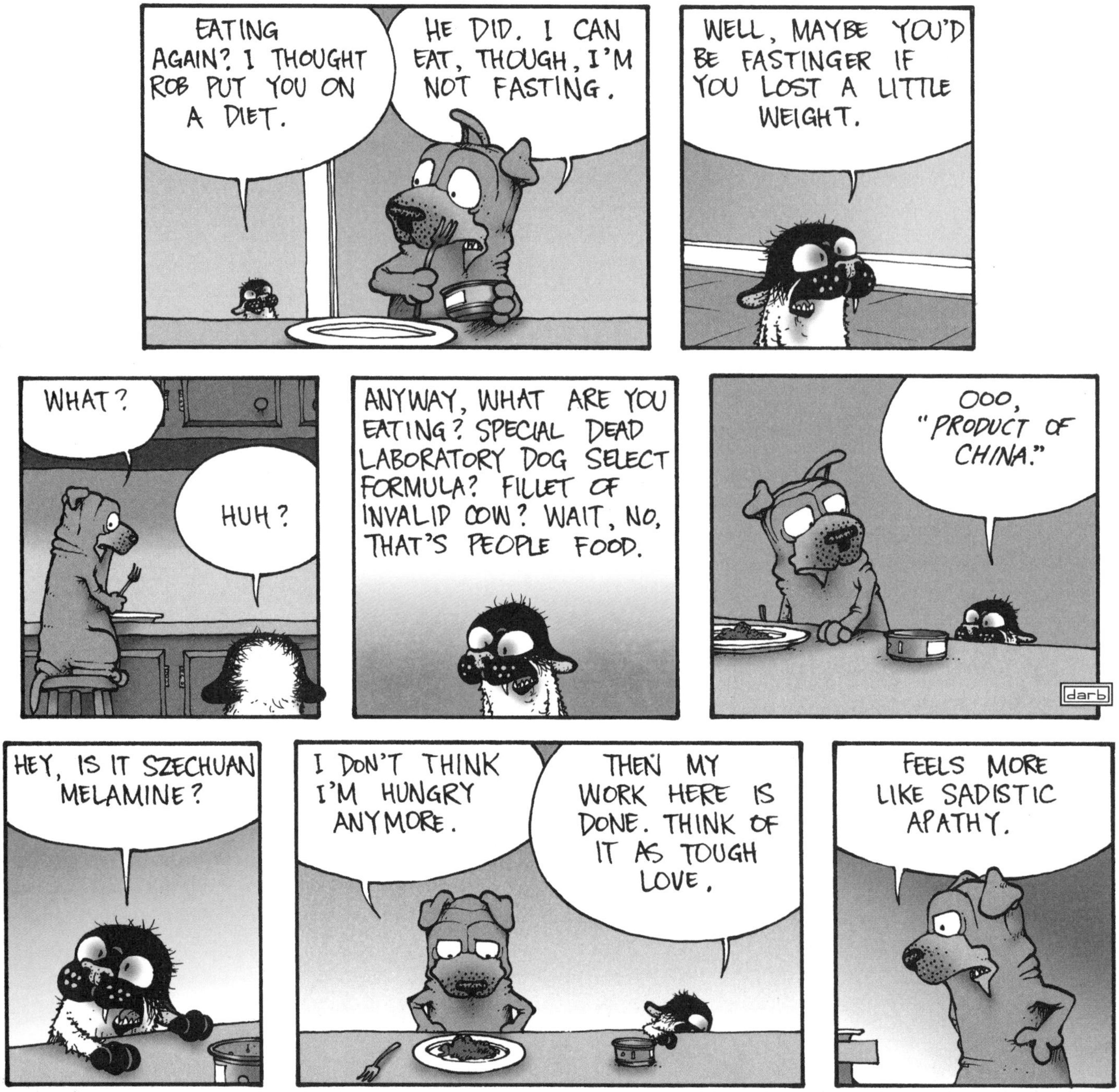
EATING AGAIN? I THOUGHT ROB PUT YOU ON A DIET.
HE DID. I CAN EAT, THOUGH, I'M NOT FASTING.
WELL, MAYBE YOU'D BE FASTINGER IF YOU LOST A LITTLE WEIGHT.
WHAT?
HUH?
ANYWAY, WHAT ARE YOU EATING? SPECIAL DEAD LABORATORY DOG SELECT FORMULA? FILLET OF INVALID COW? WAIT, NO, THAT'S PEOPLE FOOD.
OOO, "PRODUCT OF CHINA."
darb
HEY, IS IT SZECHUAN MELAMINE?
I DON'T THINK I'M HUNGRY ANYMORE.
THEN MY WORK HERE IS DONE. THINK OF IT AS TOUGH LOVE.
FEELS MORE LIKE SADISTIC APATHY.

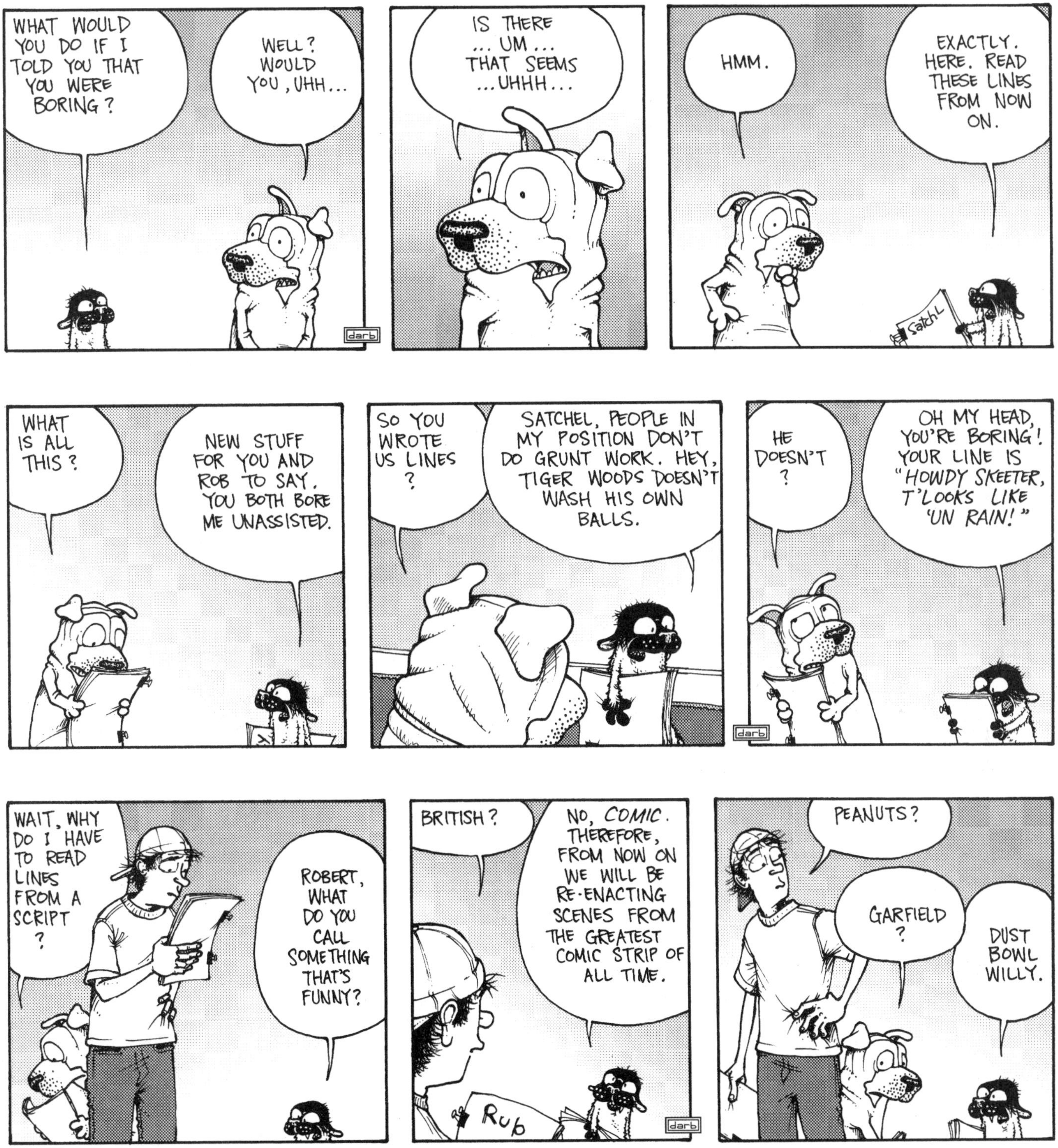
WHAT WOULD YOU DO IF I TOLD YOU THAT YOU WERE BORING?
WELL? WOULD YOU, UHH...
IS THERE ... UM ... THAT SEEMS ...UHHH...
HMM.
EXACTLY. HERE. READ THESE LINES FROM NOW ON.
Satchel
WHAT IS ALL THIS?
NEW STUFF FOR YOU AND ROB TO SAY. YOU BOTH BORE ME UNASSISTED.
SO YOU WROTE US LINES?
SATCHEL, PEOPLE IN MY POSITION DON'T DO GRUNT WORK. HEY, TIGER WOODS DOESN'T WASH HIS OWN BALLS.
HE DOESN'T?
OH MY HEAD, YOU'RE BORING! YOUR LINE IS "HOWDY SKEETER, T'LOOKS LIKE 'UN RAIN!"
WAIT, WHY DO I HAVE TO READ LINES FROM A SCRIPT?
ROBERT, WHAT DO YOU CALL SOMETHING THAT'S FUNNY?
BRITISH?
NO, COMIC. THEREFORE, FROM NOW ON WE WILL BE RE-ENACTING SCENES FROM THE GREATEST COMIC STRIP OF ALL TIME.
Rob
PEANUTS?
GARFIELD?
DUST BOWL WILLY.
darb

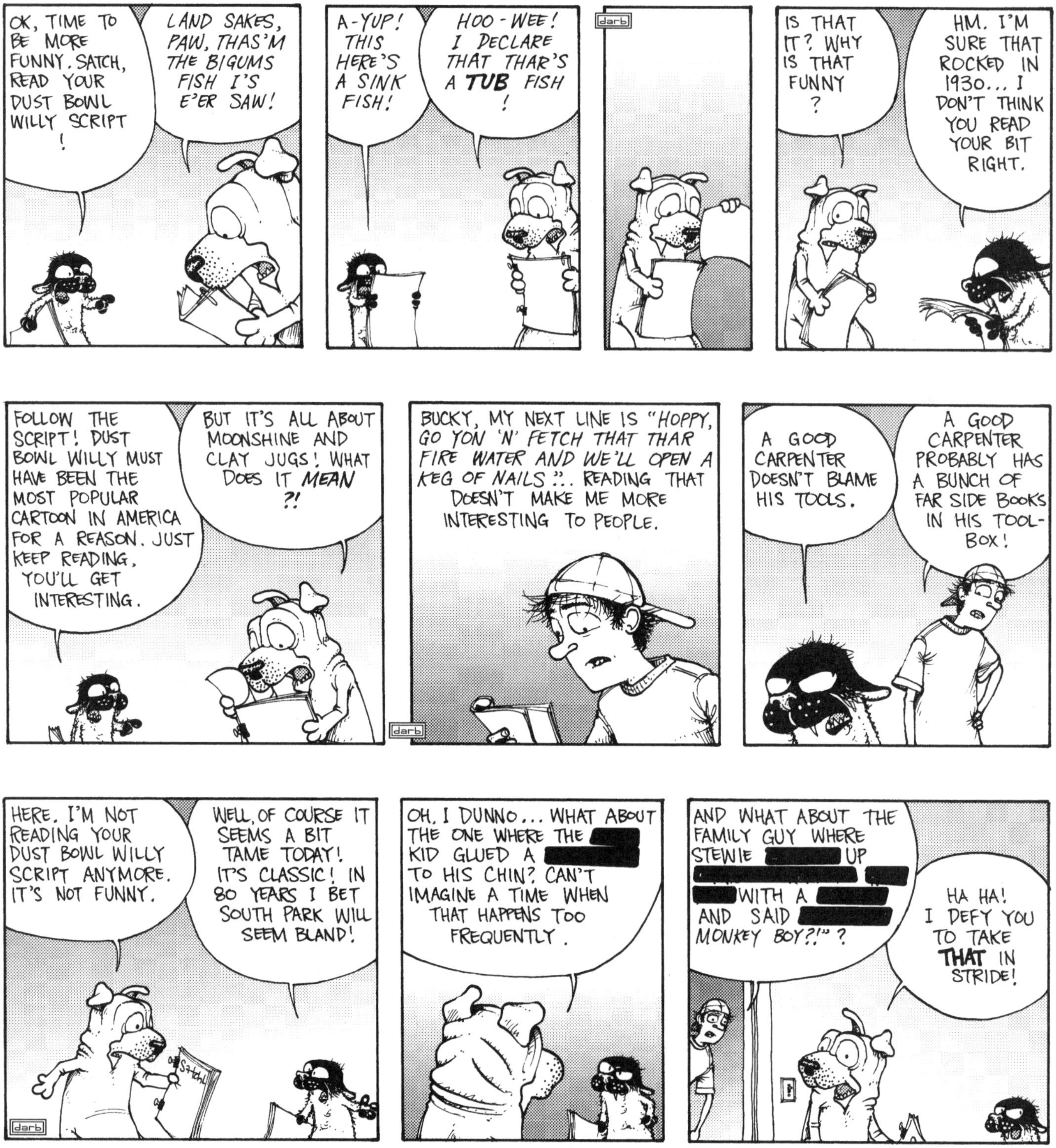
OK, TIME TO BE MORE FUNNY. SATCH, READ YOUR DUST BOWL WILLY SCRIPT!
LAND SAKES, PAW, THAS'M THE BIGUMS FISH I'S E'ER SAW!
A-YUP! THIS HERE'S A SINK FISH!
HOO-WEE! I DECLARE THAT THAR'S A TUB FISH!
darb
IS THAT IT? WHY IS THAT FUNNY?
HM. I'M SURE THAT ROCKED IN 1930... I DON'T THINK YOU READ YOUR BIT RIGHT.
FOLLOW THE SCRIPT! DUST BOWL WILLY MUST HAVE BEEN THE MOST POPULAR CARTOON IN AMERICA FOR A REASON. JUST KEEP READING. YOU'LL GET INTERESTING.
BUT IT'S ALL ABOUT MOONSHINE AND CLAY JUGS! WHAT DOES IT MEAN?!
darb
BUCKY, MY NEXT LINE IS "HOPPY, GO YON 'N' FETCH THAT THAR FIRE WATER AND WE'LL OPEN A KEG OF NAILS!".. READING THAT DOESN'T MAKE ME MORE INTERESTING TO PEOPLE.
A GOOD CARPENTER DOESN'T BLAME HIS TOOLS.
A GOOD CARPENTER PROBABLY HAS A BUNCH OF FAR SIDE BOOKS IN HIS TOOL-BOX!
HERE. I'M NOT READING YOUR DUST BOWL WILLY SCRIPT ANYMORE. IT'S NOT FUNNY.
WELL, OF COURSE IT SEEMS A BIT TAME TODAY! IT'S CLASSIC! IN 80 YEARS I BET SOUTH PARK WILL SEEM BLAND!
darb
OH, I DUNNO... WHAT ABOUT THE ONE WHERE THE [redacted] KID GLUED A [redacted] TO HIS CHIN? CAN'T IMAGINE A TIME WHEN THAT HAPPENS TOO FREQUENTLY.
AND WHAT ABOUT THE FAMILY GUY WHERE STEWIE [redacted] UP [redacted] WITH A [redacted] AND SAID [redacted] MONKEY BOY?!"?
HA HA! I DEFY YOU TO TAKE THAT IN STRIDE!

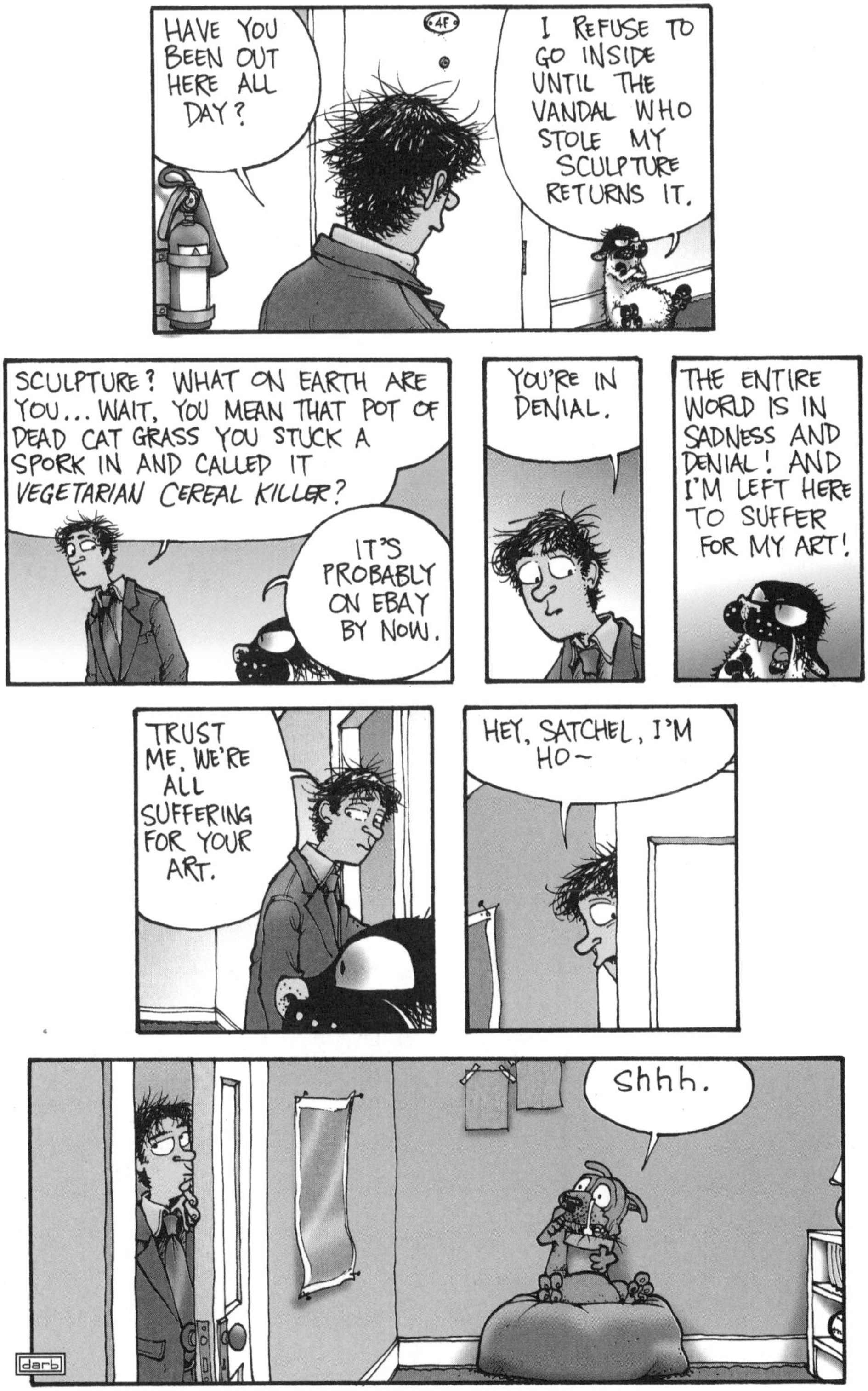
HAVE YOU BEEN OUT HERE ALL DAY?
I REFUSE TO GO INSIDE UNTIL THE VANDAL WHO STOLE MY SCULPTURE RETURNS IT.
SCULPTURE? WHAT ON EARTH ARE YOU... WAIT, YOU MEAN THAT POT OF DEAD CAT GRASS YOU STUCK A SPORK IN AND CALLED IT *VEGETARIAN CEREAL KILLER*?
IT'S PROBABLY ON EBAY BY NOW.
YOU'RE IN DENIAL.
THE ENTIRE WORLD IS IN SADNESS AND DENIAL! AND I'M LEFT HERE TO SUFFER FOR MY ART!
TRUST ME, WE'RE ALL SUFFERING FOR YOUR ART.
HEY, SATCHEL, I'M HO~
Shhh.
darb

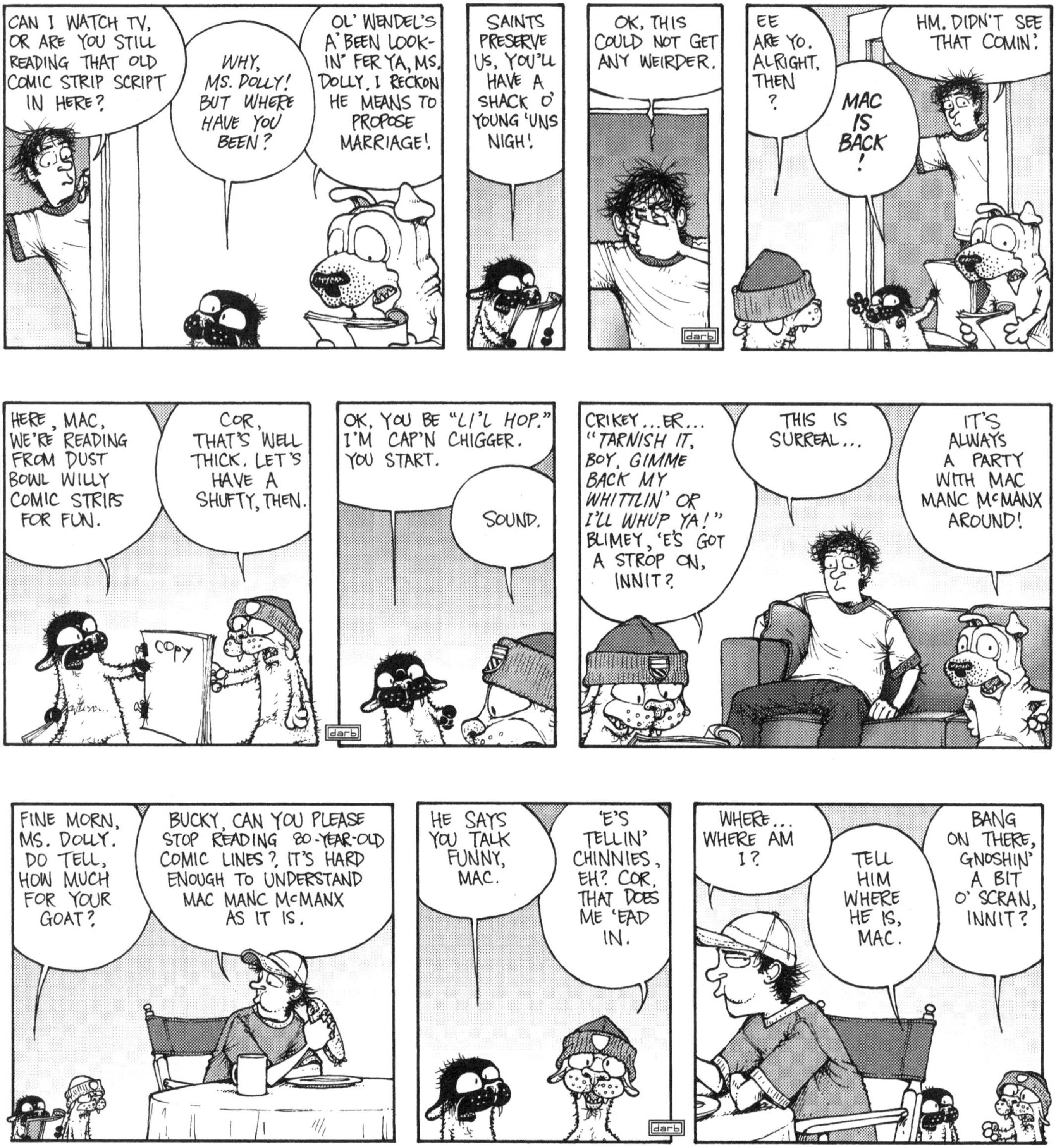
CAN I WATCH TV, OR ARE YOU STILL READING THAT OLD COMIC STRIP SCRIPT IN HERE?
WHY, MS. DOLLY! BUT WHERE HAVE YOU BEEN?
OL' WENDEL'S A'BEEN LOOKIN' FER YA, MS. DOLLY. I RECKON HE MEANS TO PROPOSE MARRIAGE!
SAINTS PRESERVE US, YOU'LL HAVE A SHACK O' YOUNG 'UNS NIGH!
OK, THIS COULD NOT GET ANY WEIRDER.
darb
EE ARE YO. ALRIGHT, THEN?
MAC IS BACK!
HM. DIDN'T SEE THAT COMIN'.
HERE, MAC, WE'RE READING FROM DUST BOWL WILLY COMIC STRIPS FOR FUN.
COR, THAT'S WELL THICK. LET'S HAVE A SHUFTY, THEN.
COPY
darb
OK, YOU BE "LI'L HOP." I'M CAP'N CHIGGER. YOU START.
SOUND.
CRIKEY... ER... "TARNISH IT, BOY, GIMME BACK MY WHITTLIN' OR I'LL WHUP YA!" BLIMEY, 'E'S GOT A STROP ON, INNIT?
THIS IS SURREAL...
IT'S ALWAYS A PARTY WITH MAC MANC McMANX AROUND!
FINE MORN, MS. DOLLY. DO TELL, HOW MUCH FOR YOUR GOAT?
BUCKY, CAN YOU PLEASE STOP READING 80-YEAR-OLD COMIC LINES? IT'S HARD ENOUGH TO UNDERSTAND MAC MANC McMANX AS IT IS.
HE SAYS YOU TALK FUNNY, MAC.
'E'S TELLIN' CHINNIES, EH? COR, THAT DOES ME 'EAD IN.
darb
WHERE... WHERE AM I?
TELL HIM WHERE HE IS, MAC.
BANG ON THERE, GNOSHIN' A BIT O' SCRAN, INNIT?

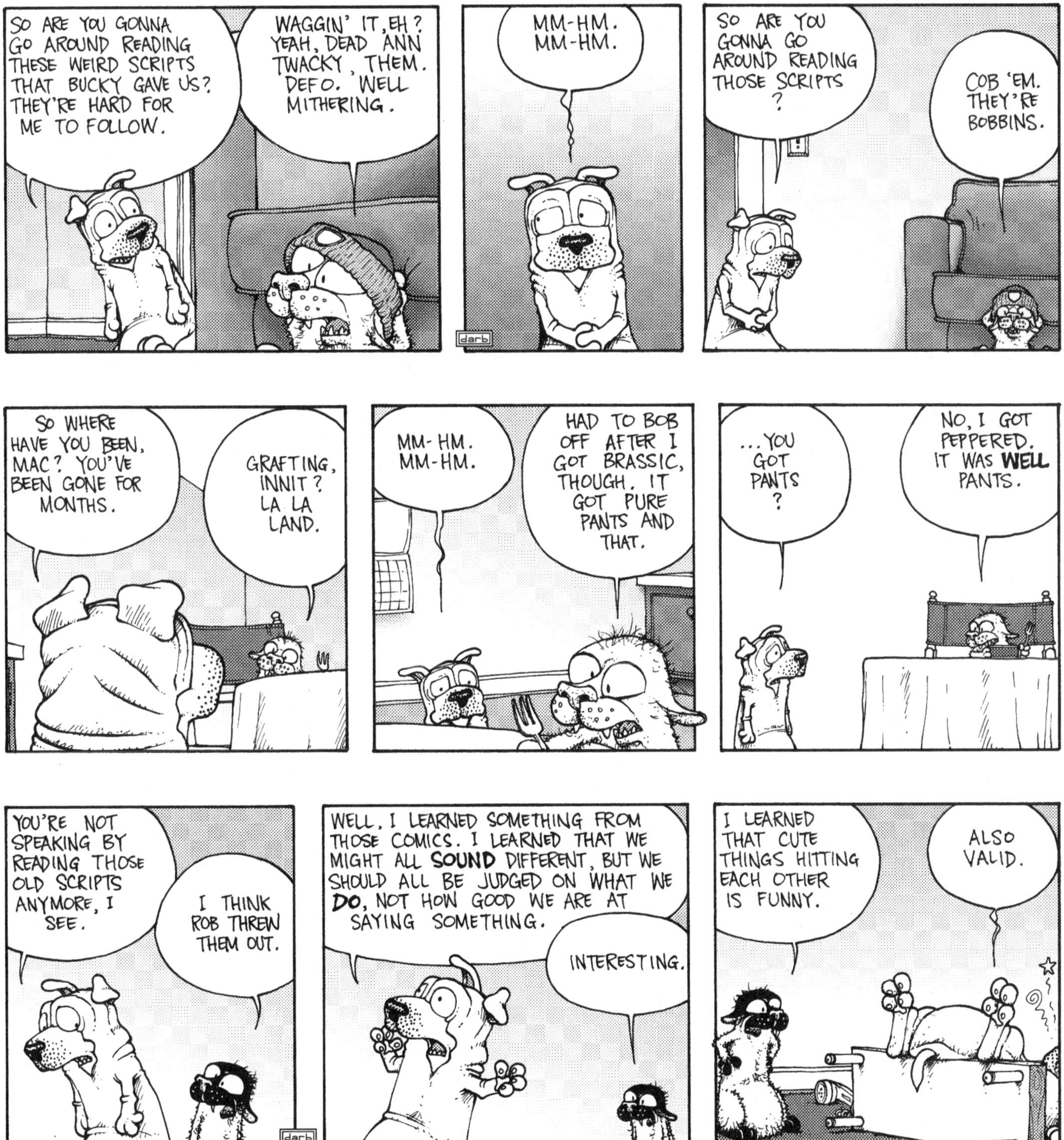
SO ARE YOU GONNA GO AROUND READING THESE WEIRD SCRIPTS THAT BUCKY GAVE US? THEY'RE HARD FOR ME TO FOLLOW.
WAGGIN' IT, EH? YEAH, DEAD ANN TWACKY, THEM. DEFO. WELL MITHERING.
MM-HM. MM-HM.
darb
SO ARE YOU GONNA GO AROUND READING THOSE SCRIPTS ?
COB 'EM. THEY'RE BOBBINS.
SO WHERE HAVE YOU BEEN, MAC? YOU'VE BEEN GONE FOR MONTHS.
GRAFTING, INNIT? LA LA LAND.
MM-HM. MM-HM.
HAD TO BOB OFF AFTER I GOT BRASSIC, THOUGH. IT GOT PURE PANTS AND THAT.
...YOU GOT PANTS ?
NO, I GOT PEPPERED. IT WAS **WELL** PANTS.
YOU'RE NOT SPEAKING BY READING THOSE OLD SCRIPTS ANYMORE, I SEE.
I THINK ROB THREW THEM OUT.
darb
WELL, I LEARNED SOMETHING FROM THOSE COMICS. I LEARNED THAT WE MIGHT ALL **SOUND** DIFFERENT, BUT WE SHOULD ALL BE JUDGED ON WHAT WE **DO**, NOT HOW GOOD WE ARE AT SAYING SOMETHING.
INTERESTING.
I LEARNED THAT CUTE THINGS HITTING EACH OTHER IS FUNNY.
ALSO VALID.

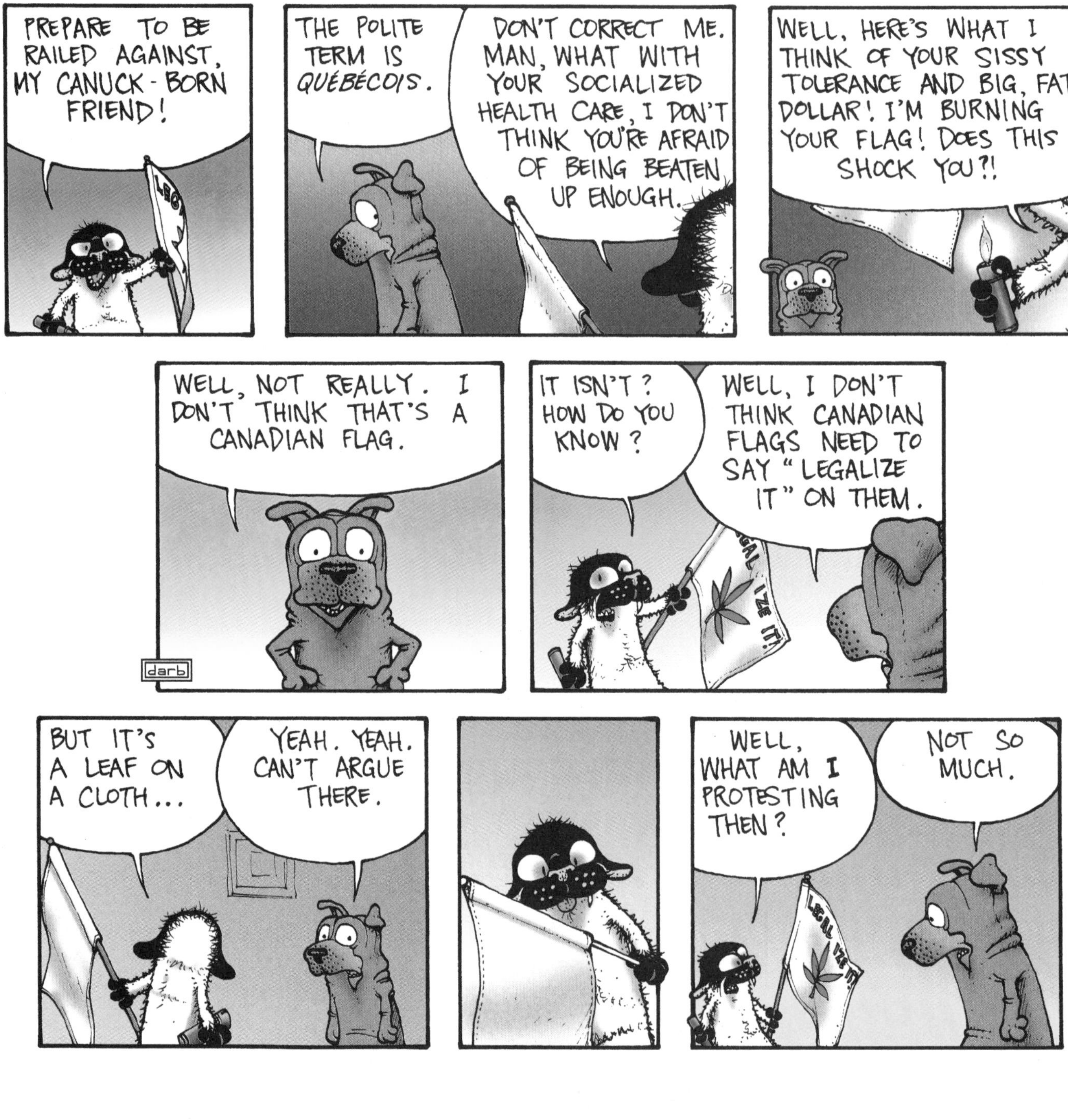
PREPARE TO BE RAILED AGAINST, MY CANUCK-BORN FRIEND!
THE POLITE TERM IS *QUÉBÉCOIS*.
DON'T CORRECT ME. MAN, WHAT WITH YOUR SOCIALIZED HEALTH CARE, I DON'T THINK YOU'RE AFRAID OF BEING BEATEN UP ENOUGH.
WELL, HERE'S WHAT I THINK OF YOUR SISSY TOLERANCE AND BIG, FAT DOLLAR! I'M BURNING YOUR FLAG! DOES THIS SHOCK YOU?!
WELL, NOT REALLY. I DON'T THINK THAT'S A CANADIAN FLAG.
darb
IT ISN'T? HOW DO YOU KNOW?
WELL, I DON'T THINK CANADIAN FLAGS NEED TO SAY "LEGALIZE IT" ON THEM.
LEGAL IZE IT!
BUT IT'S A LEAF ON A CLOTH...
YEAH. YEAH. CAN'T ARGUE THERE.
WELL, WHAT AM **I** PROTESTING THEN?
NOT SO MUCH.

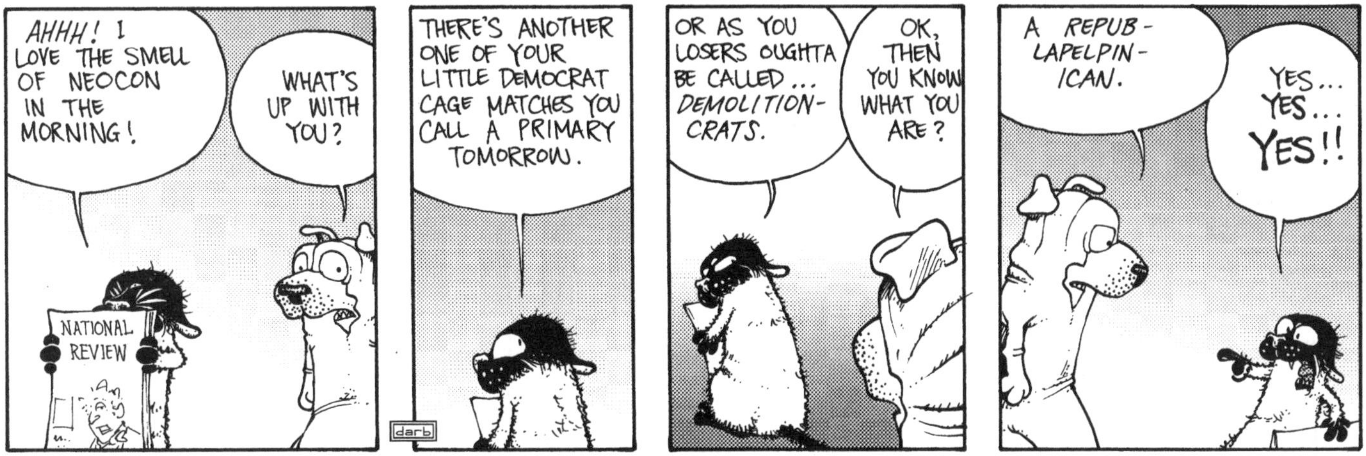
AHHH! I LOVE THE SMELL OF NEOCON IN THE MORNING!
NATIONAL REVIEW
WHAT'S UP WITH YOU?
THERE'S ANOTHER ONE OF YOUR LITTLE DEMOCRAT CAGE MATCHES YOU CALL A PRIMARY TOMORROW.
darb
OR AS YOU LOSERS OUGHTA BE CALLED... *DEMOLITION-CRATS.*
OK, THEN YOU KNOW WHAT YOU ARE?
A *REPUB-LAPELPIN-ICAN.*
YES... YES... YES!!

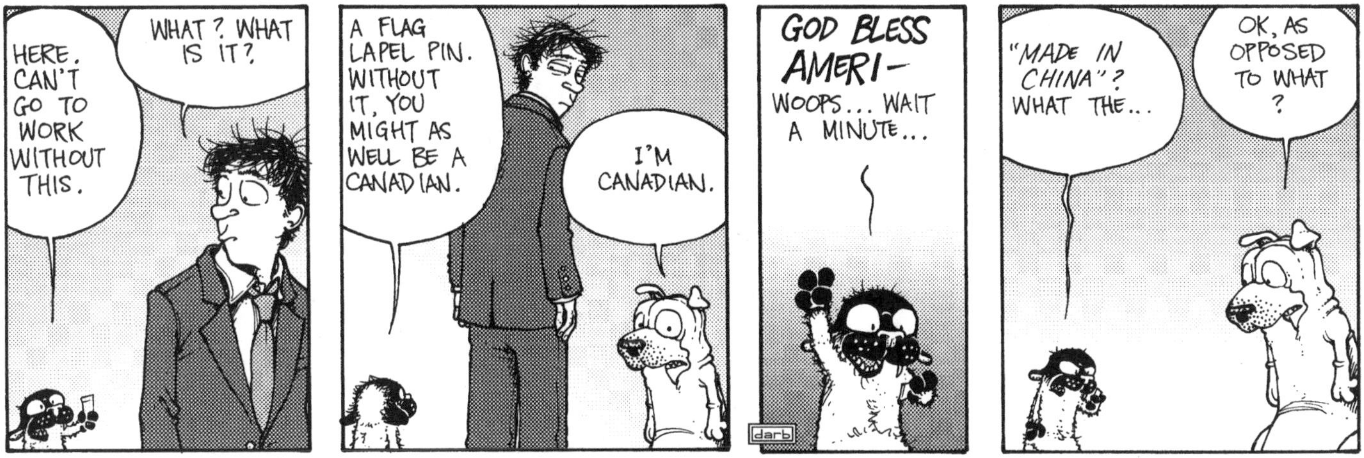
HERE. CAN'T GO TO WORK WITHOUT THIS.
WHAT? WHAT IS IT?
A FLAG LAPEL PIN. WITHOUT IT, YOU MIGHT AS WELL BE A CANADIAN.
I'M CANADIAN.
GOD BLESS AMERI-
WOOPS... WAIT A MINUTE...
darb
"*MADE IN CHINA*"? WHAT THE...
OK, AS OPPOSED TO WHAT?

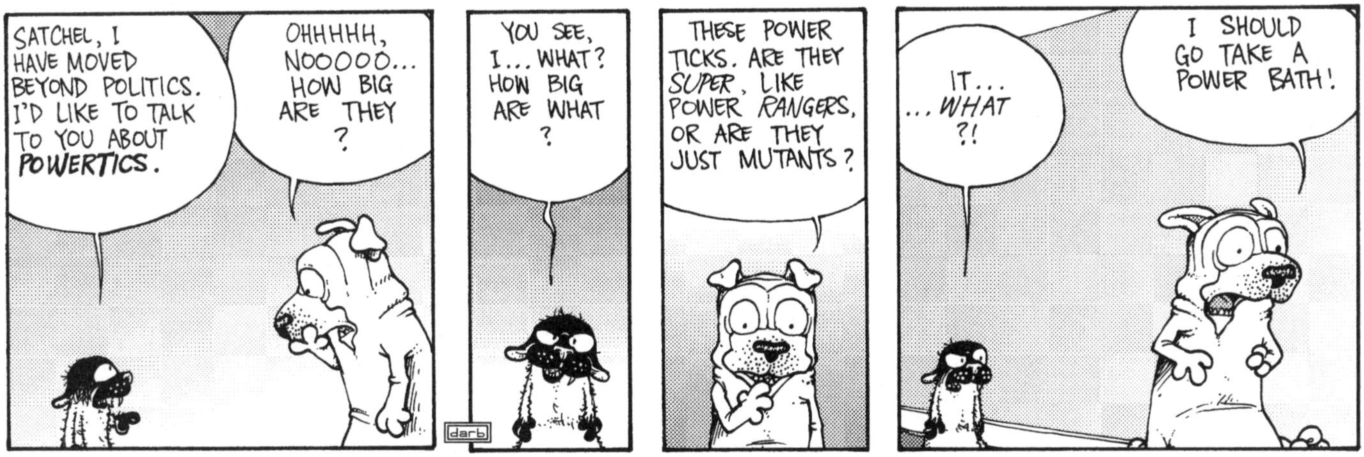
SATCHEL, I HAVE MOVED BEYOND POLITICS. I'D LIKE TO TALK TO YOU ABOUT **POWERTICS.**
OHHHHH, NOOOOO... HOW BIG ARE THEY?
darb
YOU SEE, I... WHAT? HOW BIG ARE WHAT?
THESE POWER TICKS. ARE THEY *SUPER*, LIKE POWER *RANGERS*, OR ARE THEY JUST MUTANTS?
IT... ...*WHAT*?!
I SHOULD GO TAKE A POWER BATH!

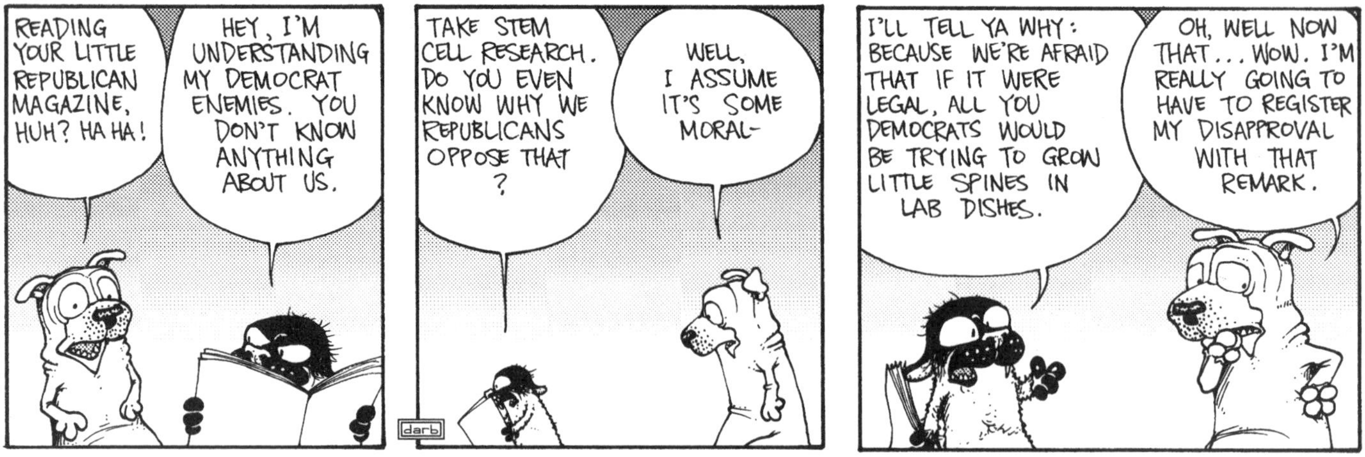
READING YOUR LITTLE REPUBLICAN MAGAZINE, HUH? HA HA!
HEY, I'M UNDERSTANDING MY DEMOCRAT ENEMIES. YOU DON'T KNOW ANYTHING ABOUT US.
TAKE STEM CELL RESEARCH. DO YOU EVEN KNOW WHY WE REPUBLICANS OPPOSE THAT?
WELL, I ASSUME IT'S SOME MORAL-
darb
I'LL TELL YA WHY: BECAUSE WE'RE AFRAID THAT IF IT WERE LEGAL, ALL YOU DEMOCRATS WOULD BE TRYING TO GROW LITTLE SPINES IN LAB DISHES.
OH, WELL NOW THAT... WOW. I'M REALLY GOING TO HAVE TO REGISTER MY DISAPPROVAL WITH THAT REMARK.

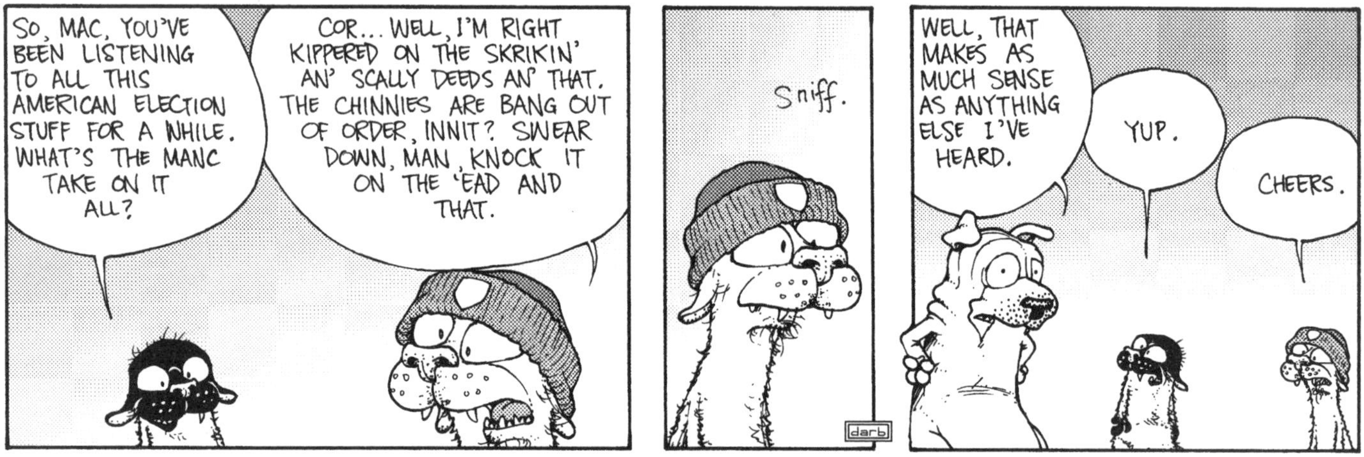
SO, MAC, YOU'VE BEEN LISTENING TO ALL THIS AMERICAN ELECTION STUFF FOR A WHILE. WHAT'S THE MANC TAKE ON IT ALL?
COR... WELL, I'M RIGHT KIPPERED ON THE SKRIKIN' AN' SCALLY DEEDS AN' THAT. THE CHINNIES ARE BANG OUT OF ORDER, INNIT? SWEAR DOWN, MAN, KNOCK IT ON THE 'EAD AND THAT.
Sniff.
darb
WELL, THAT MAKES AS MUCH SENSE AS ANYTHING ELSE I'VE HEARD.
YUP.
CHEERS.

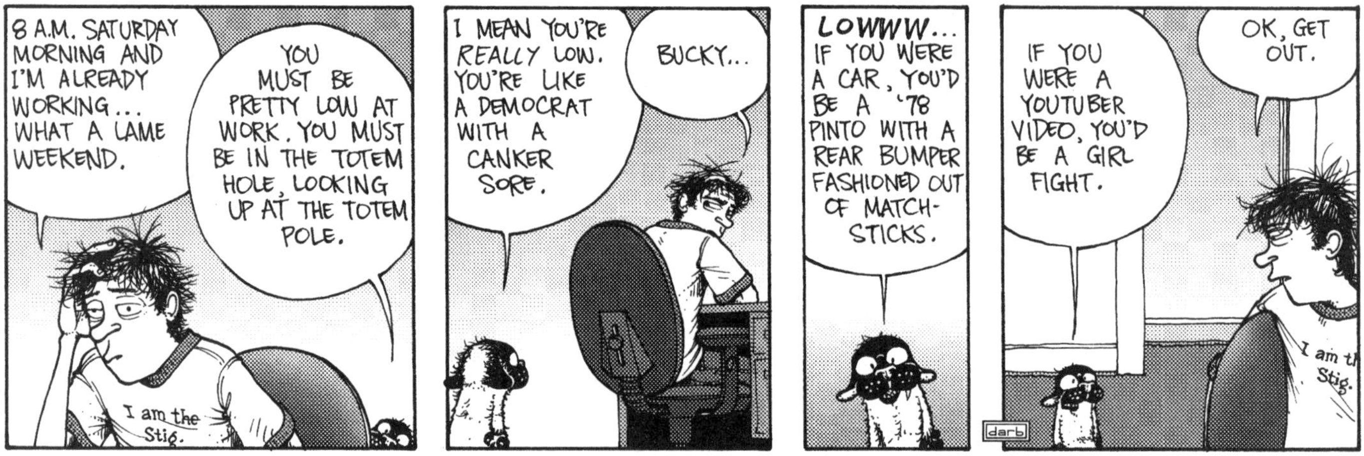
8 A.M. SATURDAY MORNING AND I'M ALREADY WORKING... WHAT A LAME WEEKEND.
YOU MUST BE PRETTY LOW AT WORK. YOU MUST BE IN THE TOTEM HOLE, LOOKING UP AT THE TOTEM POLE.
I am the Stig.
I MEAN YOU'RE REALLY LOW. YOU'RE LIKE A DEMOCRAT WITH A CANKER SORE.
BUCKY...
LOWWW... IF YOU WERE A CAR, YOU'D BE A '78 PINTO WITH A REAR BUMPER FASHIONED OUT OF MATCH-STICKS.
darb
IF YOU WERE A YOUTUBER VIDEO, YOU'D BE A GIRL FIGHT.
OK, GET OUT.

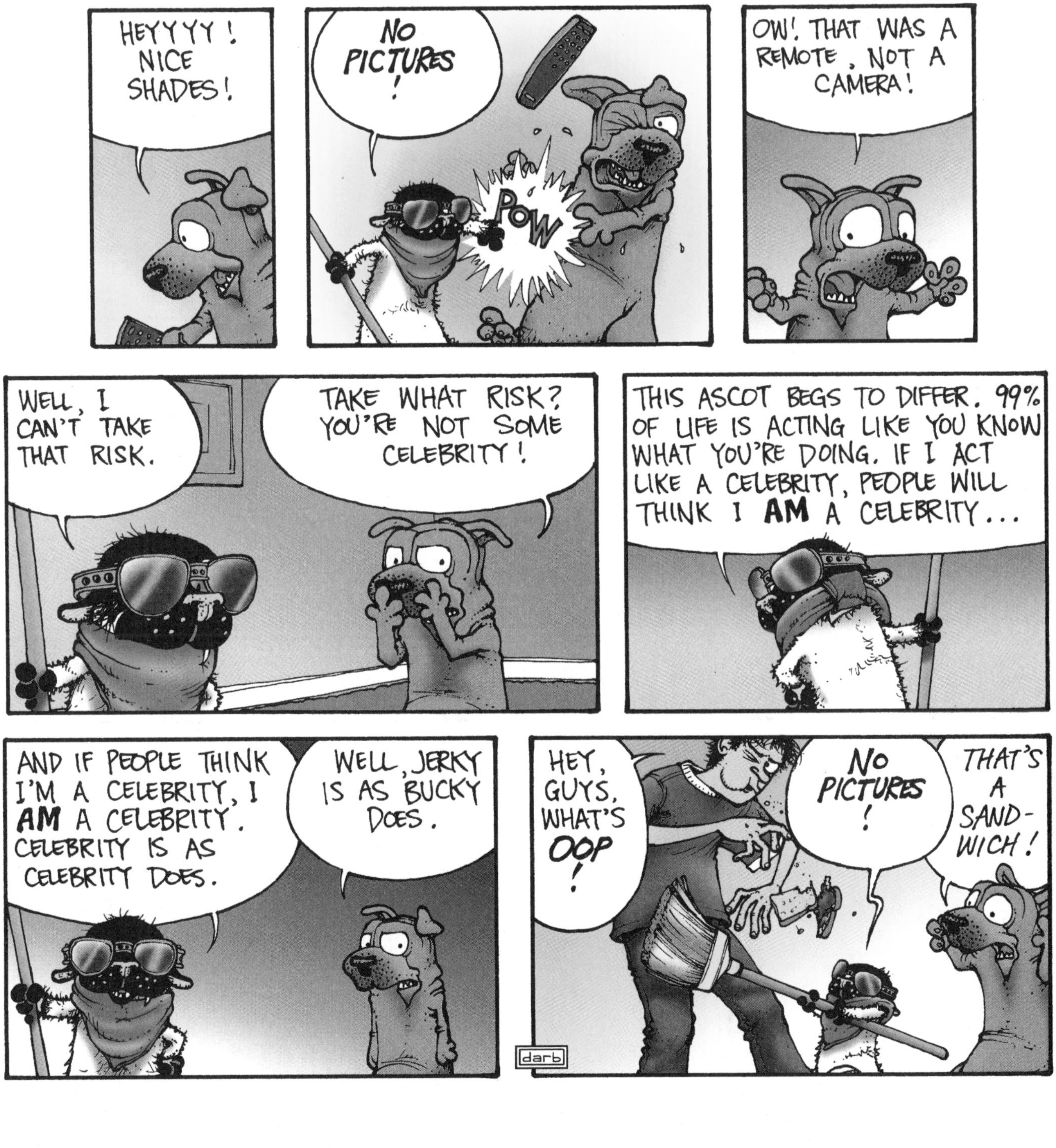
HEYYYY! NICE SHADES!
NO PICTURES!
POW
OW! THAT WAS A REMOTE, NOT A CAMERA!
WELL, I CAN'T TAKE THAT RISK.
TAKE WHAT RISK? YOU'RE NOT SOME CELEBRITY!
THIS ASCOT BEGS TO DIFFER. 99% OF LIFE IS ACTING LIKE YOU KNOW WHAT YOU'RE DOING. IF I ACT LIKE A CELEBRITY, PEOPLE WILL THINK I **AM** A CELEBRITY...
AND IF PEOPLE THINK I'M A CELEBRITY, I **AM** A CELEBRITY. CELEBRITY IS AS CELEBRITY DOES.
WELL, JERKY IS AS BUCKY DOES.
HEY, GUYS, WHAT'S OOP!
NO PICTURES!
THAT'S A SAND-WICH!
darb

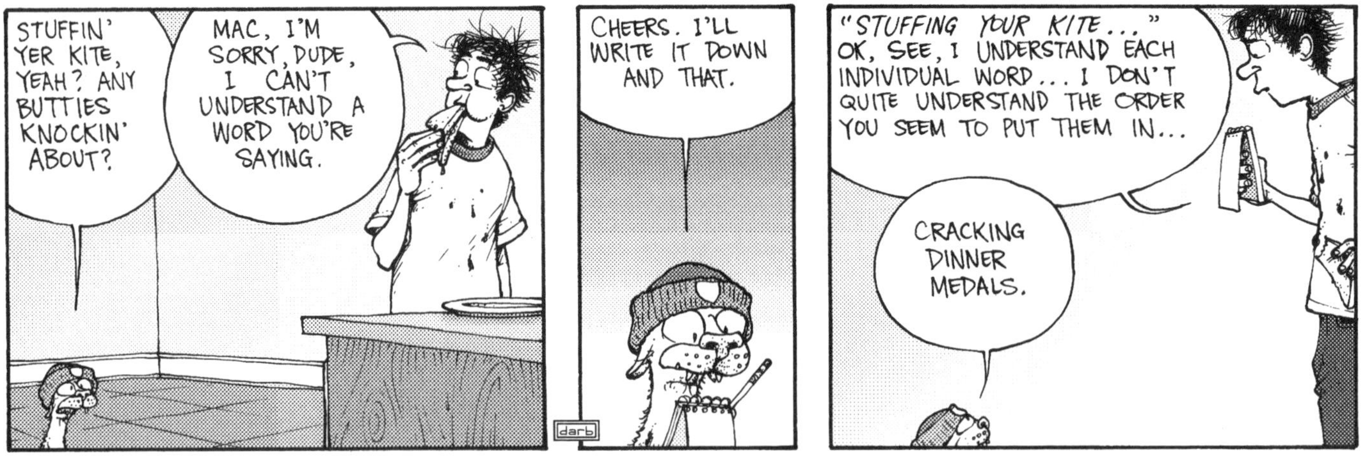
STUFFIN' YER KITE, YEAH? ANY BUTTIES KNOCKIN' ABOUT?
MAC, I'M SORRY, DUDE, I CAN'T UNDERSTAND A WORD YOU'RE SAYING.
CHEERS. I'LL WRITE IT DOWN AND THAT.
darb
"STUFFING YOUR KITE..." OK, SEE, I UNDERSTAND EACH INDIVIDUAL WORD... I DON'T QUITE UNDERSTAND THE ORDER YOU SEEM TO PUT THEM IN...
CRACKING DINNER MEDALS.

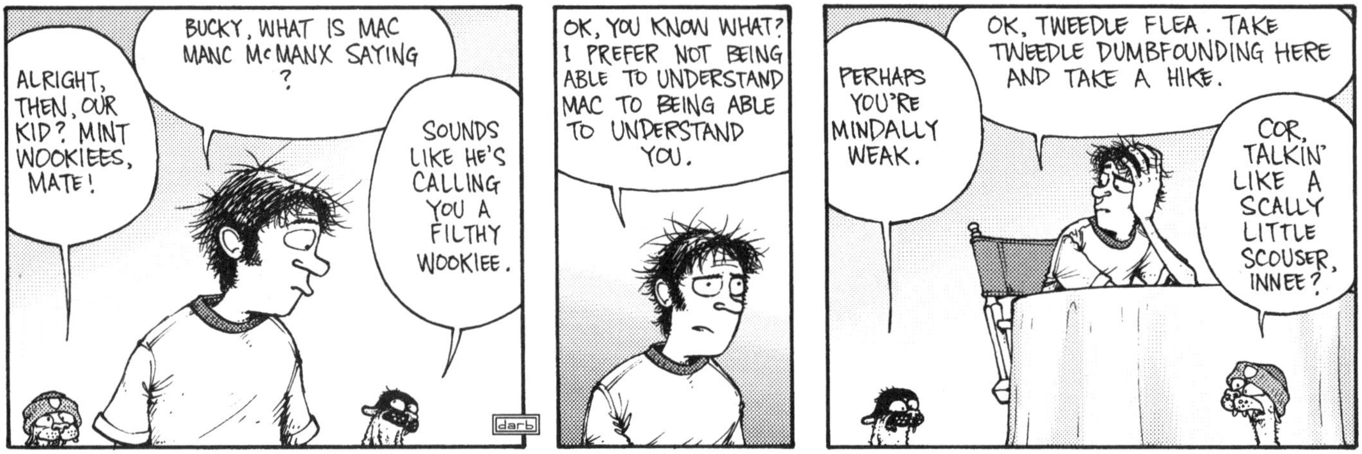
ALRIGHT, THEN, OUR KID? MINT WOOKIEES, MATE!
BUCKY, WHAT IS MAC MANC McMANX SAYING?
SOUNDS LIKE HE'S CALLING YOU A FILTHY WOOKIEE.
darb
OK, YOU KNOW WHAT? I PREFER NOT BEING ABLE TO UNDERSTAND MAC TO BEING ABLE TO UNDERSTAND YOU.
PERHAPS YOU'RE MINDALLY WEAK.
OK, TWEEDLE FLEA. TAKE TWEEDLE DUMBFOUNDING HERE AND TAKE A HIKE.
COR, TALKIN' LIKE A SCALLY LITTLE SCOUSER, INNEE?

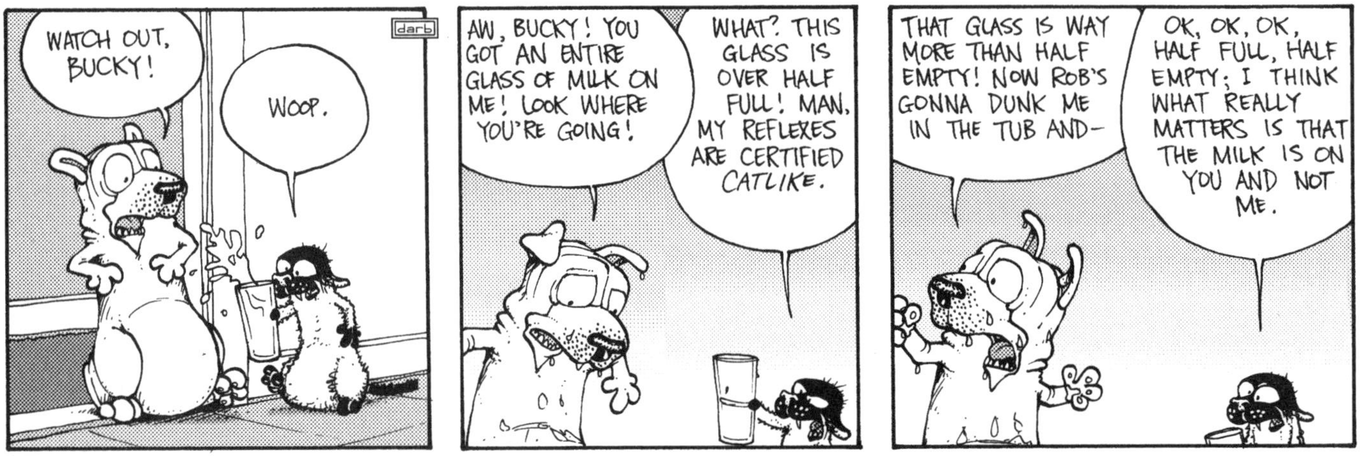
darb
WATCH OUT, BUCKY!
WOOP.
AW, BUCKY! YOU GOT AN ENTIRE GLASS OF MILK ON ME! LOOK WHERE YOU'RE GOING!
WHAT? THIS GLASS IS OVER HALF FULL! MAN, MY REFLEXES ARE CERTIFIED CATLIKE.
THAT GLASS IS WAY MORE THAN HALF EMPTY! NOW ROB'S GONNA DUNK ME IN THE TUB AND-
OK, OK, OK, HALF FULL, HALF EMPTY; I THINK WHAT REALLY MATTERS IS THAT THE MILK IS ON YOU AND NOT ME.

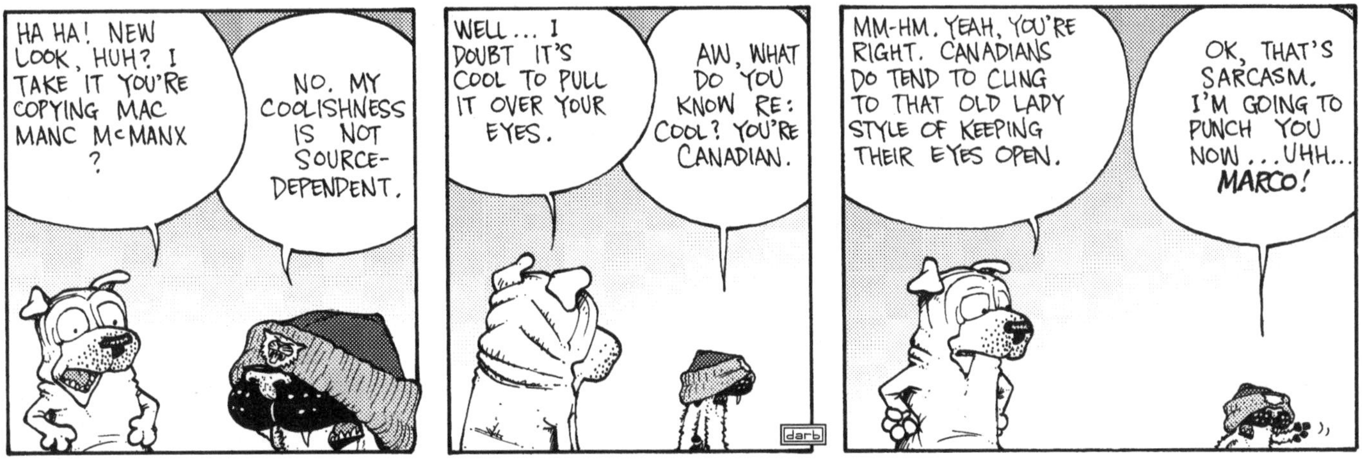
HA HA! NEW LOOK, HUH? I TAKE IT YOU'RE COPYING MAC MANC McMANX ?
NO. MY COOLISHNESS IS NOT SOURCE-DEPENDENT.
WELL... I DOUBT IT'S COOL TO PULL IT OVER YOUR EYES.
AW, WHAT DO YOU KNOW RE: COOL? YOU'RE CANADIAN.
darb
MM-HM. YEAH, YOU'RE RIGHT. CANADIANS DO TEND TO CLING TO THAT OLD LADY STYLE OF KEEPING THEIR EYES OPEN.
OK, THAT'S SARCASM. I'M GOING TO PUNCH YOU NOW...UHH... MARCO!

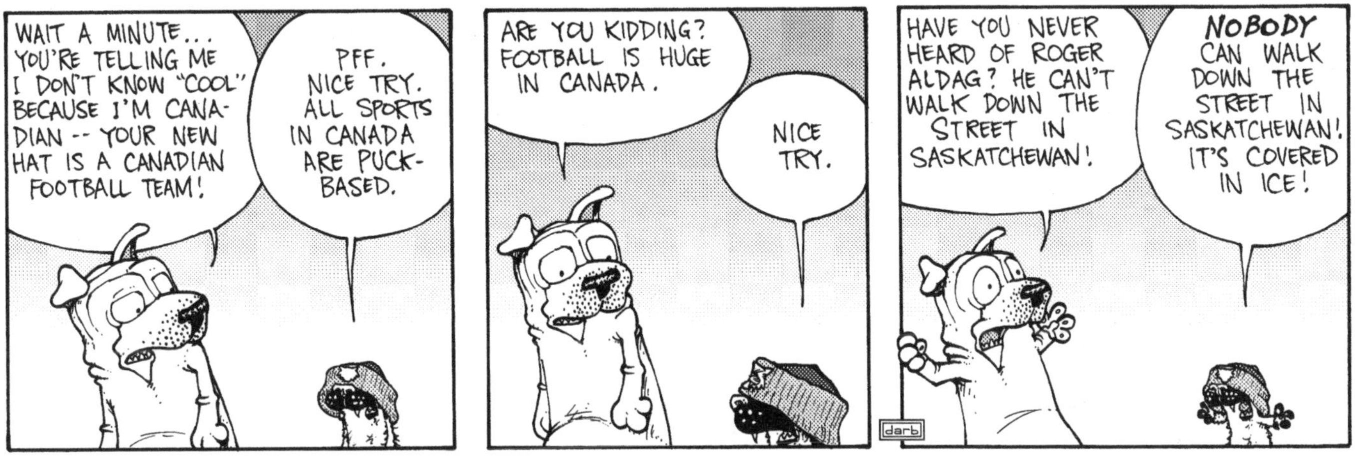
WAIT A MINUTE... YOU'RE TELLING ME I DON'T KNOW "COOL" BECAUSE I'M CANADIAN -- YOUR NEW HAT IS A CANADIAN FOOTBALL TEAM!
PFF. NICE TRY. ALL SPORTS IN CANADA ARE PUCK-BASED.
ARE YOU KIDDING? FOOTBALL IS HUGE IN CANADA.
NICE TRY.
darb
HAVE YOU NEVER HEARD OF ROGER ALDAG? HE CAN'T WALK DOWN THE STREET IN SASKATCHEWAN!
NOBODY CAN WALK DOWN THE STREET IN SASKATCHEWAN! IT'S COVERED IN ICE!

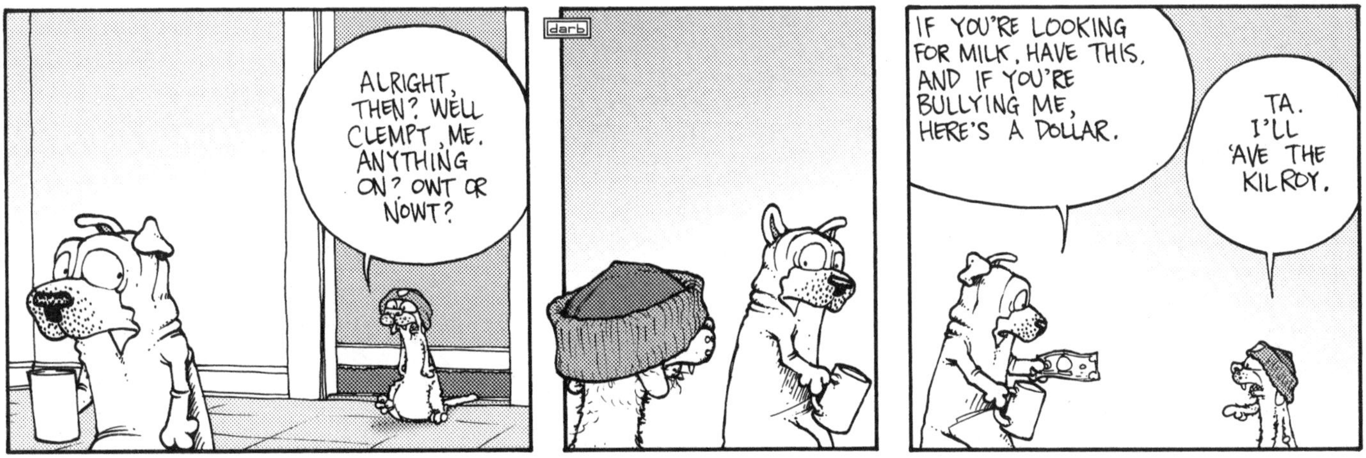
ALRIGHT, THEN? WELL CLEMPT ME. ANYTHING ON? OWT OR NOWT?
darb
IF YOU'RE LOOKING FOR MILK, HAVE THIS. AND IF YOU'RE BULLYING ME, HERE'S A DOLLAR.
TA. I'LL 'AVE THE KILROY.

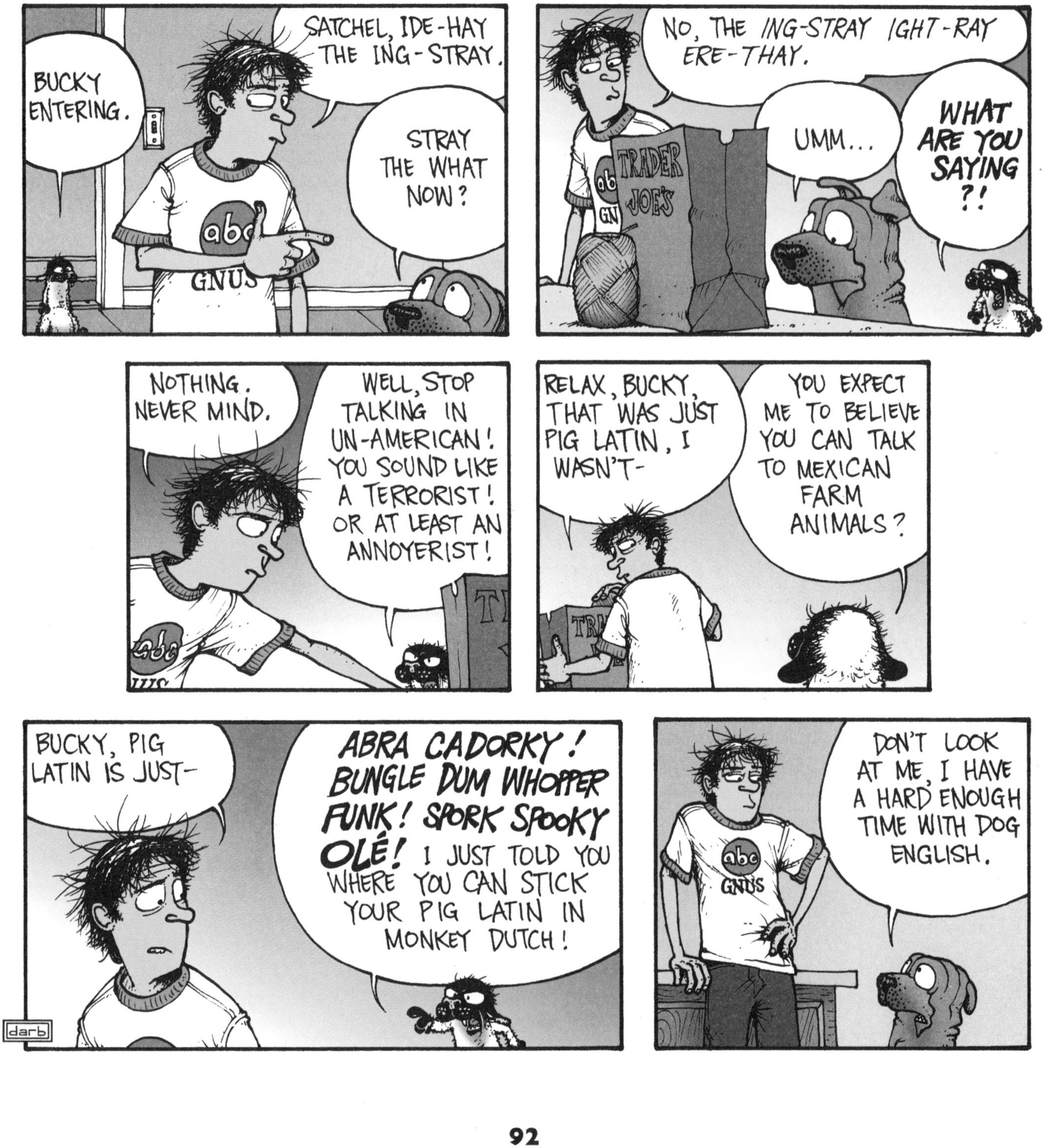
SATCHEL, IDE-HAY THE ING-STRAY.
BUCKY ENTERING.
STRAY THE WHAT NOW?
NO, THE ING-STRAY IGHT-RAY ERE-THAY.
UMM...
WHAT ARE YOU SAYING ?!
TRADER JOE'S
NOTHING. NEVER MIND.
WELL, STOP TALKING IN UN-AMERICAN! YOU SOUND LIKE A TERRORIST! OR AT LEAST AN ANNOYERIST!
RELAX, BUCKY, THAT WAS JUST PIG LATIN, I WASN'T-
YOU EXPECT ME TO BELIEVE YOU CAN TALK TO MEXICAN FARM ANIMALS?
BUCKY, PIG LATIN IS JUST-
ABRA CADORKY! BUNGLE DUM WHOPPER FUNK! SPORK SPOOKY OLÉ! I JUST TOLD YOU WHERE YOU CAN STICK YOUR PIG LATIN IN MONKEY DUTCH!
darb
DON'T LOOK AT ME, I HAVE A HARD ENOUGH TIME WITH DOG ENGLISH.

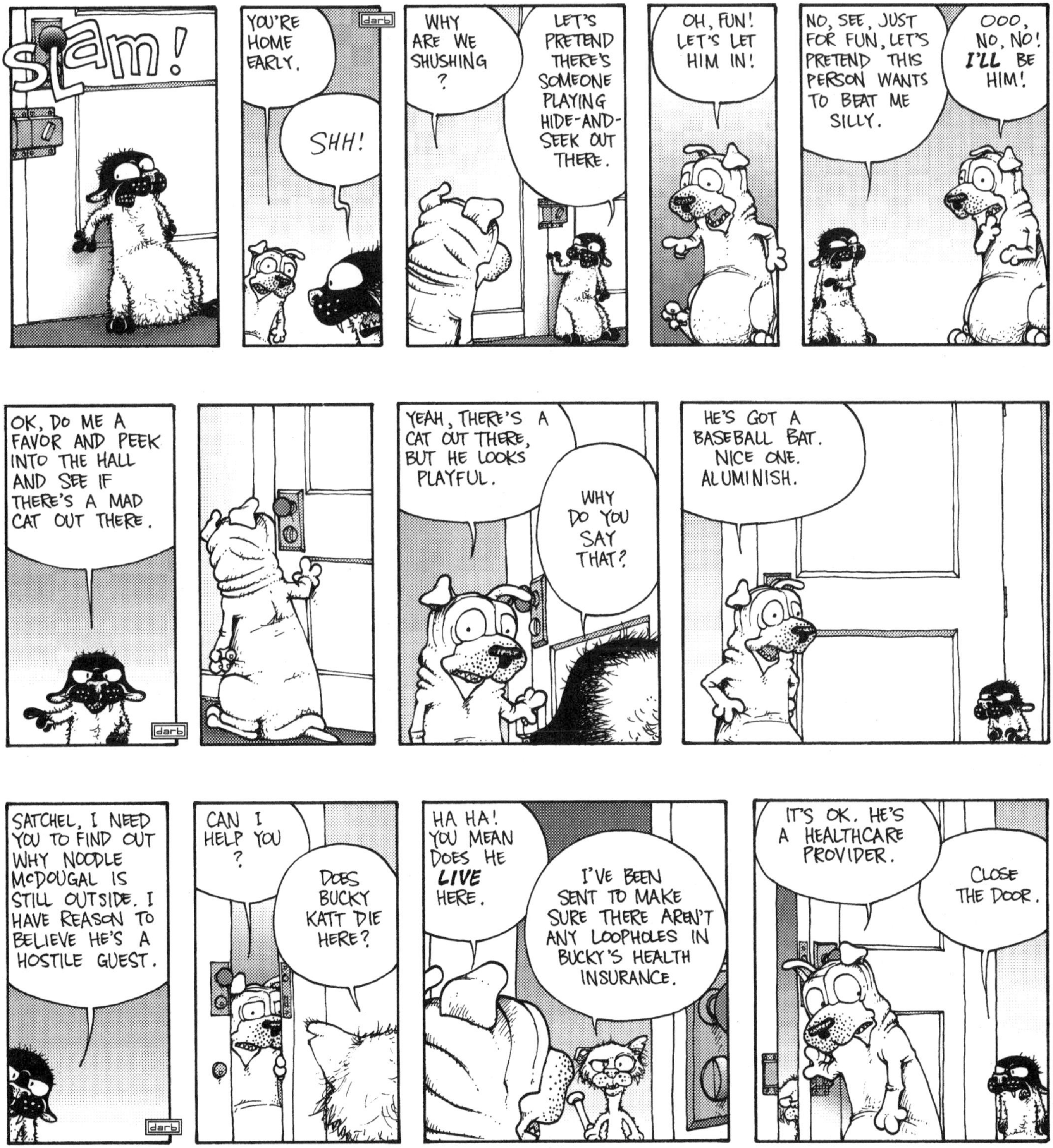
SLAM!
YOU'RE HOME EARLY.
SHH!
WHY ARE WE SHUSHING?
LET'S PRETEND THERE'S SOMEONE PLAYING HIDE-AND-SEEK OUT THERE.
OH, FUN! LET'S LET HIM IN!
NO, SEE, JUST FOR FUN, LET'S PRETEND THIS PERSON WANTS TO BEAT ME SILLY.
OOO, NO, NO! I'LL BE HIM!
OK, DO ME A FAVOR AND PEEK INTO THE HALL AND SEE IF THERE'S A MAD CAT OUT THERE.
YEAH, THERE'S A CAT OUT THERE, BUT HE LOOKS PLAYFUL.
WHY DO YOU SAY THAT?
HE'S GOT A BASEBALL BAT. NICE ONE. ALUMINISH.
SATCHEL, I NEED YOU TO FIND OUT WHY NOODLE McDOUGAL IS STILL OUTSIDE. I HAVE REASON TO BELIEVE HE'S A HOSTILE GUEST.
CAN I HELP YOU?
DOES BUCKY KATT DIE HERE?
HA HA! YOU MEAN DOES HE LIVE HERE.
I'VE BEEN SENT TO MAKE SURE THERE AREN'T ANY LOOPHOLES IN BUCKY'S HEALTH INSURANCE.
IT'S OK. HE'S A HEALTHCARE PROVIDER.
CLOSE THE DOOR.

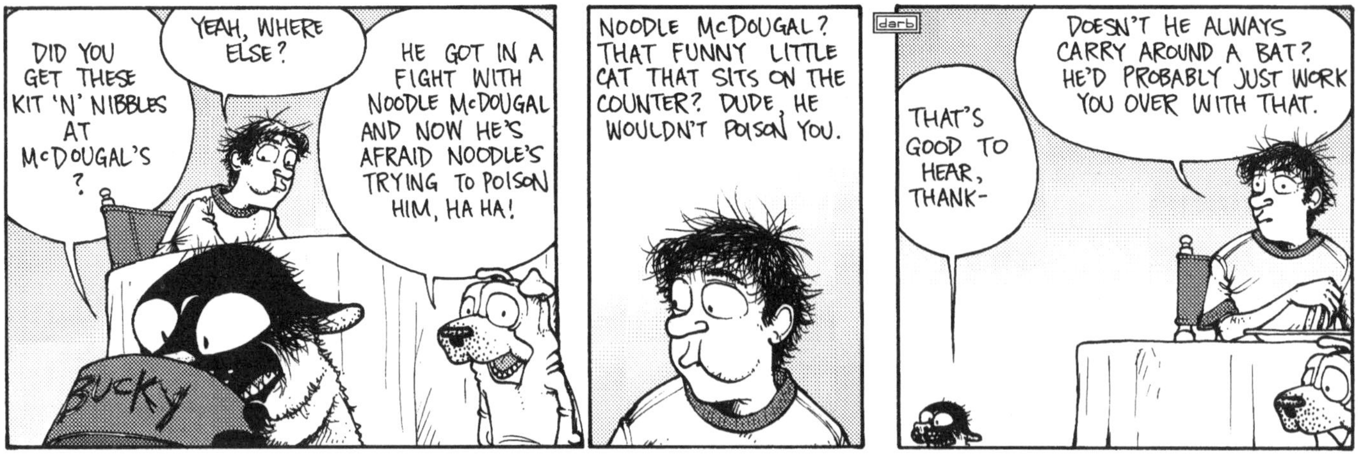
DID YOU GET THESE KIT 'N' NIBBLES AT McDOUGAL'S?
YEAH, WHERE ELSE?
HE GOT IN A FIGHT WITH NOODLE McDOUGAL AND NOW HE'S AFRAID NOODLE'S TRYING TO POISON HIM, HA HA!
BUCKY
NOODLE McDOUGAL? THAT FUNNY LITTLE CAT THAT SITS ON THE COUNTER? DUDE, HE WOULDN'T POISON YOU.
THAT'S GOOD TO HEAR, THANK-
DOESN'T HE ALWAYS CARRY AROUND A BAT? HE'D PROBABLY JUST WORK YOU OVER WITH THAT.

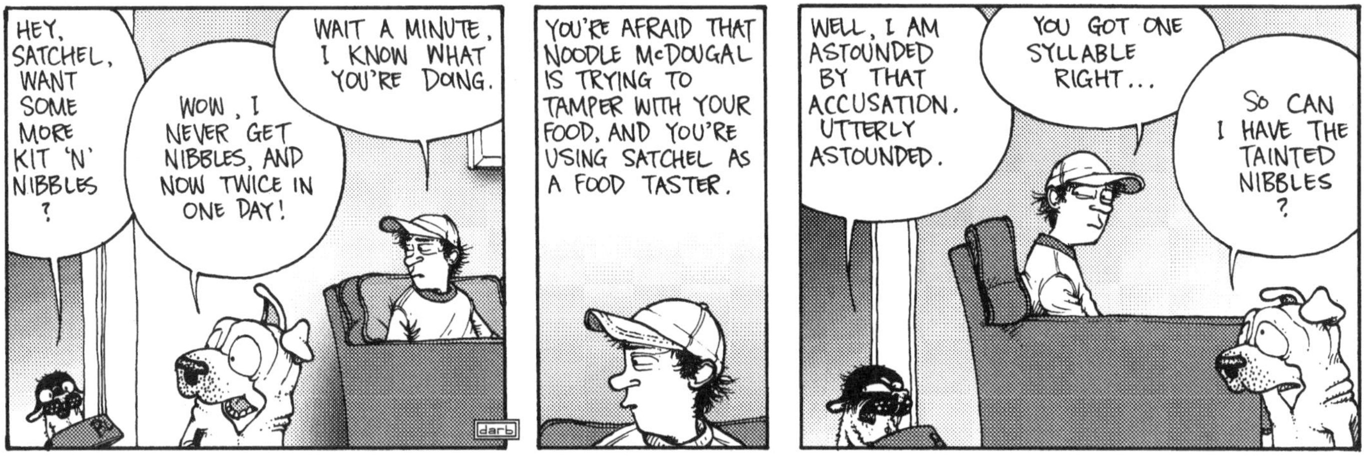
HEY, SATCHEL, WANT SOME MORE KIT 'N' NIBBLES?
WOW, I NEVER GET NIBBLES, AND NOW TWICE IN ONE DAY!
WAIT A MINUTE, I KNOW WHAT YOU'RE DOING.
YOU'RE AFRAID THAT NOODLE McDOUGAL IS TRYING TO TAMPER WITH YOUR FOOD, AND YOU'RE USING SATCHEL AS A FOOD TASTER.
WELL, I AM ASTOUNDED BY THAT ACCUSATION. UTTERLY ASTOUNDED.
YOU GOT ONE SYLLABLE RIGHT...
SO CAN I HAVE THE TAINTED NIBBLES?

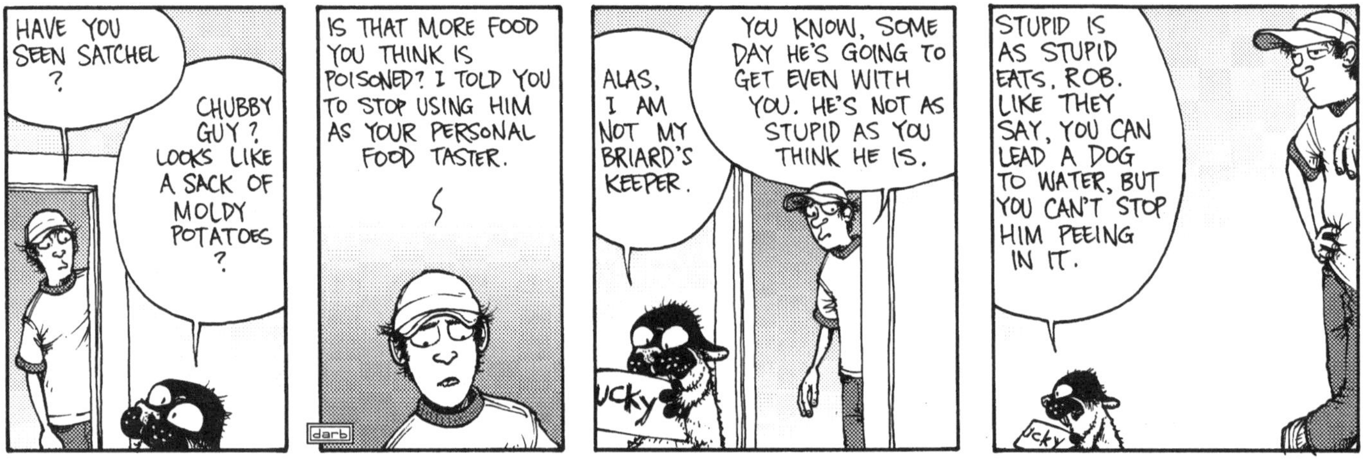
HAVE YOU SEEN SATCHEL?
CHUBBY GUY? LOOKS LIKE A SACK OF MOLDY POTATOES?
IS THAT MORE FOOD YOU THINK IS POISONED? I TOLD YOU TO STOP USING HIM AS YOUR PERSONAL FOOD TASTER.
ALAS, I AM NOT MY BRIARD'S KEEPER.
YOU KNOW, SOME DAY HE'S GOING TO GET EVEN WITH YOU. HE'S NOT AS STUPID AS YOU THINK HE IS.
STUPID IS AS STUPID EATS, ROB. LIKE THEY SAY, YOU CAN LEAD A DOG TO WATER, BUT YOU CAN'T STOP HIM PEEING IN IT.

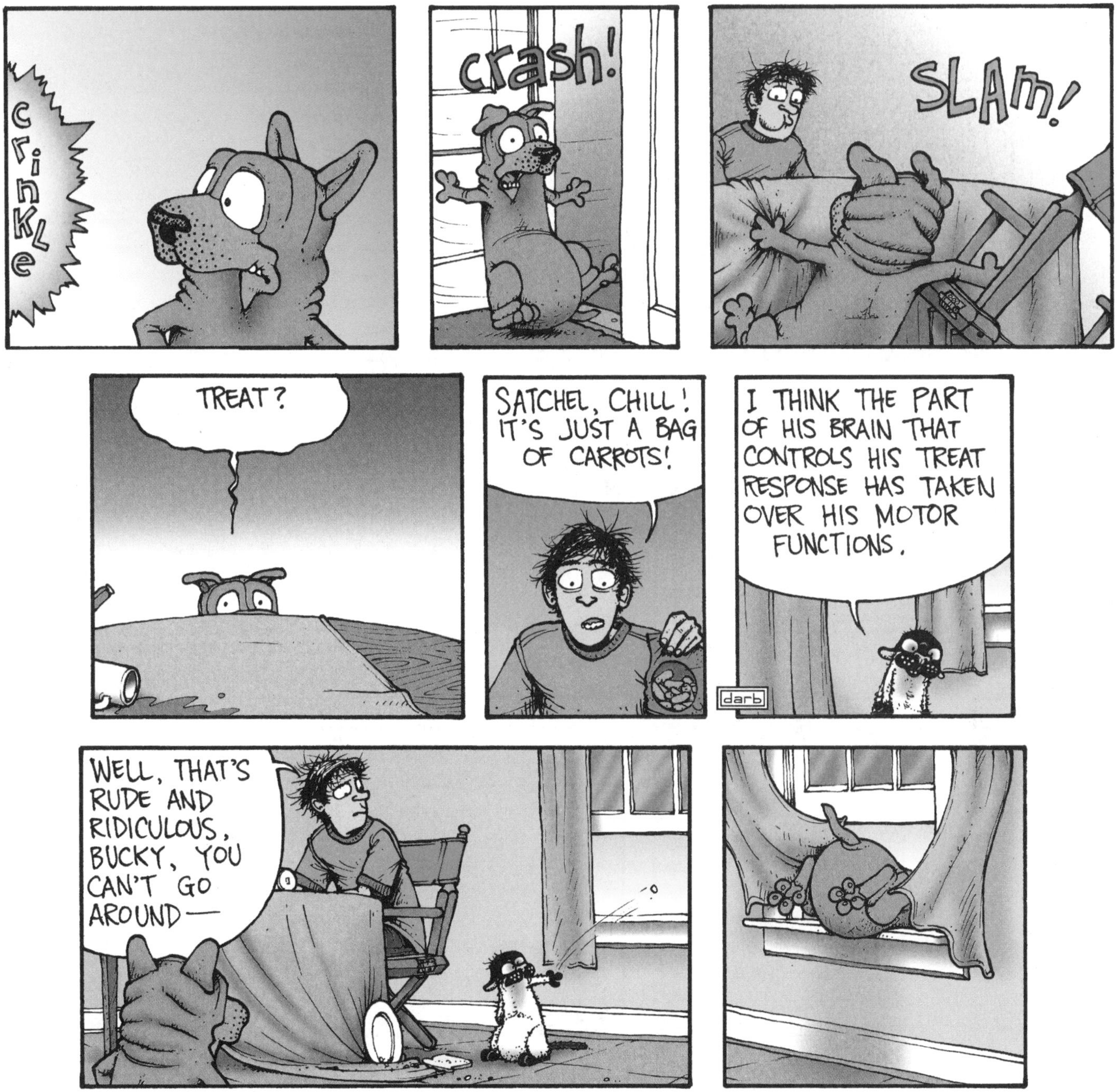
crinkle
crash!
SLAM!
TREAT?
SATCHEL, CHILL! IT'S JUST A BAG OF CARROTS!
I THINK THE PART OF HIS BRAIN THAT CONTROLS HIS TREAT RESPONSE HAS TAKEN OVER HIS MOTOR FUNCTIONS.
darb
WELL, THAT'S RUDE AND RIDICULOUS, BUCKY, YOU CAN'T GO AROUND—

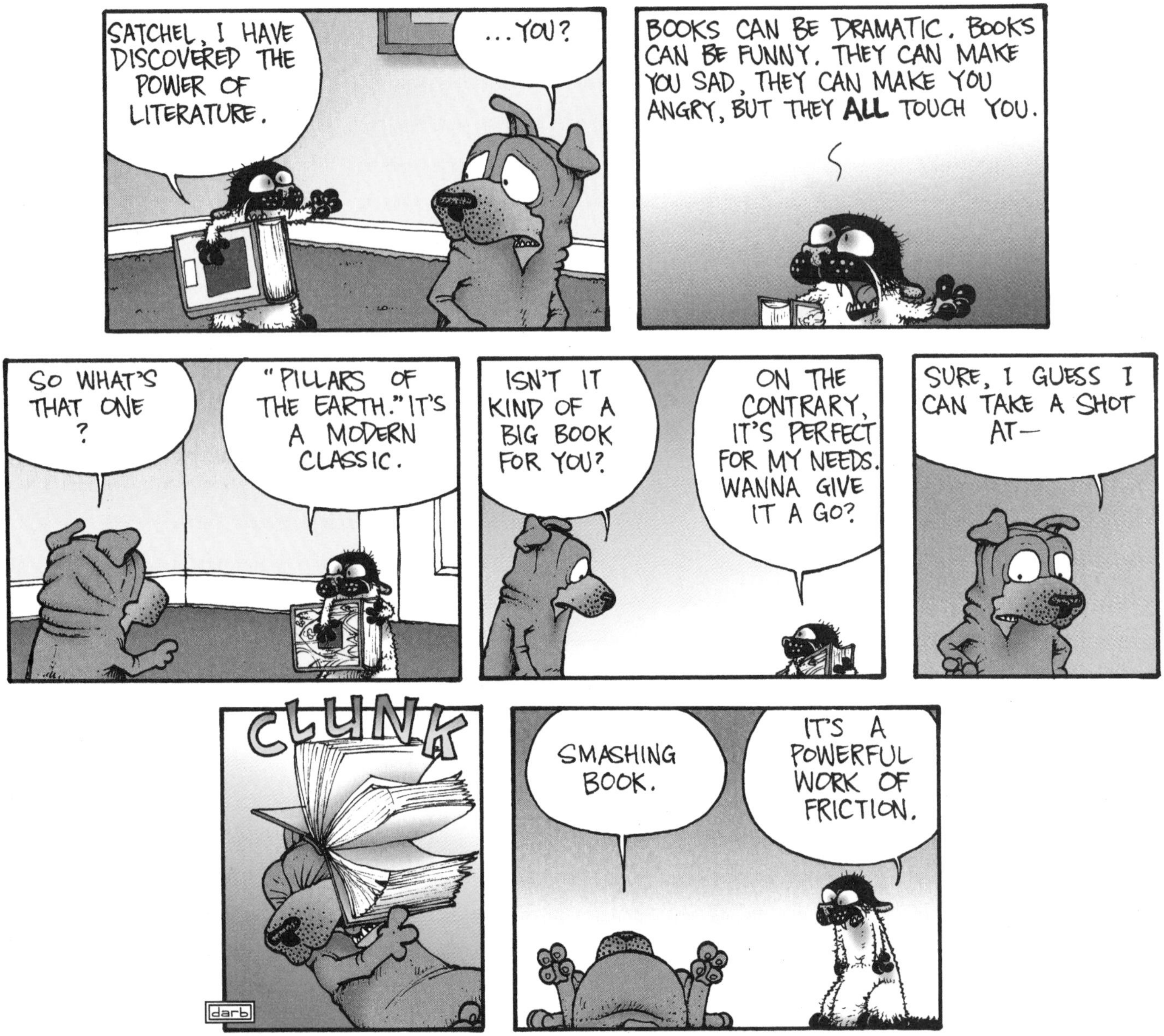
SATCHEL, I HAVE DISCOVERED THE POWER OF LITERATURE.
...YOU?
BOOKS CAN BE DRAMATIC. BOOKS CAN BE FUNNY. THEY CAN MAKE YOU SAD, THEY CAN MAKE YOU ANGRY, BUT THEY ALL TOUCH YOU.
SO WHAT'S THAT ONE ?
"PILLARS OF THE EARTH." IT'S A MODERN CLASSIC.
ISN'T IT KIND OF A BIG BOOK FOR YOU?
ON THE CONTRARY, IT'S PERFECT FOR MY NEEDS. WANNA GIVE IT A GO?
SURE, I GUESS I CAN TAKE A SHOT AT—
CLUNK
darb
SMASHING BOOK.
IT'S A POWERFUL WORK OF FRICTION.

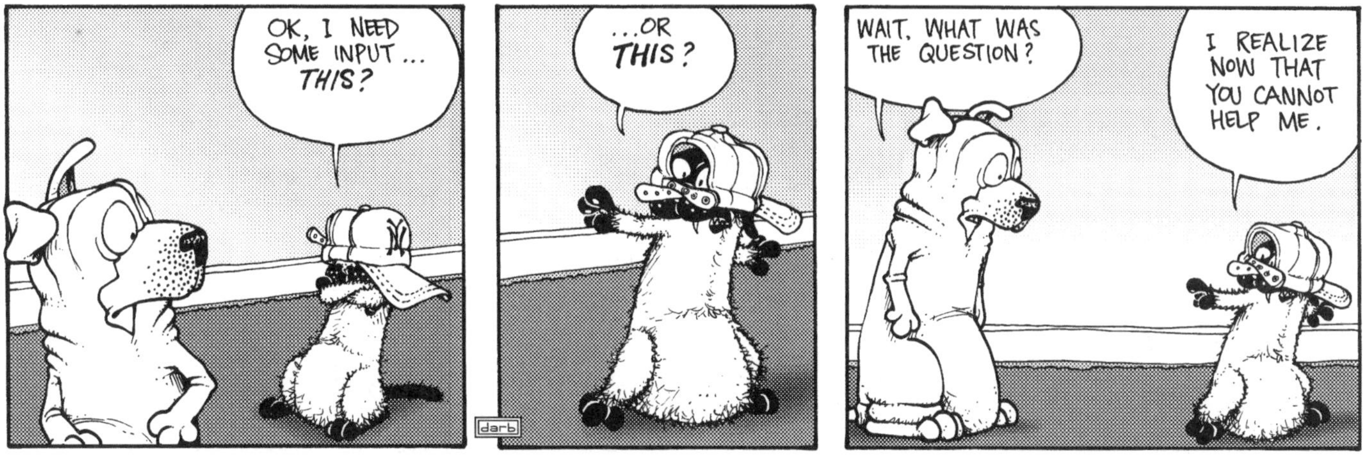
OK, I NEED SOME INPUT... *THIS?*
...OR *THIS?*
WAIT, WHAT WAS THE QUESTION?
I REALIZE NOW THAT YOU CANNOT HELP ME.

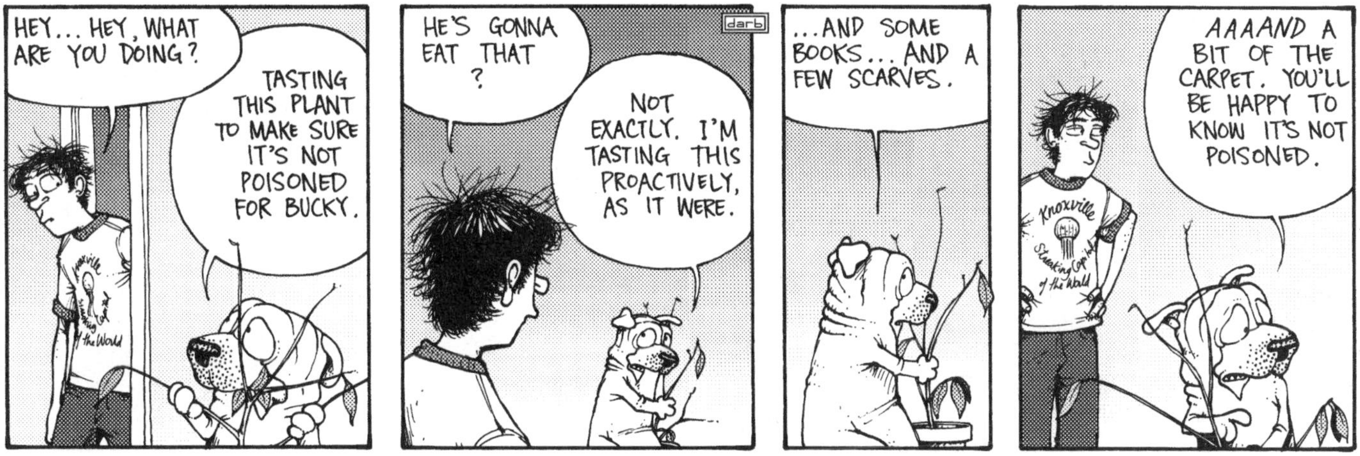
HEY... HEY, WHAT ARE YOU DOING?
TASTING THIS PLANT TO MAKE SURE IT'S NOT POISONED FOR BUCKY.
HE'S GONNA EAT THAT ?
NOT EXACTLY. I'M TASTING THIS PROACTIVELY, AS IT WERE.
...AND SOME BOOKS... AND A FEW SCARVES.
AAAAND A BIT OF THE CARPET. YOU'LL BE HAPPY TO KNOW IT'S NOT POISONED.

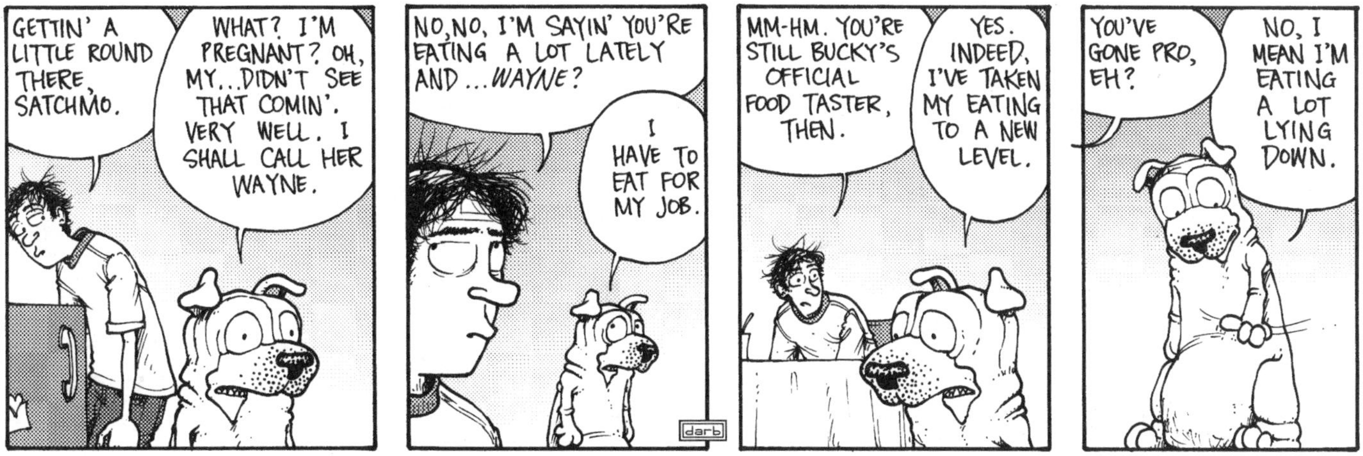
GETTIN' A LITTLE ROUND THERE, SATCHMO.
WHAT? I'M PREGNANT? OH, MY...DIDN'T SEE THAT COMIN'. VERY WELL. I SHALL CALL HER WAYNE.
NO, NO, I'M SAYIN' YOU'RE EATING A LOT LATELY AND ...*WAYNE?*
I HAVE TO EAT FOR MY JOB.
MM-HM. YOU'RE STILL BUCKY'S OFFICIAL FOOD TASTER, THEN.
YES. INDEED, I'VE TAKEN MY EATING TO A NEW LEVEL.
YOU'VE GONE PRO, EH?
NO, I MEAN I'M EATING A LOT LYING DOWN.

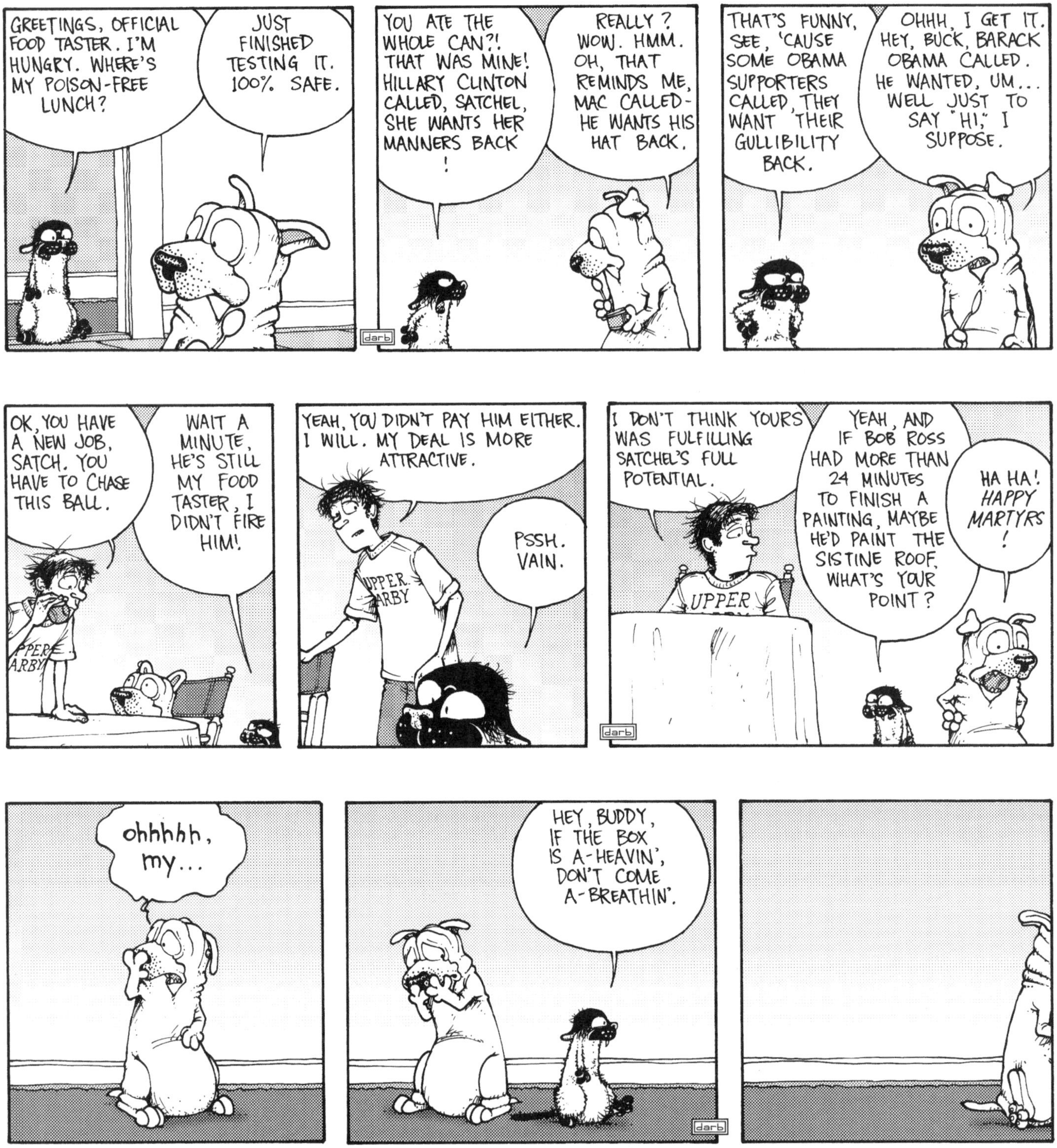
GREETINGS, OFFICIAL FOOD TASTER. I'M HUNGRY. WHERE'S MY POISON-FREE LUNCH?
JUST FINISHED TESTING IT. 100% SAFE.
darb
YOU ATE THE WHOLE CAN?! THAT WAS MINE! HILLARY CLINTON CALLED, SATCHEL, SHE WANTS HER MANNERS BACK !
REALLY? WOW. HMM. OH, THAT REMINDS ME, MAC CALLED- HE WANTS HIS HAT BACK.
THAT'S FUNNY, SEE, 'CAUSE SOME OBAMA SUPPORTERS CALLED, THEY WANT THEIR GULLIBILITY BACK.
OHHH, I GET IT. HEY, BUCK, BARACK OBAMA CALLED. HE WANTED, UM... WELL JUST TO SAY "HI," I SUPPOSE.
OK, YOU HAVE A NEW JOB, SATCH. YOU HAVE TO CHASE THIS BALL.
WAIT A MINUTE, HE'S STILL MY FOOD TASTER, I DIDN'T FIRE HIM!
YEAH, YOU DIDN'T PAY HIM EITHER. I WILL. MY DEAL IS MORE ATTRACTIVE.
PSSH. VAIN.
darb
I DON'T THINK YOURS WAS FULFILLING SATCHEL'S FULL POTENTIAL.
YEAH, AND IF BOB ROSS HAD MORE THAN 24 MINUTES TO FINISH A PAINTING, MAYBE HE'D PAINT THE SISTINE ROOF. WHAT'S YOUR POINT?
HA HA! HAPPY MARTYRS !
ohhhhh, my...
HEY, BUDDY, IF THE BOX IS A-HEAVIN', DON'T COME A-BREATHIN'.
darb

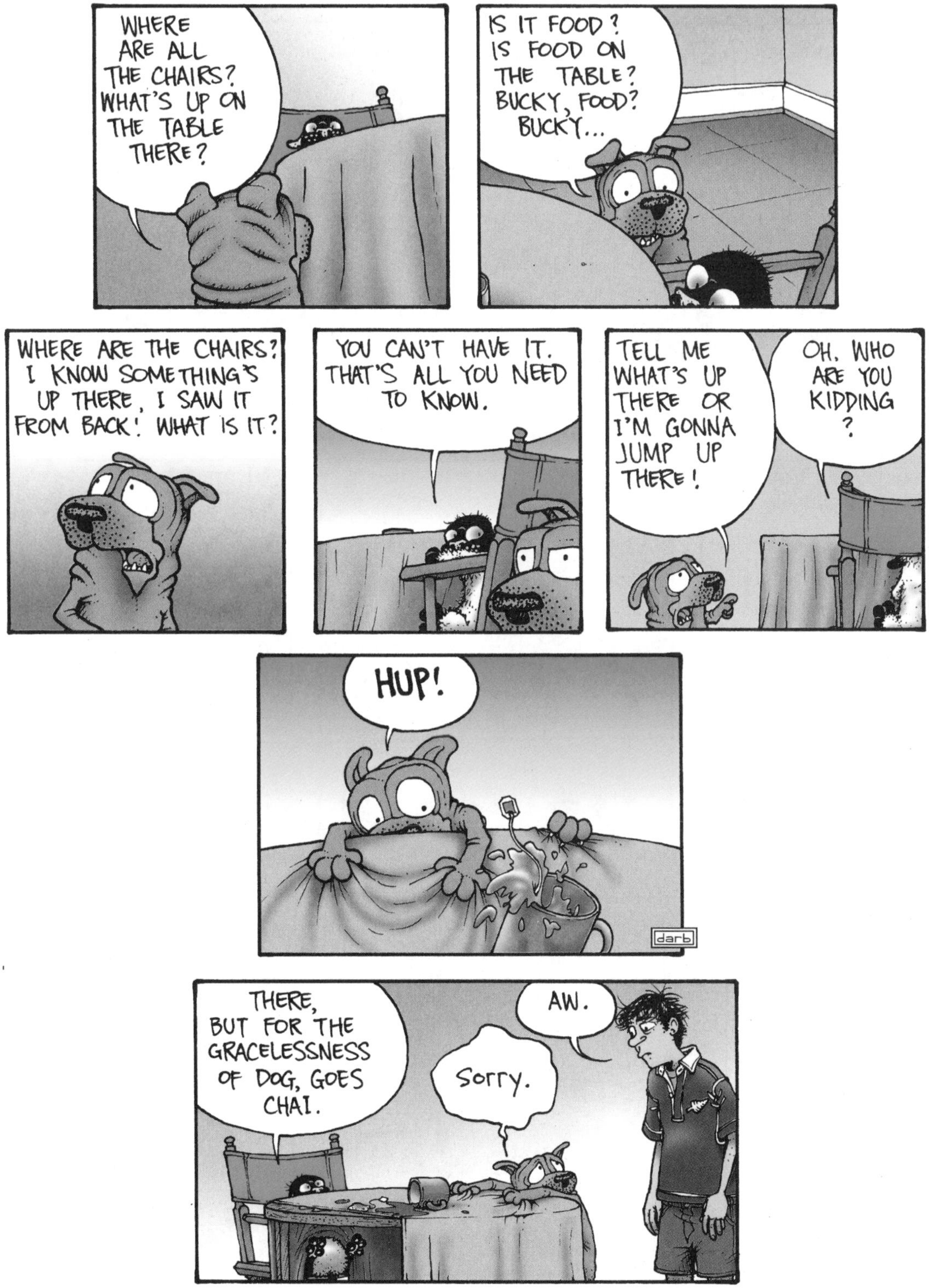
WHERE ARE ALL THE CHAIRS? WHAT'S UP ON THE TABLE THERE?
IS IT FOOD? IS FOOD ON THE TABLE? BUCKY, FOOD? BUCKY...
WHERE ARE THE CHAIRS? I KNOW SOMETHING'S UP THERE, I SAW IT FROM BACK! WHAT IS IT?
YOU CAN'T HAVE IT. THAT'S ALL YOU NEED TO KNOW.
TELL ME WHAT'S UP THERE OR I'M GONNA JUMP UP THERE!
OH. WHO ARE YOU KIDDING?
HUP!
darb
THERE, BUT FOR THE GRACELESSNESS OF DOG, GOES CHAI.
AW.
Sorry.

Panel 1:

HEY... WHERE'D YOU GET THAT CHEESE?

THE VENDING CUPBOARD.

Panel 2:

VENDING CUPBOARD? WHAT'S A VENDING CUPBOARD?

THE DRAWER IN THE KITCHEN WITH ALL THAT PRE-TASTED FOOD IN IT.

Panel 3:

Panel 4:

...YOU'RE EATING GARBAGE?

I THINK IT'S CALLED GOUDA.

Panel 5:

SATCHEL, THERE WAS A MOLDY BAGEL IN HERE, DID YOU SEE IT?

DEFINE THIS TERM "BAGEL" OF WHICH YOU SPEAK.

Panel 6:

ROUND THING... HOLE IN THE MIDDLE... MOLDY...

OK, YEAH, I ATE THAT.

Panel 7:

YOU ATE THE WHOLE THING?

NO, NO, I ATE THE THING AROUND THE HOLE.

Panel 8:

WHY THE "NO FOOD" SIGN ON THE TRASH DRAWER, BIG PINK?

SATCHEL'S BEEN EATING OUT OF THE CAN. THAT'S TO REMIND HIM NOT TO.

NO FOOD INSIDE!

Panel 9:

OK. SO WHEN DOES THE "NO BEVERAGE" SIGN GO ON THE TOILET? OR THE "NO GUM" SIGN ON THE NEWSPAPER?

Panel 10:

AND DO THEY MAKE "NO GIRLFRIEND" IRON-ON PATCHES FOR YOUR PANT LEGS OR DO YOU—

I'M EATING HERE.

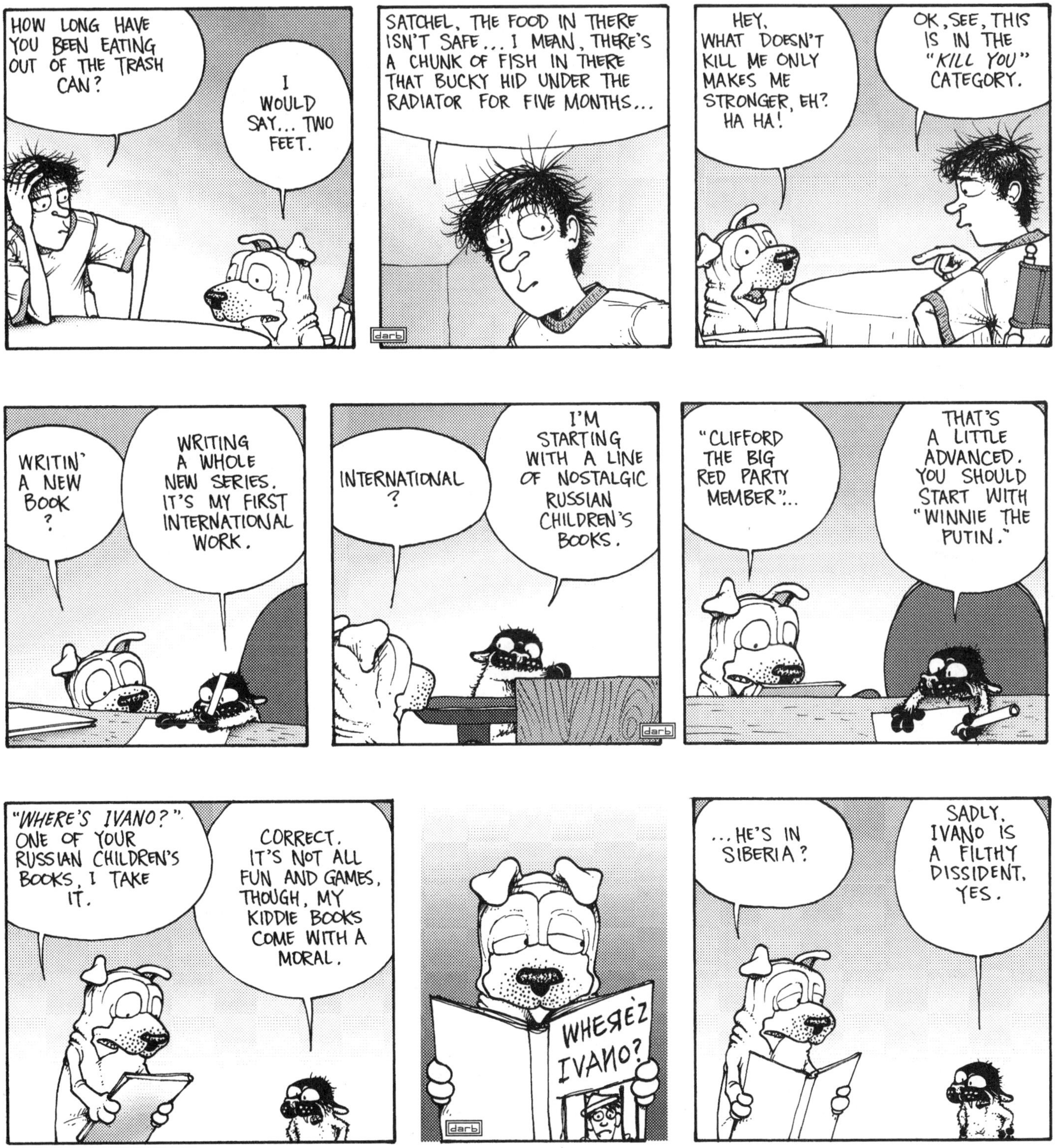
HOW LONG HAVE YOU BEEN EATING OUT OF THE TRASH CAN?
I WOULD SAY... TWO FEET.
SATCHEL, THE FOOD IN THERE ISN'T SAFE... I MEAN, THERE'S A CHUNK OF FISH IN THERE THAT BUCKY HID UNDER THE RADIATOR FOR FIVE MONTHS...
darb
HEY, WHAT DOESN'T KILL ME ONLY MAKES ME STRONGER, EH? HA HA!
OK, SEE, THIS IS IN THE "KILL YOU" CATEGORY.
WRITIN' A NEW BOOK?
WRITING A WHOLE NEW SERIES. IT'S MY FIRST INTERNATIONAL WORK.
INTERNATIONAL?
I'M STARTING WITH A LINE OF NOSTALGIC RUSSIAN CHILDREN'S BOOKS.
darb
"CLIFFORD THE BIG RED PARTY MEMBER"...
THAT'S A LITTLE ADVANCED. YOU SHOULD START WITH "WINNIE THE PUTIN."
"WHERE'S IVANO?" ONE OF YOUR RUSSIAN CHILDREN'S BOOKS, I TAKE IT.
CORRECT. IT'S NOT ALL FUN AND GAMES, THOUGH, MY KIDDIE BOOKS COME WITH A MORAL.
WHEЯE'Z IVAИO?
darb
...HE'S IN SIBERIA?
SADLY, IVANO IS A FILTHY DISSIDENT, YES.

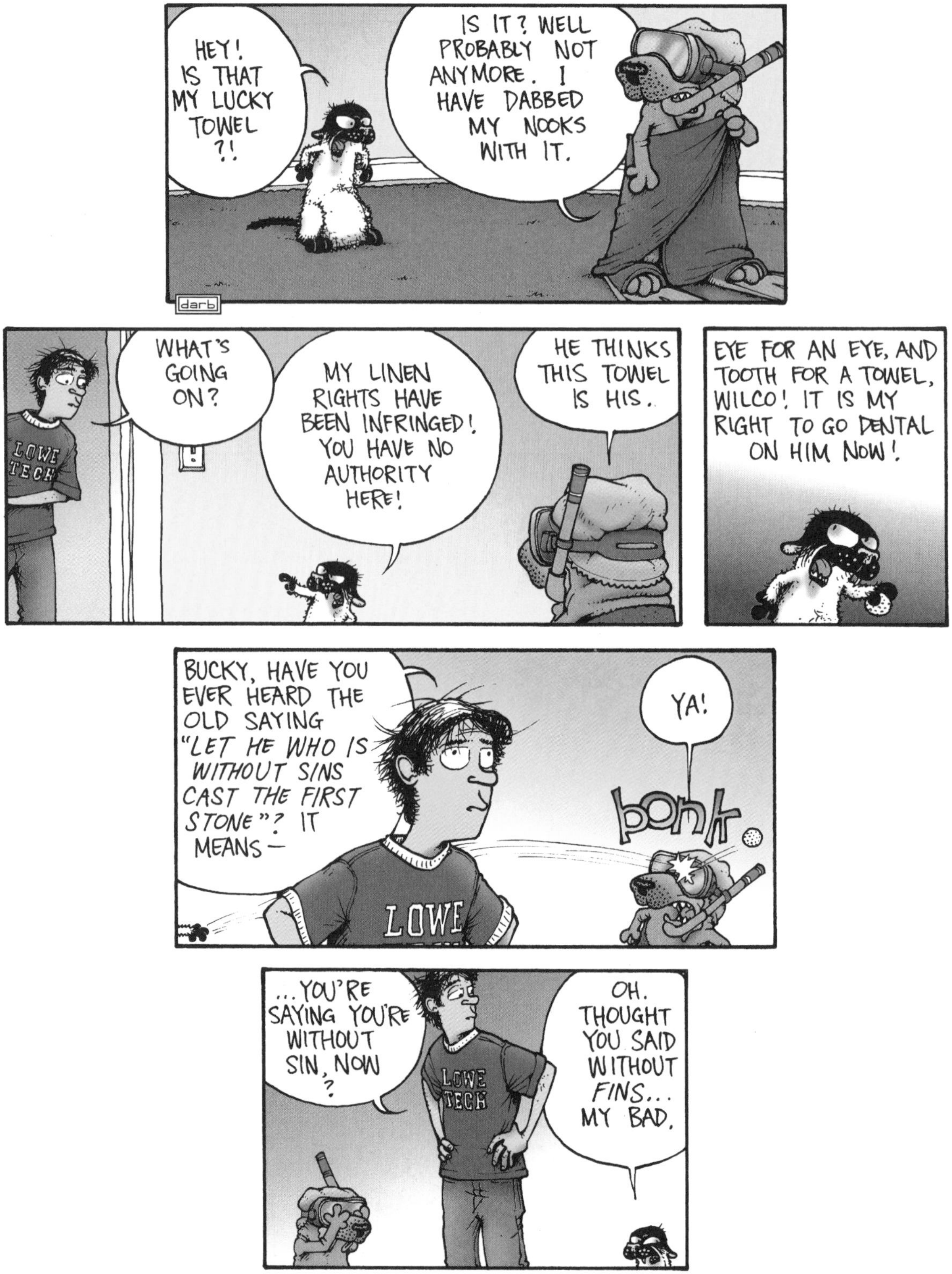
HEY! IS THAT MY LUCKY TOWEL ?!
IS IT? WELL PROBABLY NOT ANYMORE. I HAVE DABBED MY NOOKS WITH IT.
darb
WHAT'S GOING ON?
MY LINEN RIGHTS HAVE BEEN INFRINGED! YOU HAVE NO AUTHORITY HERE!
HE THINKS THIS TOWEL IS HIS.
LOWE TECH
EYE FOR AN EYE, AND TOOTH FOR A TOWEL, WILCO! IT IS MY RIGHT TO GO DENTAL ON HIM NOW!
BUCKY, HAVE YOU EVER HEARD THE OLD SAYING *"LET HE WHO IS WITHOUT SINS CAST THE FIRST STONE"*? IT MEANS—
YA!
bonk
LOWE
...YOU'RE SAYING YOU'RE WITHOUT SIN, NOW ?
LOWE TECH
OH. THOUGHT YOU SAID WITHOUT *FINS*... MY BAD.

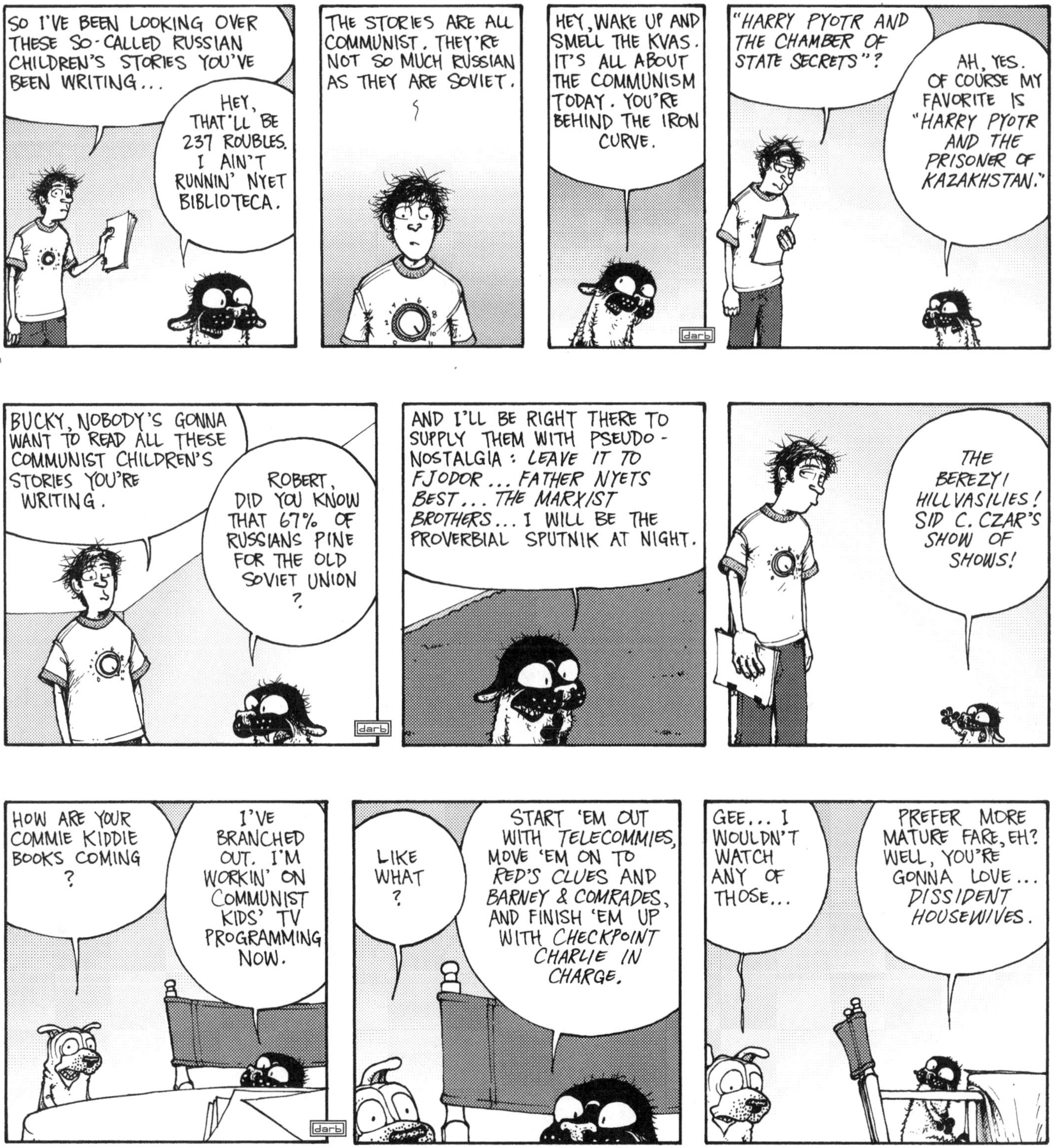
SO I'VE BEEN LOOKING OVER THESE SO-CALLED RUSSIAN CHILDREN'S STORIES YOU'VE BEEN WRITING...
HEY, THAT'LL BE 237 ROUBLES. I AIN'T RUNNIN' NYET BIBLIOTECA.
THE STORIES ARE ALL COMMUNIST. THEY'RE NOT SO MUCH RUSSIAN AS THEY ARE SOVIET.
HEY, WAKE UP AND SMELL THE KVAS. IT'S ALL ABOUT THE COMMUNISM TODAY. YOU'RE BEHIND THE IRON CURVE.
darb
"HARRY PYOTR AND THE CHAMBER OF STATE SECRETS"?
AH, YES. OF COURSE MY FAVORITE IS "HARRY PYOTR AND THE PRISONER OF KAZAKHSTAN."
BUCKY, NOBODY'S GONNA WANT TO READ ALL THESE COMMUNIST CHILDREN'S STORIES YOU'RE WRITING.
ROBERT, DID YOU KNOW THAT 67% OF RUSSIANS PINE FOR THE OLD SOVIET UNION?
darb
AND I'LL BE RIGHT THERE TO SUPPLY THEM WITH PSEUDO-NOSTALGIA: LEAVE IT TO FJODOR... FATHER NYETS BEST... THE MARXIST BROTHERS... I WILL BE THE PROVERBIAL SPUTNIK AT NIGHT.
THE BEREZYI HILLVASILIES! SID C. CZAR'S SHOW OF SHOWS!
HOW ARE YOUR COMMIE KIDDIE BOOKS COMING?
I'VE BRANCHED OUT. I'M WORKIN' ON COMMUNIST KIDS' TV PROGRAMMING NOW.
darb
LIKE WHAT?
START 'EM OUT WITH TELECOMMIES, MOVE 'EM ON TO RED'S CLUES AND BARNEY & COMRADES, AND FINISH 'EM UP WITH CHECKPOINT CHARLIE IN CHARGE.
GEE... I WOULDN'T WATCH ANY OF THOSE...
PREFER MORE MATURE FARE, EH? WELL, YOU'RE GONNA LOVE... DISSIDENT HOUSEWIVES.

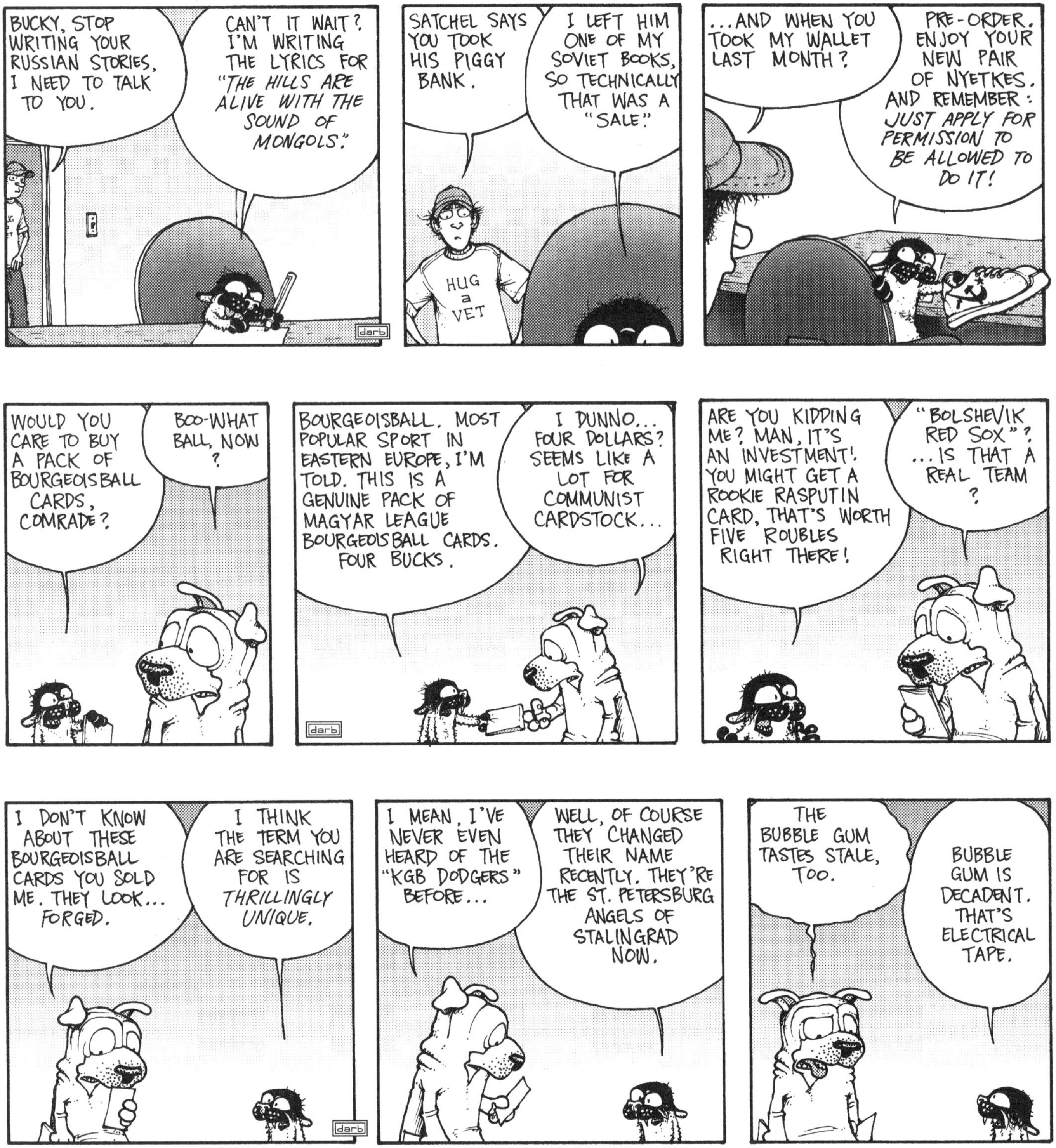
BUCKY, STOP WRITING YOUR RUSSIAN STORIES. I NEED TO TALK TO YOU.
CAN'T IT WAIT? I'M WRITING THE LYRICS FOR "THE HILLS ARE ALIVE WITH THE SOUND OF MONGOLS."
darb
SATCHEL SAYS YOU TOOK HIS PIGGY BANK.
I LEFT HIM ONE OF MY SOVIET BOOKS, SO TECHNICALLY THAT WAS A "SALE."
HUG a VET
...AND WHEN YOU TOOK MY WALLET LAST MONTH?
PRE-ORDER. ENJOY YOUR NEW PAIR OF NYETKES. AND REMEMBER: JUST APPLY FOR PERMISSION TO BE ALLOWED TO DO IT!
WOULD YOU CARE TO BUY A PACK OF BOURGEOISBALL CARDS, COMRADE?
BOO-WHAT BALL, NOW?
BOURGEOISBALL. MOST POPULAR SPORT IN EASTERN EUROPE, I'M TOLD. THIS IS A GENUINE PACK OF MAGYAR LEAGUE BOURGEOISBALL CARDS. FOUR BUCKS.
I DUNNO... FOUR DOLLARS? SEEMS LIKE A LOT FOR COMMUNIST CARDSTOCK...
darb
ARE YOU KIDDING ME? MAN, IT'S AN INVESTMENT! YOU MIGHT GET A ROOKIE RASPUTIN CARD, THAT'S WORTH FIVE ROUBLES RIGHT THERE!
"BOLSHEVIK RED SOX"? ...IS THAT A REAL TEAM?
I DON'T KNOW ABOUT THESE BOURGEOISBALL CARDS YOU SOLD ME. THEY LOOK... FORGED.
I THINK THE TERM YOU ARE SEARCHING FOR IS THRILLINGLY UNIQUE.
darb
I MEAN, I'VE NEVER EVEN HEARD OF THE "KGB DODGERS" BEFORE...
WELL, OF COURSE THEY CHANGED THEIR NAME RECENTLY. THEY'RE THE ST. PETERSBURG ANGELS OF STALINGRAD NOW.
THE BUBBLE GUM TASTES STALE, TOO.
BUBBLE GUM IS DECADENT. THAT'S ELECTRICAL TAPE.

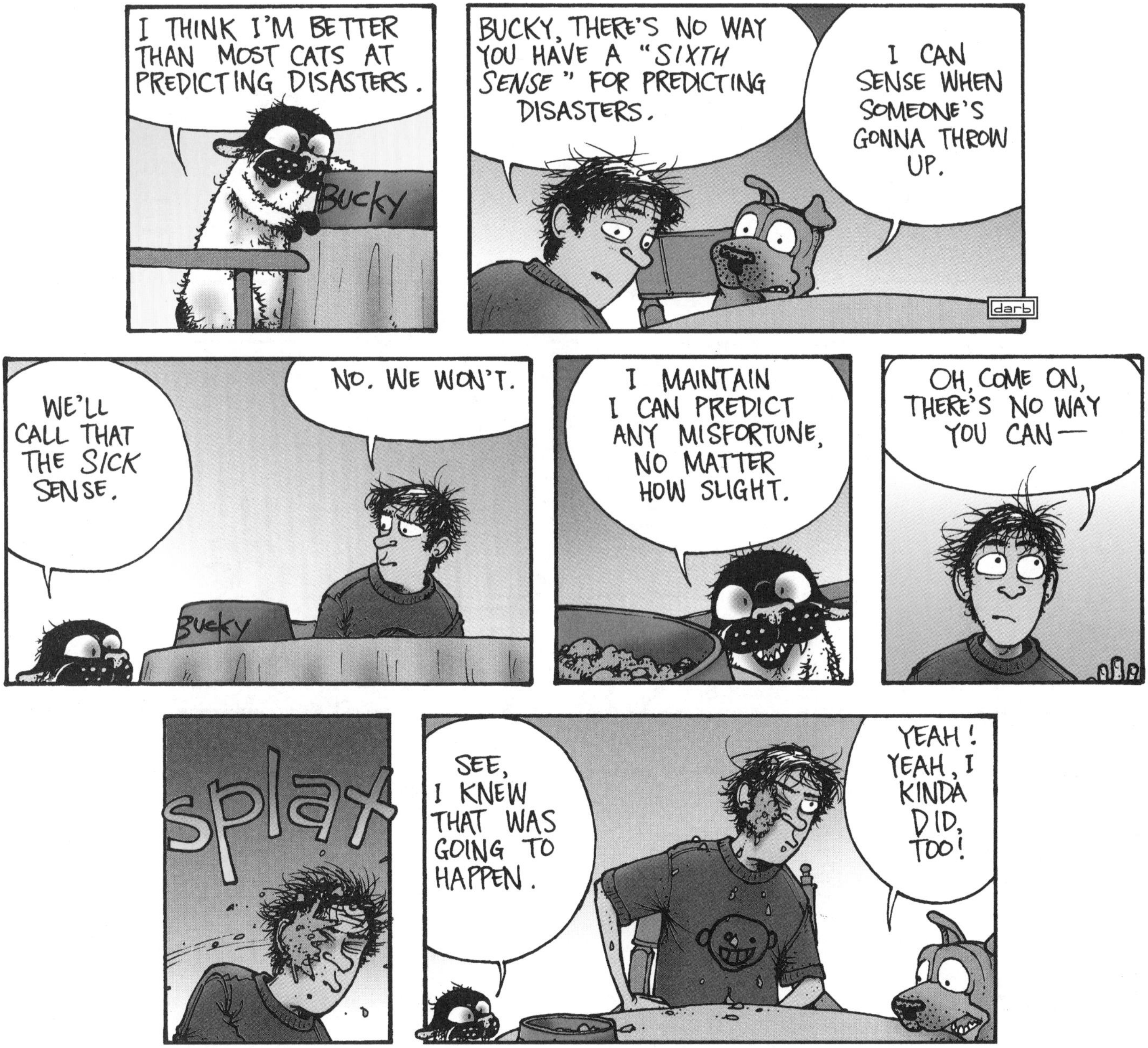
I THINK I'M BETTER THAN MOST CATS AT PREDICTING DISASTERS.
BUCKY
BUCKY, THERE'S NO WAY YOU HAVE A "SIXTH SENSE" FOR PREDICTING DISASTERS.
I CAN SENSE WHEN SOMEONE'S GONNA THROW UP.
darb
WE'LL CALL THAT THE SICK SENSE.
NO. WE WON'T.
BUCKY
I MAINTAIN I CAN PREDICT ANY MISFORTUNE, NO MATTER HOW SLIGHT.
OH, COME ON, THERE'S NO WAY YOU CAN—
splat
SEE, I KNEW THAT WAS GOING TO HAPPEN.
YEAH! YEAH, I KINDA DID, TOO!

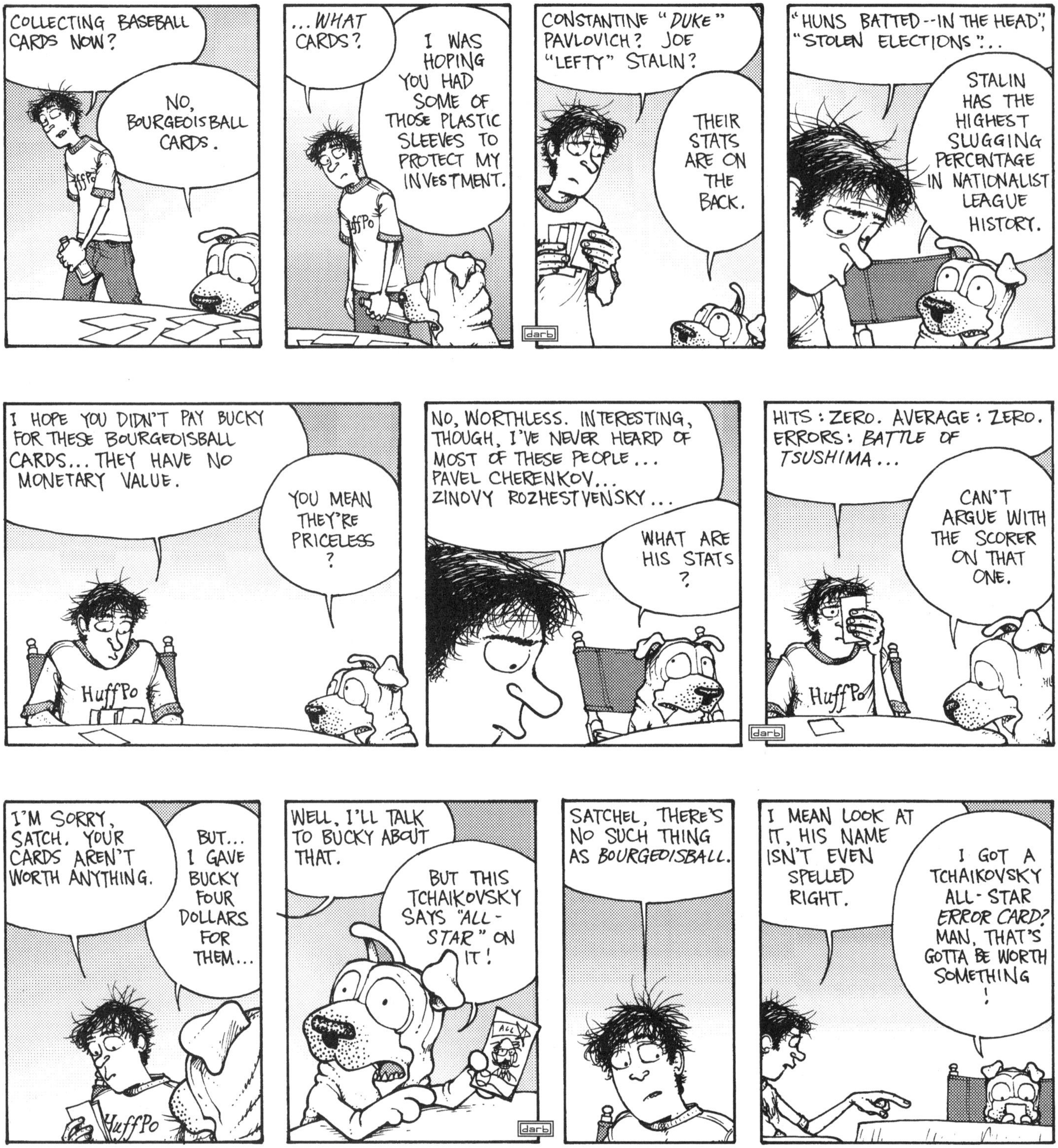
COLLECTING BASEBALL CARDS NOW?
NO, BOURGEOISBALL CARDS.
...WHAT CARDS?
I WAS HOPING YOU HAD SOME OF THOSE PLASTIC SLEEVES TO PROTECT MY INVESTMENT.
CONSTANTINE "DUKE" PAVLOVICH? JOE "LEFTY" STALIN?
THEIR STATS ARE ON THE BACK.
"HUNS BATTED--IN THE HEAD", "STOLEN ELECTIONS"...
STALIN HAS THE HIGHEST SLUGGING PERCENTAGE IN NATIONALIST LEAGUE HISTORY.
darb
I HOPE YOU DIDN'T PAY BUCKY FOR THESE BOURGEOISBALL CARDS... THEY HAVE NO MONETARY VALUE.
YOU MEAN THEY'RE PRICELESS?
NO, WORTHLESS. INTERESTING, THOUGH, I'VE NEVER HEARD OF MOST OF THESE PEOPLE... PAVEL CHERENKOV... ZINOVY ROZHESTVENSKY...
WHAT ARE HIS STATS?
HITS: ZERO. AVERAGE: ZERO. ERRORS: BATTLE OF TSUSHIMA...
CAN'T ARGUE WITH THE SCORER ON THAT ONE.
darb
I'M SORRY, SATCH. YOUR CARDS AREN'T WORTH ANYTHING.
BUT... I GAVE BUCKY FOUR DOLLARS FOR THEM...
WELL, I'LL TALK TO BUCKY ABOUT THAT.
BUT THIS TCHAIKOVSKY SAYS "ALL-STAR" ON IT!
darb
SATCHEL, THERE'S NO SUCH THING AS BOURGEOISBALL.
I MEAN LOOK AT IT, HIS NAME ISN'T EVEN SPELLED RIGHT.
I GOT A TCHAIKOVSKY ALL-STAR ERROR CARD? MAN, THAT'S GOTTA BE WORTH SOMETHING!

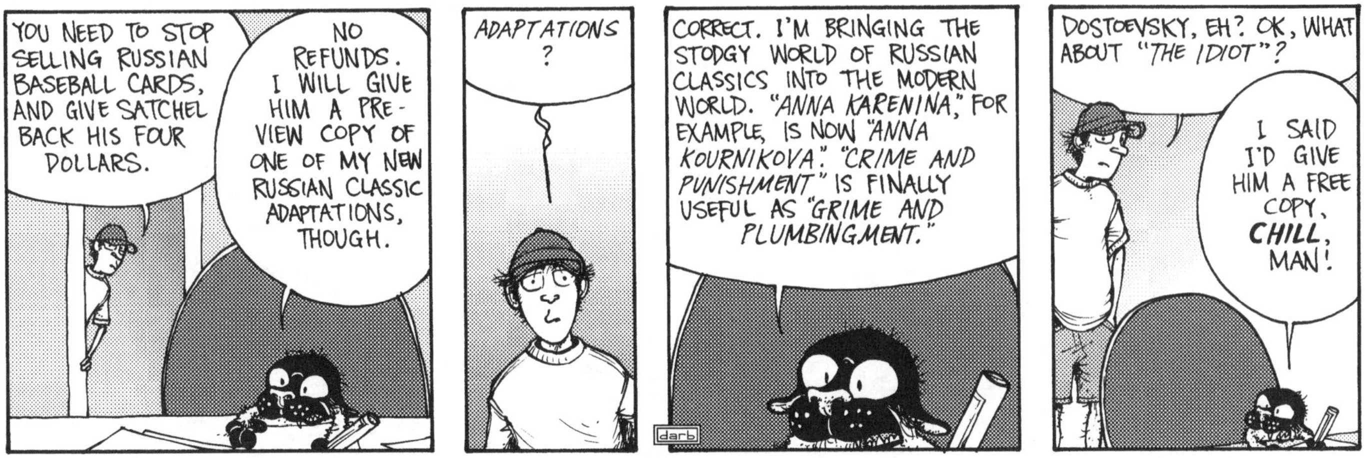
YOU NEED TO STOP SELLING RUSSIAN BASEBALL CARDS, AND GIVE SATCHEL BACK HIS FOUR DOLLARS.
NO REFUNDS. I WILL GIVE HIM A PRE-VIEW COPY OF ONE OF MY NEW RUSSIAN CLASSIC ADAPTATIONS, THOUGH.
ADAPTATIONS?
CORRECT. I'M BRINGING THE STODGY WORLD OF RUSSIAN CLASSICS INTO THE MODERN WORLD. "ANNA KARENINA," FOR EXAMPLE, IS NOW "ANNA KOURNIKOVA." "CRIME AND PUNISHMENT" IS FINALLY USEFUL AS "GRIME AND PLUMBINGMENT."
DOSTOEVSKY, EH? OK, WHAT ABOUT "THE IDIOT"?
I SAID I'D GIVE HIM A FREE COPY. CHILL, MAN!

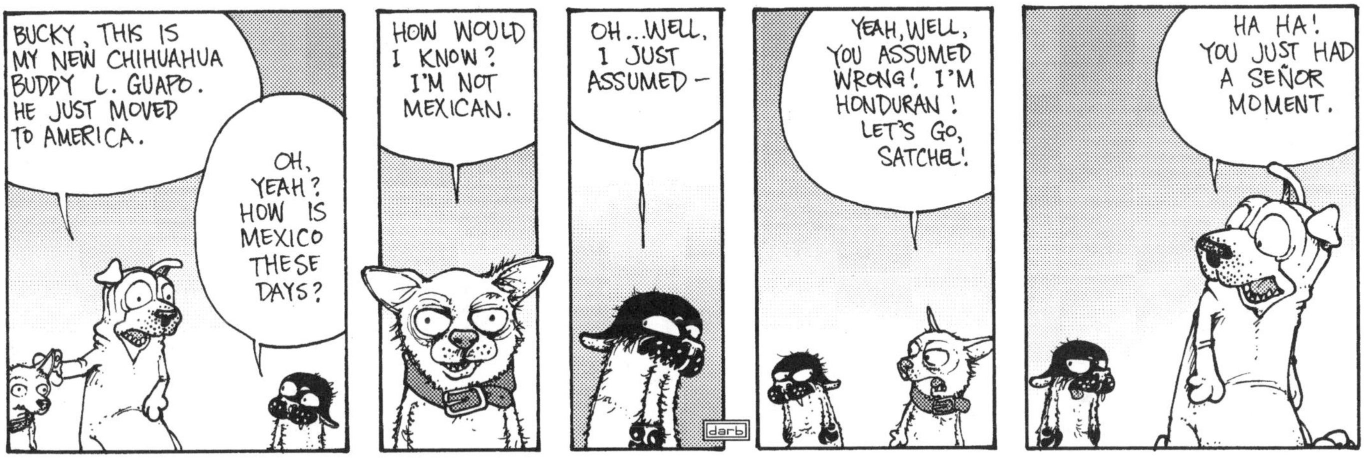
BUCKY, THIS IS MY NEW CHIHUAHUA BUDDY L. GUAPO. HE JUST MOVED TO AMERICA.
OH, YEAH? HOW IS MEXICO THESE DAYS?
HOW WOULD I KNOW? I'M NOT MEXICAN.
OH...WELL, I JUST ASSUMED—
YEAH, WELL, YOU ASSUMED WRONG! I'M HONDURAN! LET'S GO, SATCHEL!
HA HA! YOU JUST HAD A SEÑOR MOMENT.

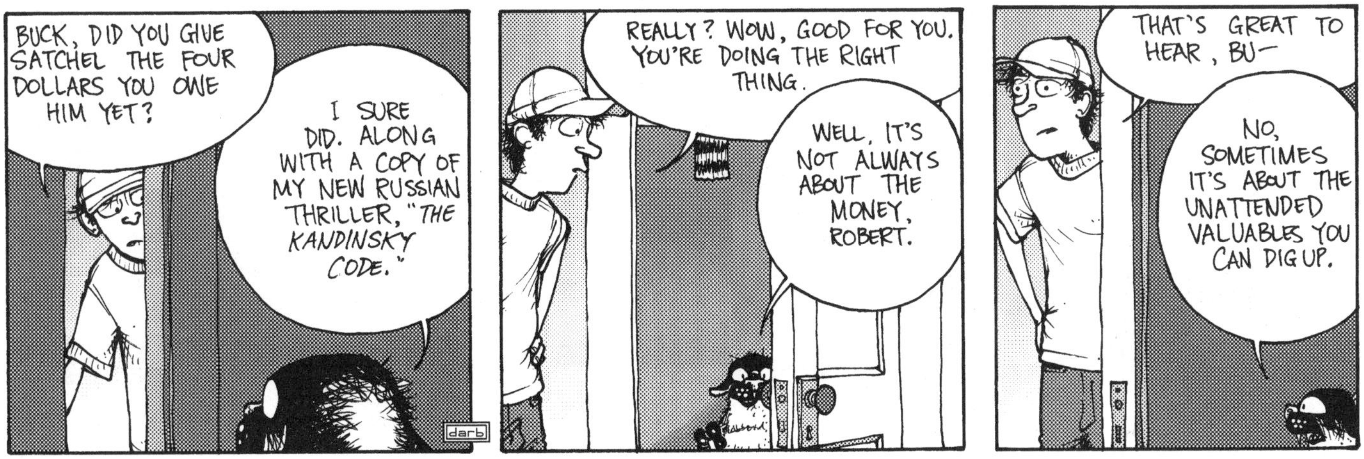
BUCK, DID YOU GIVE SATCHEL THE FOUR DOLLARS YOU OWE HIM YET?
I SURE DID. ALONG WITH A COPY OF MY NEW RUSSIAN THRILLER, "THE KANDINSKY CODE."
REALLY? WOW, GOOD FOR YOU. YOU'RE DOING THE RIGHT THING.
WELL, IT'S NOT ALWAYS ABOUT THE MONEY, ROBERT.
THAT'S GREAT TO HEAR, BU—
NO, SOMETIMES IT'S ABOUT THE UNATTENDED VALUABLES YOU CAN DIG UP.

WHAT IS THAT?

SUPPOSED TO BE A VIDEO OF THE FIRST REAL SPACE ALIEN.

AW, FOR THE LOVE OF... NOW WE HAVE TO BUILD A △@#% ROOF!

WHO DOES?

WE DO! U.S. AMERICANS! FIRST THE WALL IN TEXAZONA AND NOW THIS!

A ROOF? OVER THE ENTIRE COUNTRY?

YOU GOT A BETTER IDEA, WHINESTEIN?! WALL AIN'T GONNA KEEP OUT **SKY CRITTERS**!

darb

ROOF AIN'T GONNA BE EASY, EITHER, CONNECTICUT IS **SOFT**.

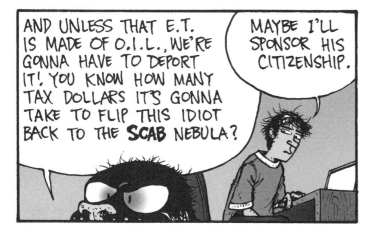

AND UNLESS THAT E.T. IS MADE OF O.I.L., WE'RE GONNA HAVE TO DEPORT IT! YOU KNOW HOW MANY TAX DOLLARS IT'S GONNA TAKE TO FLIP THIS IDIOT BACK TO THE **SCAB** NEBULA?

MAYBE I'LL SPONSOR HIS CITIZENSHIP.

...THEY SAY THAT LIBERALS ARE ELITE, BUT YOU'RE A LIBERAL AND YOU'RE JUST ANOTHER MORON.

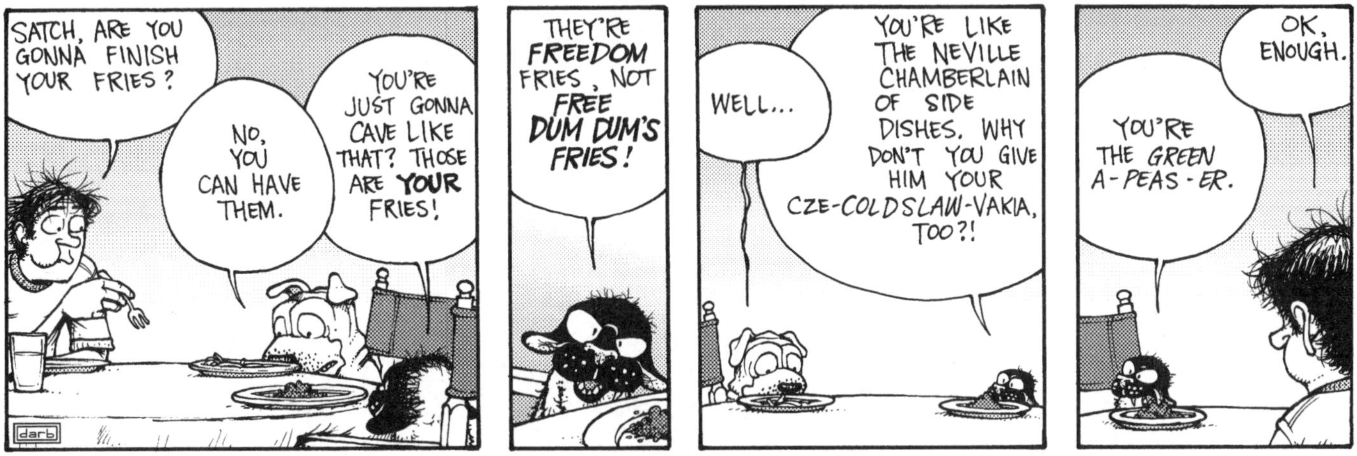
SATCH, ARE YOU GONNA FINISH YOUR FRIES?
NO, YOU CAN HAVE THEM.
YOU'RE JUST GONNA CAVE LIKE THAT? THOSE ARE **YOUR** FRIES!
darb
THEY'RE ***FREEDOM*** FRIES, NOT ***FREE DUM DUM'S FRIES!***
WELL...
YOU'RE LIKE THE NEVILLE CHAMBERLAIN OF SIDE DISHES. WHY DON'T YOU GIVE HIM YOUR CZE-*COLDSLAW*-VAKIA, TOO?!
OK, ENOUGH.
YOU'RE THE *GREEN A-PEAS-ER*.

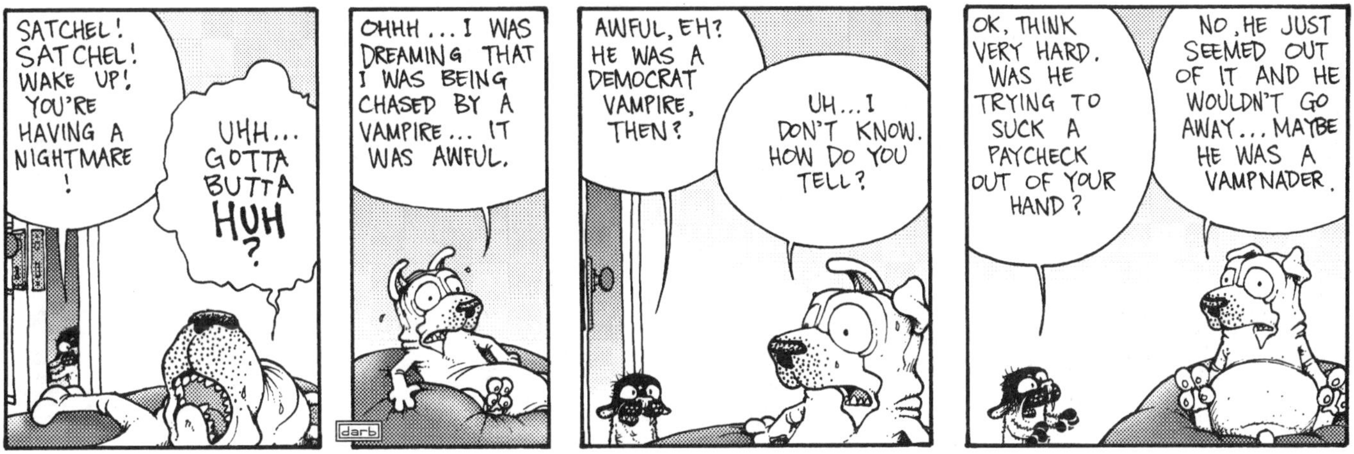
SATCHEL! SATCHEL! WAKE UP! YOU'RE HAVING A NIGHTMARE!
UHH... GOTTA BUTTA HUH?
OHHH... I WAS DREAMING THAT I WAS BEING CHASED BY A VAMPIRE... IT WAS AWFUL.
darb
AWFUL, EH? HE WAS A DEMOCRAT VAMPIRE, THEN?
UH... I DON'T KNOW. HOW DO YOU TELL?
OK, THINK VERY HARD. WAS HE TRYING TO SUCK A PAYCHECK OUT OF YOUR HAND?
NO, HE JUST SEEMED OUT OF IT AND HE WOULDN'T GO AWAY... MAYBE HE WAS A VAMPNADER.

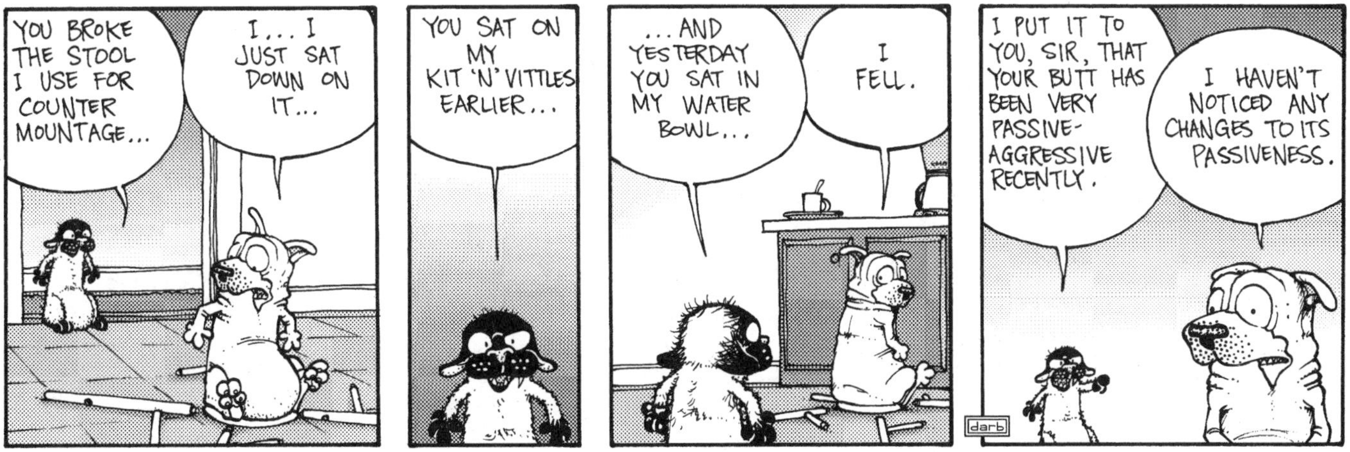
YOU BROKE THE STOOL I USE FOR COUNTER MOUNTAGE...
I... I JUST SAT DOWN ON IT...
YOU SAT ON MY KIT 'N' VITTLES EARLIER...
...AND YESTERDAY YOU SAT IN MY WATER BOWL...
I FELL.
I PUT IT TO YOU, SIR, THAT YOUR BUTT HAS BEEN VERY PASSIVE-AGGRESSIVE RECENTLY.
I HAVEN'T NOTICED ANY CHANGES TO ITS PASSIVENESS.
darb

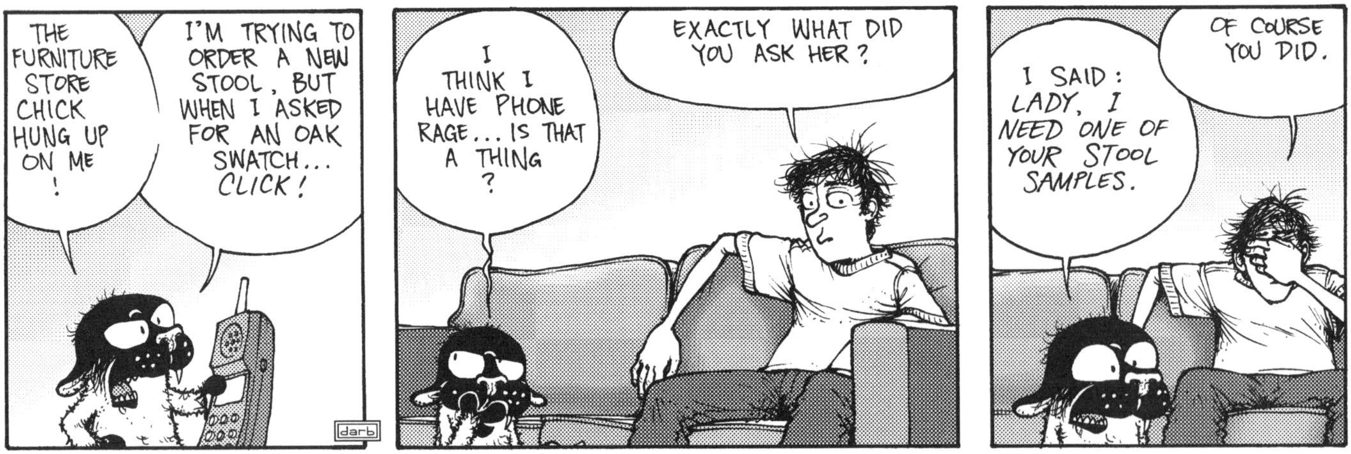
THE FURNITURE STORE CHICK HUNG UP ON ME!
I'M TRYING TO ORDER A NEW STOOL, BUT WHEN I ASKED FOR AN OAK SWATCH... CLICK!
darb
I THINK I HAVE PHONE RAGE... IS THAT A THING?
EXACTLY WHAT DID YOU ASK HER?
I SAID: LADY, I NEED ONE OF YOUR STOOL SAMPLES.
OF COURSE YOU DID.

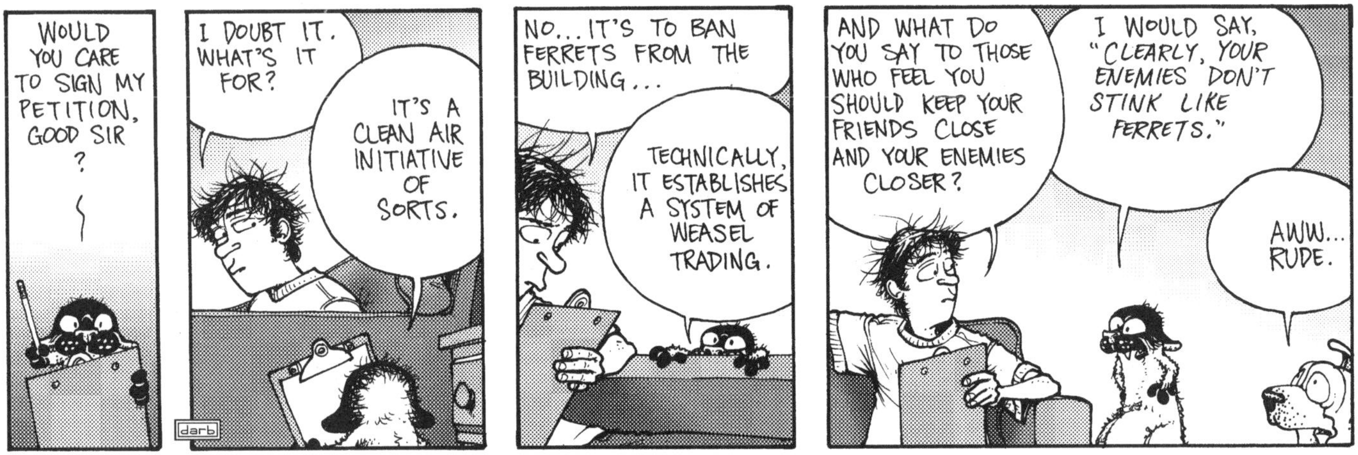
WOULD YOU CARE TO SIGN MY PETITION, GOOD SIR?
darb
I DOUBT IT. WHAT'S IT FOR?
IT'S A CLEAN AIR INITIATIVE OF SORTS.
NO... IT'S TO BAN FERRETS FROM THE BUILDING...
TECHNICALLY, IT ESTABLISHES A SYSTEM OF WEASEL TRADING.
AND WHAT DO YOU SAY TO THOSE WHO FEEL YOU SHOULD KEEP YOUR FRIENDS CLOSE AND YOUR ENEMIES CLOSER?
I WOULD SAY, "CLEARLY, YOUR ENEMIES DON'T STINK LIKE FERRETS."
AWW... RUDE.

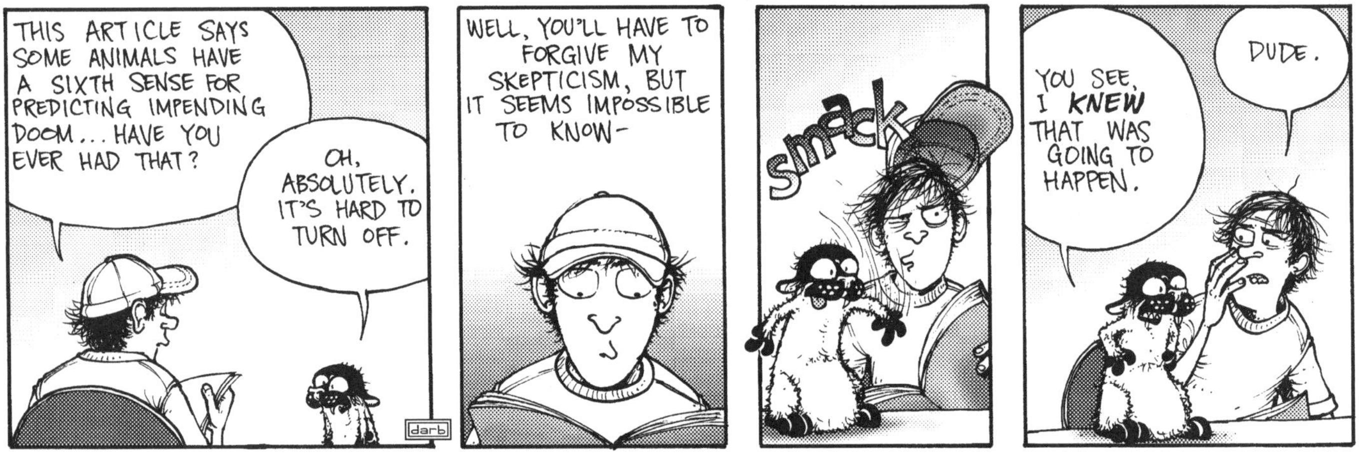
THIS ARTICLE SAYS SOME ANIMALS HAVE A SIXTH SENSE FOR PREDICTING IMPENDING DOOM... HAVE YOU EVER HAD THAT?
OH, ABSOLUTELY. IT'S HARD TO TURN OFF.
darb
WELL, YOU'LL HAVE TO FORGIVE MY SKEPTICISM, BUT IT SEEMS IMPOSSIBLE TO KNOW-
smack
YOU SEE, I **KNEW** THAT WAS GOING TO HAPPEN.
DUDE.

OW! STUPID COFFEE MAKER BURNED ME!
KRAPS
darb
POW
KRAPS
HA HA! 'ATTA BOY, BUCK! RAGE AGAINST THE COFFEE MACHINE!
NOT SO TOUGH NOW, ARE YA, FLOORBUCKS?!

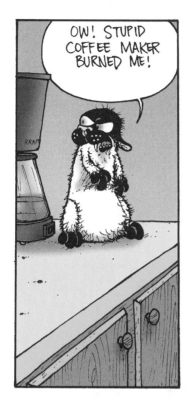

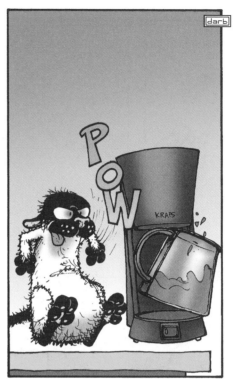

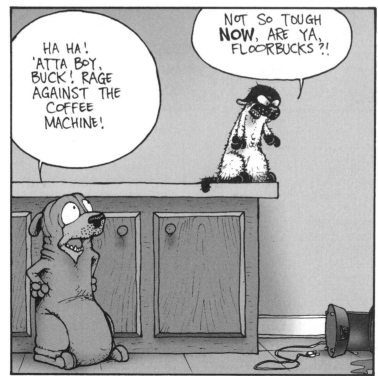

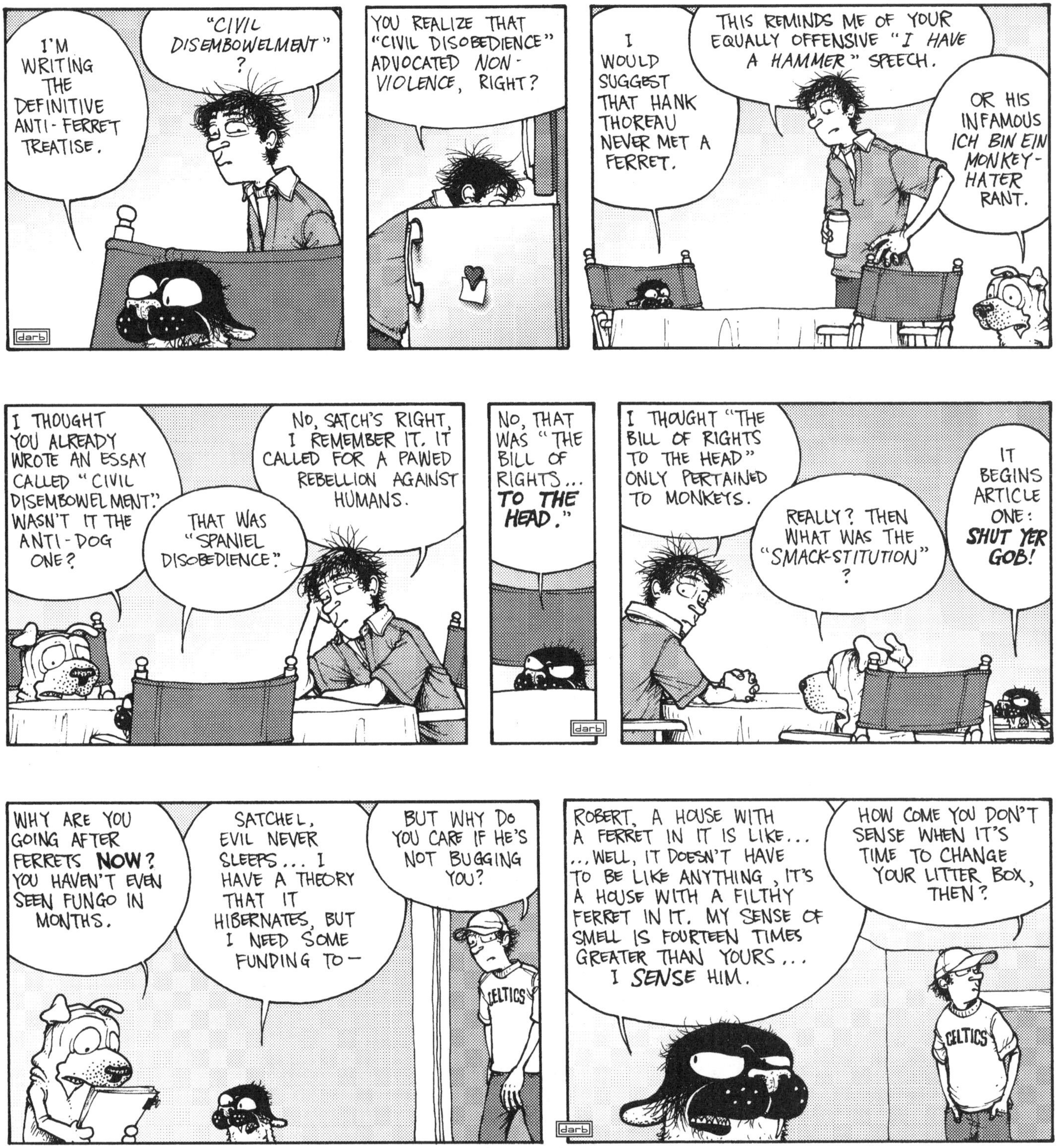
I'M WRITING THE DEFINITIVE ANTI-FERRET TREATISE.
"CIVIL DISEMBOWELMENT"?
YOU REALIZE THAT "CIVIL DISOBEDIENCE" ADVOCATED NON-VIOLENCE, RIGHT?
I WOULD SUGGEST THAT HANK THOREAU NEVER MET A FERRET.
THIS REMINDS ME OF YOUR EQUALLY OFFENSIVE "I HAVE A HAMMER" SPEECH.
OR HIS INFAMOUS ICH BIN EIN MONKEY-HATER RANT.
darb
I THOUGHT YOU ALREADY WROTE AN ESSAY CALLED "CIVIL DISEMBOWELMENT." WASN'T IT THE ANTI-DOG ONE?
THAT WAS "SPANIEL DISOBEDIENCE."
NO, SATCH'S RIGHT, I REMEMBER IT. IT CALLED FOR A PAWED REBELLION AGAINST HUMANS.
NO, THAT WAS "THE BILL OF RIGHTS... TO THE HEAD."
I THOUGHT "THE BILL OF RIGHTS TO THE HEAD" ONLY PERTAINED TO MONKEYS.
REALLY? THEN WHAT WAS THE "SMACK-STITUTION"?
IT BEGINS ARTICLE ONE: SHUT YER GOB!
darb
WHY ARE YOU GOING AFTER FERRETS NOW? YOU HAVEN'T EVEN SEEN FUNGO IN MONTHS.
SATCHEL, EVIL NEVER SLEEPS... I HAVE A THEORY THAT IT HIBERNATES, BUT I NEED SOME FUNDING TO—
BUT WHY DO YOU CARE IF HE'S NOT BUGGING YOU?
CELTICS
ROBERT, A HOUSE WITH A FERRET IN IT IS LIKE... ...WELL, IT DOESN'T HAVE TO BE LIKE ANYTHING, IT'S A HOUSE WITH A FILTHY FERRET IN IT. MY SENSE OF SMELL IS FOURTEEN TIMES GREATER THAN YOURS... I SENSE HIM.
HOW COME YOU DON'T SENSE WHEN IT'S TIME TO CHANGE YOUR LITTER BOX, THEN?
CELTICS
darb

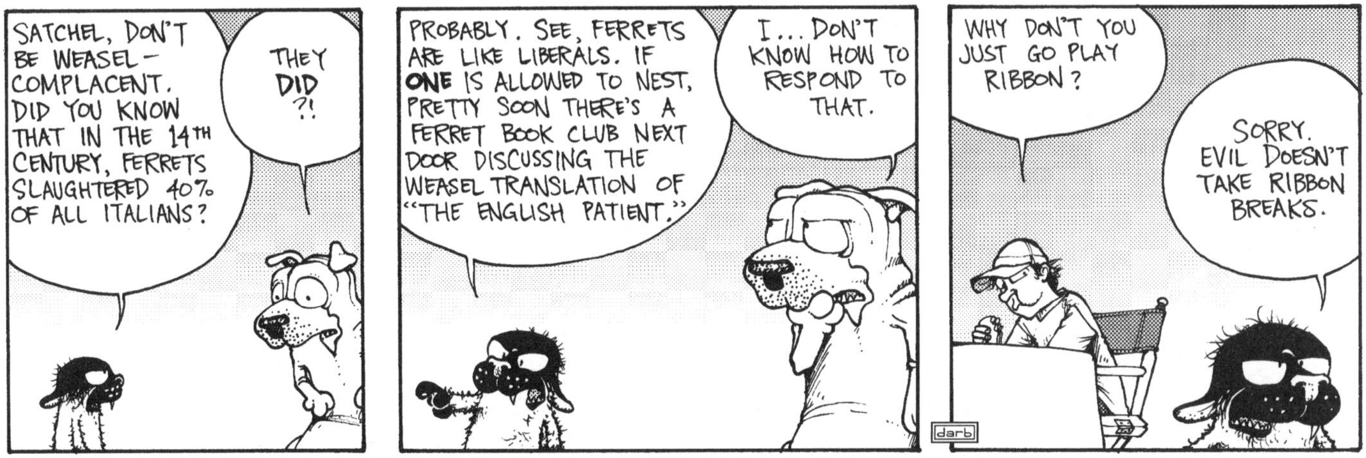
SATCHEL, DON'T BE WEASEL-COMPLACENT. DID YOU KNOW THAT IN THE 14TH CENTURY, FERRETS SLAUGHTERED 40% OF ALL ITALIANS?
THEY DID?!
PROBABLY. SEE, FERRETS ARE LIKE LIBERALS. IF ONE IS ALLOWED TO NEST, PRETTY SOON THERE'S A FERRET BOOK CLUB NEXT DOOR DISCUSSING THE WEASEL TRANSLATION OF "THE ENGLISH PATIENT."
I... DON'T KNOW HOW TO RESPOND TO THAT.
WHY DON'T YOU JUST GO PLAY RIBBON?
SORRY. EVIL DOESN'T TAKE RIBBON BREAKS.
darb

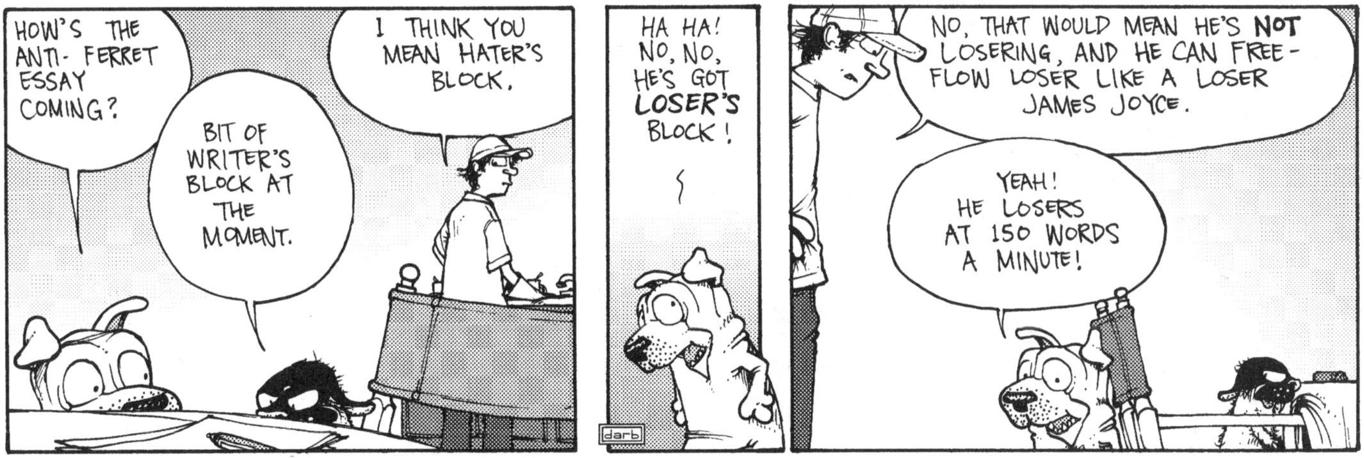
HOW'S THE ANTI-FERRET ESSAY COMING?
BIT OF WRITER'S BLOCK AT THE MOMENT.
I THINK YOU MEAN HATER'S BLOCK.
HA HA! NO, NO, HE'S GOT LOSER'S BLOCK!
darb
NO, THAT WOULD MEAN HE'S NOT LOSERING, AND HE CAN FREE-FLOW LOSER LIKE A LOSER JAMES JOYCE.
YEAH! HE LOSERS AT 150 WORDS A MINUTE!

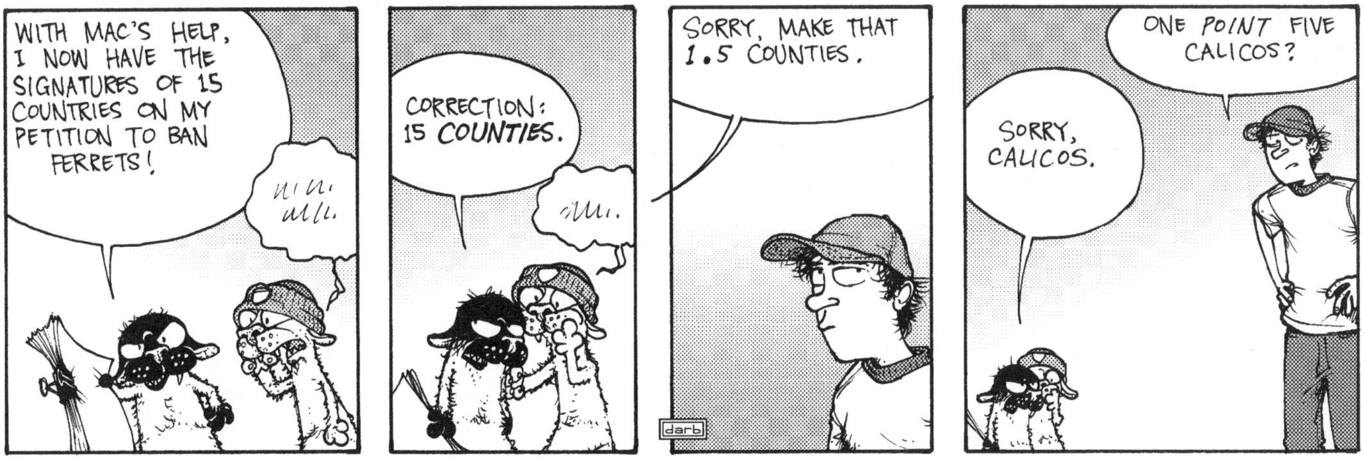
WITH MAC'S HELP, I NOW HAVE THE SIGNATURES OF 15 COUNTRIES ON MY PETITION TO BAN FERRETS!
CORRECTION: 15 COUNTIES.
SORRY, MAKE THAT 1.5 COUNTIES.
darb
ONE POINT FIVE CALICOS?
SORRY, CALICOS.

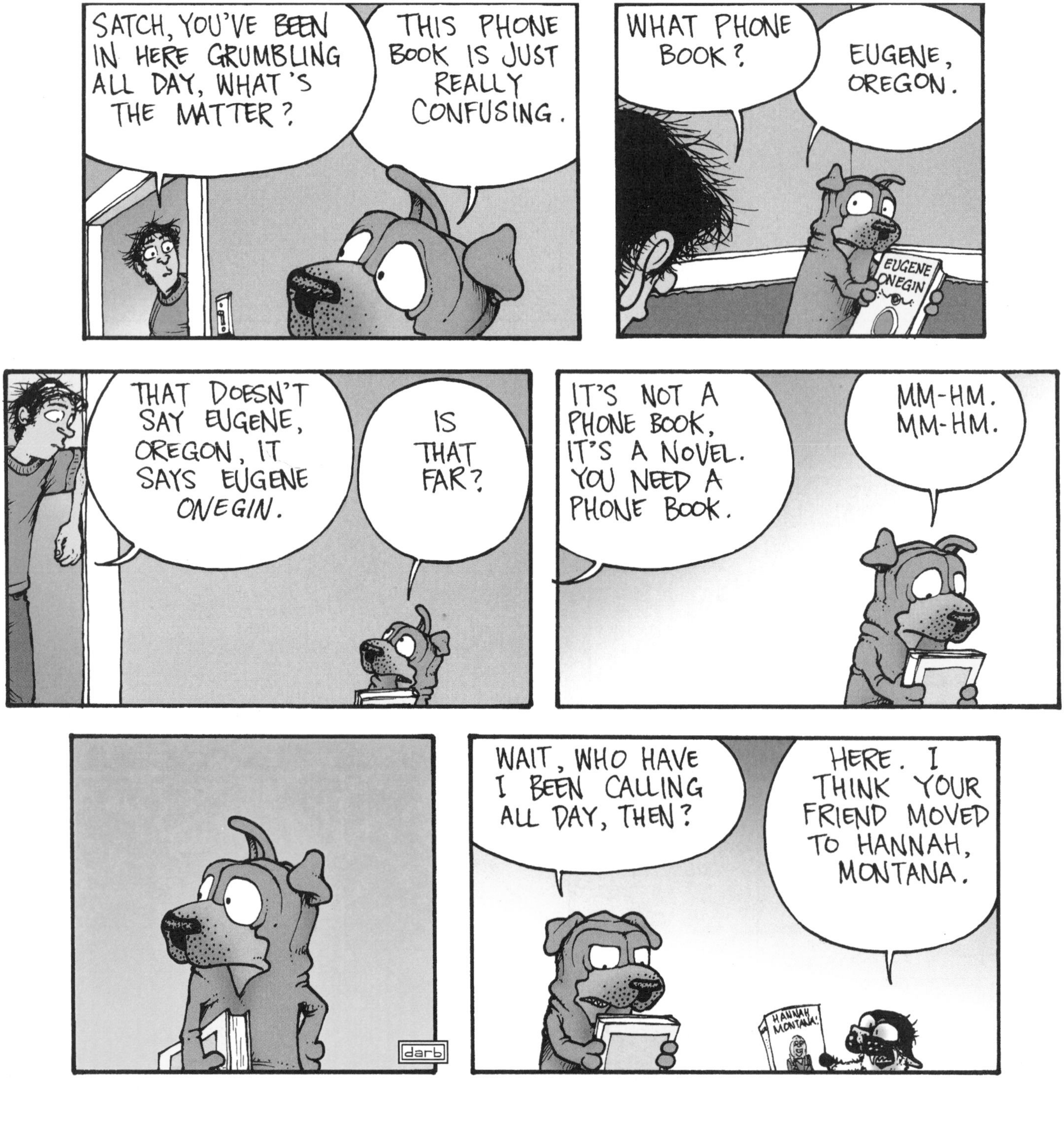
SATCH, YOU'VE BEEN IN HERE GRUMBLING ALL DAY, WHAT'S THE MATTER?
THIS PHONE BOOK IS JUST REALLY CONFUSING.
WHAT PHONE BOOK?
EUGENE, OREGON.
EUGENE ONEGIN
THAT DOESN'T SAY EUGENE, OREGON, IT SAYS EUGENE ONEGIN.
IS THAT FAR?
IT'S NOT A PHONE BOOK, IT'S A NOVEL. YOU NEED A PHONE BOOK.
MM-HM. MM-HM.
darb
WAIT, WHO HAVE I BEEN CALLING ALL DAY, THEN?
HERE. I THINK YOUR FRIEND MOVED TO HANNAH, MONTANA.
HANNAH MONTANA!

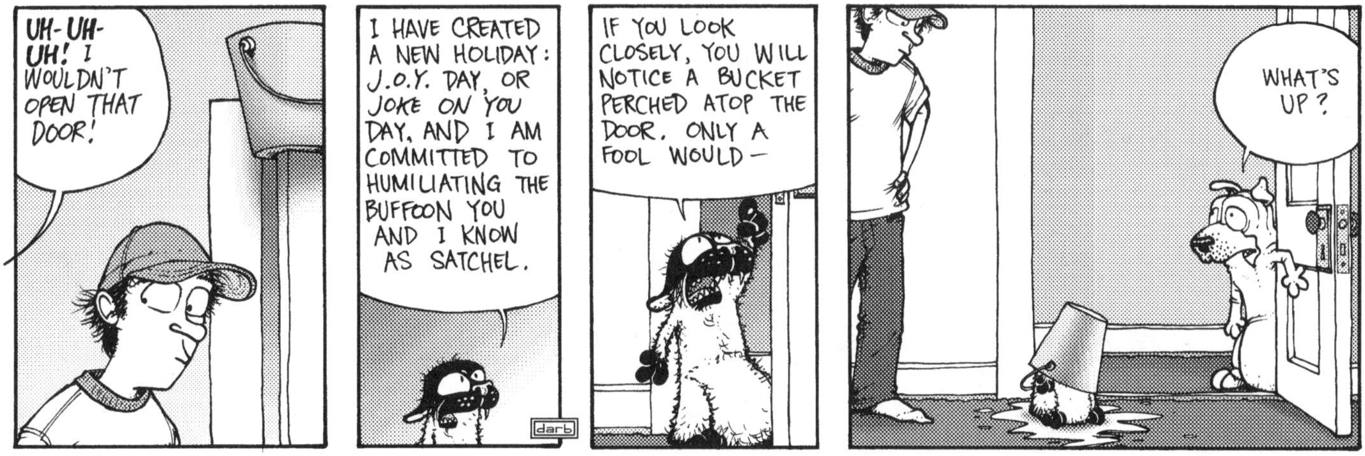
UH-UH-UH! I WOULDN'T OPEN THAT DOOR!
I HAVE CREATED A NEW HOLIDAY: J.O.Y. DAY, OR JOKE ON YOU DAY, AND I AM COMMITTED TO HUMILIATING THE BUFFOON YOU AND I KNOW AS SATCHEL.
IF YOU LOOK CLOSELY, YOU WILL NOTICE A BUCKET PERCHED ATOP THE DOOR. ONLY A FOOL WOULD—
WHAT'S UP?
darb

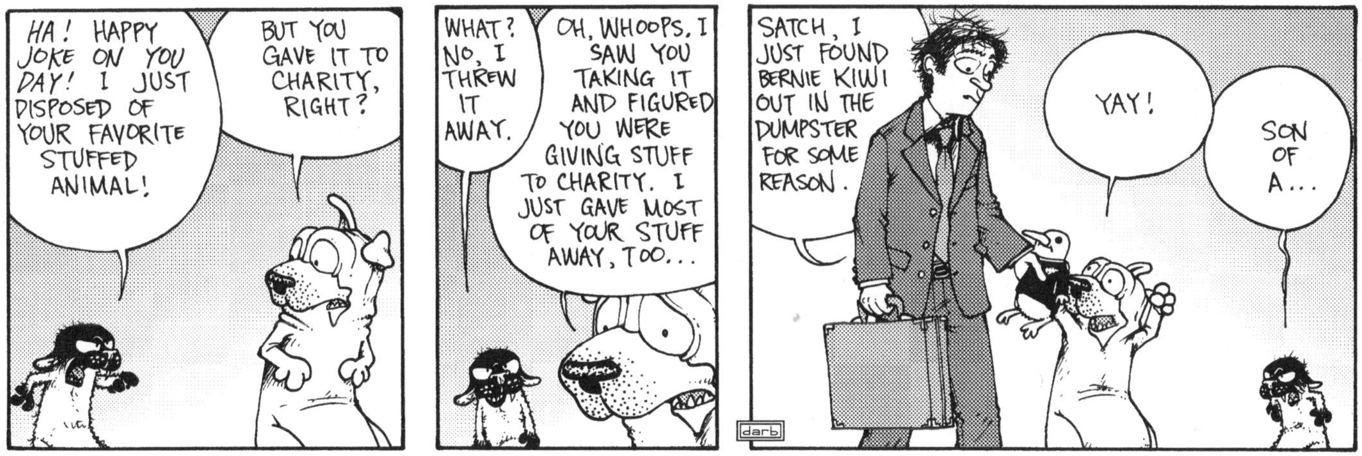
HA! HAPPY JOKE ON YOU DAY! I JUST DISPOSED OF YOUR FAVORITE STUFFED ANIMAL!
BUT YOU GAVE IT TO CHARITY, RIGHT?
WHAT? NO, I THREW IT AWAY.
OH, WHOOPS. I SAW YOU TAKING IT AND FIGURED YOU WERE GIVING STUFF TO CHARITY. I JUST GAVE MOST OF YOUR STUFF AWAY, TOO...
SATCH, I JUST FOUND BERNIE KIWI OUT IN THE DUMPSTER FOR SOME REASON.
YAY!
SON OF A...
darb

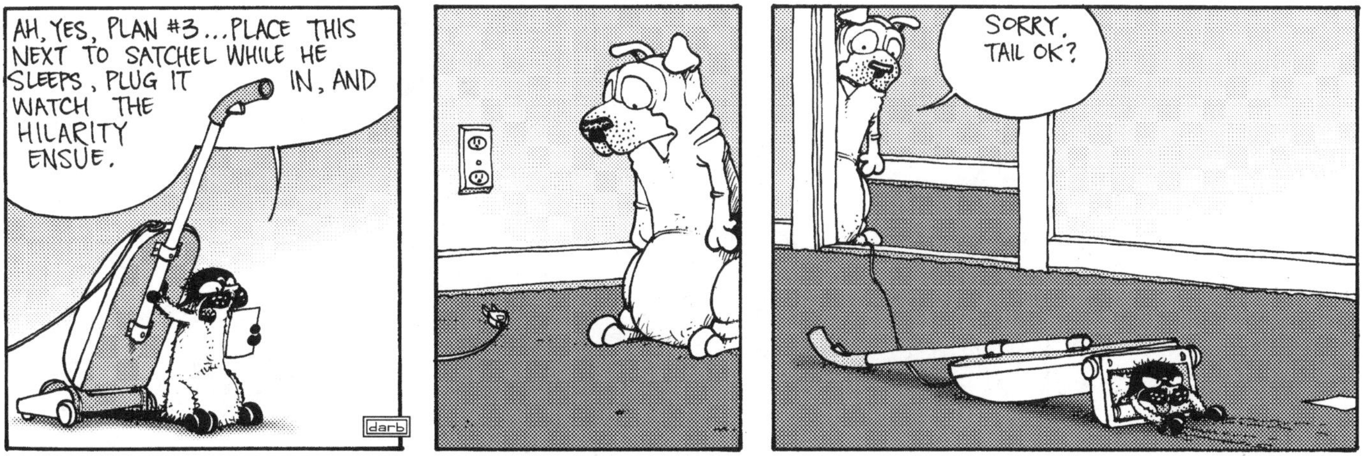
AH, YES, PLAN #3...PLACE THIS NEXT TO SATCHEL WHILE HE SLEEPS, PLUG IT IN, AND WATCH THE HILARITY ENSUE.
SORRY. TAIL OK?
darb

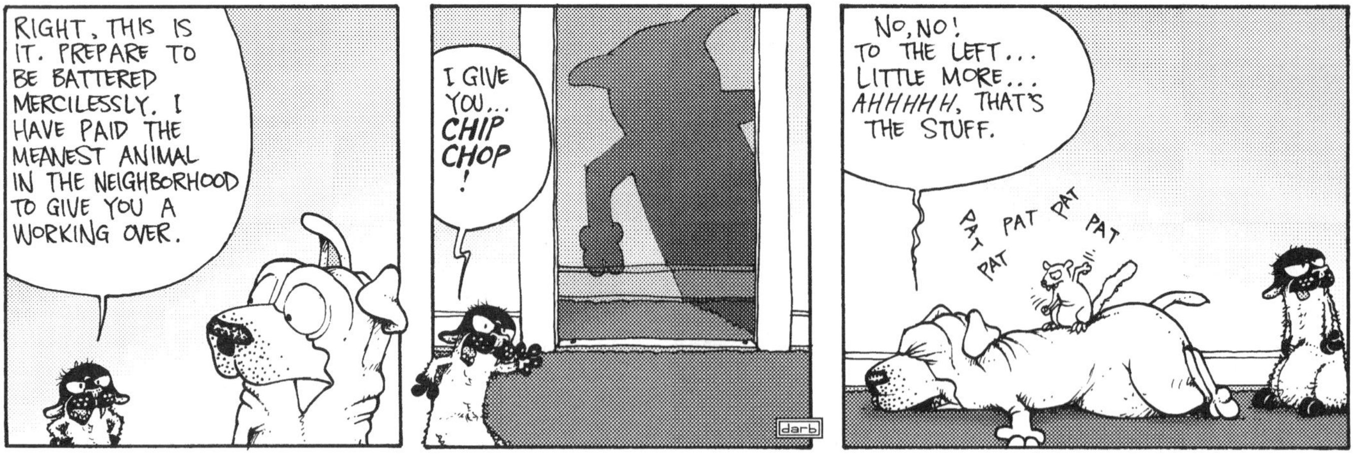
RIGHT, THIS IS IT. PREPARE TO BE BATTERED MERCILESSLY. I HAVE PAID THE MEANEST ANIMAL IN THE NEIGHBORHOOD TO GIVE YOU A WORKING OVER.
I GIVE YOU... CHIP CHOP !
NO, NO! TO THE LEFT... LITTLE MORE... AHHHHH, THAT'S THE STUFF.
PAT PAT PAT PAT PAT
darb

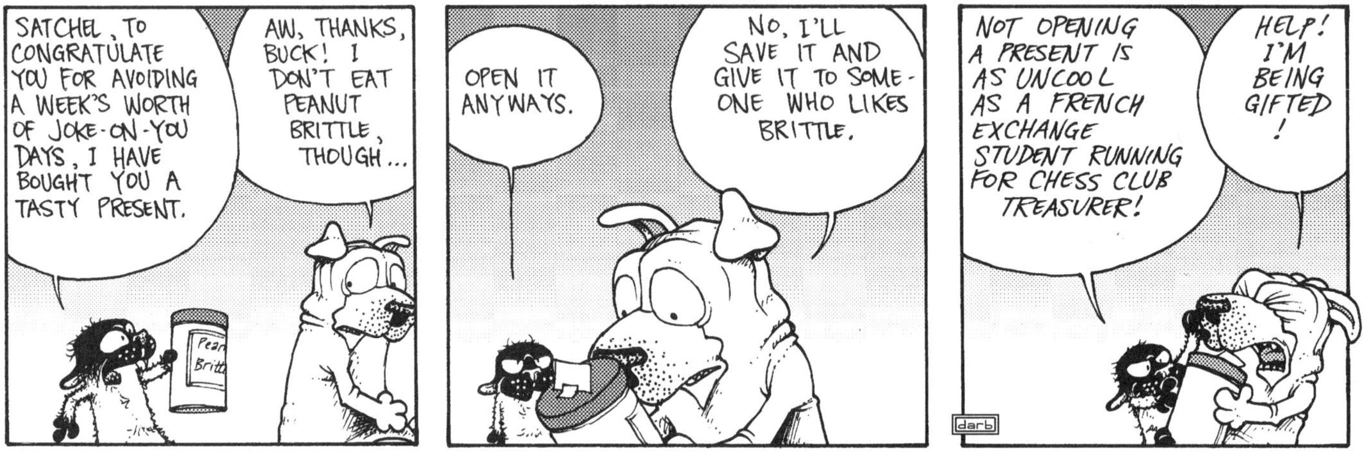
SATCHEL, TO CONGRATULATE YOU FOR AVOIDING A WEEK'S WORTH OF JOKE-ON-YOU DAYS, I HAVE BOUGHT YOU A TASTY PRESENT.
AW, THANKS, BUCK! I DON'T EAT PEANUT BRITTLE, THOUGH...
OPEN IT ANYWAYS.
NO, I'LL SAVE IT AND GIVE IT TO SOME-ONE WHO LIKES BRITTLE.
NOT OPENING A PRESENT IS AS UNCOOL AS A FRENCH EXCHANGE STUDENT RUNNING FOR CHESS CLUB TREASURER!
HELP! I'M BEING GIFTED !
darb

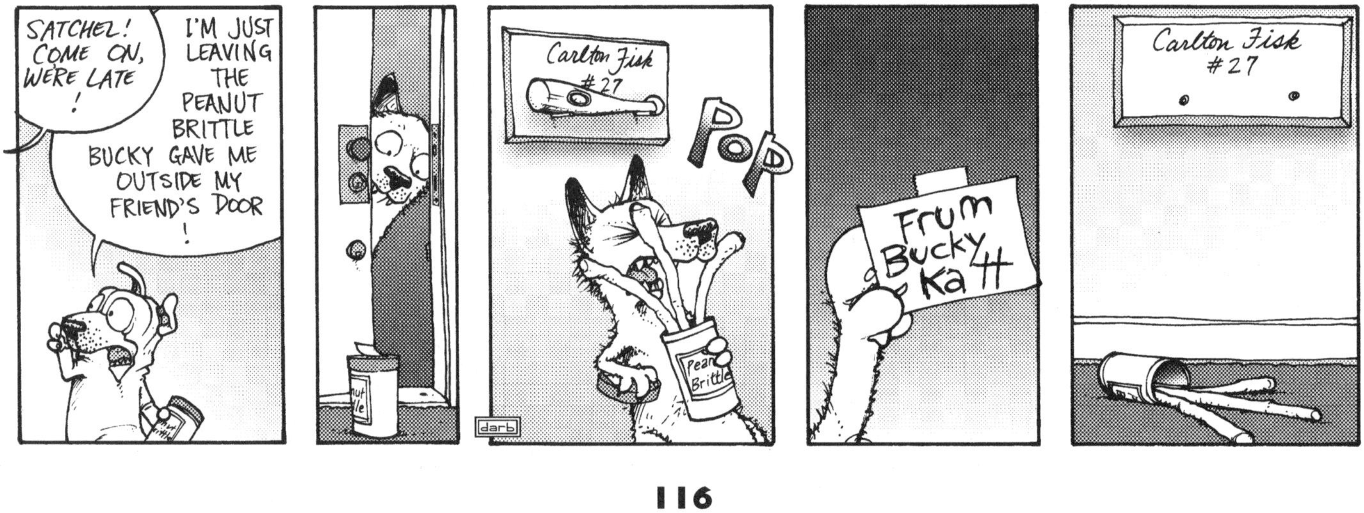
SATCHEL! COME ON, WE'RE LATE !
I'M JUST LEAVING THE PEANUT BRITTLE BUCKY GAVE ME OUTSIDE MY FRIEND'S DOOR !
darb
Carlton Fisk #27
POP
Peanut Brittle
Frum Bucky Katt
Carlton Fisk #27

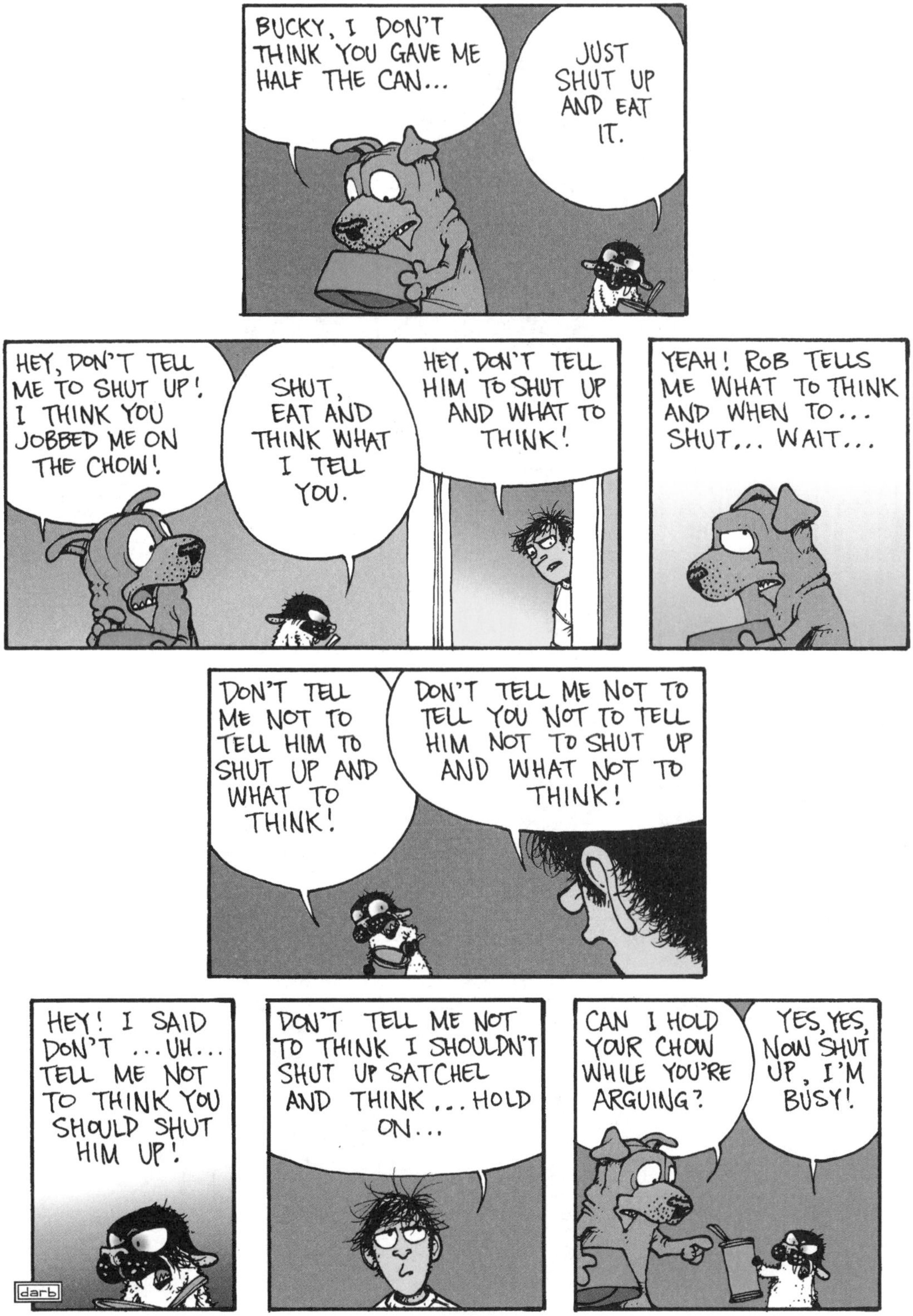
BUCKY, I DON'T THINK YOU GAVE ME HALF THE CAN...
JUST SHUT UP AND EAT IT.
HEY, DON'T TELL ME TO SHUT UP! I THINK YOU JOBBED ME ON THE CHOW!
SHUT, EAT AND THINK WHAT I TELL YOU.
HEY, DON'T TELL HIM TO SHUT UP AND WHAT TO THINK!
YEAH! ROB TELLS ME WHAT TO THINK AND WHEN TO... SHUT,... WAIT...
DON'T TELL ME NOT TO TELL HIM TO SHUT UP AND WHAT TO THINK!
DON'T TELL ME NOT TO TELL YOU NOT TO TELL HIM NOT TO SHUT UP AND WHAT NOT TO THINK!
HEY! I SAID DON'T ...UH... TELL ME NOT TO THINK YOU SHOULD SHUT HIM UP!
darb
DON'T TELL ME NOT TO THINK I SHOULDN'T SHUT UP SATCHEL AND THINK... HOLD ON...
CAN I HOLD YOUR CHOW WHILE YOU'RE ARGUING?
YES, YES, NOW SHUT UP, I'M BUSY!

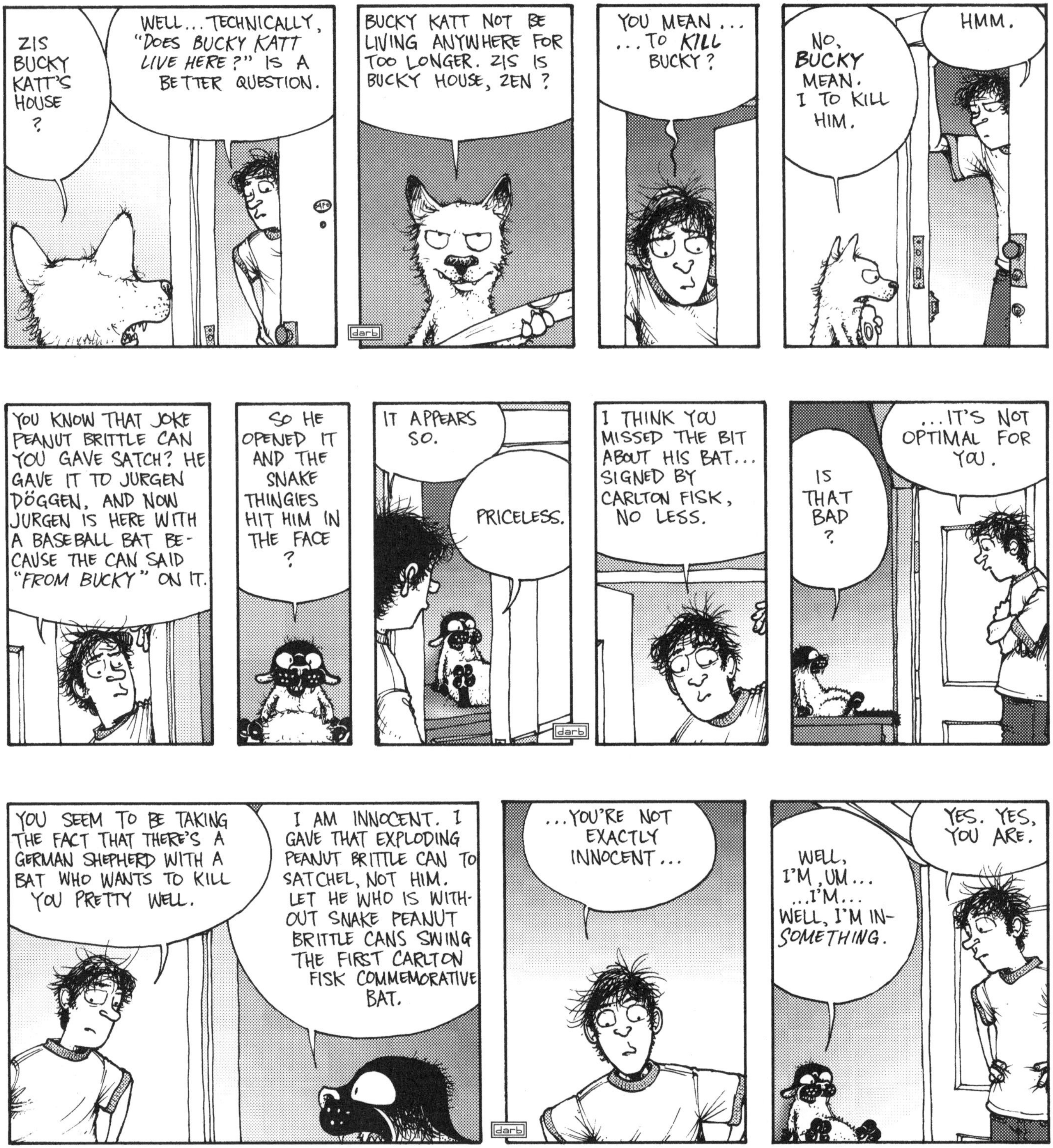
ZIS BUCKY KATT'S HOUSE ?
WELL... TECHNICALLY, "DOES BUCKY KATT LIVE HERE?" IS A BETTER QUESTION.
BUCKY KATT NOT BE LIVING ANYWHERE FOR TOO LONGER. ZIS IS BUCKY HOUSE, ZEN ?
YOU MEAN ... ...TO KILL BUCKY?
NO, BUCKY MEAN. I TO KILL HIM.
HMM.
YOU KNOW THAT JOKE PEANUT BRITTLE CAN YOU GAVE SATCH? HE GAVE IT TO JURGEN DÖGGEN, AND NOW JURGEN IS HERE WITH A BASEBALL BAT BECAUSE THE CAN SAID "FROM BUCKY" ON IT.
SO HE OPENED IT AND THE SNAKE THINGIES HIT HIM IN THE FACE ?
IT APPEARS SO.
PRICELESS.
I THINK YOU MISSED THE BIT ABOUT HIS BAT... SIGNED BY CARLTON FISK, NO LESS.
IS THAT BAD ?
...IT'S NOT OPTIMAL FOR YOU.
YOU SEEM TO BE TAKING THE FACT THAT THERE'S A GERMAN SHEPHERD WITH A BAT WHO WANTS TO KILL YOU PRETTY WELL.
I AM INNOCENT. I GAVE THAT EXPLODING PEANUT BRITTLE CAN TO SATCHEL, NOT HIM. LET HE WHO IS WITHOUT SNAKE PEANUT BRITTLE CANS SWING THE FIRST CARLTON FISK COMMEMORATIVE BAT.
...YOU'RE NOT EXACTLY INNOCENT...
WELL, I'M, UM... ...I'M... WELL, I'M IN-SOMETHING.
YES. YES, YOU ARE.
darb

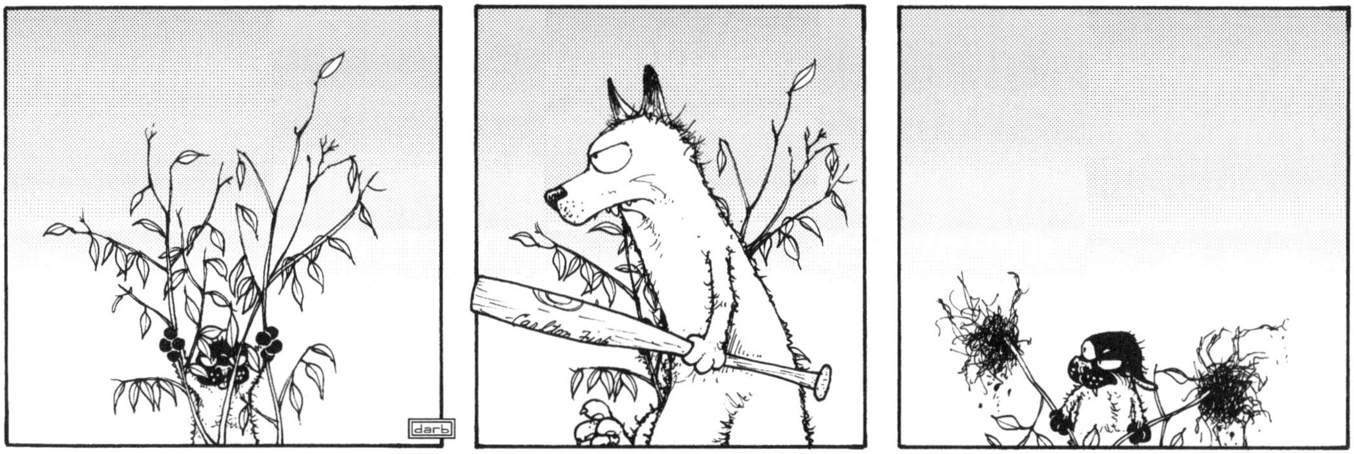

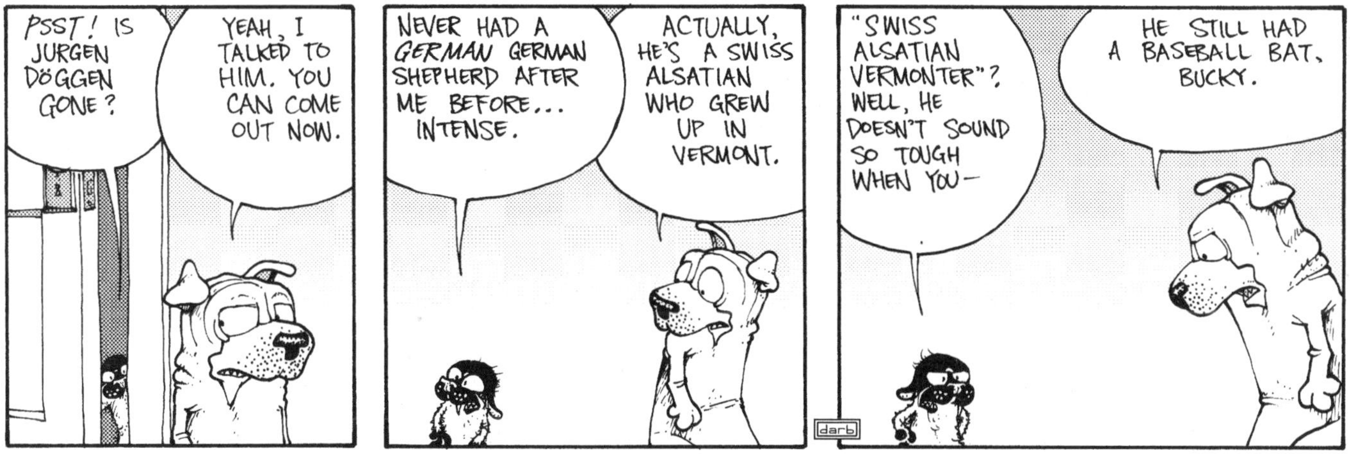
PSST! IS JURGEN DÖGGEN GONE?
YEAH, I TALKED TO HIM. YOU CAN COME OUT NOW.
NEVER HAD A GERMAN GERMAN SHEPHERD AFTER ME BEFORE... INTENSE.
ACTUALLY, HE'S A SWISS ALSATIAN WHO GREW UP IN VERMONT.
"SWISS ALSATIAN VERMONTER"? WELL, HE DOESN'T SOUND SO TOUGH WHEN YOU—
HE STILL HAD A BASEBALL BAT, BUCKY.

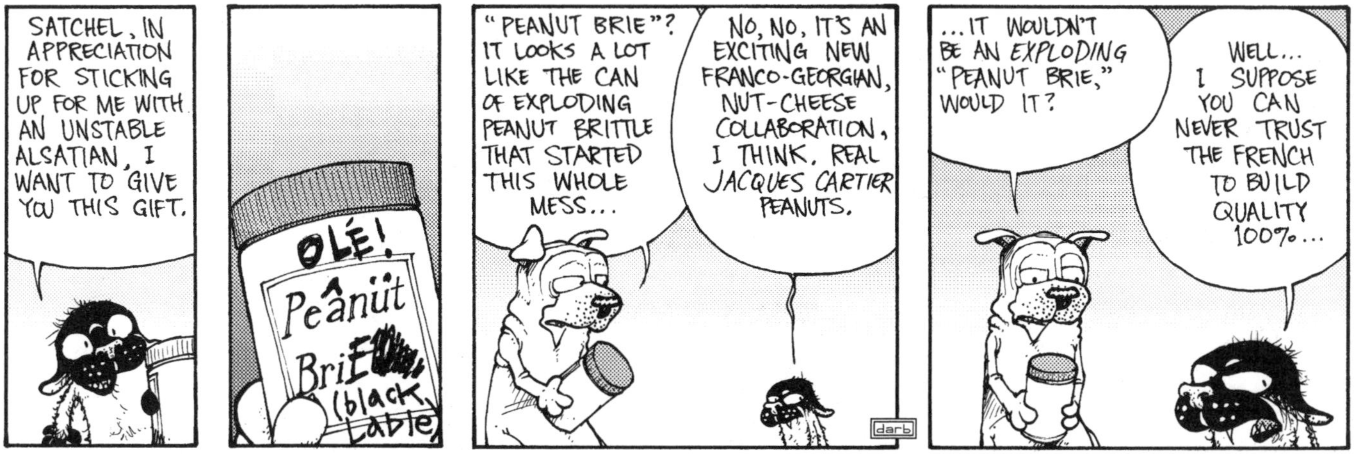
SATCHEL, IN APPRECIATION FOR STICKING UP FOR ME WITH AN UNSTABLE ALSATIAN, I WANT TO GIVE YOU THIS GIFT.
OLÉ! Peânüt BriE (black Lable)
"PEANUT BRIE"? IT LOOKS A LOT LIKE THE CAN OF EXPLODING PEANUT BRITTLE THAT STARTED THIS WHOLE MESS...
NO, NO, IT'S AN EXCITING NEW FRANCO-GEORGIAN, NUT-CHEESE COLLABORATION, I THINK. REAL JACQUES CARTIER PEANUTS.
...IT WOULDN'T BE AN EXPLODING "PEANUT BRIE," WOULD IT?
WELL... I SUPPOSE YOU CAN NEVER TRUST THE FRENCH TO BUILD QUALITY 100%...

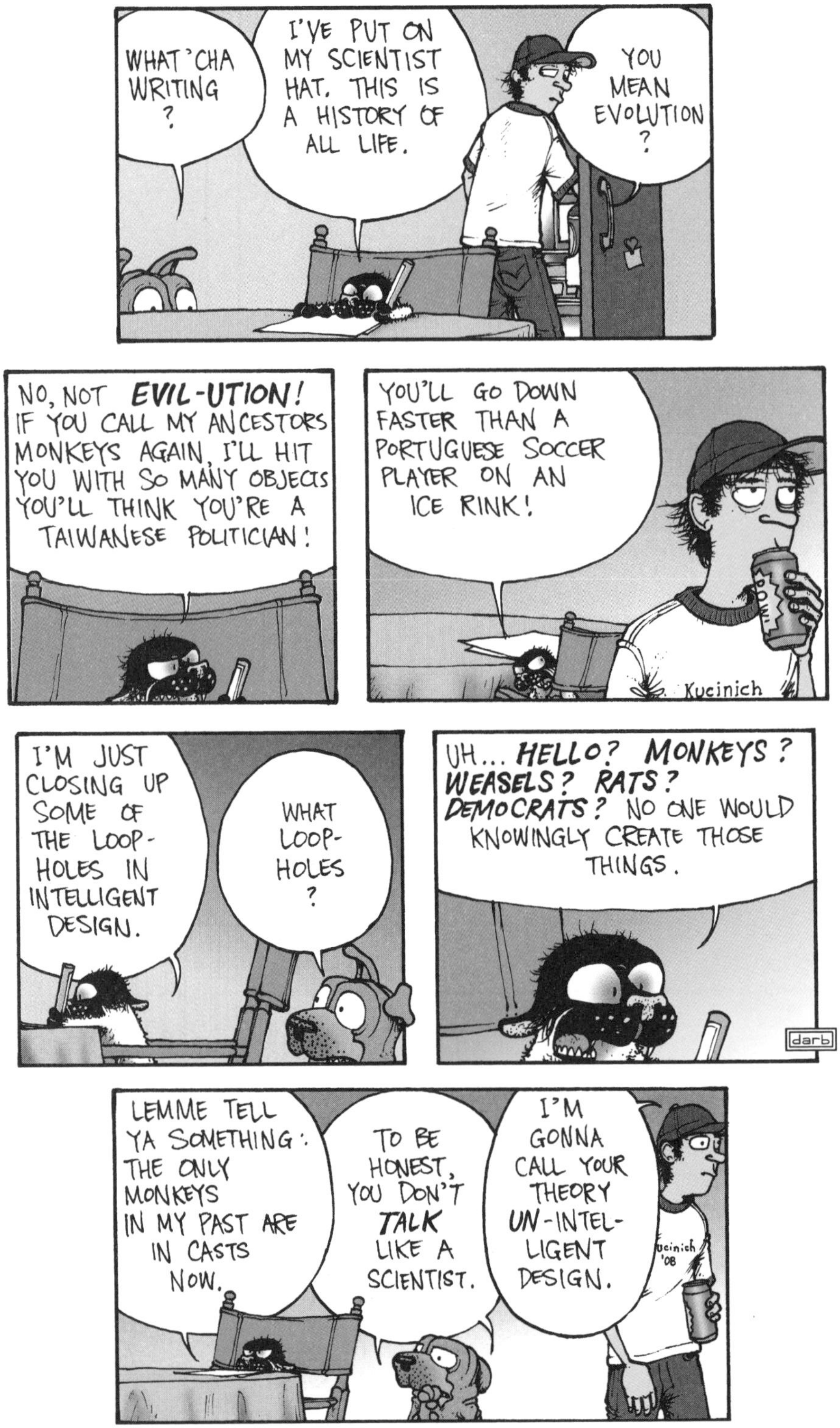
WHAT'CHA WRITING ?
I'VE PUT ON MY SCIENTIST HAT. THIS IS A HISTORY OF ALL LIFE.
YOU MEAN EVOLUTION ?
NO, NOT EVIL-UTION! IF YOU CALL MY ANCESTORS MONKEYS AGAIN, I'LL HIT YOU WITH SO MANY OBJECTS YOU'LL THINK YOU'RE A TAIWANESE POLITICIAN!
YOU'LL GO DOWN FASTER THAN A PORTUGUESE SOCCER PLAYER ON AN ICE RINK!
Kucinich
I'M JUST CLOSING UP SOME OF THE LOOP-HOLES IN INTELLIGENT DESIGN.
WHAT LOOP-HOLES ?
UH... HELLO? MONKEYS? WEASELS? RATS? DEMOCRATS? NO ONE WOULD KNOWINGLY CREATE THOSE THINGS.
darb
LEMME TELL YA SOMETHING: THE ONLY MONKEYS IN MY PAST ARE IN CASTS NOW.
TO BE HONEST, YOU DON'T TALK LIKE A SCIENTIST.
I'M GONNA CALL YOUR THEORY UN-INTEL-LIGENT DESIGN.
Kucinich '08

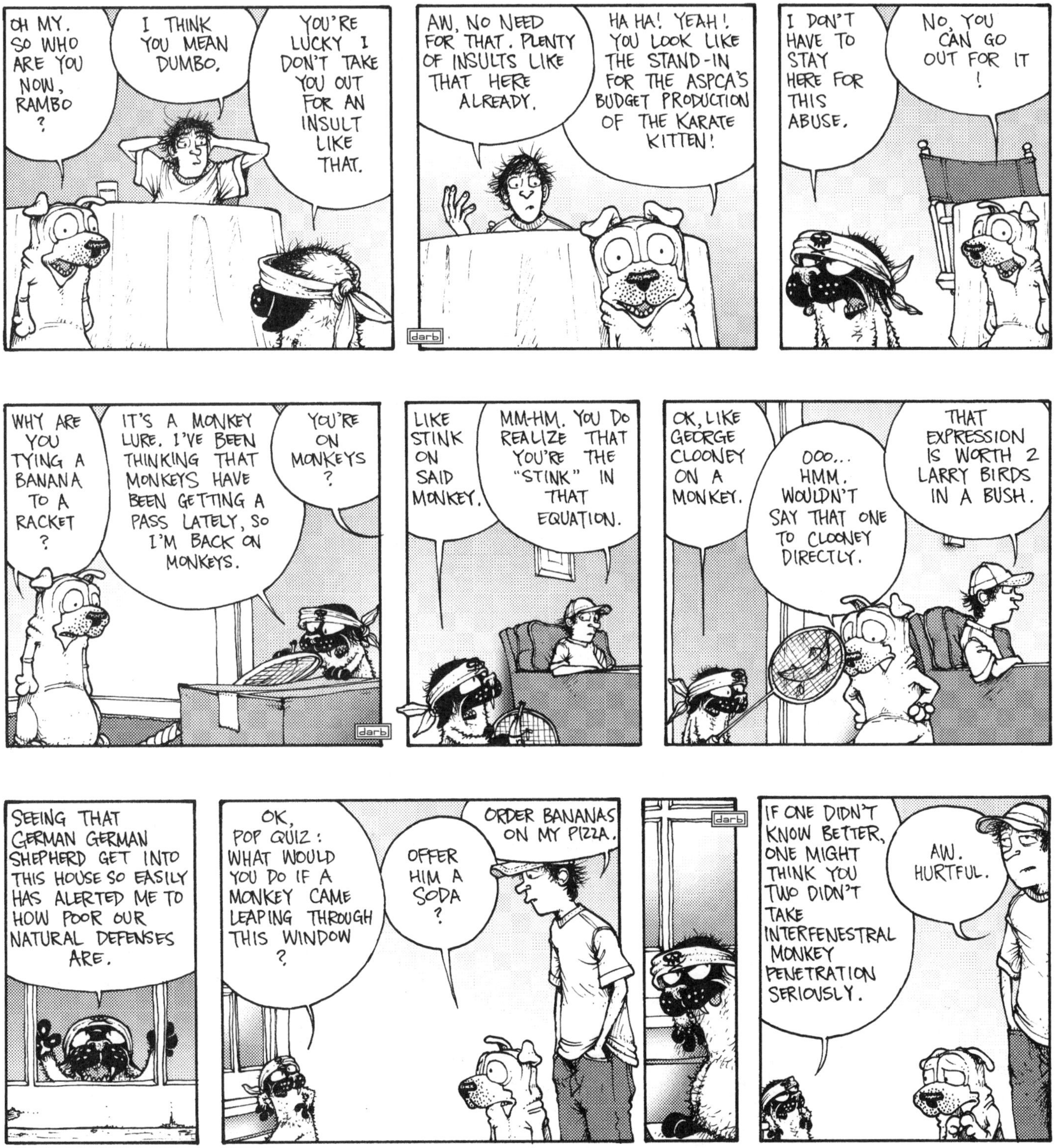
OH MY. SO WHO ARE YOU NOW, RAMBO?
I THINK YOU MEAN DUMBO.
YOU'RE LUCKY I DON'T TAKE YOU OUT FOR AN INSULT LIKE THAT.
AW, NO NEED FOR THAT. PLENTY OF INSULTS LIKE THAT HERE ALREADY.
HA HA! YEAH! YOU LOOK LIKE THE STAND-IN FOR THE ASPCA'S BUDGET PRODUCTION OF THE KARATE KITTEN!
I DON'T HAVE TO STAY HERE FOR THIS ABUSE.
NO, YOU CAN GO OUT FOR IT!
darb
WHY ARE YOU TYING A BANANA TO A RACKET?
IT'S A MONKEY LURE. I'VE BEEN THINKING THAT MONKEYS HAVE BEEN GETTING A PASS LATELY, SO I'M BACK ON MONKEYS.
YOU'RE ON MONKEYS?
LIKE STINK ON SAID MONKEY.
MM-HM. YOU DO REALIZE THAT YOU'RE THE "STINK" IN THAT EQUATION.
OK, LIKE GEORGE CLOONEY ON A MONKEY.
OOO... HMM. WOULDN'T SAY THAT ONE TO CLOONEY DIRECTLY.
THAT EXPRESSION IS WORTH 2 LARRY BIRDS IN A BUSH.
darb
SEEING THAT GERMAN GERMAN SHEPHERD GET INTO THIS HOUSE SO EASILY HAS ALERTED ME TO HOW POOR OUR NATURAL DEFENSES ARE.
OK, POP QUIZ: WHAT WOULD YOU DO IF A MONKEY CAME LEAPING THROUGH THIS WINDOW?
OFFER HIM A SODA?
ORDER BANANAS ON MY PIZZA.
darb
IF ONE DIDN'T KNOW BETTER, ONE MIGHT THINK YOU TWO DIDN'T TAKE INTERFENESTRAL MONKEY PENETRATION SERIOUSLY.
AW. HURTFUL.

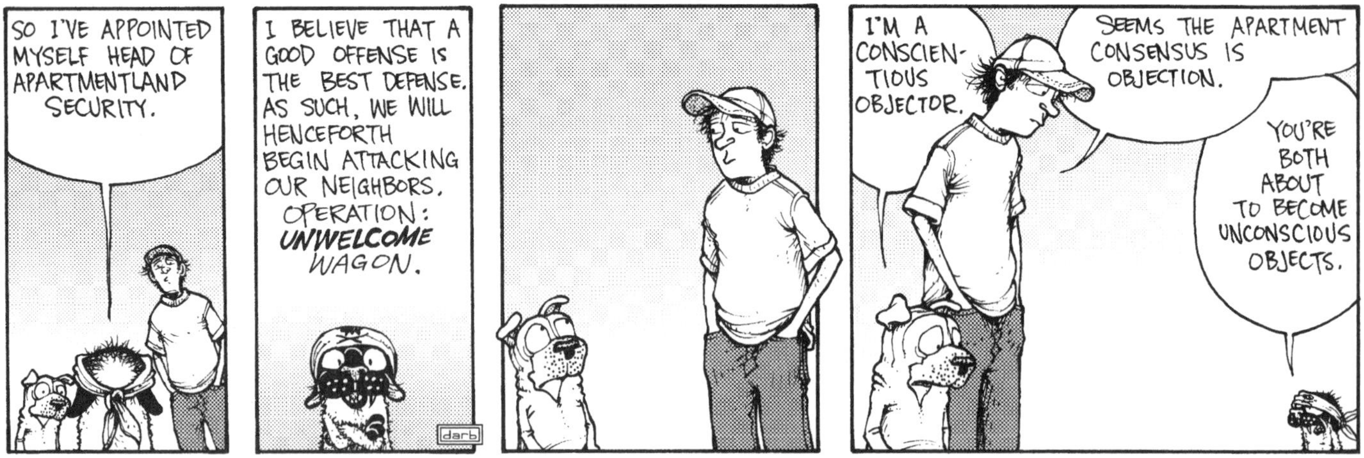
SO I'VE APPOINTED MYSELF HEAD OF APARTMENTLAND SECURITY.
I BELIEVE THAT A GOOD OFFENSE IS THE BEST DEFENSE. AS SUCH, WE WILL HENCEFORTH BEGIN ATTACKING OUR NEIGHBORS. OPERATION: UNWELCOME WAGON.
I'M A CONSCIENTIOUS OBJECTOR.
SEEMS THE APARTMENT CONSENSUS IS OBJECTION.
YOU'RE BOTH ABOUT TO BECOME UNCONSCIOUS OBJECTS.

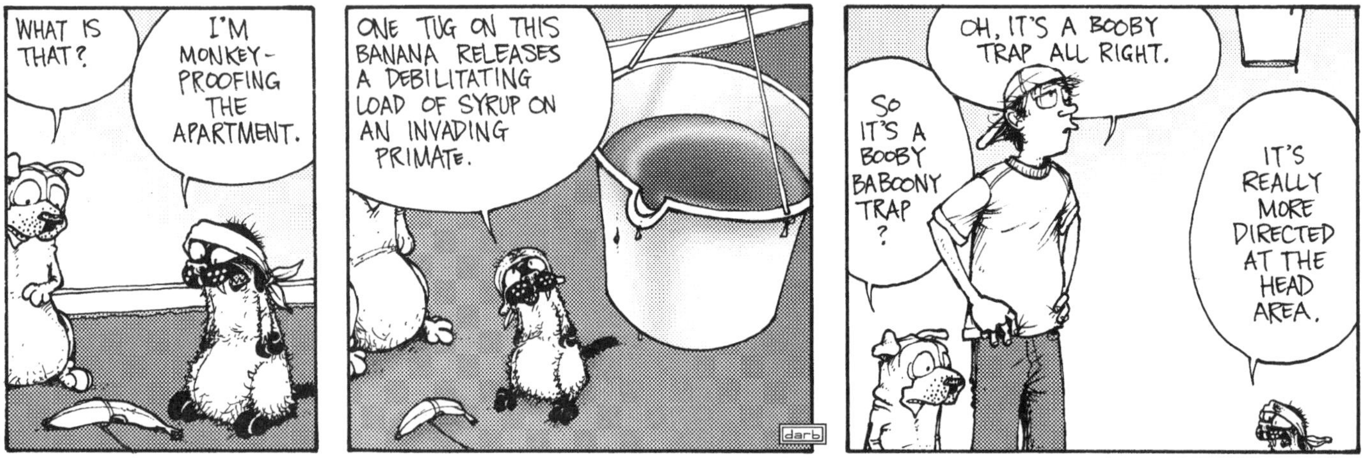
WHAT IS THAT?
I'M MONKEY-PROOFING THE APARTMENT.
ONE TUG ON THIS BANANA RELEASES A DEBILITATING LOAD OF SYRUP ON AN INVADING PRIMATE.
SO IT'S A BOOBY BABOONY TRAP?
OH, IT'S A BOOBY TRAP ALL RIGHT.
IT'S REALLY MORE DIRECTED AT THE HEAD AREA.

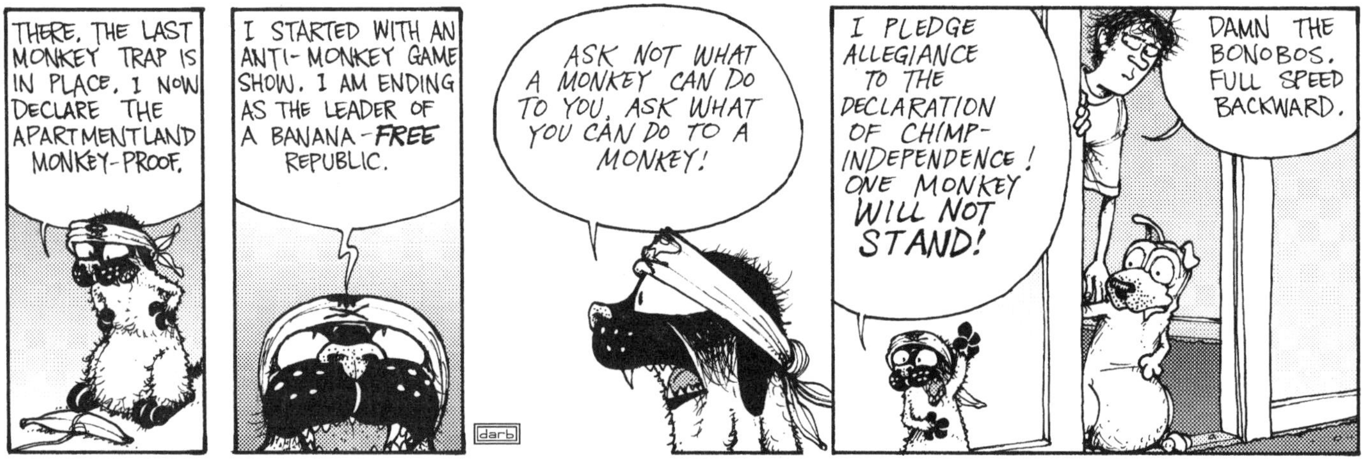
THERE. THE LAST MONKEY TRAP IS IN PLACE. I NOW DECLARE THE APARTMENTLAND MONKEY-PROOF.
I STARTED WITH AN ANTI-MONKEY GAME SHOW. I AM ENDING AS THE LEADER OF A BANANA-FREE REPUBLIC.
ASK NOT WHAT A MONKEY CAN DO TO YOU, ASK WHAT YOU CAN DO TO A MONKEY!
I PLEDGE ALLEGIANCE TO THE DECLARATION OF CHIMP-INDEPENDENCE! ONE MONKEY WILL NOT STAND!
DAMN THE BONOBOS. FULL SPEED BACKWARD.

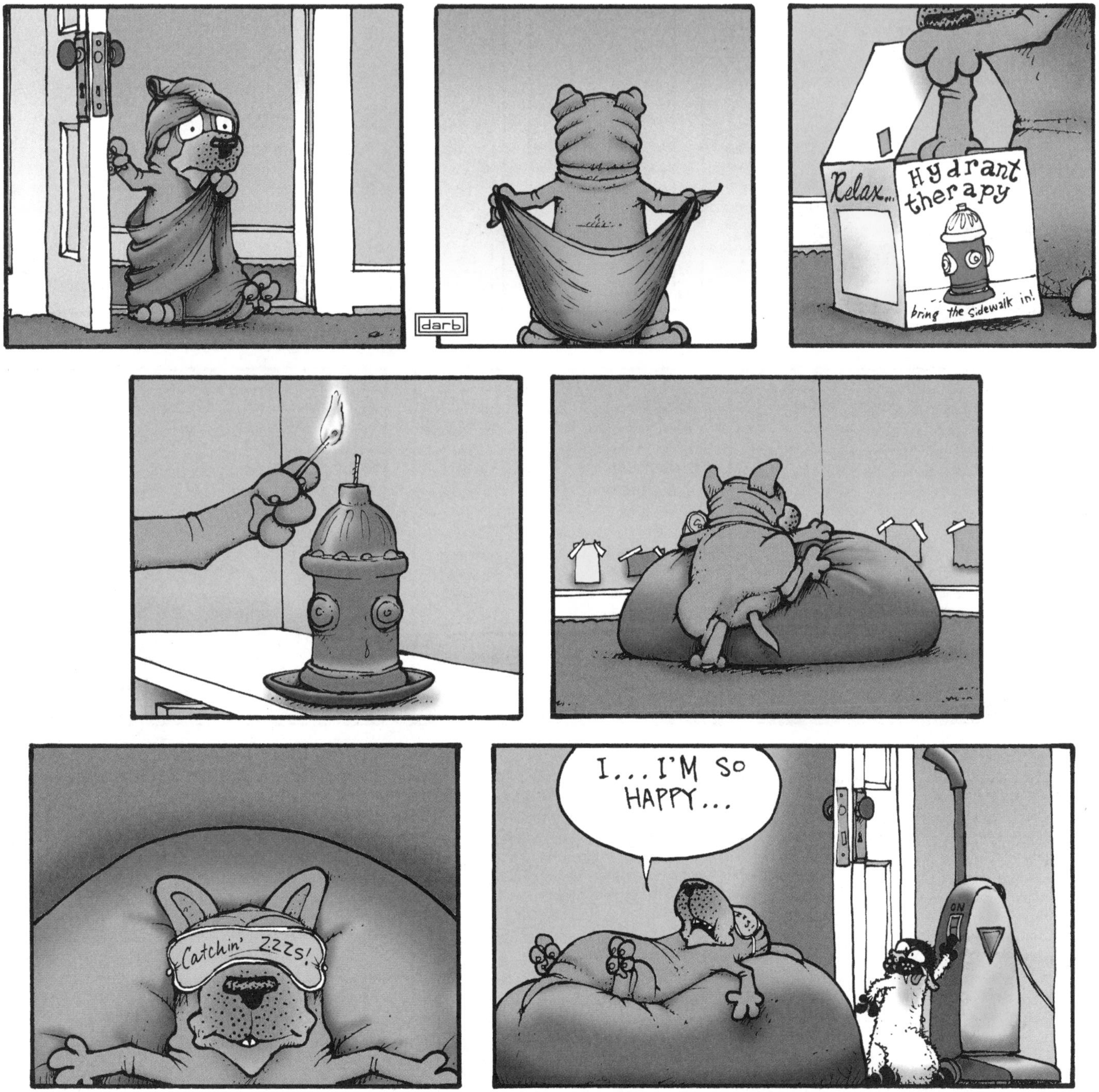
darb
Relax...
Hydrant therapy
bring the sidewalk in!
Catchin' ZZZs!
I... I'M SO HAPPY...
ON

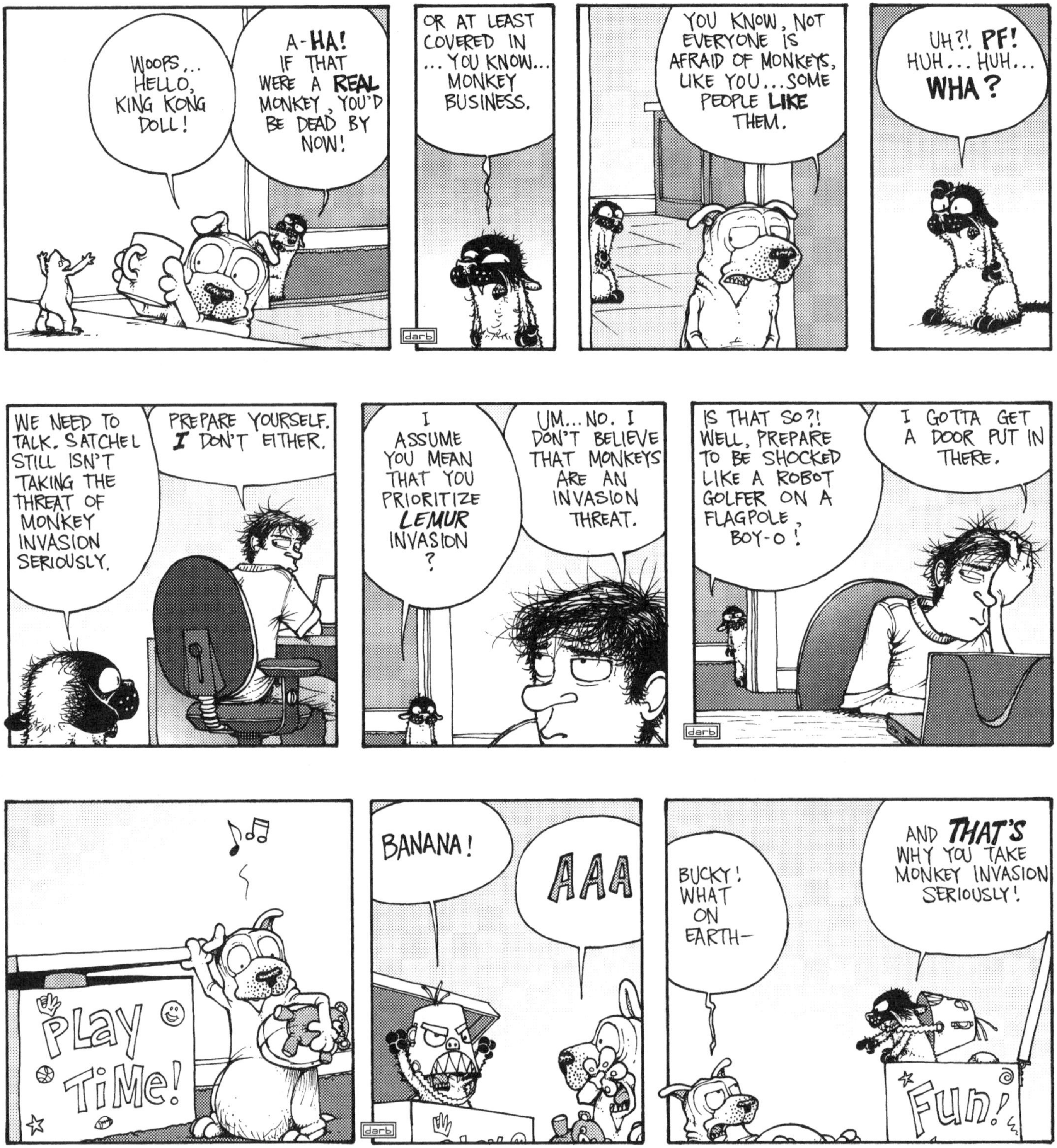
WOOPS,.. HELLO, KING KONG DOLL!
A-HA! IF THAT WERE A REAL MONKEY, YOU'D BE DEAD BY NOW!
OR AT LEAST COVERED IN ... YOU KNOW... MONKEY BUSINESS.
YOU KNOW, NOT EVERYONE IS AFRAID OF MONKEYS, LIKE YOU...SOME PEOPLE LIKE THEM.
UH?!. PF! HUH... HUH... WHA?
darb
WE NEED TO TALK. SATCHEL STILL ISN'T TAKING THE THREAT OF MONKEY INVASION SERIOUSLY.
PREPARE YOURSELF. I DON'T EITHER.
I ASSUME YOU MEAN THAT YOU PRIORITIZE LEMUR INVASION?
UM... NO. I DON'T BELIEVE THAT MONKEYS ARE AN INVASION THREAT.
IS THAT SO?! WELL, PREPARE TO BE SHOCKED LIKE A ROBOT GOLFER ON A FLAGPOLE, BOY-O!
I GOTTA GET A DOOR PUT IN THERE.
darb
PLAY TIME!
BANANA!
AAA
darb
BUCKY! WHAT ON EARTH-
AND THAT'S WHY YOU TAKE MONKEY INVASION SERIOUSLY!
FUN!

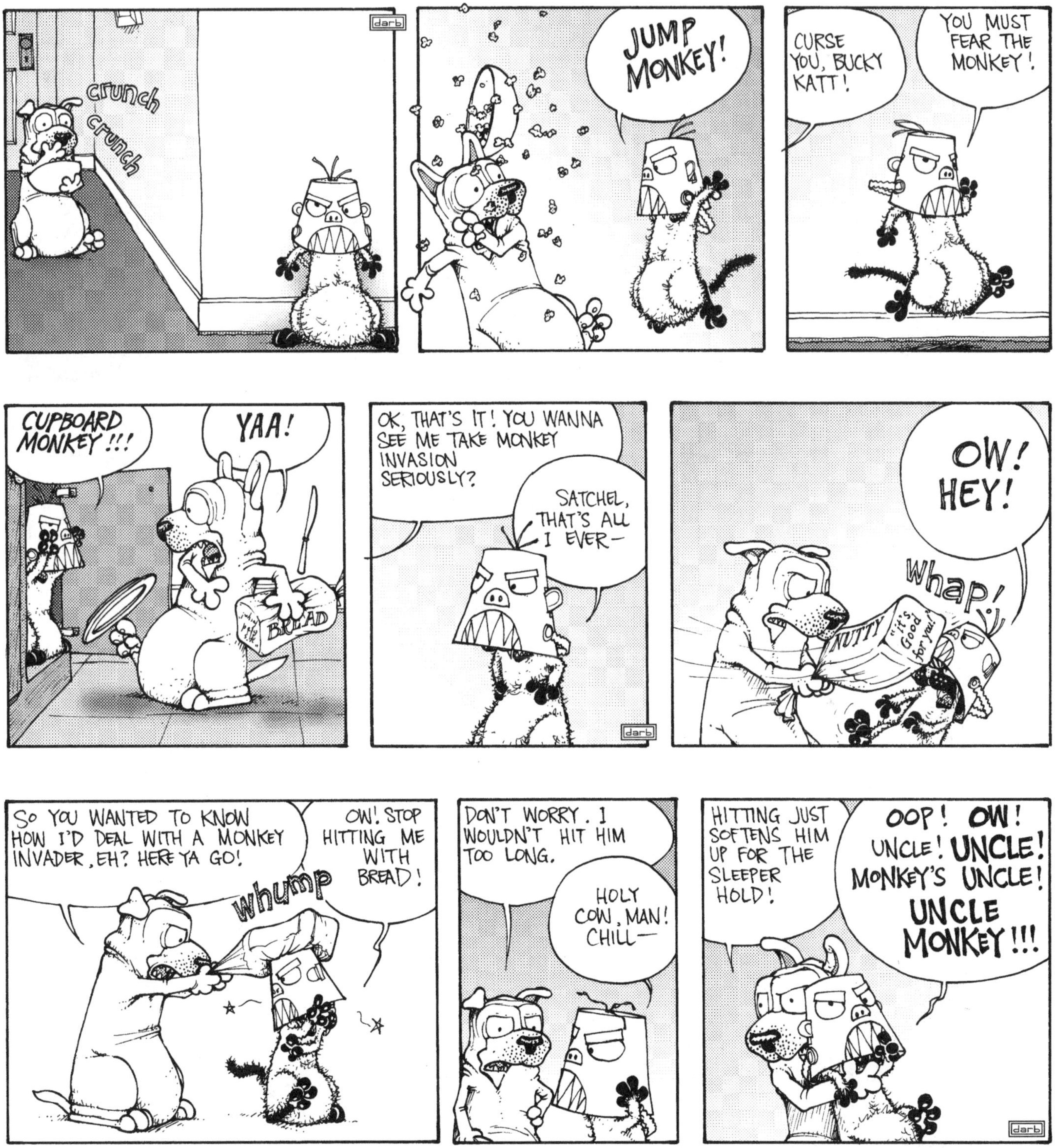
crunch
crunch
darb
JUMP MONKEY!
CURSE YOU, BUCKY KATT!
YOU MUST FEAR THE MONKEY!
CUPBOARD MONKEY!!!
YAA!
BREAD
OK, THAT'S IT! YOU WANNA SEE ME TAKE MONKEY INVASION SERIOUSLY?
SATCHEL, THAT'S ALL I EVER—
darb
OW! HEY!
Whap!
NUTTY
"it's Good for you!"
SO YOU WANTED TO KNOW HOW I'D DEAL WITH A MONKEY INVADER, EH? HERE YA GO!
OW! STOP HITTING ME WITH BREAD!
whump
DON'T WORRY. I WOULDN'T HIT HIM TOO LONG.
HOLY COW, MAN! CHILL—
HITTING JUST SOFTENS HIM UP FOR THE SLEEPER HOLD!
OOP! OW! UNCLE! UNCLE! MONKEY'S UNCLE! UNCLE MONKEY!!!
darb

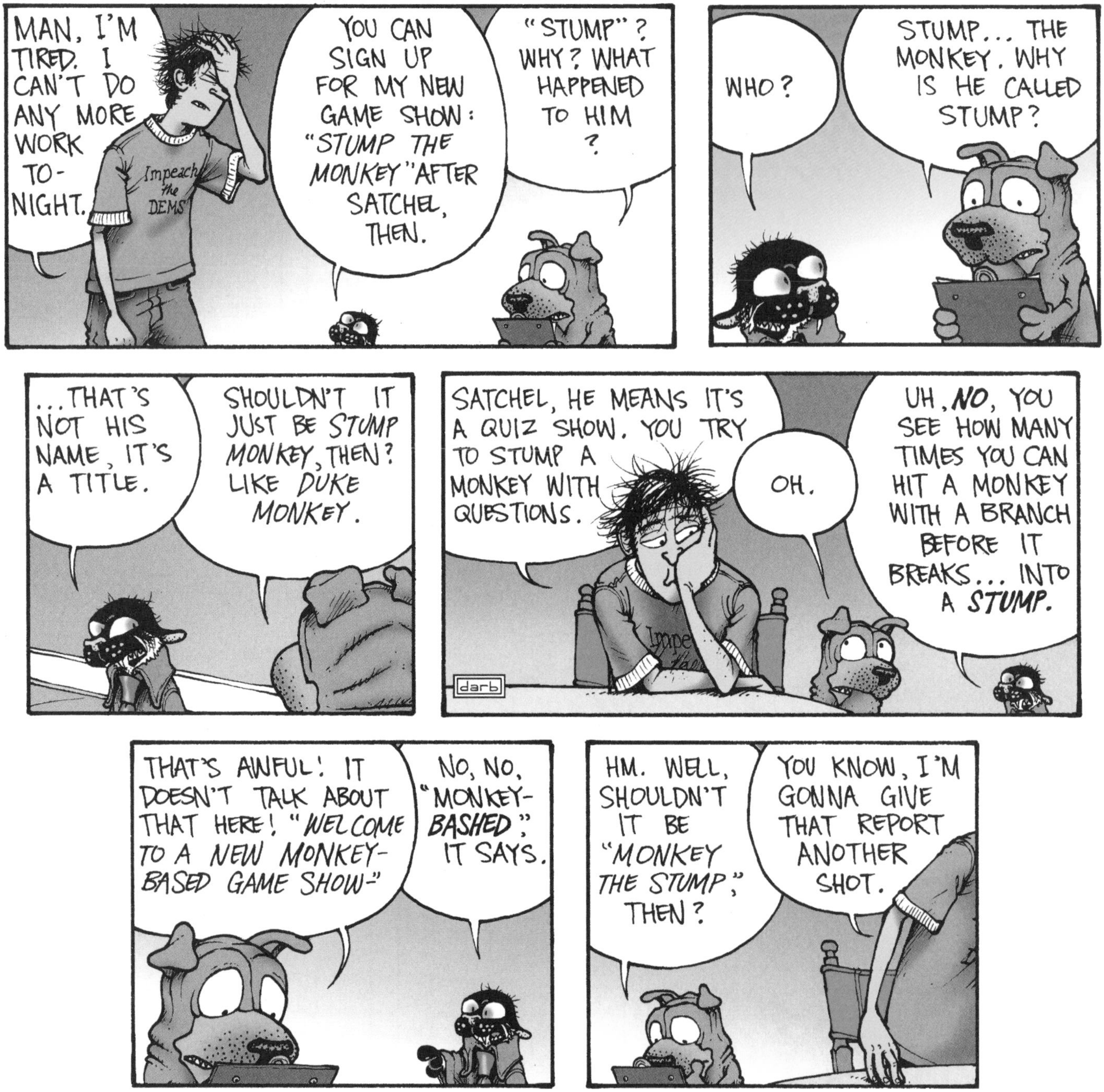
MAN, I'M TIRED. I CAN'T DO ANY MORE WORK TO-NIGHT.
Impeach the DEMS
YOU CAN SIGN UP FOR MY NEW GAME SHOW: "STUMP THE MONKEY" AFTER SATCHEL, THEN.
"STUMP"? WHY? WHAT HAPPENED TO HIM?
WHO?
STUMP... THE MONKEY. WHY IS HE CALLED STUMP?
...THAT'S NOT HIS NAME, IT'S A TITLE.
SHOULDN'T IT JUST BE STUMP MONKEY, THEN? LIKE DUKE MONKEY.
SATCHEL, HE MEANS IT'S A QUIZ SHOW. YOU TRY TO STUMP A MONKEY WITH QUESTIONS.
OH.
UH, NO, YOU SEE HOW MANY TIMES YOU CAN HIT A MONKEY WITH A BRANCH BEFORE IT BREAKS... INTO A STUMP.
darb
THAT'S AWFUL! IT DOESN'T TALK ABOUT THAT HERE! "WELCOME TO A NEW MONKEY-BASED GAME SHOW-"
NO, NO, "MONKEY-BASHED," IT SAYS.
HM. WELL, SHOULDN'T IT BE "MONKEY THE STUMP," THEN?
YOU KNOW, I'M GONNA GIVE THAT REPORT ANOTHER SHOT.

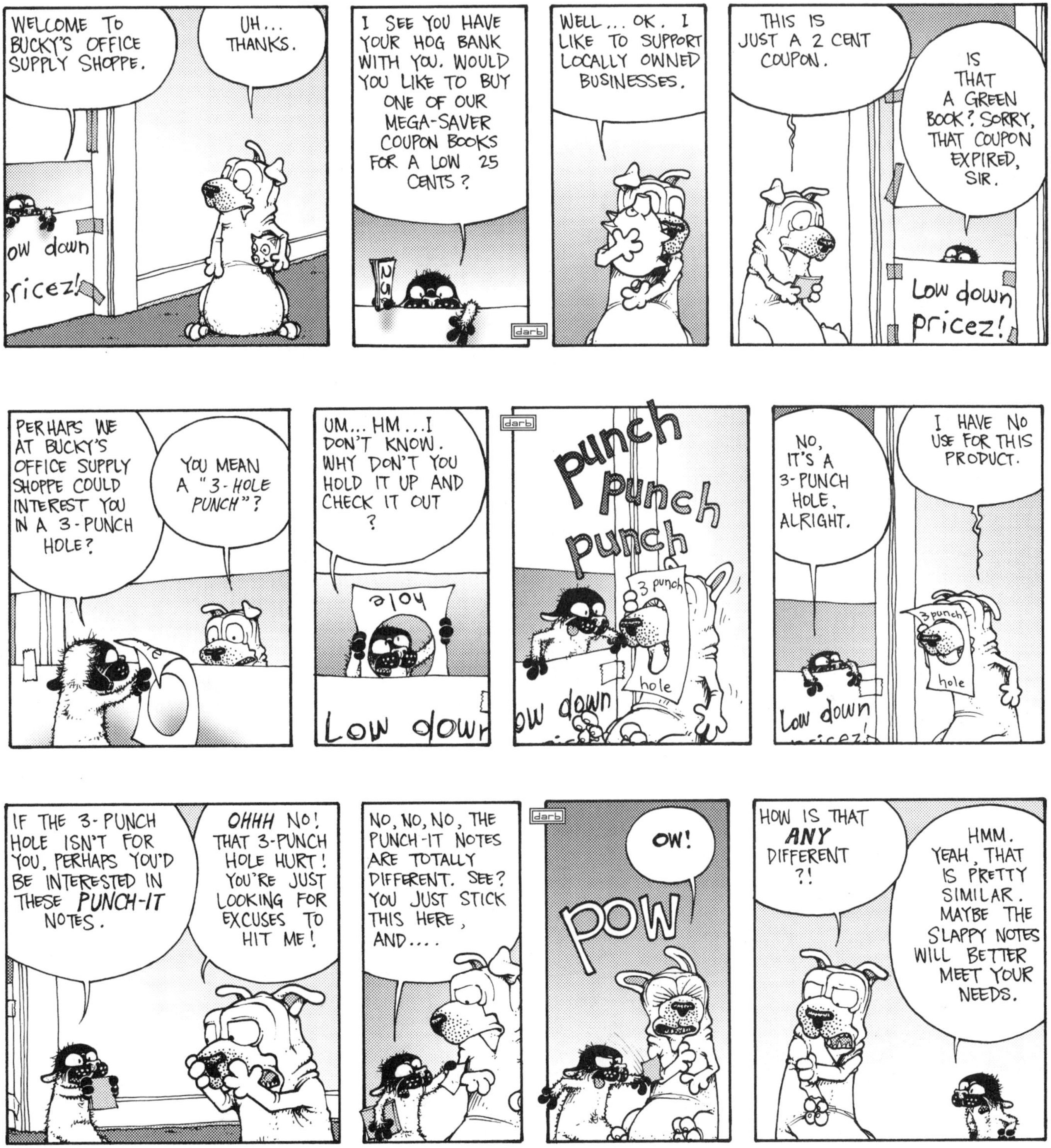
WELCOME TO BUCKY'S OFFICE SUPPLY SHOPPE.
UH... THANKS.
I SEE YOU HAVE YOUR HOG BANK WITH YOU. WOULD YOU LIKE TO BUY ONE OF OUR MEGA-SAVER COUPON BOOKS FOR A LOW 25 CENTS?
WELL... OK. I LIKE TO SUPPORT LOCALLY OWNED BUSINESSES.
THIS IS JUST A 2 CENT COUPON.
IS THAT A GREEN BOOK? SORRY, THAT COUPON EXPIRED, SIR.
Low down pricez!
PERHAPS WE AT BUCKY'S OFFICE SUPPLY SHOPPE COULD INTEREST YOU IN A 3-PUNCH HOLE?
YOU MEAN A "3-HOLE PUNCH"?
UM... HM... I DON'T KNOW. WHY DON'T YOU HOLD IT UP AND CHECK IT OUT ?
hole
punch punch punch
3 punch
hole
NO, IT'S A 3-PUNCH HOLE, ALRIGHT.
I HAVE NO USE FOR THIS PRODUCT.
IF THE 3-PUNCH HOLE ISN'T FOR YOU, PERHAPS YOU'D BE INTERESTED IN THESE PUNCH-IT NOTES.
OHHH NO! THAT 3-PUNCH HOLE HURT! YOU'RE JUST LOOKING FOR EXCUSES TO HIT ME!
NO, NO, NO, THE PUNCH-IT NOTES ARE TOTALLY DIFFERENT. SEE? YOU JUST STICK THIS HERE, AND....
OW!
POW
HOW IS THAT ANY DIFFERENT ?!
HMM. YEAH, THAT IS PRETTY SIMILAR. MAYBE THE SLAPPY NOTES WILL BETTER MEET YOUR NEEDS.

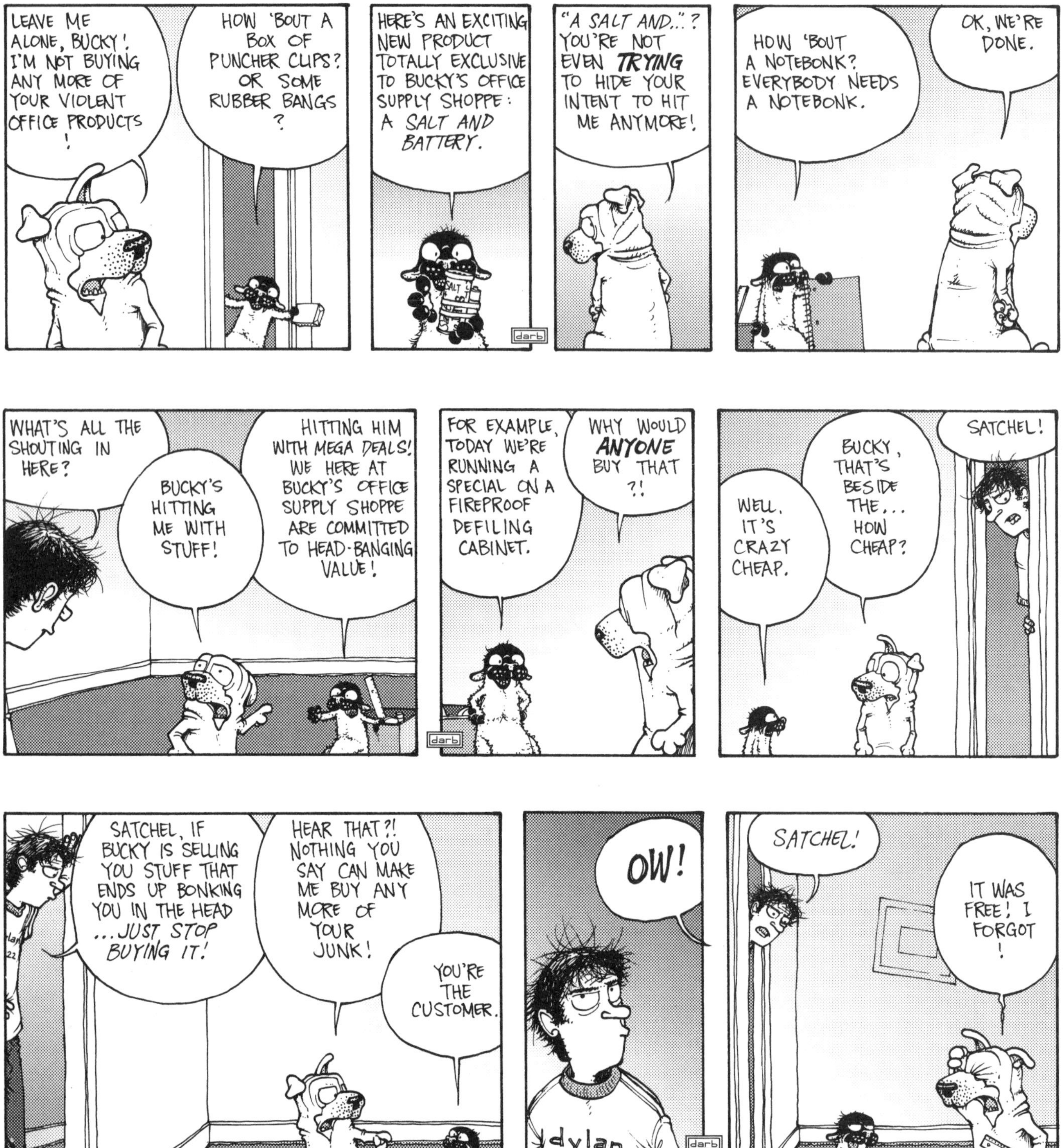
LEAVE ME ALONE, BUCKY! I'M NOT BUYING ANY MORE OF YOUR VIOLENT OFFICE PRODUCTS!
HOW 'BOUT A BOX OF PUNCHER CLIPS? OR SOME RUBBER BANGS?
HERE'S AN EXCITING NEW PRODUCT TOTALLY EXCLUSIVE TO BUCKY'S OFFICE SUPPLY SHOPPE: A *SALT AND BATTERY*.
darb
"*A SALT AND...*"? YOU'RE NOT EVEN **TRYING** TO HIDE YOUR INTENT TO HIT ME ANYMORE!
HOW 'BOUT A NOTEBONK? EVERYBODY NEEDS A NOTEBONK.
OK, WE'RE DONE.
WHAT'S ALL THE SHOUTING IN HERE?
BUCKY'S HITTING ME WITH STUFF!
HITTING HIM WITH *MEGA DEALS!* WE HERE AT BUCKY'S OFFICE SUPPLY SHOPPE ARE COMMITTED TO HEAD-BANGING VALUE!
darb
FOR EXAMPLE, TODAY WE'RE RUNNING A SPECIAL ON A FIREPROOF DEFILING CABINET.
WHY WOULD **ANYONE** BUY THAT?!
WELL, IT'S CRAZY CHEAP.
BUCKY, THAT'S BESIDE THE... HOW CHEAP?
SATCHEL!
SATCHEL, IF BUCKY IS SELLING YOU STUFF THAT ENDS UP BONKING YOU IN THE HEAD *...JUST STOP BUYING IT!*
HEAR THAT?! NOTHING YOU SAY CAN MAKE ME BUY ANY MORE OF YOUR JUNK!
YOU'RE THE CUSTOMER.
OW!
dylan
darb
SATCHEL!
IT WAS FREE! I FORGOT!